MW00584346

Challenging the Status Quo

in the New Testament Debate

THE

QUESTION

OF

CANON

MICHAEL J. KRUGER

IVP Academic

An imprint of InterVarsity Press
Downers Grove, Illinois

InterVarsity Press
P.O. Box 1400, Downers Grove, IL 60515-1426
World Wide Web: www.ivpress.com
Email: email@ivpress.com

InterVarsity Press® is the book-publishing division of InterVarsity Christian Fellowship/USA®, a movement of students and faculty active on campus at hundreds of universities, colleges and schools of nursing in the United States of America, and a member movement of the International Fellowship of Evangelical Students. For information about local and regional activities, write Public Relations Dept., InterVarsity Christian Fellowship/USA, 6400 Schroeder Rd., P.O. Box 7895, Madison, WI 53707-7895, or visit the IVCF website at www.intervarsity.org.

Chapter one of this book was published in a slighty different form as "The Definition of the Term 'Canon': Exclusive or Multi-Dimensional?" Tyndale Bulletin 63 (2012): 1-20. Permission to republish courtesy of Tyndale Bulletin.

Scripture quotations, unless otherwise noted, are from The Holy Bible, English Standard Version, copyright © 2001 by Crossway Bibles, a division of Good News Publishers. Used by permission. All rights reserved.

While all stories in this book are true, some names and identifying information in this book have been changed to protect the privacy of the individuals involved.

Cover design: Cindy Kiple
Interior design: Beth Hagenberg
Image: Brother Pedro Machado by Francisco de Zurburan at Real Academia de Bellas Artes de San Fernando, Madrid, Spain. Giraudon / The Bridgeman Art Library

ISBN 978-0-8308-4031-1 (print)
ISBN 978-0-8308-6497-3 (digital)

Printed in the United States of America ∞

Library of Congress Cataloging-in-Publication Data
Kruger, Michael J.
  The question of Canon : challenging the status quo in the New Testament
  debate / Michael J. Kruger.
    pages cm
  Includes bibliographical references and index.
  ISBN 978-0-8308-4031-1 (pbk. : alk. paper)
  1. Bible. New Testament—Canon. I. Title.
  BS2320.K785 2013
  225.1'2--dc23

                                                       2013029158

P   21   20   19   18   17   16   15   14   13   12   11   10   9   8   7   6

Y   31   30   29   28   27   26   25   24   23   22   21   20   19   18   17

CONTENTS

Preface 7

Abbreviations 9

Introduction 15

   1. THE DEFINITION OF CANON 27
      Must We Make a Sharp Distinction Between
      the Definitions of *Canon* and *Scripture*?

   2. THE ORIGINS OF CANON 47
      Was There Really Nothing in Early Christianity
      That May Have Led to a Canon?

   3. THE WRITING OF CANON 79
      Were Early Christians Averse to Written Documents?

   4. THE AUTHORS OF CANON 119
      Were the New Testament Authors Unaware
      of Their Own Authority?

   5. THE DATE OF CANON 155
      Were the New Testament Books First Regarded
      as Scripture at the End of the Second Century?

Conclusion 204

Bibliography 211

Author Index 249

Subject Index 251

Scripture Index 253

PREFACE

⚜

FOR MANY YEARS NOW, the topic of the New Testament canon has been the main focus of my research and writing. It is an exciting field of study that probes into questions that have long fascinated scholars and laypeople alike, namely when and how these twenty-seven books came to be regarded as a new scriptural deposit. But the story of the New Testament canon is bigger than just the *when* and the *how*. It is also, and perhaps most fundamentally, about the *why*. Why did Christians have a canon at all? Does the canon exist because of some later decision or action of the second- or third-century church? Or did it arise more naturally from within the early Christian faith itself? Was the canon an extrinsic phenomenon or an intrinsic one? These are the questions this book is designed to address. And these are not micro questions but macro ones. They address foundational and paradigmatic issues about the way we view the canon. They force us to consider the larger framework through which we conduct our research—whether we realized we had such a framework or not.

Of course, we are not the first to ask such questions about why we have a canon. Indeed, for many scholars this question has already been settled. The dominant view today, as we shall see below, is that the New Testament is an extrinsic phenomenon: a later ecclesiastical development imposed on books originally written for another purpose. This is the framework through which much of modern scholarship operates. And it is the goal of this volume to ask whether it is a compelling one. To be sure, it is no easy task challenging the status quo in any academic field. But we should not be afraid to ask tough questions. Likewise, the consensus position should not be afraid for them to be asked.

In any project like this one, there are many people and institutions that deserve thanks. I am grateful for the support of Dan Reid at IVP Academic for his keen interest in this project. It has been a pleasure to work with him and all the folks at InterVarsity Press. Although chapter one below was originally written for this volume, it was published last year (in a slightly different form) in *Tyndale Bulletin* 63 (2012): 1-20, under the title "The Definition of the Term 'Canon': Exclusive or Multi-Dimensional?" Thanks to *Tyndale Bulletin* for permission to republish it here. I am grateful for the many colleagues who have given feedback and input to this book, including Larry Hurtado, Paul Foster, Chris Keith and Don Hagner. It is a better volume as a result of their thoughtful comments, though its shortcomings are still my own. My teaching assistants, Alan Gay and Aaron Gray, also deserve a word of thanks. Their tireless attention to detail was a great help to me as this book was edited. Most of all, I would like to thank my wife, Melissa, and my three children, Emma, John and Kate. They are always a joy to my heart when I return home from a long day of writing books such as this one.

ABBREVIATIONS

Apocrypha and Septuagint

Bar	Baruch
1-2 Macc	1-2 Maccabees
Sir	Sirach
Tob	Tobit
Wis	Wisdom of Solomon

Old Testament Pseudepigrapha

1 En.	*1 Enoch*
2 En.	*2 Enoch*
2 Bar.	*2 Baruch*
Apoc. Ab.	*Apocalypse of Abraham*
Jub	*Jubilees*
T. Mos.	*Testament of Moses*

Dead Sea Scrolls

1QH^a	*1QHodayot^a*
1QM	*1QWar Scroll*
1QpHab	*1QPesher to Habakkuk*
1QS	*1QRule of the Community*
1QSa	*1QRule of the Congregation*
1QSb	*1QRule of Benedictions*
4Q52	*4QSamuel^b*
4Q175	*4QTestimonia*
4Q504	*4QWords of the Luminaries^a*
4QMMT^c	*4QHalakhic Letter^c*
11Q13	*11QMelchizedek*
11QT^a	*11QTemple^a*
CD	*Damascus Document*

Tractates in the Mishnah, Tosefta and Talmud

b. Meg.	Babylonian Talmud Megillah
b. Soṭah	Babylonian Talmud Soṭah
m. Kelim	Mishnah Kelim

Apostolic Fathers

1 Clem.	1 Clement
2 Clem	2 Clement
Barn.	Epistle of Barnabas
Did.	Didache
Herm. Vis.	Shepherd of Hermas, Vision(s)
Ign. Eph.	Ignatius, To the Ephesians
Ign. Magn.	Ignatius, To the Magnesians
Ign. Phld.	Ignatius, To the Philadelphians
Ign. Pol.	Ignatius, To Polycarp
Ign. Smyrn.	Ignatius, To the Smyrnaeans
Ign. Rom.	Ignatius, To the Romans
Polycarp	
Phil.	To the Philippians

Greek and Latin Works

Cicero	
Tusc.	Tusculanae disputationes
Clement of Alexandria	
Exc.	Excerpta ex Theodoto (Excerps from Theodotus)
Strom.	Stromata (Miscellanies)
Eusebius	
Hist. eccl.	Historia Ecclesiastica (Ecclesiastical History)
Galen	
Temp. Med.	De simplicium medicamentorum temperamentis et facultatibus (On the Mixtures and Powers of Simple Drugs)
Irenaeus	
Haer.	Adversus Haereses (Against Heresies)
Jerome	
Epist.	Epistles

Josephus
  Ag. Ap.   *Contra Apionem (Against Apion)*
  Ant.   *Antiquitates judaicae (Jewish Antiquities)*
Justin
  1 Apol.   *Apologia i (First Apology)*
  Dial.   *Dialogus cum Tryphone (Dialogue with Trypho)*
Lucian
  Hist. Conscr. *(How to Write History)*
  Peregr.   *de Morte Peregrini (The Death of Peregrinus)*
Martial
  Epigr.   *Epigrammata (Epigrams)*
Minucius Felix
  Oct.   *Octavius*
Origen
  Cels.   *Contra Celsum (Against Celsus)*
Philo
  Contempl. Life *On the Contemplative Life*
Pliny
  Ep.   *Epistulae*
Quintilian
  Inst. Or.   *Institutio oratoria*
Seneca
  Ep.   *Epistulae Morales*
Tacitus
  Ann.   *Annales*
  Hist.   *Historiae*
Theophilus of Antioch
  Autol.   *To Autolycus*
Tertullian
  Adv. Jud.   *Adversus Judaios (Against the Jews)*
  Marc.   *Adversus Marcionem (Against Marcion)*
  Prax.   *Adversus Praxean (Against Praxeas)*
  Pud.   *De puditicia (On Modesty)*

Periodicals, Reference Works and Serials

ABD   *Anchor Bible Dictionary*, ed. D. N. Freedman (6 vols.; New York: Doubleday, 1992)

AJP	*American Journal of Philology*
ANRW	*Aufstieg und Niedergang der römischen Welt: Geschichte und Kultur Roms im Spiegel der neueren Forschung*, ed. W. Haase and H. Temporini (Berlin: de Gruyter, 1972–)
ASOR	American Schools of Oriental Research
AThR	*Anglican Theological Review*
ATR	*Australasian Theological Review*
BA	*Biblical Archaeologist*
BBR	*Bulletin for Biblical Research*
BECNT	Baker Exegetical Commentary on the New Testament
Bib	*Biblica*
BJA	*British Journal of Aesthetics*
BJRL	*Bulletin of the John Rylands University Library of Manchester*
BR	*Biblical Research*
BSac	*Bibliotheca sacra*
CBQ	*Catholic Biblical Quarterly*
CBR	*Currents in Biblical Research*
CI	*Critical Inquiry*
CTM	*Concordia Theological Monthly*
CurTM	*Currents in Theology and Missions*
DBSJ	*Detroit Baptist Seminary Journal*
EvQ	*Evangelical Quarterly*
ETL	*Ephemerides theologicae lovanienses*
Exp	*Expositor*
ExpT	*Expository Times*
HR	*History of Religions*
HTR	*Harvard Theological Review*
HvTSt	*Hervormde teologiese studies*
ICC	International Critical Commentary
Int	*Interpretation*
IVPNTC	IVP New Testament Commentary
JBL	*Journal of Biblical Literature*
JETS	*Journal of the Evangelical Theological Society*
JSJ	*Journal for the Study of Judaism in the Persian, Hellenistic and Roman Periods*

JSNT	*Journal for the Study of the New Testament*
JSOT	*Journal for the Study of the Old Testament*
JTS	*Journal of Theological Studies*
NCBC	New Century Bible Commentary
Neot	*Neotestamentica*
NIBC	New International Biblical Commentary
NICNT	New International Commentary on the New Testament
NIGTC	New International Greek Testament Commentary
NIVAC	New International Version Application Commentary
NovT	*Novum Testamentum*
NTS	*New Testament Studies*
PNTC	Pillar New Testament Commentary
Presb	*Presbyterion*
QJS	*Quarterly Journal of Speech*
RB	*Revue biblique*
RBL	*Review of Biblical Literature*
RevExp	*Review and Expositor*
RevQ	*Revue de Qumran*
RHA	*Revue Hittite et asianique*
RQ	*Römische Quartalschrift für christliche Altertumskunde und Kirchengeschichte*
SBL	Society of Biblical Literature
SecCent	*Second Century*
Sem	*Semitica*
SJT	*Scottish Journal of Theology*
SNTSMS	Society for New Testament Studies Monograph Series
SPap	*Studia papyrologica*
SPCK	Society for Promoting Christian Knowledge
TDNT	*Theological Dictionary of the New Testament*, ed. G. Kittel and G. Friedrich, trans. G. W. Bromiley (10 vols.; Grand Rapids: Eerdmans, 1964–1976)
Them	*Themelios*
TNTC	Tyndale New Testament Commentaries
TrinJ	*Trinity Journal*
TS	*Theological Studies*

TynBul	*Tyndale Bulletin*
VC	*Vigiliae christianae*
VT	*Vetus Testamentum*
WBC	Word Biblical Commentary
WTJ	*Westminster Theological Journal*
ZAW	*Zeitschrift für die alttestamentliche Wissenschaft*
ZKG	*Zeitschrift für Kirchengeschichte*
ZNW	*Zeitschrift für die neutestamentliche Wissenschaft und die Kunde der älteren Kirche*
ZPE	*Zeitschrift für Papyrologie und Epigraphik*
ZST	*Zeitschrift für systematische Theologie*

INTRODUCTION

No greater creative act can be mentioned in the whole history
of the Church than the formation of the apostolic collection
and the assigning to it of a position of equal
rank with the Old Testament.

ADOLF VON HARNACK
History of Dogma, vol. 2

⚕

THE STORY OF THE NEW TESTAMENT CANON is a bit of a conundrum.
Despite the fact that the contours of the New Testament canon were, for
the most part, decided by the fourth century, vibrant and vigorous discussions about the authenticity of these books has persisted well into the
twenty-first century—nearly seventeen hundred years later. The question
of canon simply will not go away. While the actual New Testament canon
of the Christian church has been largely unchanged during this time
frame,[1] scholars and laypeople alike never seem to tire of discussions about
ancient Christian writings and what role they might have played within
the infant church.[2] And the reason for this fascination with the canon is

---

[1] While there has been a wide consensus on these books, there are still modern-day exceptions:
e.g., the Syrian Orthodox church still uses a lectionary that presupposes the twenty-two-book
canon of the Peshitta.

[2] More recent studies on canon include: Gerd Theissen, *The New Testament: A Literary History*
(Minneapolis: Fortress, 2012); Michael J. Kruger, *Canon Revisited: Establishing the Origins and*

not hard to find. Previously unknown gospel writings continue to be discovered,[3] the authorship and date of New Testament books continue to be challenged,[4] and the diversity of early Christian "Scriptures" continues to be highlighted.[5] And rather than satisfying the scholarly appetite for all things canonical, each new discovery or discussion actually seems to increase it. Thus, Kurt Aland was right when he recognized the inevitable centrality of the canon issue: "The question of Canon will make its way to the centre of the theological and ecclesiastical debate . . . [because] the question is one which confronts not only the New Testament scholar, but every Christian theologian."[6]

Authority of the New Testament Books (Wheaton, IL: Crossway, 2012); Charles E. Hill, *Who Chose the Gospels? Probing the Great Gospel Conspiracy* (Oxford: Oxford University Press, 2010); Einar Thomassen, ed., *Canon and Canonicity: The Formation and Use of Scripture* (Copenhagen: Museum Tusculanum Press, 2010); Michael Bird and Michael Pahl, eds., *The Sacred Text* (Piscataway, NJ: Gorgias, 2010); Lee M. McDonald, *The Biblical Canon: Its Origin, Transmission, and Authority* (Peabody, MA: Hendrickson, 2007); Lee M. McDonald, *Forgotten Scriptures: The Selection and Rejection of Early Religious Writings* (Louisville: Westminster John Knox, 2009); David L. Dungan, *Constantine's Bible: Politics and the Making of the New Testament* (Philadelphia: Fortress, 2006); Christopher Seitz, *The Goodly Fellowship of the Prophets: The Achievement of Association in Canon Formation* (Grand Rapids: Baker Academic, 2009); Craig Bartholomew et al., eds., *Canon and Biblical Interpretation* (Carlisle: Paternoster, 2006); David R. Nienhuis, *Not by Paul Alone: The Formation of the Catholic Epistle Collection and the Christian Canon* (Waco: Baylor University Press, 2007); Craig A. Evans and Emanuel Tov, eds., *Exploring the Origins of the Bible: Canon Formation in Historical, Literary, and Theological Perspectives* (Grand Rapids: Baker Academic, 2008).

[3]The most recent example is the so-called *Gospel of Jesus's Wife*, which is now regarded by many as a forgery. Before this, it was the *Gospel of Judas* that garnered all the attention; see Herbert Krosney, *The Lost Gospel: The Quest for the Gospel of Judas Iscariot* (Hanover, PA: National Geographic Society, 2006); James M. Robinson, *The Secrets of Judas: The Story of the Misunderstood Disciple and His Lost Gospel* (San Francisco: HarperSanFrancisco, 2006); and Bart D. Ehrman, *The Lost Gospel of Judas Iscariot: A New Look at Betrayer and Betrayed* (New York: Oxford University Press, 2006). In addition, there continue to be new publications on previously discovered apocryphal gospels: e.g., Mark S. Goodacre, *Thomas and the Gospels: The Case for Thomas's Familiarity with the Synoptics* (Grand Rapids: Eerdmans, 2012); Simon Gathercole, *The Composition of the Gospel of Thomas: Original Language and Influences* (Cambridge: Cambridge University Press, 2012); and Paul Foster, *The Gospel of Peter: Introduction, Critical Edition and Commentary* (Leiden: E. J. Brill, 2010).

[4]For the most updated work on pseudonymity in the New Testament, see Bart D. Ehrman, *Forgery and Counterforgery: The Use of Literary Deceit in Early Christian Polemics* (New York: Oxford University Press, 2012).

[5]Heikki Räisänen, *Beyond New Testament Theology: A Story and a Program* (London: SCM, 1990); James D. G. Dunn, *Unity and Diversity in the New Testament: An Inquiry into the Character of Early Christianity*, 3rd ed. (London: SCM, 2006); Bart D. Ehrman, *Lost Christianities: The Battles for Scripture and the Faiths We Never Knew* (New York: Oxford University Press, 2002).

[6]Kurt Aland, *The Problem of the New Testament Canon* (London: A. R. Mowbray & Co., 1962), p. 31.

In the midst of all this scholarly attention on the question of canon, serious questions have been raised about the integrity of the New Testament. Most of these questions have centered on the problem of canonical boundaries. How do we know we have the right books? Why these books and not other books? And what about apocryphal books used by other Christian groups? But, in recent years, a new and more foundational question has begun to take center stage (though it is really not new at all). While the validity of the canon's boundaries is still an area of concern, the attention has shifted to the validity of the canon's very *existence*. The question now is, why is there a New Testament at all? If there are no real distinctions between "canonical" books and "apocryphal" books, and if some books were forged by authors pretending to be apostles, then what can account for the emergence of an authoritative canon? The answer, according to some scholars, is not to be found in the first century—there was nothing about earliest Christianity (or the books themselves) that would naturally lead to the development of a canon.[7] Instead, we are told, the answer is to be found in the later Christian church. The canon was an ecclesiastical product that was designed to meet ecclesiastical needs. Sure, the books themselves were produced at a much earlier point, but the idea of a canon was something that was retroactively imposed upon these books at a later time. Books are not written as canon—they *become* canon.[8]

This idea that the New Testament canon was not a natural development within early Christianity, but a later artificial development that is out of sync with Christianity's original purpose, is, I shall argue, a central framework that dominates much of modern canonical (and biblical) studies.

[7]Harry Y. Gamble, *The New Testament Canon: Its Making and Meaning* (Philadelphia: Fortress, 1985), p. 12. As we shall see below, there are variations of this sort of argument. Some scholars have argued that there was nothing about early Christianity that would have naturally led to the *kind* of canon Christianity ended up with (namely a closed, authoritative canon). See David Brakke, "Canon Formation and Social Conflict in Fourth Century Egypt: Athanasius of Alexandria's Thirty-Ninth Festal Letter," *HTR* 87 (1994): pp. 395-419, esp. 408-9.

[8]Eugene Ulrich, "The Notion and Definition of Canon," in *The Canon Debate*, ed. Lee M. McDonald and James A. Sanders (Peabody, MA: Hendrickson, 2002), p. 35. Cf. Hugo Lundhaug, "Canon and Interpretation: A Cognitive Perspective," in *Canon and Canonicity: The Formation and Use of Scripture*, pp. 67-90, at p. 68; and Wilfred C. Smith, *What Is Scripture? A Comparative Approach* (London: SPCK, 1993), p. 237. For further discussion on this concept, see John Webster, "'A Great and Meritorious Act of the Church'? The Dogmatic Location of the Canon," in *Die Einheit der Schrift und die Vielfalt des Kanons*, ed. John Barton and Michael Wolter (Berlin: Walter de Gruyter, 2003), pp. 95-126, at pp. 98-101.

We will call this the *extrinsic* model of canon—the idea that the canon was, to some degree, imposed upon the Christian faith.[9] Or, as Harnack has argued, the New Testament was something the church was "compelled" to do by the rise of Marcionism.[10] Loren Johns, in his article "Was 'Canon' Ever God's Will?" states the question clearly: "Is canon . . . a function of *Christendom* or of a certain kind of ecclesiastical *power?*"[11] For Johns, the answer is clearly the latter. In a similar fashion, Christopher Evans, in his book *Is "Holy Scripture" Christian?* argues that the production of a canon is due to the "worldliness of the church" and the "secularization of Christianity."[12] Lee McDonald also indicates that the idea of a New Testament canon may be inconsistent with the founding of Christianity: "We must ponder the question of whether the notion of a biblical canon is necessarily Christian. The best available information about the earliest followers of Jesus shows that they did not have such canons as the church presently possesses today, nor did they indicate that their successors should draw them up."[13]

It is worth noting that this extrinsic model of the canon's origins was criticized a number of years ago by Brevard Childs (though he used different terminology). Childs described this same view: "It is assumed by many that the formation of a canon is a late, ecclesiastical activity, external to the biblical literature itself, which was subsequently imposed on the

---

[9]Karl Barth, *Church Dogmatics* (Edinburgh: T & T Clark, 1975), I/1:107, makes a very similar statement when he declares, "The Bible constitutes itself the Canon. It is the Canon because it imposed itself upon the Church." However, the difference is that Barth is referring to something the Scripture itself does, whereas the extrinsic model is referring to what the church (or another ecclesiastical group) does.

[10]Adolf von Harnack, *Origin of the New Testament and the Most Important Consequences of a New Creation* (London: Williams & Northgate, 1925), p. 31.

[11]Loren L. Johns, "Was 'Canon' Ever God's Will?," in *Jewish and Christian Scriptures: The Function of "Canonical" and "Non-Canonical" Religious Texts*, ed. James H. Charlesworth and Lee M. McDonald (London: T & T Clark, 2010), p. 42 (emphasis his). For more on the canon as a demonstration of power, see Alan K. Bowman and Greg Wolf, eds., *Literacy and Power in the Ancient World* (Cambridge: Cambridge University Press, 1994); Gerald L. Bruns, "Canon and Power in the Hebrew Scriptures," *CI* 10 (1984): 462-80; Kim Haines-Eitzen, *Guardians of Letters: Literacy, Power, and the Transmitters of Early Christian Literature* (Oxford: Oxford University Press, 2000); and Robert P. Coote and Mary P. Coote, *Power, Politics, and the Making of the Bible* (Minneapolis: Fortress, 1990).

[12]Christopher Evans, *Is "Holy Scripture" Christian?* (London: SCM, 1971), pp. 7 and 34. See also C. F. Evans, "The New Testament in the Making," in *The Cambridge History of the Bible: From the Beginnings to Jerome*, ed. P. R. Ackroyd and C. F. Evans (Cambridge: Cambridge University Press, 1970), pp. 232-83, at p. 235.

[13]McDonald, *Biblical Canon*, p. 426.

writings."[14] In similar language, he says this model views the canon as "simply a post-apostolic development undertaken by the early catholic church which could be sharply separated from the formation of the New Testament literature."[15] Childs refers to this as a "modern consensus" which has led to "the almost universal rejection of a traditionally earlier dating for the first stage of the New Testament's canonization during the first half of the second century."[16]

If the New Testament canon was a later ecclesiastical creation, as the extrinsic model suggests, then what were the specific circumstances that led Christians to do such a thing? As can be imagined, the answers to this question vary widely. David Dungan, in his book *Constantine's Bible*, pins the origins of the canon on the influence of Greek philosophy and its emphasis on possessing a list of genuine writings that contain true doctrine.[17] According to Dungan, this influence culminated when the pagan emperor Constantine converted to Christianity and then "powerfully intruded" into the affairs of the church and determined the canon through "coercive enforcement."[18] Koester takes a different route, arguing along with Harnack that "the impelling force for the formation of the canon" was the second-century heretic Marcion.[19] Thus, in an attempt to counter Marcion, the "New Testament canon of Holy Scripture . . . was thus essentially *created* by

---

[14]Brevard S. Childs, *The New Testament as Canon: An Introduction* (London: SCM, 1984), p. 21.

[15]Ibid., p. 12.

[16]Ibid., p. 19.

[17]Dungan, *Constantine's Bible*, pp. 32-53.

[18]Ibid., p. 120.

[19]Helmut Koester, *Introduction to the New Testament*, vol. 2, *History and Literature of Early Christianity* (Philadelphia: Fortress, 1982), p. 8. The idea that Marcion was responsible for the origins of the New Testament canon can be found most notably in Adolf von Harnack, *Marcion: Das Evangelium von fremden Gott* (Leipzig: J. C. Hinrichs, 1924); Hans von Campenhausen, *The Formation of the Christian Bible* (London: Adam & Charles Black, 1972); and John Knox, *Marcion and the New Testament: An Essay in the Early History of the Canon* (Chicago: University of Chicago Press, 1942). However, Marcion's role in the formation of the canon has been minimized in recent years: e.g., John Barton, "Marcion Revisited," in *Canon Debate*, pp. 341-54; John Barton, *The Spirit and the Letter: Studies in the Biblical Canon* (London: SPCK, 1997), pp. 35-62; Franz Stuhlhofer, *Der Gebrauch Der Bibel Von Jesus Bis Euseb: Eine Statistische Untersuchung Zur Kanonsgeschichte* (Wuppertal: R. Brockhaus, 1988), pp. 73-75; David L. Balás, "Marcion Revisited: A 'Post-Harnack' Perspective," in *Texts and Testaments: Critical Essays on the Bible and the Early Church Fathers*, ed. W. Eugene March (San Antonio: Trinity University Press, 1980), pp. 95-107; and Robert M. Grant, *The Formation of the New Testament* (New York: Harper & Row, 1965), p. 126.

Irenaeus."[20] Elaine Pagels follows a similar path as Koester and lays the origins of the canon at the feet of Irenaeus.[21] Regardless of the specific *raison d'être* given to the canon, a dominant position in critical scholarship today is that the idea of canon is not a natural and original part of the early Christian faith.

Now, it should be noted from the outset that there is much that is correct in the extrinsic model. Indeed, these scholars are correct to observe that a New Testament was not an instantaneous development within early Christianity—it took time for this collection to be developed and shaped. And, they are correct to remind us that the entire process took several centuries to complete, and the church played an influential role in this process (as did heretics like Marcion).[22] However, are we really to think that "*nothing* dictated that there should be a NT"[23] prior to these later ecclesiastical actions? Was there nothing about earliest Christianity that might have given rise to such a collection? Was the idea of new Scriptures entirely foreign to the early followers of Jesus? It is the purpose of this volume to suggest otherwise. Our goal is not to deny the truth of the extrinsic model in its entirety, but to offer a well-intended corrective to its assessment and interpretation of some of the historical evidence. Paradigms always need adjustments and refinement, and this volume hopes to take a helpful step forward in that direction. This brief study, therefore, is not designed to offer the final word on the very complex subject of canon, but to reopen dialogue on a number of key topics where the dialogue, at least in appearance, seems to be closed. Thus, the format of this book will be unique. Rather than being yet another introduction to canon, it will focus narrowly upon five tenets of the extrinsic model. Each chapter will focus on one of these tenets, offering an assessment and response.

---

[20]Koester, *Introduction to the New Testament*, vol. 2, p. 10 (emphasis mine). There are other versions of this hypothesis; some suggest the canon was created to counteract the flood of apocryphal literature in the second century. See Kenneth L. Carroll, "The Earliest New Testament," *BJRL* 38 (1955): 45-57.

[21]Elaine Pagels, *Beyond Belief: The Secret Gospel of Thomas* (New York: Random House, 2003), pp. 114-42.

[22]For a study that emphasizes the role of the church in the development of the canon, see Craig D. Allert, *A High View of Scripture? The Authority of the Bible and the Formation of the New Testament Canon* (Grand Rapids: Baker Academic, 2007).

[23]Gamble, *New Testament Canon*, p. 12 (emphasis mine).

By responding to the major tenets of the extrinsic model, this volume will effectively be offering an alternative approach—what we might call an *intrinsic* model. This model suggests that the idea of canon is not something imposed from the outside but develops more organically from within the early Christian religion itself. The earliest Christian communities had certain characteristics and also held a number of theological beliefs that, especially when taken in tandem, would have made a new collection of sacred books (what we could call a "canon"[24]) a more natural development. As Everett Ferguson put it, "A canon of New Testament writings placed alongside the scriptures of Judaism resulted primarily from the *internal dynamics of the Christian faith*."[25] Childs argues in a similar fashion when he says:

> Canon consciousness thus arose at the inception of the Christian church and lies deep within the New Testament literature itself. There is an organic continuity in the historical process of the development of an established canon of sacred writings from the earliest stages of the New Testament to the final canonical stabilization of its scope.[26]

In other words, we shall argue that the makeup of first-century Christianity created a favorable environment for the growth of a new written revelational deposit. And when we look at the historical evidence of how this new written deposit developed—particularly the early date by which many of these books were received and the self-awareness of the New Testament authors—it is quite consistent with what we would expect if the intrinsic model were true. If that is the case, then we can agree with Childs that we should not make an overly sharp division between the early and late stages of the canon.

At this point, two clarifications are in order. First, as noted above, it is important to remember that the intrinsic model does not reject all the claims of the extrinsic model. The two models should not be unnecessarily polarized. Indeed, we can agree that the canon was a long, drawn-out process that was

---

[24]Obviously, we are using the functional definition for "canon" here. For further discussions of definition, see chapter one.

[25]Everett Ferguson, "Factors Leading to the Selection and Closure of the New Testament Canon," in *Canon Debate*, pp. 295-320, at p. 295.

[26]Childs, *New Testament as Canon*, p. 21.

not finalized until the fourth century or later—and the extrinsic model rightly recognizes this point. The canon did not pop into existence overnight. However, the intrinsic model is not denying this lengthy canonical process. Rather, it is simply arguing that the idea of a canon, and the beginning of the canonical process, cannot be laid solely at the feet of later ecclesiastical figures (or groups) who sought to solidify their power. There is something about the canon that seems more innate to the early Christian movement. Second, it is important to recognize that both the extrinsic and intrinsic models are *historical* models that do not require a commitment to any particular theological perspective.[27] One might be inclined to think of the extrinsic model as a historical model and the intrinsic model as the theological model—as if the latter required a belief in something like inspiration. But that is not the case. The intrinsic model has theological aspects to be sure (as we shall see below[28]), but it is essentially making a historical argument, namely that the canon developed early and naturally out of the Christian religion. One need not believe in inspiration to hold such a position.

David Meade provides a helpful way of describing the differences between the intrinsic and extrinsic models. Using different terminology, he refers to each model as the "push" and the "pull" respectively:

> A central question that arises out of the morass of controversy is the question of the direction from which the canonical process of the New Testament proceeds. In other words, is the formation of the New Testament "pushed" from elements inherent within itself or its Jewish origins or is it "pulled" into being by forces of the church and society largely external to the texts themselves?[29]

---

[27]John C. Peckham, "The Canon and Biblical Authority: A Critical Comparison of Two Models of Canonicity," *TrinJ* 28 (2007): 229-49, contrasts two models, which he calls the "community" model and the "intrinsic" model. Although the terminology is similar to what we are using here, Peckham's two models are very different because he is addressing the question of where the *authority* of the canon comes from—whether from the community or from the canon itself. In contrast, this volume is not using the term "intrinsic" to speak of the authority of the canon but is using it to speak of the *historical development* of the canon.

[28]When we deal with the definition of *canon* in chapter one, we shall argue that the ontological definition is a legitimate option and should not be disallowed simply because it is theological. However, one does not need to hold the ontological definition of canon in order to affirm the intrinsic model. The latter can exist without the former.

[29]David G. Meade, "Ancient Near Eastern Apocalypticism and the Origins of the New Testament Canon of Scripture," in *The Bible as a Human Witness: Hearing the Word of God Through Historically Dissimilar Traditions*, ed. Randall Heskett and Brian Irwin (London: T & T Clark, 2010), pp. 302-21, at p. 304.

Of course, the answer is that the canon is, to some extent, the result of *both* push and pull. But, the purpose of this volume is to argue that the extrinsic model (the "pull") has unduly dominated modern canonical studies and needs to be corrected by a recovery and new appreciation of the intrinsic model (the "push"). When it comes to explaining the formation of the New Testament, we cannot ignore the "elements inherent within itself or its Jewish origins" that gave it birth.

With the basic contours of these two models in mind, let us now turn to the five major tenets of the extrinsic model that this book will address. As we do so, it is important that we are clear about the limitations we face when expressing the tenets of any particular model. Models, by definition, are generalized descriptions and therefore subject to exceptions. Thus, by listing these five tenets we are not suggesting that everyone in the extrinsic camp would hold all of them without exception, nor are we suggesting that they exhaustively capture the beliefs of the extrinsic camp. Rather we are simply making a general observation that these five tenets are often (though not always) found together among those who see the canon as a later ecclesiastical development, and therefore they warrant our attention here. In addition to this, we must be careful to avoid another misconception, namely that merely addressing these five tenets would somehow prove the intrinsic model. To be clear, the goal of this volume is not to prove the intrinsic model—our purpose here is not nearly so ambitious. But if we can show that these five tenets are problematic (and that is the goal of this volume), then that would raise serious questions about the viability of the extrinsic model and at least pave the way for a reconsideration of the intrinsic model. Here are the five tenets:

- Tenet one: *We must make a sharp distinction between* Scripture *and* canon. Central to the extrinsic model is the insistence that the term *canon* can only be used after the church has acted to create a final, closed list of books. To use only this definition gives the impression that the canon is a late ecclesiastical creation. We shall argue in chapter one that this definition is correct as far as it goes, but that we should not rule out other definitions that bring more balance to our understanding of canon.

- Tenet two: *There was nothing in earliest Christianity that might have led to a canon.* While the extrinsic model insists that the idea of a canon was nowhere in the mind of the earliest Christians, chapter two will suggest that there was a matrix of theological beliefs held by early Christians that gives us good reason to think that a canon might have developed quite naturally.

- Tenet three: *Early Christians were averse to written documents.* A core tenet of the extrinsic model is that the whole idea of canon had to be a later ecclesiastical development because the earliest Christians were illiterate and uninterested in books. On the contrary, we shall argue in chapter three that while most Christians were illiterate (as were most people in the world at this time), they were characterized by a robust textuality—the knowledge, use and appreciation of written texts.

- Tenet four: *The New Testament authors were unaware of their own authority.* A frequent claim of those in the extrinsic camp is that the authors of the New Testament did not conceive of themselves as producing authoritative texts—they were merely producing occasional documents that were only *later* regarded as Scripture. Indeed, such a claim is critical for establishing the canon as an artificial ecclesiastical creation. However, in response, we shall argue in chapter four that the New Testament writers actually do provide substantial indications that they understood their message as authoritative, and often do so quite plainly.

- Tenet five: *The New Testament books were first regarded as Scripture at the end of the second century.* If the extrinsic model were true, we would expect that it would have taken a while for the New Testament writings to attain a scriptural status. And many advocates of the extrinsic model argue that the end of the second century was when this status was first acquired—most fundamentally due to the influence of Irenaeus. Although this date is often used, it is subject to serious question. In chapter five, we will examine the state of the canon in the second century and will argue that many of these writings were regarded as Scripture at a much earlier point.

Now that we have an overview of the questions that lay before us, we can begin to see that they have significant implications for the field of canonical studies. We are not dealing here with the standard questions about canon—

for example, how do we know these are the right books?—but instead we are dealing with more foundational and more fundamental questions about where the canon comes from. The issue is not so much which books, but whether Christianity should even be defined by books. For that reason, we have an opportunity here to consider (or reconsider) the macro direction we might take in the field of canonical studies. While much of modern scholarship is committed to the extrinsic model—and the five tenets to which it holds—we must remain open to the possibility that it may be in need of some modification. And we should not be surprised if it turns out that it does. The field of biblical studies, just like other fields, is sometimes in need of a paradigm shift. It is these shifts that allow the discipline to move forward in productive ways. So let us turn our attention now to the following chapters and explore that possibility.

1

THE DEFINITION OF CANON

Must We Make a Sharp Distinction
Between the Definitions of
Canon and Scripture?

Once a distinction is made between scripture and canon,
the idea of a New Testament canon does not appear
applicable until the fourth century.

GEOFFREY M. HAHNEMAN
The Muratorian Fragment and
the Development of the Canon

🜍

BREVARD CHILDS ONCE DECLARED, "Much of the present confusion over the problem of canon turns on the failure to reach an agreement regarding the terminology."[1] Although Childs made this statement in 1979, it could just as easily been written in our current day. As scholars continue to probe into the origins and development of the biblical canon, debates and disagreements about canonical semantics have not abated.[2] What exactly

---

[1]Brevard S. Childs, *Introduction to the Old Testament as Scripture* (Philadelphia: Fortress, 1979), p. 51.
[2]Some recent studies on the definition of canon include: John Barton, *The Spirit and the Letter: Studies in the Biblical Canon* (London: SPCK, 1997), pp. 1-34; Stephen B. Chapman, *The Law and the Prophets: A Study in Old Testament Canon Formation* (Tübingen: Mohr Siebeck, 2000), pp. 71-110; idem, "How the Biblical Canon Began: Working Models and Open Questions," in Margalit Finkelberg and Guy G. Strousma, eds., *Homer, the Bible, and Beyond* (Leiden: E. J. Brill,

do we mean by the term *canon*?[3] Does it refer to books that were widely used by early Christians? Does it refer to books that function as Scripture? Or does it refer only to books that are included in a final, closed list? While these discussions over the definition of canon will certainly continue, and no universal agreement appears to be forthcoming, something does seem to have changed since Childs's original observation. The definition of canon as a final, closed list of books has begun to emerge as the more dominant one—at least in some circles. In particular, advocates of an "extrinsic" model of canon are typically committed to this particular definition and insistent that all scholars must adopt it, lest the entire field become plagued by confusion and anachronism.[4]

2003), pp. 29-51; John Webster, "'A Great and Meritorious Act of the Church'? The Dogmatic Location of the Canon," in *Die Einheit der Schrift und die Vielfalt des Kanons*, ed. John Barton and Michael Wolter (Berlin: Walter de Gruyter, 2003), pp. 95-126; Eugene Ulrich, "The Notion and Definition of Canon," in *The Canon Debate*, ed. Lee M. McDonald and James A. Sanders (Peabody, MA: Hendrickson, 2002), pp. 21-35; idem, "Qumran and the Canon of the Old Testament," in *The Biblical Canons*, ed. J.-M. Auwers and H. J. de Jonge (Leuven: Leuven University Press, 2003), pp. 57-80; Jonathan Z. Smith, "Canons, Catalogues, and Classics," in *Canonization and Decanonization*, pp. 295-311; Kendall W. Folkert, "The 'Canons' of 'Scripture,'" in *Rethinking Scripture: Essays from a Comparative Perspective*, ed. Miriam Levering (Albany: State University of New York Press, 1989), pp. 170-79; James A. Sanders, *Torah and Canon* (Philadelphia: Fortress, 1972), pp. 91-98; Gerald T. Sheppard, "Canon," in *Encyclopedia of Religion*, ed. Lindsay Jones (Detroit: Thomson Gale, 1987), 3:62-69; John C. Peckham, "The Canon and Biblical Authority: A Critical Comparison of Two Models of Canonicity," *TrinJ* 28 (2007): 229-49; John Goldingay, *Models for Scripture* (Grand Rapids: Eerdmans, 1994), pp. 85-197.

[3]Our concern throughout this chapter is not the word *canon* itself (κανών, borrowed from the Hebrew כנה), but the *concept* of canon. Put differently, we are asking what sociohistorical or theological phenomenon is referred to when we use the word *canon*, not the etymology or history of the term. This is unfortunate, because considering only the term itself can bring confusion rather than clarity. For example, Geoffrey M. Hahneman, in "The Muratorian Fragment and the Origins of the New Testament Canon," in *Canon Debate*, p. 406, has attempted to argue for a late date for the canon by appealing to the fact that the term *canon* (in either Greek or Latin) was not used to refer to a list of Christian Scriptures until the fourth century or later. However, there is no reason to think the appearance of the term itself is decisive—it is the concept behind the term that must be clarified and considered. Although others do not go to the extreme of Hahneman, there seems to be a fascination with the etymology of the term: e.g., Bruce M. Metzger, *The Canon of the New Testament: Its Origin, Development, and Significance* (Oxford: Clarendon, 1987), pp. 289-93; Harry Y. Gamble, *The New Testament Canon: Its Making and Meaning* (Philadelphia: Fortress, 1985), pp. 15-18; and Ulrich, "Notion and Definition of Canon," pp. 21-35. In fact, Alexander Souter, in *The Text and Canon of the New Testament* (London: Duckworth, 1954), declares, "The word 'Canon' has had a history unsurpassed in interest, perhaps, by any other word in the Greek language" (p. 141).

[4]On this point, see Ulrich, "Notion and Definition of Canon," p. 34; and Craig D. Allert, *A High View of Scripture? The Authority of the Bible and the Formation of the New Testament Canon* (Grand Rapids: Baker Academic, 2007), pp. 49-51. Once again, it should be noted that not all scholars in the extrinsic camp necessarily adopt this definition, nor do all scholars outside the

Such claims are difficult to resist—after all, no one wants to plunge canonical studies into disarray. Moreover, there is certainly something attractive about having a single, unified definition of canon on which we can all agree (and build upon). Nevertheless, we must ask whether this "consensus" position, and the attitude with which it is held, is justified. Does this single definition adequately capture the complexities and nuances of the concept of canon? And are we required to adopt only this definition to the exclusion of all others?

THE EXCLUSIVE DEFINITION OF CANON

The definition of canon as a fixed, final and closed list of books—what might be called the *exclusive* definition[5]—was put forth originally by A. C. Sundberg in 1968.[6] Sundberg drew a sharp distinction between the terms *Scripture* and *canon* and, on this basis, argued that we cannot speak of the idea of canon until at least the fourth century or later. Although Scripture would have existed prior to this time period, Sundberg argues that we must reserve the term canon until the end of the entire process. It would be anachronistic to use the term canon to speak of any second- or third-century historical realities. Thus, simply marshaling evidence of a book's scriptural status in the early church—as is so often done in canonical studies—is not enough to consider it canonical. The book must be part of a list from which nothing can be added or taken away.

Sundberg's exclusive definition of canon was initially supported by a

---

extrinsic camp reject it. The point of this chapter is that this definition is a *general* tenet of the extrinsic model and therefore warrants our careful examination.

[5]Chapman, "How the Biblical Canon Began," pp. 34-35, uses the term "extrinsic" instead of "exclusive." The former term is also used in Smith, "Canons, Catalogues, and Classics," p. 297. But Chapman does use the latter term in Stephen B. Chapman, "The Canon Debate: What It Is and Why It Matters" (presented at SBL, San Diego, 2007).

[6]Albert C. Sundberg, "Towards a Revised History of the New Testament Canon," *Studia Evangelica* 4 (1968): 452-61; idem, "The Making of the New Testament Canon," in *The Interpreter's One-Volume Commentary on the Bible* (Nashville: Abingdon, 1971), pp. 1216-24. Of course, Sundberg is not the first scholar to propose a sharp distinction between Scripture and canon. Its roots can be traced to W. Staerk, "Der Schrift- und Kanonbegriff der jüdischen Bibel," *ZST* 6 (1929): 101-19; Gustav Hölscher, *Kanonisch und Apokryph. Ein Kapitel aus der Geschichte des alttestamentlichen Kanons* (Naumburg: Lippert, 1905); and arguably back to Semler's original critique of canon, *Abhandlung von freier Untersuchung des Canon* (Halle, 1771–1775). See discussion in Iain Provan, "Canons to the Left of Him: Brevard Childs, His Critics, and the Future of Old Testament Theology," *SJT* 50 (1997): 9-11; and Chapman, *Law and the Prophets*, p. 34.

number of key scholars such as D. H. Kelsey,[7] James Barr[8] and Harry Gamble,[9] and, in more recent years, has continued to gather adherents. John Barton, while rightly recognizing that multiple definitions of canon have some validity,[10] still seems to prefer the exclusive definition: "Much clarity could be gained if we agreed to distinguish sharply between these two concepts [of Scripture and canon]."[11] Geoffrey Hahneman has been a vigorous advocate of the exclusive definition, declaring, "Once a distinction is made between scripture and canon, the idea of a New Testament canon does not appear applicable until the fourth century."[12] Lee McDonald has consistently promoted Sundberg's definition in his many writings over the last twenty years and is no doubt one of the reasons for its recent popularity.[13] Eugene Ulrich is quite forceful in his approach, arguing that unless scholars accept the exclusive definition, discussions will be "confusing and counterproductive." [14] Likewise, the recent work of Craig Allert insists on the "*necessity* of proper distinction between the terms 'Scripture' and 'canon.'"[15] Even this brief survey of scholars (and more could be added[16])

---

[7]David H. Kelsey, *The Uses of Scripture in Recent Theology* (Philadelphia: Fortress, 1975), pp. 104-5.

[8]James Barr, *The Scope and Authority of the Bible* (Philadelphia: Westminster, 1980), p. 120.

[9]Gamble, *New Testament Canon*, pp. 18-19. Elsewhere, Gamble nuances his view further and acknowledges that other definitions have some validity: e.g., Harry Y. Gamble, "The Canon of the New Testament," in *The New Testament and Its Modern Interpreters*, ed. Eldon J. Epp and George MacRae (Philadelphia: Fortress, 1989), pp. 201-43; idem, "The New Testament Canon: Recent Research and the Status Quaestionis," in *Canon Debate*, pp. 267-94.

[10]Barton, *Spirit and the Letter*, pp. 1-34.

[11]John Barton, "Canonical Approaches Ancient and Modern," in *Biblical Canons*, p. 202; see also idem, *Oracles of God: Perceptions of Ancient Prophecy in Israel After the Exile* (London: Darton, Longman, and Todd, 1985), pp. 55-82.

[12]Geoffrey M. Hahneman, *The Muratorian Fragment and the Development of the Canon* (Oxford: Clarendon, 1992), pp. 129-30.

[13]Lee M. McDonald, *The Biblical Canon: Its Origin, Transmission, and Authority* (Peabody, MA: Hendrickson, 2007), pp. 38-69; idem, *Forgotten Scriptures: The Selection and Rejection of Early Religious Writings* (Louisville: Westminster John Knox, 2009), pp. 11-33. As a whole, McDonald is more balanced in the way he holds Sundberg's definition, recognizing that other definitions have some validity.

[14]Ulrich, "Notion and Definition of Canon," pp. 21-35.

[15]Allert, *High View of Scripture?*, p. 51 (emphasis mine).

[16]E.g., George Aichele, "Canon, Ideology, and the Emergence of an Imperial Church," in *Canon and Canonicity: The Formation and Use of Scripture*, ed. Einar Thomassen (Copenhagen: Museum Tusculanum Press, 2010), pp. 45-65; Julio Trebolle-Barrera, "Origins of a Tripartite Old Testament Canon," in *Canon Debate*, pp. 128-45; David L. Dungan, *Constantine's Bible: Politics and the Making of the New Testament* (Philadelphia: Fortress, 2006), pp. 1-10; H. J. de Jonge, "The New Testament Canon," in *Biblical Canons*, pp. 309-19; and John C. Poirier, "Scripture and Canon," in *The Sacred Text*, ed. Michael Bird and Michael Pahl (Piscataway, NJ: Gorgias, 2010), pp. 83-98.

suggests that David Nienhuis was correct when he observed that "Sundberg's position has enjoyed widespread acceptance."[17]

But is the widespread acceptance of this position justified? We begin our analysis by noting that there are many positives to this position that ought to be acknowledged. For one, the exclusive definition of canon rightly captures the reality of the canon's "fluid" edges prior to the fourth century. It took some time for the boundaries of the canon to solidify, and the exclusive definition accommodates this historical fact by using different terms for different stages. Moreover, this definition helps remind us of the important role played by the church in the recognition and reception of the canon. By restricting the term *canon* to only the final stage when the church has decisively responded, the exclusive definition keeps church and canon from being unduly divorced from one another—the two concepts go hand in hand. However, there are a number of concerns about this definition that need to be explored.

First, it is difficult to believe that the sharp Scripture-canon distinction drawn by modern advocates of the exclusive definition would have been so readily shared by their historical counterparts in the second century. Would early Christians have regarded "Scripture" as fluid and open-ended and only "canon" as limited and restricted? If they were able to say that certain books in their library were Scripture, then that implies they would have been able to say that other books in their library were *not* Scripture. But, if they are able to say which books are (and are not) Scripture, then how is that materially different than saying which books are in (or not in) a canon? Thus, it seems some degree of limitation and exclusion is already implied in the term *Scripture*. As Iain Provan observes, "The question I am asking is whether the idea of scripture does not itself imply the idea of limitation, of canon, even if it is not yet conceived that the limits have been reached. I believe that it does so imply."[18] If so, then the necessity of a strict demarcation between Scripture and canon largely disappears.

Second, while the exclusive definition insists the term *canon* cannot be used until the New Testament collection has been officially "closed,"

---

[17]David R. Nienhuis, *Not by Paul Alone: The Formation of the Catholic Epistle Collection and the Christian Canon* (Waco: Baylor University Press, 2007), p. 235.

[18]Provan, "Canons to the Left of Him," pp. 9-10.

significant ambiguity remains on what, exactly, constitutes this closing.
If it is absolute uniformity of practice, across all of Christendom, then,
on those terms, there was still not a canon even in the fourth century.
Indeed, on those terms we *still* do not have a canon even today.[19] If the
closing of the canon refers to a formal, official act of the early church,
then we are hard pressed to find such an act before the Council of Trent
in the sixteenth century.[20] The fact of the matter is that when we look
into the history of the canon we realize that there was never a time when
the boundaries of the New Testament were closed in the way the exclusive definition would require. Stephen Chapman comments on this
problem: "Rather than being a minor problem, this inconsistency casts
significant doubt upon the appropriateness of the entire approach. Why
should scholars adopt as the correct usage of the term 'canon' a meaning
that does not correspond fully to any historical reality?"[21] Ironically,
then, the exclusive definition is as guilty of anachronism as any of the
views that it critiques.

This leads us to the third, and arguably the most foundational, problem
for this definition. Inherent to the exclusive definition is an insistence that
the fourth century represents such a profoundly different stage in the development of the New Testament that it warrants a decisive change in terminology. Indeed, Dungan refers to the stage of Scripture and the stage of
canon as "very different."[22] But was the canon so very different in the fourth
century? While a broader degree of consensus was no doubt achieved by
this point, the core books of the New Testament—the four Gospels and the
majority of Paul's epistles—had already been recognized and received for
centuries. Whatever supposedly happened in the fourth century neither al-

---

[19]E.g., as noted in the introduction, the modern-day lectionary of the Syrian Orthodox Church
still operates on the twenty-two-book canon of the Peshitta. For further discussion see Metzger,
Canon of the New Testament, pp. 218-28.

[20]Harry Y. Gamble, "Christianity: Scripture and Canon," in *The Holy Book in Comparative Perspective*, ed. Frederick M. Denny and Rodney L. Taylor (Columbia: University of South Carolina
Press, 1985), pp. 46-47. Gamble argues that church councils such as Laodicea (in 360) were
local, not ecumenical, and therefore had no binding authority. Lee M. McDonald, "The Integrity of the Biblical Canon in Light of Its Historical Development," *BBR* 6 (1996): 131-32, agrees:
"There was never a time when the church as a whole concluded that these writings and no others could help the church carry out its mission in the world."

[21]Chapman, "Canon Debate," p. 14.

[22]Dungan, *Constantine's Bible*, p. 133.

tered the status of these books nor increased their authority.[23] It is precisely at this point that the limitations of the exclusive definition become clear. The abrupt change in terminology gives the impression that these books bore some lesser status prior to this point; it communicates that Christians *only* had Scripture and not a canon. Or, as one scholar put it, prior to the fourth century Christians only had a "boundless, living mass of heterogenous" texts.[24] At best this is obscurant, and at worst misleading. Moreover, it feeds the notion that the canon was somehow the result of "a great and meritorious act of the church."[25] And this is why this definition is a core tenet of the extrinsic model—it implies there was no (and could be no) canon until the church officially acted. Stephen Dempster highlights this problem: "Reserving the terminology 'canon' for only the final collection of books obscures the continuity that exists at earlier times. To accept such a limiting definition might suggest that the canon did not have a history, only to be created *ex nihilo*, the result of a [church] council."[26]

An example of this third issue can be seen clearly in the recent work of Craig Allert. The stated goal of his volume is to "emphasize the centrality of the church in the formation of the New Testament."[27] It is no surprise, then, that he is such a strong advocate of Sundberg's definition of canon because, as he acknowledges, "Sundberg's work has had the effect of pushing the decisive period, that of formal canonization, into the fourth and fifth centuries."[28] Such a late date for canon allows Allert to raise the profile of the church—it was there from the beginning, whereas the canon only arrives late on the scene. He declares, "The Bible was not always 'there' in early Christianity. Yet the church still continued to function in its absence."[29] While Allert is right to remind us of the important role of the church, this whole approach to the development of the canon raises some concerns. If the core books of the New Testament were functioning as authoritative Scripture by the middle of the second century, then is it really helpful to

---

[23]Barton, *Spirit and the Letter*, pp. 18-19. We will explore this issue further in chapter five.

[24]Dungan, *Constantine's Bible*, pp. 132-33.

[25]Webster, "Dogmatic Location of the Canon," pp. 96-97.

[26]Stephen G. Dempster, "Canons on the Right and Canons on the Left: Finding a Resolution in the Canon Debate," *JETS* 52 (2009): 51.

[27]Allert, *High View of Scripture?*, p. 67.

[28]Ibid., p. 88.

[29]Ibid., p. 12.

claim that early Christians did not have a "Bible"? This sort of language seems to bring more confusion than clarity. Although it may prevent one kind of misperception (that the canon was neat and tidy in the second century), it ends up promulgating what is arguably a bigger one (that early Christians had little interest in a New Testament until the fourth century).

With these concerns on the table (and more could be added), one might get the impression that this critique has been offered to challenge the overall legitimacy of the exclusive definition. However, that is not the intent here. If the above concerns are addressed, then the exclusive definition still has an important role to play. After all, the exclusive definition is correct that the boundaries of the canon were not solidified until the fourth century—and, in this sense, we did not have a "canon" until that time. The exclusive definition just needs to acknowledge that this is a general consensus and not an official act of "closing" with airtight boundaries that somehow increased the authority of these books.[30] Thus, the main point of this critique is not to do away with the exclusive definition entirely but to challenge those advocates of the exclusive view who claim that it is the *only* legitimate perspective on canon. Given the limitations and weaknesses of the exclusive definition we have observed, we should be hesitant to think it completely exhausts the meaning of the term. If we are to fully appreciate the depth and complexity of *canon*, we must also let other definitions have a voice.

THE FUNCTIONAL DEFINITION OF CANON

Although the exclusive definition of canon may be the dominant one at the current time (or at least the one that has enjoyed increasing popularity), it is not the only option on the table. Childs has played a central role in promoting an alternative definition, arguing, in contrast to Sundberg, that the term *canon* need not be restricted to a final, closed list but can "encompass the entire process by which the formation of the church's sacred writings took place."[31] If a collection of books functions as a religious norm, regardless of whether that collection is open or closed, then Childs is comfortable

---

[30]By "general consensus" I mean that the vast majority of the church was in agreement about the boundaries of the canon, even though there may have been pockets of the church that still had differing views.

[31]Brevard S. Childs, *The New Testament as Canon: An Introduction* (London: SCM, 1984), p. 25.

using the term *canon*. Or, put differently, the term *canon* can be employed as soon as a book is regarded as "Scripture" by early Christian communities. Thus, Childs argues against any rigid separation between Scripture and canon, saying that they are "very closely related, indeed often identical."[32] For our purposes here, we shall refer to this definition as the *functional* definition of canon.[33]

Of course, the pedigree of this functional definition goes back further than Childs. Barton points out how Harnack's entire reconstruction of the origins of the New Testament canon is predicated upon this very definition.[34] Harnack argued that a book could be considered canonical when it was expressly regarded as "Scripture"—which usually required the use of formulaic markers such as γραφή or γέγραπται. On this definition, the origins of the New Testament canon would be dated to the middle of the second century, dramatically earlier than the fourth/fifth century date advocated by Sundberg. Barton also distinguishes Harnack's approach from that of Zahn, who was willing to regard a book as canonical apart from formulaic markers, as long as it enjoyed some degree of widespread use by early Christians (allowing for an even earlier date for canon).[35] However, the distinction between Zahn and Harnack should not be overplayed. Their disagreement hinged upon the *way* to determine the church's view of a book (formulaic markers versus widespread use), not whether the church's view of a book was the key factor in deciding canonical status. The definitions of Harnack and Zahn are in agreement on the critical point: canon is

---

[32]Idem, "On Reclaiming the Bible for Christian Theology," in *Reclaiming the Bible for the Church*, ed. Carl E. Braaten and Robert W. Jenson (Grand Rapids: Eerdmans, 1995), p. 9.

[33]Chapman, "How the Biblical Canon Began," pp. 34-35, uses the term "intrinsic" for the functional definition, as does Smith, "Canons, Catalogues, and Classics," p. 297. Elsewhere, Chapman uses the term "inclusive" ("Canon Debate," p. 12).

[34]Barton, *Spirit and the Letter*, pp. 4-8. For Harnack's original thesis, see Adolf von Harnack, *Origin of the New Testament and the Most Important Consequences of a New Creation* (London: Williams & Northgate, 1925). Harnack is a good example of someone who is clearly in the extrinsic camp but does not, for whatever set of reasons, follow the exclusive definition of canon. Thus, we are reminded again that there is not a one-to-one correspondence between the extrinsic model and this definition of canon.

[35]Barton, *Spirit and the Letter*, pp. 1-14. As observed by Barton, Zahn's emphasis on the early Christian use of canonical books (instead of just formulaic markers) has found some support in the recent statistical work of Franz Stuhlhofer, *Der Gebrauch Der Bibel Von Jesus Bis Euseb: Eine Statistische Untersuchung Zur Kanonsgeschichte* (Wuppertal: R. Brockhaus, 1988). Stuhlhofer argues that the core canonical books of the New Testament were used substantially more often (in proportion to their size) than noncanonical books (and even the Old Testament).

determined by the *function* of a book in the church and not whether it was regarded as part of a final, closed list. In this sense, Harnack and Zahn really hold to the same general approach to canon.

The functional definition has also found support from a number of modern scholars, particularly those who have an association with Childs and/or the "canonical criticism" camp.[36] James Sanders recognizes that the functional perspective on canon is valid because it is the predecessor of the exclusive perspective: "Canon as *function* antedates canon as *shape*."[37] G. T. Sheppard provides a helpful distinction between canon as a "rule, standard, ideal, norm" and canon as "fixation, standardization, enumeration."[38] He designates the former "Canon 1" and the latter "Canon 2," recognizing the legitimacy of both. Chapman has persistently critiqued the exclusive definition while suggesting that the functional definition should have its place at the table,[39] as have Provan,[40] Meade,[41] Riekert[42] and Dempster.[43]

The functional definition has many positives and provides a welcome balance to the exclusive definition. For one, it accurately captures the historical reality that early Christians did possess an authoritative corpus of books long before the fourth century, even if the edges were not entirely solidified. Thus, it does not run the risk of unduly diminishing the perceived authority of these books in pre-fourth-century context. In this sense, the functional definition would fit well with an intrinsic model of canon. In addition, this definition seems less prone to artificially inflate the role of official church declarations about the canon—as if those declarations somehow "created" or "established" the authority of these books.

That said, however, the functional definition still has its weaknesses. Two of these can be noted here. First, McDonald has pointed out that the func-

---

[36]Of course, Childs himself does not prefer the term "canonical criticism" (*Introduction to the Old Testament*, p. 82), but that term has been used to refer to this approach since it was apparently coined by Sanders (*Torah and Canon*, pp. ix-xx).

[37]James Sanders, "Canon: Hebrew Bible," in *ABD* 1:843 (emphasis his).

[38]Sheppard, "Canon," p. 64.

[39]Chapman, *Law and the Prophets*, pp. 71-110; Chapman, "How the Biblical Canon Began," pp. 29-51.

[40]Provan, "Canons to the Left of Him," pp. 9-11.

[41]D. Meade, *Pseudepigrapha and Canon* (Tübingen: J. C. B. Mohr, 1986), p. 24.

[42]Stephanus J. P. K. Riekert, "Critical Research and the One Christian Canon Comprising Two Testaments," *Neot* 14 (1981): 21-41.

[43]Dempster, "Canons on the Right and Canons on the Left," pp. 50-51.

tional definition struggles to account for books that were regarded as Scripture by some early Christian communities but never made it into the final, closed canon: for example, the *Shepherd of Hermas*, *Apocalypse of Peter*, and so on.[44] What shall we call these books? McDonald argues that the functional definition leads to confusion because it is forced to call these books "canonical." How can a book be canonical and then cease to be canonical? If we would only use the exclusive definition, he argues, then such confusion could be avoided.[45] McDonald is correct to point out this issue, and it should be acknowledged that there is some imprecision in the functional definition here. However, it is not clear that the issue is as serious as McDonald suggests, nor that it mandates the sole use of the exclusive definition. For one, there does not appear to be anything particularly problematic or confusing about saying that some early Christian communities had different functional canons. There was widespread agreement about the core canonical books, but some disagreement over the peripheral books was inevitable. Some books were "canonical" in the eyes of certain communities, even though they would never become part of the church's permanent collection. The functional definition appropriately captures this reality. The exclusive definition claims to avoid the problem of imprecision because it waits until the fourth century when the canonical boundaries were finally fixed. But, as noted above, the boundaries of the canon were not absolute even in the fourth or fifth centuries. Indeed, disagreements continue to the modern day. Thus, we are reminded that all definitions, including the exclusive definition, suffer from a level of imprecision—that is unavoidable whenever a definition seeks to capture an evolving historical situation (such as the development of the canon).

The second weakness of the functional definition is more significant and is also one that is shared by the exclusive definition. Both of these definitions fail to adequately address the *ontology* of canon. That is, these definitions do not incorporate what canon *is* in and of itself, apart from what it does in the church (functional) or how it is delineated by the church (ex-

---

[44]McDonald, *Forgotten Scriptures*, pp. 23-25.
[45]McDonald argues that terms like "decanonization" or "temporary canonization" are nonsensical (*Forgotten Scriptures*, pp. 23-25). For more on this issue, see A. van der Kooij and K. van der Toorn, eds., *Canonization and Decanonization* (Leiden: E. J. Brill, 1998).

clusive). If we only have the functional and exclusive definitions, then we can only conclude that this thing we call *canon* cannot exist prior to it being used as Scripture or prior to the church reaching a final consensus. The church must act for there to be a canon. In this regard, the functional and exclusive definitions seem to confuse (or at least are prone to confuse) the church's reception of the canon with that which *makes* a book canon. A book can become canonical, but on its own it is nothing. Of course, for some modern scholars, this would not be viewed as a problem. Viewing the canon as a purely community-dependent entity is central to the extrinsic model we are discussing in this volume—it is what John Webster calls the "naturalization" of canon.[46] If the canon is nothing in and of itself, then it must be the result of contingent (and to some extent, arbitrary) human processes. Harnack is a prime example of this naturalization as he attributes the existence of the canon to the church's "creative act"[47] in response to Marcion.[48] Others have argued that the canon is merely a sociocultural concept that reflects the relationship between a religious society and its texts.[49] Still others have suggested canon is just a social phenomenon that arises when a community desires to express its identity.[50] As Kelsey notes,

---

[46]Webster, "Dogmatic Location of the Canon," p. 101.

[47]Harnack, *History of Dogma*, vol. 2 (New York: Dover, 1961), p. 62n1.

[48]Harnack's core thesis regarding Marcion was supported by Hans von Campenhausen, *The Formation of the Christian Bible* (London: Adam & Charles Black, 1972) (German title: *Die Entstehung der christlichen Bibel* [Tubingen: J. C. B. Mohr, 1968]). For other assessments of Marcion's influence on the canon, see R. Joseph Hoffmann, *Marcion: On the Restitution of Christianity: An Essay on the Development of Radical Paulinist Theology in the Second Century* (Chico, CA: Scholars Press, 1984); Barton, *Spirit and the Letter*, pp. 35-62; and Robert Grant, *The Formation of the New Testament* (New York: Harper & Row, 1965), p. 126.

[49]Smith, "Canons, Catalogues, and Classics," pp. 295-311; H. J. Adriaanse, "Canonicity and the Problem of the Golden Mean," in *Canonization and Decanonization*, pp. 313-30; Aleida Assmann and Jan Assmann, eds., *Kanon und Zensur, Archäologie der literarischen Kommunikation II* (München: Wilhelm Fink Verlag, 1987); Paul Davies, *Whose Bible Is It Anyway?* (Sheffield: Sheffield Academic Press, 1995), pp. 17-27.

[50]Paul Ricoeur, "The 'Sacred' Text and the Community," in *The Critical Study of Sacred Texts*, ed. Wendy D. O'Flaherty (Berkeley: Graduate Theological Union, 1979), pp. 271-76. A number of recent studies of canon have taken on a *comparative* dimension, showing how other religions, groups and communities have their own sorts of "canons." E.g., Margalit Finkelberg and Guy G. Stroumsa, eds., *Homer, the Bible and Beyond*; Tomas Hägg, "Canon Formation in Greek Literary Culture," in *Canon and Canonicity*, pp. 109-28; Wilfred C. Smith, *What Is Scripture? A Comparative Approach* (London: SPCK, 1993); Loveday Alexander, "Canon and Exegesis in the Medical Schools of Antiquity," in *The Canon of Scripture in Jewish and Christian Tradition*, ed. Philip S. Alexander and Kaestli Jean-Daniel (Lausanne: Éditions du Zèbre, 2007), pp. 115-53; Armin Lange, "Oracle Collection and Canon: A Comparison Between Judah and Greece in

canon is the church's "self-description."[51] And always popular is the idea that "canon" is just a political construct, an ideological instrument, created to wield power and control.[52]

The problem with these community-dependent views is that they do not represent the historical Christian position on the canon. Although it is out of vogue in some critical circles today, Christians have traditionally believed that the canon is a collection of books that are given by God to his corporate church. And if the canonical books are what they are by virtue of the divine purpose for which they were given, and not by virtue of their use or acceptance by the community of faith, then, in principle, they can exist as such apart from that community. After all, aren't God's books still God's books—and therefore still authoritative—*prior* to anyone using them or recognizing them? Surely, the existence of canon and the recognition of canon are two distinguishable phenomena. Why, then, should the term *canon* be restricted to only the latter and not the former? Thus, our definition of canon cannot be limited to only the functional or exclusive definitions because neither of them account for this phenomenon; neither allow for the ontology of canon to play a role. Now, this doesn't mean that all those who use the functional or exclusive definitions do not have an ontology of canon. It simply means that these definitions *themselves* do not allow for an ontology of canon. Unless this limitation is ad-

---

Persian Times," in *Jewish and Christian Scripture as Artifact and Canon*, ed. Craig A. Evans and H. Daniel Zacharias (London: T & T Clark, 2009), pp. 9-47; and many of the essays in *Religion and Normativity, Vol 1: The Discursive Fight Over Religious Texts in Antiquity*, ed. Anders-Christian Jacobson (Aarhus: Aarhus University Press, 2009).

[51]Kelsey, *Uses of Scripture in Recent Theology*, p. 106.

[52]On this general topic, see Alan K. Bowman and Greg Wolf, eds., *Literacy and Power in the Ancient World* (Cambridge: Cambridge University Press, 1994); George Aichele, *The Control of Biblical Meaning: Canon As Semiotic Mechanism* (Harrisburg, PA: Trinity Press International, 2001); James E. Brenneman, *Canons in Conflict: Negotiating Texts in True and False Prophecy* (New York: Oxford University Press, 1997), pp. 52-80; Robert P. Coote and Mary P. Coote, *Power, Politics, and the Making of the Bible* (Minneapolis: Fortress, 1990); Gerald L. Bruns, "Canon and Power in the Hebrew Scriptures," *CI* 10 (1984): 462-80; Kim Haines-Eitzen, *Guardians of Letters: Literacy, Power, and the Transmitters of Early Christian Literature* (Oxford: Oxford University Press, 2000); Max Weber, *The Sociology of Religion* (Boston: Beacon, 1993), p. 68; David Brakke, "Canon Formation and Social Conflict in Fourth Century Egypt: Athanasius of Alexandria's Thirty-Ninth Festal Letter," *HTR* 87 (1994): 395-419; and Aichele, "Canon, Ideology, and the Emergence of an Imperial Church," pp. 45-65. In response to the idea that canons always represent those in power, see Willie van Peer, "Canon Formation: Ideology or Aesthetic Quality?," *British Journal of Aesthetics* 36 (1996): 97-108.

dressed, such definitions, whether intended or not, inevitably encourage the "naturalization" of canon.[53]

THE ONTOLOGICAL DEFINITION OF CANON

In order to accommodate the historical Christian approach to the canon, we need a definition that moves beyond the functional and exclusive ones. So, we shall call this the *ontological* definition. The ontological definition focuses on what the canon is in and of itself, namely *the authoritative books that God gave his corporate church*. One might say that this definition looks at canon from a divine perspective, rather than from only an ecclesiological perspective. Books do not *become* canonical—they are canonical because they are the books God has given as a permanent guide for his church. Thus, from this perspective, it is the existence of the canonical books that is determinative, not their function or reception. On this definition, there would be a canon even in the first century, as soon as the New Testament books were written. Of course, such a definition is inevitably retrospective in nature. The Gospel of John would have been "canon" ten minutes after it was written, but the early church would not yet have known it. It was only at a later point, when the corporate church had finally recognized which books belonged in the canon, that it could then look back and realize that there was a "canon" even in the first century.[54] But, there is nothing illegit-

---

[53] Adherents of the exclusive definition may respond that their definition does not necessarily encourage the "naturalization" of canon because it allows for books to be regarded as "Scripture" prior to their recognition by the church. While this is certainly true, two concerns still remain: (1) As we noted above, the strict demarcation between Scripture and canon tends to diminish the authority of the former; i.e., it suggests there was *only* a loose, unbounded collection of Scripture prior to the church's formal decisions. Thus, whatever ontology the exclusive definition might grant to "Scripture," it is still understood to be different from the ontology of "canon." (2) What is still lacking in the exclusive definition is an ontology of canon where the *limits* are determined by the purpose for which they were given, apart from the actions of the church. If God really gave certain books to serve as a permanent guide for the church—as the ontological definition maintains—then there is nothing incoherent about arguing that those limits are already there *in principle*. The "canon" is always the books God intended as a permanent foundation for his church; no more and no less. In this sense, the canon is "closed" as soon as the last book is given by God.

[54] In light of the ontological definition, one might wonder what language should be used to describe "lost" apostolic books (e.g., Paul's other letter to the Corinthians). Are we obligated to call these books "canon"? Not at all. C. Stephen Evans, "Canonicity, Apostolicity, and Biblical Authority: Some Kierkegaardian Reflections," in *Canon and Biblical Interpretation*, ed. Craig Bartholomew, et al. (Carlisle: Paternoster, 2006), p. 155, makes the argument that we have good reasons to think that lost books were not intended by God to be in the canon. He declares, "It

imate about affirming this reality. If canonicity is not merely something that *happens* to a book, then we can affirm a book is canonical when that book is produced. B. B. Warfield employs the ontological definition when he says, "The Canon of the New Testament was completed when the last authoritative book was given to any church by the apostles, and that was when John wrote the apocalypse, about A.D. 98."[55]

No doubt, those committed to a rigid historical-critical approach to the study of the canon will balk at the ontological definition as inappropriately theological.[56] One cannot use a definition for canon that involves any theological considerations, we might be told.[57] But why are we obligated to study the canon on purely historical-critical terms? Why should we be obligated to use the term *canon* in a way that prohibits the very approach to the canon that Christians have held for two millennia? Indeed, one might argue that, in this sense, the historical-critical approach is offering its own theological perspective—just in the opposite direction. More and more,

---

seems highly plausible, then, that if God is going to see that an authorized revelation is given, he will also see that this revelation is recognized. . . . On this view, then, the fact that the church recognized the books of the New Testament as canonical is itself a powerful reason to believe that these books are indeed the revelation God intended humans to have." If God did not intend these lost books to be in the canon, then we have little reason to call them "canon." As for what to call these lost books, we could refer to them simply as "other apostolic books" or even as "Scripture." In regard to the latter term, this would be the one place where a distinction between "canon" and "Scripture" would be useful. Whereas Sundberg advocates a more permanent distinction between Scripture and canon, we would argue that this distinction would only apply to the narrow issue of lost apostolic books. When that issue is in view, canon is rightly a subset of Scripture—all canonical books are Scripture, but not all scriptural books are canonical. However, outside of this particular issue, there seems to be little reason to make a sharp distinction between Scripture and canon.

[55]B. B. Warfield, "The Formation of the Canon of the New Testament," in *The Inspiration and Authority of the Bible* (Phillipsburg, NJ: P & R, 1948), p. 415.

[56]For examples of those who argue theological perspectives have no place in biblical studies, see Davies, *Whose Bible Is It Anyway?*, pp. 51-52; and also John J. Collins, "Is a Critical Biblical Theology Possible?," in *The Hebrew Bible and Its Interpreters*, ed. William H. Propp (Winona Lake, IN: Eisenbrauns, 1990), pp. 1-17.

[57]At this point, it is important that we are clear about the role of the ontological definition of canon within the overall "intrinsic" model we are advocating in this volume. As said in the introduction, the intrinsic model, as a whole, does not require any particular theological commitments about the divine origins of these books. Thus, one need not affirm the ontological definition of canon in order to hold to the intrinsic model. Although I am arguing that these three different definitions of canon work best as a unit, a person who wants to avoid theological commitments could just affirm the validity of the functional definition. The key point of this chapter is simply that the exclusive definition of canon—a major tenet of the extrinsic model— is problematic when it stands as the only definition of canon.

scholars have recognized that theological and historical concerns are not easily separated, nor should they be. Iain Provan makes the point that, "All the great giants of biblical study in the last 200 years have worked within certain dogmatic and philosophical positions."[58] Francis Watson has pressed the case that, "Theological concerns should have an acknowledged place within the field of biblical scholarship."[59] This is especially true in the field of canonical studies. Floyd Filson has made the simple, but often overlooked, observation that, "The canon is a theological issue."[60] Kevin Vanhoozer concurs, "History alone cannot answer the question of what the canon finally is; theology alone can do that."[61]

Although the ontological definition brings a healthy balance to our definition of canon, we are not arguing here that it should be the *only* definition of canon. On the contrary, the ontological definition is being offered to complement (or round out) the functional and exclusive definitions. All three of these definitions make important contributions to our understanding of canon and therefore all three should be used in an integrative and multidimensional manner. The exclusive definition rightly reminds us that the canon did not fall in place overnight; it took several centuries for the edges of the canon to solidify.[62] The functional definition reminds us that prior to the determination of the final shape of the canon there was a core collection of books that functioned with supreme authority in early Christian communities. And the ontological definition reminds us that books do not just *become* authoritative because of the actions of the church— they bear authority by virtue of what they are, books given by God. When all three perspectives on the canon are considered in tandem, a more bal-

---

[58]Provan, "Canons to the Left of Him," p. 23. See also Iain Provan, "Ideologies, Literary and Critical: Reflections on Recent Writings on the History of Israel," *JBL* 114 (1995): 585-606.

[59]Francis Watson, *Text and Truth: Redefining Biblical Theology* (Grand Rapids: Eerdmans, 1997), p. 3. See also idem, "Bible, Theology and the University: A Response to Philip Davies," *JSOT* 71 (1996): 3-16.

[60]Floyd V. Filson, *Which Books Belong in the Bible? A Study of the Canon* (Philadelphia: Westminster, 1957), p. 42.

[61]Kevin J. Vanhoozer, *The Drama of Doctrine: A Canonical-Linguistic Approach to Christian Theology* (Louisville: Westminster John Knox, 2005), p. 146.

[62]As noted above, the exclusive definition still plays a legitimate role as long as some of its weaknesses are addressed. In particular, the exclusive definition needs to view the fourth century as the time that the church reached a general consensus on the boundaries of the canon, not the time in which the church officially acted to close the canon in an airtight manner.

anced and more complete vision of the canon is realized. Thus, we should not be forced to choose between them.

In addition, this multidimensional approach to the definition of canon provides much-needed clarification to the ongoing debate over the "date" of canon. As Barton and others have already noted, the date assigned to the canon is, to some extent, correlative to the definition of canon one brings to the table.[63] On the exclusive definition, we do not have a canon until about the fourth century. On the functional definition, it seems that we have a canon at least by the middle of the second century. On the ontological definition, a New Testament book would be canonical as soon as it was written—giving a first-century date for the canon (depending on when one dates specific books). When these three definitions are viewed together they nicely capture the entire flow of canonical history: (1) the canonical books are written with divine authority; → (2) the books are recognized and used as Scripture by early Christians; → (3) the church reaches a consensus around these books. The fact that these three definitions are linked together in such a natural chronological order reminds us that the story of the canon is indeed a *process*; and therefore it should not be artificially restricted to one moment in time.[64] Put differently, the story of the canon is organic. It's like a tree at different stages of its life: the young seedling just inches high, the adolescent sapling, and the full-grown adult. Even though there are changes, at each stage we can still use the same terminology, namely a "tree." Perhaps, then, we need to rethink the whole concept of the canon's "date." Instead of discussing the date of canon, we might consider discussing the *stage* of canon. This latter term brings out the multidimensional nature of canon, whereas the former implies that canon is, and only can be, one point in time.

Once these three definitions are allowed to interface with one another, it also becomes evident that they, in some sense, imply one another. If a ca-

---

[63]Barton, *Spirit and the Letter*, pp. 1-34.

[64]The fact that certain definitions of canon tend to match with certain stages of canonical history should not be taken as an indication they cannot be used for other stages. For example, the ontological definition—defined as the books God gave his church—could still be used to refer to the canon in the second, third or fourth century (and even now!). Likewise, the functional definition could be used in any century where books were regarded as Scripture. It is actually the exclusive definition that is most limited in this regard; it cannot be used prior to the fourth century.

nonical book is a book given by God to his church (ontological definition) then we might naturally expect his church to recognize it as such and use it as an authoritative norm (functional definition). And if a canonical book is a book used as an authoritative norm (functional definition), we might naturally expect that the church would eventually reach a consensus on the boundaries around such books (exclusive definition). And if the church has reached a consensus on the boundaries around certain books (exclusive definition), then it is reasonable to think these are the books that have already been used as an authoritative norm (functional definition), and also that they are the books that God intended his church to have (ontological definition). The manner in which these definitions reinforce one another suggests that they are not contradictory as so many suppose, but instead are to be seen as complementary.

It is also worth noting that these three definitions of canon fit quite well with the established categories of modern speech-act philosophy.[65] Speaking (which would also include divine speaking) can take three different forms: (1) *locution* (making coherent and meaningful sounds or, in the case of writing, letters), (2) *illocution* (what the words are actually doing; for example, promising, warning, commanding, declaring and so on), and (3) *perlocution* (the effect of these words on the listener; for example, encouraging, challenging, persuading and so on).[66] Since any speaking act can include some or all of these attributes, it would be out of place to suggest that only one of them is the proper definition for what we call *speaking*. These three types of speech-acts generally correspond to the three definitions of canon outlined above. The ontological definition of canon refers to the actual production of these books and thus refers to a *locutionary* act. The functional definition refers to what the canonical books actually do in

[65]Kevin J. Vanhoozer, *First Theology: God, Scripture & Hermeneutics* (Downers Grove, IL: IVP Academic, 2002), pp. 159-203; Nicholas Wolterstorff, *Divine Discourse: Philosophical Reflections on the Claim That God Speaks* (Cambridge: Cambridge University Press, 1995); William P. Alston, *Illocutionary Acts and Sentence Meaning* (Ithaca: Cornell University Press, 2000); John L. Austin, *How to Do Things with Words* (Oxford: Oxford Paperbacks, 1976); and John R. Searle, *Speech Acts: An Essay in the Philosophy of Language* (Cambridge: Cambridge University Press, 1970).
[66]Austin, *How to Do Things with Words*, pp. 100-103; Michael S. Horton, *Covenant and Eschatology: The Divine Drama* (Louisville: Westminster John Knox, 2002), pp. 126-27; Wolterstorff, *Divine Discourse*, pp. 1-36.

the life of the church and thus refers to an *illocutionary* act. And the exclusive definition refers to the reception and impact of these books on the church and thus refers to a *perlocutionary* act. Again, a multidimensional approach to the definition of canon brings out these nuances in greater richness and depth.

The manner in which speech-act philosophy uses three complementary definitions for the term *speaking* can provide some practical insight into how the same can be done with the term *canon*. Speech-act philosophy sees no need to choose just one of these definitions to the exclusion of all others, nor should we do so in regard to canon. Of course, authors may employ one particular definition of canon at any given time, but this need not be viewed as problematic. The particular definition employed may be determined simply by what an author desires to emphasize. If an author wants to emphasize the ecclesiastical dimension of canon, then the exclusive definition may be most appropriate. If an author wants to emphasize the authoritative role played by canonical books, then the functional definition is best. And if an author desires to view canon from the perspective of its divine origins, then the ontological definition is most suitable. But, even when just one of the definitions is employed, the other two definitions can still be viewed as legitimate and complementary (just as in speech-act philosophy). Moreover, it should be acknowledged that it is not always necessary for an author to choose which definition he or she is using (nor feel the need to explain to the reader which definition is being used). Sometimes the term *canon*, like the term *speech*, is used in such a general manner that all three definitions could be in view. In the end, this term can be employed with a substantial amount of flexibility, and this flexibility is a reminder of the depth and richness of this thing we call *canon*.

Conclusion

Brevard Childs was correct that much of the confusion over the history of the canon has to do with differences in terminology. However, that problem is not solved, as the extrinsic model suggests, by imposing a single definition of canon on modern scholars. On the contrary, insisting that only a single definition rightly captures the depth and breadth of canon may end up bringing more distortion than clarification. While the exclusive defi-

nition correctly reminds us that a general consensus on the boundaries of
the canon was not achieved until the fourth century, it can give the misleading impression that there was little agreement over the core books prior
to this time period. While the functional definition correctly reminds us
that New Testament books served as an authoritative norm at quite an early
time, it still does not address what these books are in and of themselves.
While the ontological definition brings the necessary balance to both of
these approaches—offering a reminder that these books do not *become* canonical simply by the actions of the church—it too cannot stand alone. To
have only the ontological definition would lead us to wrongly conclude that
these books were basically lowered from heaven as a completed canon with
no development or history in the real world. Ironically, then, perhaps the
debate over canon is best addressed not by choosing one definition, but by
allowing for the legitimacy of multiple definitions that interface with one
another. If canon is a multidimensional phenomenon, then perhaps it is
best defined in a multidimensional fashion.

2

THE ORIGINS OF CANON

Was There Really Nothing in Early Christianity That May Have Led to a Canon?

The idea of a Christian faith governed by Christian written holy scriptures was not an essential part of the foundation plan of Christianity.

JAMES BARR
Holy Scripture: Canon, Authority and Criticism

⚖

As NOTED IN THE INTRODUCTION, the essential thrust of the extrinsic model of canon is that the canon was something developed by the later Christian church and subsequently imposed on writings written for another purpose. It is an ecclesiastical creation. If so, then it is no surprise that the second major tenet of this model is that there was nothing in early Christianity that would have naturally led to the development of a canon. The idea of a new set of scriptural books, we are told, did not arise from within the earliest stages of the Christian faith. Christians in the first century had no reason to think about such things. It was not in their DNA. Harry Gamble reflects this sentiment: "There is no intimation at all that the early church entertained the idea of Christian scriptures. . . . Therefore, the NT as we think of it was utterly remote from the minds of the first generation of Christian believers."[1] Likewise, C. F. Evans suggests that the earliest Christians "could hardly have conceived . . . the creation of a further Bible to go along with that already in existence."[2] Such a thought of new scriptural books, argues Morton Enslin, would have "scandalized" the first generation of believers.[3] James Barr is most direct: "Jesus in his teaching is nowhere portrayed as commanding or even sanctioning the production of . . . a written New Testament. He never even casually told his disciples to write anything down."[4]

Now, there are aspects of these observations that are certainly correct. In the Gospel accounts, Jesus never told his disciples to write anything down. We have no passage in the New Testament that explicitly states that Christians should produce a New Testament. And certainly the earliest Christians did not have in mind the full twenty-seven-book shape of the future canon. But, even if these things are true, does that necessarily mean that "*nothing* dictated that there should be a NT"?[5] Was there really nothing about earliest Christianity that might have given rise to a new corpus of sacred books? We shall argue here that the earliest Christians held a number of theological beliefs that would have naturally led to the development of a new canon of Scripture. In other words, we shall argue that the theological matrix of first-century Christianity created a favorable environment for the growth of a new written revelational deposit. This, of course, does not mean that these theological beliefs were, in fact, true. That is a separate question (and one we are not dealing with here). Our primary concern is whether there are good historical reasons for thinking Christians held these beliefs, and whether these beliefs might have naturally led to the development of a new canon.

[1]Harry Y. Gamble, *The New Testament Canon: Its Making and Meaning* (Philadelphia: Fortress, 1985), p. 57.

[2]C. F. Evans, "The New Testament in the Making," in *The Cambridge History of the Bible: From the Beginnings to Jerome*, ed. P. R. Ackroyd and C. F. Evans (Cambridge: Cambridge University Press, 1970), pp. 232-83, at p. 234.

[3]Morton S. Enslin, "Along Highways and Byways," *HTR* 44 (1951): 67-92, at p. 70.

[4]James Barr, *Holy Scripture: Canon, Authority and Criticism* (Philadelphia: Westminster, 1983), p. 12.

[5]Gamble, *New Testament Canon*, p. 12 (emphasis mine).

THE ESCHATOLOGICAL NATURE OF EARLY CHRISTIANITY

The Jews of the Second Temple period were not a settled group. Despite having returned to their promised land, they still conceived of themselves as in "exile"—they were still oppressed by foreign rulers (Bar 2:7-10; 2 Macc 2:5-18; 4Q504 2–5; *T. Mos.* 4:8-9).[6] Thus, Israel was in a posture of anticipation and longing; they were waiting for God to fulfill his promises to break into the world and redeem his people (for example, Is 49:6; 52:8; Zech 14:9; Amos 9:11-15). This new kingdom era was described in a number of Old Testament texts as a time that would be filled with forgiveness and reconciliation (for example, Is 40:1-11; 52:13–53:12; Jer 31:31-40; Ezek 36:24-28; Zeph 3:14-20). After all, forgiveness is what Israel needed most—it was still in "exile" due to its own sin and rebellion.[7] Not only is this heightened expectation of a new redemptive kingdom evident in a number of Second Temple texts (Tob 14:5-7; Bar 3:6-8; 4:36-37; *T. Mos.* 10:1-10; 2 Macc 1:27-29, 2:18; Wis 3:7; 1QSb 5.23-29; 1QH[a] 14.7-9),[8] but a number of New Testament texts show these same expectations of a new kingdom—people were looking for the Messiah (Jn 1:41; 4:25) who would bring the "redemption of Jerusalem" (Lk 2:38), "the consolation of Israel" (Lk 2:25), and would "restore the kingdom to Israel" (Acts 1:6).[9]

---

[6]For discussion of Israel as still in exile, see N. T. Wright, *The New Testament and the People of God* (Minneapolis: Fortress, 1992), pp. 268-79; Craig A. Evans, "Aspects of Exile and Restoration in the Proclamation of Jesus and the Gospels," in *Exile: Old Testament, Jewish, and Christian Conceptions*, ed. James M. Scott (Leiden: E. J. Brill, 1997), pp. 299-328; idem, "Jesus and the Continuing Exile of Israel," in *Jesus and the Restoration of Israel*, ed. Carey C. Newman (Downers Grove, IL: IVP Academic, 1999), pp. 77-100; and Stephen G. Dempster, *Dominion and Dynasty: A Biblical Theology of the Hebrew Bible* (Downers Grove, IL: IVP Academic, 2003), pp. 224-27.

[7]Wright, *New Testament and the People of God*, pp. 272-79.

[8]For more on messianic-redemptive expectations at Qumran, see Emile Puech, "Messianism, Resurrection, and Eschatology at Qumran and in the New Testament," in *The Community of the Renewed Covenant: The Notre Dame Symposium on the Dead Sea Scrolls*, ed. Eugene Ulrich and James C. VanderKam (Notre Dame: University of Notre Dame Press, 1994), pp. 235-56.

[9]Heightened expectations of a new redemptive kingdom are also evident in the varied attempts to lead a revolution during the first century; e.g., Theudas (Josephus, *Ant.* 20.5.1); Judas the Galilean (*Ant.* 18.1-10; Acts 5:37); the Jew from Egypt (*Ant.* 20.8.6). The fact that Theudas wanted people to follow him to the Jordan where "the river would be parted" (*Ant.* 20.5.1; cf. Josh 3:14-17) suggests that he was looking for Israel to be delivered from exile. Likewise, the Jew from Egypt sought to lead his revolution in the desert (*J.W.* 2.13.4-5), which also indicates an exilic motif. For further discussion, see P. W. Barnett, "The Jewish Sign Prophets—A.D. 40–70: Their Intentions and Origin," *NTS* 27 (1980): 679-97; Eric Eve, *The Jewish Context of Jesus' Miracles* (London: Sheffield Academic Press, 2002), pp. 296-325; and E. P. Sanders, *Judaism: Practice and Belief 63BCE–66CE* (London: SCM, 1992), pp. 280-89.

Another way to articulate Second Temple expectations of a future divine inbreaking is to say that the Jews of this period viewed the story of the Old Testament books as incomplete. When the Old Testament story of Israel was viewed as a whole, it was not viewed as something that was finished but as something that was waiting to be finished.[10] N. T. Wright observes, "The great story of the Hebrew scriptures was therefore inevitably read in the Second Temple period as a story in search of a conclusion."[11] Indeed, some scholars have argued that the Old Testament canon ended with Chronicles[12] as a reminder to the reader that Israel's return from exile documented in Ezra–Nehemiah is not the full story—it is only a physical return, not a spiritual one.[13] The hearts of the people still needed to be changed. Such an ending places the reader in a posture of eschatological expectation, *looking ahead* to the time when the Messiah, the son of David, will come to Jerusalem and bring full deliverance to his people.[14] The Davidic focus of Chronicles is also borne out by its extensive genealogies with David at the very center (1 Chron 3:1-24).

With this Second Temple Jewish context in mind, we are now in a position to understand the eschatological nature of early Christianity. When we speak of early Christianity as "eschatological" we are not speaking here simply of the Christian belief that Jesus would one day return to judge the world; rather, we are speaking of the belief that, in some sense, Israel's long-

---

[10]Evidence that Second Temple groups were looking for a proper conclusion to the Old Testament story can be found in Wis 11–19; *Jub* 36; and Sir 50:1-21.

[11]Wright, *New Testament and the People of God*, p. 217.

[12]Although this is disputed by some scholars, there are good reasons to think the threefold canonical structure of the Old Testament would have been established by the time of Jesus; see Luke 24:44; Sir 39:1; 4QMMT^c (10); Philo, *Contempl. Life*, 25. For discussion see Rolf Rendtorff, *Theologie des Altens Testaments: Ein kanonischer Entwurf* (Neukirchen-Vluyn: Neukirchener Verlag, 1999); Roger T. Beckwith, *The Old Testament Canon of the New Testament Church, and Its Background in Early Judaism* (Grand Rapids: Eerdmans, 1986), pp. 110-80; Stephen B. Chapman, "The Old Testament Canon and Its Authority for the Christian Church," *Ex Auditu* 19 (2003): 125-48; Christopher Seitz, *The Goodly Fellowship of the Prophets: The Achievement of Association in Canon Formation* (Grand Rapids: Baker Academic, 2009), pp. 97-99. However, some scholars are less sure the order of the Old Testament canon was secure by this time: e.g., Craig A. Evans, "The Scriptures of Jesus and His Earliest Followers," in *The Canon Debate*, ed. Lee M. McDonald and James A. Sanders (Peabody, MA: Hendrickson, 2002), pp. 185-95; and Julio C. Trebolle-Barrera, "Origins of a Tripartite Old Testament Canon," in *Canon Debate*, pp. 128-45.

[13]Dempster, *Dominion and Dynasty*, pp. 224-27.

[14]Nahum Sarna, "Bible," in *Encyclopedia Judaica* III:832.

awaited eschatological redemption had occurred in the person and work of Jesus of Nazareth. Through Jesus, forgiveness of sins was now possible, and Israel's "exile" could come to an end. The kingdom of God had arrived. For early Christians, "Israel's history has reached its climax."[15] Of course, our earliest Christian writings indicate that this was Jesus' own understanding of his mission. The eschatological nature of Jesus' message is evident in his early preaching: "The time is fulfilled, and the kingdom of God is at hand" (Mk 1:15),[16] and in his declarations that these Old Testament promises were fulfilled in his coming (Lk 4:16-30; compare Is 61:1-2). Other early Christian writers agree. Paul indicated that in Christ "the end of the ages has come" (1 Cor 10:11) and the time of "the promised Spirit" (Gal 3:14; compare Is 44:3) has arrived, and the writer to the Hebrews understood that "in these last days [God] has spoken to us by his Son" (Heb 1:2). Moreover, Jesus is often described as the second Moses who is bringing about a new "exodus."[17] He recapitulates the original exodus (Mt 2:14-15; Hos 11:1), begins his ministry in the desert (Mt 3:1-7; Is 40:3), presents himself as a new lawgiver on the mountaintop (Mt 5:1), is a great prophet like Moses (Lk 24:19; Acts 3:22-23), provides the true manna from heaven (Jn 6:32), and even directly speaks of his ἔξοδος with Moses at the transfiguration (Lk 9:31).[18]

How do such eschatological beliefs about Jesus fulfilling the Old Testament promises to Israel affect the development of a new canon of Scripture? Three considerations are worth noting. First, the fact that Second Temple Jews regarded the Old Testament story as incomplete and in need of a proper conclusion has significant implications for the production of a new corpus of biblical books. If some Second Temple Jews

---

[15]Wright, *New Testament and the People of God*, p. 401.

[16]For more on the theme of kingdom, see George Eldon Ladd, *Jesus and the Kingdom: The Eschatology of Biblical Realism* (New York: Harper & Row, 1964); Herman Ridderbos, *The Coming of the Kingdom* (Phillipsburg, NJ: P & R, 1962); and Thomas Schreiner, *New Testament Theology: Magnifying God in Christ* (Grand Rapids: Baker Academic, 2008), pp. 41-116.

[17]Vern S. Poythress, *The Shadow of Christ in the Law of Moses* (Phillipsburg, NJ: P & R, 1991), pp. 252-55; John Lierman, *The New Testament Moses* (Tübingen: Mohr Siebeck, 2004), pp. 258-88; Dale C. Allison, *The New Moses: A Matthean Typology* (Edinburgh: T & T Clark, 1993); and Wayne A. Meeks, *The Prophet-King: Moses Traditions and the Johannine Christology* (Leiden: E. J. Brill, 1967).

[18]For more on this theme, see Tremper Longman III and Daniel G. Reid, "Jesus: New Exodus, New Conquest," in *God Is a Warrior* (Grand Rapids: Zondervan, 1995), pp. 91-118; and David Pao, *Acts and the Isaianic New Exodus* (Tübingen: Mohr Siebeck, 2000).

became convinced that the story was completed in the life and ministry of
Jesus of Nazareth—such as the earliest Christians did—then it is not unreasonable to think that the proper conclusion to the Old Testament might
then be written. Indeed, the very structure of the Old Testament itself,
with its truncated and forward-looking ending, naturally leads to the expectation that there would be a second installment of writings to finish the
job. Otherwise, one would be left with a play that had no final act. This
possibility finds confirmation in the fact that some of the New Testament
writings seem to be intentionally completing the Old Testament story. It is
noteworthy that the first book of the New Testament begins with a genealogy with a strong Davidic theme (Mt 1:1), and the (likely) last book of the
Hebrew canon begins with a genealogy that has a strong Davidic theme (1
Chron 1–2).[19] This structural feature led D. Moody Smith to declare, "In
doing so, Matthew makes clear that Jesus represents the restoration of that
dynasty and therefore the history of Israel and the history of salvation.
Thus, Jesus continues the biblical narrative."[20] W. D. Davies and Dale Allison agree that Matthew "thought of his gospel as a continuation of the
biblical history."[21]

Second, the Old Testament writings themselves—from which the earliest Christians have drawn these promises—indicate that God often brings
new Word-revelation *after* he acts to redeem his people. In other words, the
story of Israel indicates that there is a tight connection between God's major
redemptive acts and God's new installments of revelation. When God
breaks into the world to redeem, he typically follows that redemption with
a new revelation that interprets those redemptive acts.[22] Richard Lints observes, "For whatever reasons, God has chosen to bring redemption to his
people in a progressive and epochal manner. This being the case, it should
come as no surprise that the revelation of God's redemptive activity also has

---

[19]Evans, "Jesus and the Continuing Exile of Israel," p. 99.

[20]D. Moody Smith, "When Did the Gospels Become Scripture?," *JBL* 119 (2000): 7. Although
Genesis does not begin with a genealogy, the fact that the first and last books of the Old Testament contain genealogies is further evidence of its structural unity.

[21]W. D. Davies and Dale C. Allison, *The Gospel According to Saint Matthew* (ICC; Edinburgh:
T & T Clark, 1997), 1:187.

[22]Michael S. Horton, *Covenant and Eschatology: The Divine Drama* (Louisville: Westminster John
Knox, 2002), p. 233; Geerhardus Vos, *Biblical Theology* (Edinburgh: Banner of Truth, 1975),
p. 5. Examples of these redemptive epochs can be found in the latter volume.

an epochal structure, manifested and marked in the canonical Scriptures."[23] Richard Gaffin argues the same point: "Revelation never stands by itself, but is always concerned either explicitly or implicitly with redemptive accomplishment. . . . It is not going too far to say that redemption is the *raison d'être* of revelation."[24] This historical connection between redemption and revelation is particularly evident in the exodus event, arguably the archetypal redemptive event of the story of Israel.[25] It was after God redeemed his people from Egypt that he delivered a written covenantal word to them (Ex 20:2).

Given this redemption-revelation pattern in God's prior dealings with Israel, it is not difficult to see why early Christians might have naturally expected to be given a new revelational deposit. After all, they believed that the redemption brought through Jesus of Nazareth was not just one of many redemptive installments, but the final and ultimate redemption for Israel (Heb 1:2). Early Christians believed that Jesus was not another prophet, but *the* prophet (Jn 7:52); not just a giver of the law, but the embodiment of the law (Jn 1:1); not just a king like David, but the king of David (Lk 20:44); not just one who worships at the temple, but one greater than the temple (Mt 12:6). If a covenantal revelation had been given at Israel's first exodus, then it is difficult to imagine that early Christians would not have naturally anticipated a new covenantal revelation for Israel's eschatological exodus in Christ. We can agree with David Meade that "[a] 'New Israel' . . . will require new Scriptures."[26]

François Bovon observes this same redemption-revelation pattern within the structure of the New Testament itself—but instead uses the terms *event* and *proclamation*.[27] He argues that the New Testament has a twofold structure of gospel and apostle precisely for this reason: the former

---

[23]Richard Lints, *The Fabric of Theology* (Grand Rapids: Eerdmans, 1993), p. 267.

[24]Richard B. Gaffin, *Resurrection and Redemption* (Phillipsburg, NJ: P & R, 1978), p. 22.

[25]1 Sam 8:8; 12:6; 2 Sam 7:23; Neh 9:9-10; Ps 78:12-14; 135:9; Is 11:16; Hos 11:1.

[26]David Meade, "Ancient Near Eastern Apocalypticism and the Origins of the New Testament Canon of Scripture," in *The Bible as a Human Witness: Hearing the Word of God Through Historically Dissimilar Traditions*, ed. Randall Heskett and Brian Irwin (London: T & T Clark, 2010), p. 315.

[27]François Bovon, "The Canonical Structure of Gospel and Apostle," in *Canon Debate*, pp. 516-27. His fuller arguments can be found in François Bovon, *L'Evangile et l'Apôtre: Christ inséparable de ses témoins* (Aubonne: Editions du Moulin, 1993).

describes the redemptive *event* and the latter describes the official *procla-mation* of that event.[28] This gospel-apostle, or event-proclamation, pattern is clearly visible in the earliest Christian sources—from Paul, to the Synoptics, to the Johannine writings, to Acts, and, of course, the apostolic fathers.[29] Barrett even argues that the two volume Luke–Acts was the very first embodiment of this gospel-apostle phenomenon and thus could be regarded as "The First New Testament."[30] All of these factors lead Bovon to argue that the existence of a New Testament is not due to the influence of "outside sources" but is "inscribed in the very nature of the Christian faith."[31] In other words, it is not extrinsic but intrinsic. He sums it up well: "A 'New Testament' containing Gospels and Epistles is the logical outgrowth and materialization of . . . an event and the proclamation that follows."[32]

Third, when the Old Testament refers to the future eschatological age of redemption, it explicitly states that this new era will be accompanied by a new divine message.[33] If so, then once the earliest Christians believed this new age of redemption had arrived, we should not be surprised that a new revelational deposit might emerge. Such a reality stands in opposition to Harnack's claim that early Christians would have desired (or expected) nothing beyond the revelation already found in the Old Testament (interpreted in a Christian fashion).[34] A number of passages speak to this new divine message, but we can only mention a select few here:

1. In Deuteronomy 18:18, Moses cites the promise of God that another prophet like him will arise: "I will raise up for them a prophet like you from among their brothers. And I will *put my words in his mouth*, and he shall speak to them all that I command them." A number of New Testament texts make it clear that early Christians believed Deuteronomy

---

[28]Bovon emphasizes the degree to which redemptive event and proclamation go hand in hand when he observes, "The apostolic word becomes the indispensible complement to the act of redemption" ("Canonical Structure," p. 517).

[29]Ibid., pp. 516-27.

[30]C. K. Barrett, "The First New Testament?," *NovT* 38 (1996): 94-104.

[31]Bovon, "Canonical Structure," p. 516.

[32]Ibid., p. 516 (emphasis mine).

[33]Charles E. Hill, "God's Speech in These Last Days: The New Testament Canon as an Eschatological Phenomenon," in *Resurrection and Eschatology: Theology in Service of the Church*, ed. Lane G. Tipton and Jeffrey C. Waddington (Phillipsburg, NJ: P & R, 2008), pp. 203-54.

[34]Adolf von Harnack, *Origin of the New Testament and the Most Important Consequences of a New Creation* (London: Williams & Northgate, 1925), p. 6.

18:18 was fulfilled in the ministry of Jesus Christ: Mark 9:7; John 6:14; 7:40;[35] Acts 3:23-24; 7:37.[36]

2. Similarly, Isaiah 11:1 describes the coming Messiah as "a shoot from the stump of Jesse" who "will strike the earth with the rod of his mouth" (11:4). This is a clear allusion to the fact that the Messiah will speak the Word of God and that this new Word-revelation will be the basis by which he judges the earth.[37] This passage is echoed in a number of New Testament texts that refer to the Messiah's divine speaking (2 Thess 2:8; Rev 1:16; 11:5; 19:15).[38]

3. Isaiah 61:1-2 (LXX) describes the activity of God's servant in the coming eschatological age of salvation: "The Spirit of the LORD GOD is upon me, because the LORD has anointed me to bring good news (εὐαγγελίσασθαι) to the poor; he has sent me to bind up the brokenhearted, to proclaim (κηρύξαι) liberty to the captives . . . to proclaim (καλέσαι) the year of the LORD's favor." The frequent occurrence of verbs of proclamation (εὐαγγελίσασθαι, κηρύξαι, καλέσαι) makes it clear that the era of the Messiah would be an era in which a new message of "good news" is announced.[39] In other words, the coming kingdom of God would not just be accompanied by redemptive acts from God, but also by a redemptive *message* from God. Of course, Isaiah 61:1-2 is echoed in a number of New Testament texts (Lk 7:22-23; Mt 11:5; Acts 10:36-37), but Jesus explicitly cites it and applies it to his own ministry (Lk 4:18-19), showing that he viewed his own role as the servant-prophet who would ini-

---

[35]Paul Anderson, *The Christology of the Fourth Gospel* (Tübingen: Mohr Siebeck, 1996), pp. 174-77, argues that Deuteronomy 18 provides a broad christological framework for the entire Gospel of John. This is further evidence, therefore, that Deuteronomy 18 was paradigmatic for early Christian interpretations of Jesus.

[36]See also Qumran's use of this prophecy in 4Q175 1.5-8; 1QS 9.11. Richard A. Horsley, "'Like One of the Prophets of Old': Two Types of Popular Prophets at the Time of Jesus," *CBQ* 47 (1985): 435-63, argues that there is little evidence that Deut 18:18 played a central role in Jewish messianic expectations. However, that does not affect our point here. Whether or not Horsley is correct (and one might suggest he should give more weight to the Qumran texts), we are simply arguing that Deut 18:18 was central to the *Christian* interpretation of the ministry of Jesus of Nazareth.

[37]See discussion in G. K. Beale, *The Book of Revelation* (NIGTC; Grand Rapids: Eerdmans, 1999), pp. 961-63.

[38]See also the allusions to Is 11:4 in *4 Ezra* 13:10-11, 37-38.

[39]A number of Qumran texts that show that Isaiah 61:1-2 was understood as a prophecy specifically about the coming Messiah (e.g., 4Q52; 11Q13). See discussion in Graham N. Stanton, *Jesus and Gospel* (Cambridge: Cambridge University Press, 2004), pp. 15-18; and William Horbury, "'Gospel' in Herodian Judea," in *The Written Gospel*, ed. Markus Bockmuehl and Donald A. Hagner (Cambridge: Cambridge University Press, 2005), pp. 7-30.

tially deliver this new divine message (though others would also participate in its deliverance).[40] Given that Isaiah 61:1-2 (compare Is 40:9, 52:7; Rom 10:15) refers to the message of "good news" with the verb εὐαγγελίσασθαι, it is not surprising that the written accounts of Jesus' life were eventually known by the term εὐαγγέλιον.[41]

4. Isaiah 2:2-3 speaks also of the coming age of salvation, "It shall come to pass in the latter days, that the mountain of the house of the LORD shall be established . . . all the nations shall flow to it . . . out of Zion shall go the law, and the word of the LORD from Jerusalem." In this passage there is yet another clear expression that a new "word of the LORD" will go to the "the nations" in the future messianic age.[42] This passage was interpreted by early Christians as referring to the apostolic mission to take the "word of the Lord" to the ends of the earth.[43] In fact, Pao argues that Isaiah 2 is paradigmatic for the entire book of Acts, which traces the continued expansion of the "word of the Lord."[44] Likewise, Pahl argues that this passage may have been "a significant part of the background of [Paul's] agenda," given how much Paul uses "word of God/Lord" terminology (for example, 1 Cor 14:36; 2 Cor 2:17; 4:2; 1 Thess 1:8; 2:13).[45] In addition, Isaiah 2 is likely one of the passages Jesus alludes to in Luke 24:46-47: "It is written, that the Christ

---

[40]Luke 4:18-19 modifies the LXX text at a number of points and also includes Is 58:6. Most notably, Luke changes the καλέσαι of Is 61:2 to the verb κηρύξαι –which increases further the focus on the "preaching" of the divine message. Luke's use of the latter term to focus on the preaching/proclaiming theme is evident elsewhere in his writings (Lk 3:3; 4:44; 8:1, 39; 9:2; 12:3; 24:47; Acts 8:5; 9:20; 10:37, 42; 15:21; 19:13; 20:25; 28:31).

[41]E.g., Mark 1:1; Justin Martyr, 1 Apol. 66.3; Dial. 10.2, 100.1; Ignatius, Smyrn. 5:1; Did. 8:2; 11:3. For more discussion of the origin of Gospel titles, see Martin Hengel, The Four Gospels and the One Gospel of Jesus Christ (Harrisburg, PA: Trinity Press International, 2000), pp. 90-106 ; and Helmut Koester, Ancient Christian Gospels: Their History and Development (London: SCM Press, 1990), pp. 1-31. Koester doubts that the Isaianic passages have influenced the application of the noun Gospel to written accounts (p. 3), but other scholars disagree. Richard Bauckham, in God Crucified: Monotheism and Christology in the New Testament (Grand Rapids: Eerdmans, 1999), p. 48, argues that the Isaianic themes are so prevalent in the Gospel accounts (and elsewhere) that the title "Gospel" likely came from these texts.

[42]For discussion of this text, see John T. Willis, "Isaiah 2:2-5 and the Psalms of Zion," in Writing and Reading the Scroll of Isaiah: Studies of an Interpretive Tradition, ed. Craig C. Broyles and Craig A. Evans (Leiden: E. J. Brill, 1997), pp. 295-316.

[43]Acts 1:8; Justin Martyr, Dial. 24, 1 Apol. 39; Irenaeus, Haer. 4.34.4; Tertullian, Adv. Jud. 3; Origen, Cels. 5.33; Clement of Alexandria, Protrepticus 1.

[44]Pao, Acts and the Isaianic New Exodus, pp. 156-57.

[45]Michael Pahl, "The 'Gospel' and the 'Word': Exploring Some Early Christian Patterns," JSNT 29 (2006): 219.

should suffer and on the third day rise from the dead, and that repentance and forgiveness of sins should be proclaimed (κηρυχθῆναι[46]) in his name to all nations."[47]

In sum, the eschatological nature of early Christianity provides an essential foundation on which the new canon of Scripture would be constructed. Not only was there an Old Testament pattern of new Word-revelation following God's redemptive acts, and not only was the Old Testament story viewed as incomplete and anticipating a final installment, but the above passages indicate that the Old Testament expressly predicted that the messianic age would be marked by a new revelational message from God—and the earliest Christians applied these very passages to their own time period. With all these factors combined, there appear to be ample reasons to think that a new revelational deposit might have emerged naturally/intrinsically from within the early Christian movement rather than being foisted upon it by later ecclesiastical pressures.

THE CONCEPT OF COVENANT IN EARLY CHRISTIANITY

Speaking of the first century, N. T. Wright has observed that "Covenant theology was the air breathed by the Judaism of this period."[48] Indeed, Israel continued to understand its relationship with God through the lens of the covenantal arrangement established by God in a variety of Old Testament passages (for example, Gen 12:1-3; 15:18; 17:2; Ex 34:28; Deut 27–30; Is 55:3). So central was Israel's covenantal identity that covenantal language is evident in a wide variety of Jewish literature, especially at Qumran.[49] As

---

[46]This same verb occurs here and also in Lk 4:18-19 and Is 61:1-2 LXX.

[47]Luke 24:47 probably echoes other Isaianic passages, particularly Is 49:6. See discussion in Pao, *Acts and the Isaianic New Exodus*, pp. 84-91.

[48]Wright, *New Testament and the People of God*, p. 262. Some helpful studies on covenant include: O. Palmer Robertson, *The Christ of the Covenants* (Phillipsburg, NJ: P & R, 1980); idem, *Covenants: God's Way with His People* (Philadelphia: Great Commission, 1978); Meredith G. Kline, *Treaty of the Great King* (Grand Rapids: Eerdmans, 1963); idem, *Kingdom Prologue: Genesis Foundations for a Covenantal Worldview* (Overland Park, KS: Two Age Press, 2000); Thomas E. McComiskey, *The Covenants of Promise: A Theology of the Old Testament Covenants* (Grand Rapids: Baker, 1985); William J. Dumbrell, *Covenant and Creation* (Grand Rapids: Baker, 1984); Steven L. McKenzie, *Covenant* (St. Louis: Chalice, 2000); and most recently, Michael Horton, *God of Promise: Introducing Covenant Theology* (Grand Rapids: Baker, 2006).

[49]For a helpful overview of covenant in Second Temple Judaism, see the collected essays in Stanley E. Porter and Jacqueline C. R. de Roo, eds., *The Concept of Covenant in the Second Temple Period* (Leiden: E. J. Brill, 2003); and E. P. Sanders, *Paul and Palestinian Judaism* (Minneapolis:

Geza Vermes noted, "It was this same Covenant theology that served as the Qumran Community's basic beliefs."[50] Thus, Israel interpreted its continued bondage to foreign powers as a distinctly covenantal crisis[51] (would God be faithful to his covenantal promises?), which led the Jews to anticipate God's covenantal deliverance even more strongly.[52] It should come as little surprise that Second Temple Judaism framed its identity around the covenant, given the degree to which the covenantal concept dominates the entire Old Testament corpus.[53] John Walton has observed that the covenant is "the single most important theological structure in the Old Testament."[54] Likewise, Walter Eichrodt has argued that covenant is not just one theme (of many) in the Old Testament but the very thing that provides its "structural unity."[55]

Given that the earliest Christians were distinctively Jewish in their heritage, they naturally understood the activity of Jesus and the inaugurated

---

Fortress, 1977). Some have objected to the centrality of the covenantal concept in this period on the grounds that the term itself appears infrequently (particularly in rabbinic literature). For a response, see Sanders, *Paul and Palestinian Judaism*, pp. 420-21; Geza Vermes, *The Dead Sea Scrolls: Qumran in Perspective* (Philadelphia: Fortress, 1977), pp. 169-88; and Wright, *New Testament and the People of God*, p. 262.

[50]Vermes, *Qumran in Perspective*, p. 165.

[51]E.g., 1 Macc 1:15; 2:20; 4:8-11; 2 Macc 8:14-18.

[52]E.g., 4 *Ezra* 5:21-30; *T. Mos.* 4:5; see also Qumran's expectations about God's covenantal renewal (CD^a 6.19; 8.21; CD^b 19.33-34; 20.12; 1QpHab 2.3; 1QM 1.1-3; 4Q175 14-18; 1QSb 3.25-26; 5.5, 21). More on covenant renewal at Qumran can be found in Shemaryahu Talmon, "The Community of the Renewed Covenant: Between Judaism and Christianity," in *Community of the Renewed Covenant*, pp. 3-24. Discussion of "covenant" in the Damascus Document and the Community Rule can be found in Craig A. Evans, "Covenant in the Qumran Literature," in *Concept of Covenant in the Second Temple Period*, pp. 55-80.

[53]Again, some have questioned the centrality of the covenantal theme in the Old Testament due to the sporadic appearance of the term for *covenant*: e.g., Lothar Perlitt, *Bundestheologie im Alten Testament* (Neukirchen Vluyn: Neukirchener Verlag, 1969); and Ernest W. Nicholson, *God and His People: Covenant Theology in the Old Testament* (Oxford: Oxford University Press, 1986). However, see responses from James Barr, "Some Semantic Notes on the Covenant," in *Beiträge zur Alttestamentlichen Theologie*, ed. Herbert Donner; Göttingen: Vandenhoeck & Ruprecht, 1977), pp. 23-38; Delbert R. Hillers, *Covenant: The History of a Biblical Idea* (Baltimore: Johns Hopkins University Press, 1969), pp. 120-42; and Brevard S. Childs, *Biblical Theology of the Old and New Testaments: Theological Reflection on the Christian Bible* (Philadelphia: Augsburg Fortress, 1993), pp. 413-20.

[54]John H. Walton, *Covenant: God's Purpose, God's Plan* (Grand Rapids: Zondervan, 1994), p. 10.

[55]Walter Eichrodt, *Theology of the Old Testament*, trans. J. A. Baker (Philadelphia: Westminster, 1961), p. 13. For the distinction between covenant as theme and covenant as infrastructure, see Scott Hafemann, "The Covenant Relationship," in *Central Themes in Biblical Theology: Mapping Unity in Diversity*, ed. Scott Hafemann and Paul House (Grand Rapids: Baker Academic, 2007), pp. 20-65.

kingdom of God through the category of God's covenantal promises. The Last Supper was interpreted as a covenantal meal as Jesus declared, "This cup that is poured out for you is the new covenant in my blood" (Lk 22:20; compare Mt 26:28; Mk 14:24)—a vivid echo of Jeremiah 31:31.[56] John's father Zechariah recognized that through the coming work of Christ, God will "remember his holy covenant" to Israel (Lk 1:72). Paul not only interpreted the Lord's Supper as a new covenant meal (1 Cor 11:25), but also interpreted the ministry of Christ as the fulfillment of the promises to Israel in Isaiah 59:21 where God declares, "This is my covenant with them" (Rom 11:27). In addition, Paul refers to himself and the other apostles as "ministers of a new covenant" (2 Cor 3:6), in contrast to the ministry of the "old covenant" (2 Cor 3:14).[57] And the writer of Hebrews refers to Jesus as the "guarantor of a better covenant" (Heb 7:22), the one who establishes a "new covenant" with the house of Israel (Heb 8:8; compare 10:16; 12:24), and describes believers as those who participate in the "blood of the covenant" (Heb 10:29). Moreover, Christian interest in the covenant continued into the writings of the apostolic fathers and other patristic writers.[58]

If, as we have just seen, early Christianity was distinctively covenantal in its orientation, then what impact does this have on the development of the canon? The answer lies in the very close connection between covenants and written texts. Scholars have long observed that the concept of a treaty-covenant was not unique to the Old Testament, but was prevalent in the ancient Near Eastern world out of which this corpus of books was born.[59] The

---

[56]A thorough and well-reasoned defense of the historicity of the Last Supper, along with the covenantal language, can be found in I. Howard Marshall, "The Last Supper," in *Key Events in the Life of the Historical Jesus*, ed. Darrell L. Bock and Robert L. Webb (Tübingen: Mohr Siebeck, 2009), pp. 481-588. However, even if one disputes the historicity of the event, the key point here is that *early Christians* still conceived of the Last Supper within covenantal categories, as can be seen by the fact that the covenantal theme occurs in all the Synoptics plus Paul.

[57]Peter R. Jones, "The Apostle Paul: Second Moses to the New Covenant Community. A Study in Pauline Apostolic Authority," in *God's Inerrant Word*, ed. John Warwick Montgomery (Minneapolis: Bethany Fellowship, 1974), pp. 219-41. Jones makes a compelling case that Paul is directly appealing to Jer 31:27-28 (cf. Ezek 36:36) in the texts of 2 Cor 3:6 and 13:10.

[58]*Barn.* 4:6-8; 13:1-6; 14:1-7; Justin Martyr, *Dial.* 11.1; 34.1; 43.1; 44.2; 51.3; 67.10; 122.5; Irenaeus, *Haer.* 1.10.3; 3.11.8; 4.9.1-3; 4.12.3. For more on this point, see Everett Ferguson, "The Covenant Idea in the Second Century," in *Texts and Testaments: Critical Essays on the Bible and the Early Church Fathers*, ed. W. E. March (San Antonio: Trinity University Press, 1980), pp. 135-62; and J. Ligon Duncan, "The Covenant Idea in Melito of Sardis: An Introduction and Survey," *Presb* 28 (2002): 12-33.

[59]Hillers, *Covenant*, pp. 25-71; George E. Mendenhall, *Law and Covenant in Israel and the Ancient*

structure of these ancient treaty-covenants are well known and include a variety of components such as a preamble, historical prologue, stipulations, and blessings and curses.[60] In addition, and most noteworthy for our purposes here, these treaty-covenants (especially Hittite ones) included *written texts* that documented the terms of the covenant arrangement. A suzerain king and his vassal king each received a written copy of the treaty-covenant, and provisions were made to have these texts stored in their holy shrines and read publicly at regular intervals. For this reason, these ancient treaty-covenants often included an "inscriptional curse" warning that the text was not to be altered in any way.[61] For example, Kline notes that the Hittite treaty of Tudhaliyas IV and Ulmi-Teshub states, "Whoever . . . changes but one word of this tablet . . . may the thousand gods of this tablet root that man's descendants out of the land of Hatti."[62]

It is now well-established by scholars that the structure of the Mosaic covenant—particularly Deuteronomy and the Decalogue—reflects the structure of these extrabiblical treaty-covenants.[63] When Yahweh (in the role of the suzerain king) established his treaty-covenant with Israel (in the role of the vassal), he also gave these authoritative written texts to Israel to document the terms of that covenantal arrangement. For this reason, provisions were made to have these texts stored in the tabernacle, particularly the ark (Ex 25:16; Deut 10:2; 31:9; Josh 24:26), they were to be publicly read on a periodic basis

---

Near East (Pittsburgh: The Biblical Colloquium, 1955), pp. 24-50; Meredith G. Kline, *The Structure of Biblical Authority*, 2nd ed. (Eugene, OR: Wipf & Stock, 1997), pp. 27-44; Dennis J. McCarthy, *Treaty and Covenant* (Rome: Biblical Institute Press, 1981); John A Thompson, *The Ancient Near Eastern Treaties and the Old Testament* (Grand Rapids: Tyndale, 1964).

[60]Overviews of the structure of ancient treaties (particularly Hittite ones) can be seen in George E. Mendenhall, "Covenant Forms in Israelite Tradition," *BA* 17 (1954): 50-76; and John H. Walton, *Ancient Israelite Literature in Its Cultural Context* (Grand Rapids: Zondervan, 1989), pp. 95-107.

[61]F. C. Fensham, "Common Trends in Curses of the Near Eastern Treaties and Kudurru-Inscriptions Compared with Maledictions of Amos and Isaiah," *ZAW* 75 (1963): 155-75; Stanley Gevirtz, "West-Semitic Curses and the Problem of the Origins of Hebrew Law," *VT* 11 (1961): 137-58; Hans G. Güterbock, "Mursili's Accounts of Suppiluliuma's Dealings with Egypt," *RHA* 18 (1960): 59-60; Michael A. Fishbane, "Varia Deuteronomica," *ZAW* 84, no. 3 (1972): 349-52; James B. Pritchard, *Ancient Near Eastern Texts Relating to the Old Testament*, 3rd ed. (Princeton, NJ: Princeton University Press, 1969), p. 161.

[62]Kline, *Structure of Biblical Authority*, p. 29.

[63]Hillers, *Covenant*, pp. 46-71; Kline, *Structure of Biblical Authority*, pp. 27-44; Mendenhall, *Law and Covenant*, pp. 24-50. For a more updated discussion, see Kenneth A. Kitchen, *On the Reliability of the Old Testament* (Grand Rapids: Eerdmans, 2003), pp. 283-312.

(Deut 31:10-13), and even an "inscriptional curse" was attached to them: "You shall not add to the word that I command you, nor take from it, that you may keep the commandments of the LORD your God" (Deut 4:2).[64] Thus, the very idea of an Old Testament canon has its roots in the covenant God made with Israel—*the canon is a treaty document.* Kline puts it this way: "The very treaty that formally established the Israelite theocracy was itself the beginning and the nucleus of the total cluster of writings which constitutes the Old Testament canon."[65] All of this indicates that the religious system of Israel understood there to be a tight connection between the giving of covenants and the production of canonical texts. Just as extrabiblical treaty-covenants of this kind had written documentation, so Yahweh's biblical treaty-covenant with Israel had written documentation. As Hillers has observed, when it comes to biblical covenants between God and Israel, "there is a written document in connection with it, the familiar 'text of the covenant.'"[66]

Indeed, so close is the relationship between the covenant and the written documentation of the covenant that Old Testament authors would frequently equate the two—the covenant, in one sense, *is* a written text. For instance: "Then he took the Book of the Covenant and read it" (Ex 24:7; compare 1 Macc 1:57); "And he read in their hearing all the words of the Book of the Covenant" (2 Kings 23:2; compare 2 Chron 34:30); "He declared to you his covenant . . . that is, the Ten Commandments, and he wrote them on two tablets" (Deut 4:13); "He wrote on the tablets the words of the covenant" (Ex 34:28); and "The covenant written in this Book" (Deut 29:21).[67]

---

[64]Cf. Deut 12:32; Prov 30:5-6. The influence of inscriptional curses is notable in other Jewish literature: e.g., *Aristeas* 310-11; *1 Enoch* 104:9-10; 1 Macc 8:30; Josephus, *Ag. Ap.* 1.42; 11QT^a 54.5-7; *b. Meg.* 14a. David E. Aune, *Revelation 17-22* (WBC; Nashville: Thomas Nelson, 1998), pp. 1208-16, refers to this type of language as an "integrity formula."

[65]Kline, *Structure of Biblical Authority*, p. 43. Kline argues that the rest of the Old Testament, beyond these initial Mosaic documents, is also covenantal in nature (pp. 45-68). The other Old Testament books perform critical covenantal functions: the prophets prosecute the terms of the covenant, the historical books outline the history of God's covenant relationship with Israel, the wisdom literature is the way to live inside the covenant, etc.

[66]Hillers, *Covenant*, p. 145. Of course, this is not to say that every "covenant" in biblical history has a written document (e.g., the Noahic covenant did not). The critical distinction here is that covenants *between God and Israel* involve written texts. Kline makes a similar point, "where there is a divine covenant of the *classic Old Testament kind* there is a divine covenantal document" (*Structure of Biblical Authority*, p. 39; emphasis mine).

[67]Wolfram Kinzig, "καινὴ Διαθήκη: The Title of the New Testament in the Second and Third Centuries," *JTS* 45 (1994): 526.

These passages indicate that covenants were largely conceived as something written or read; that is, something in a book. It is precisely for this reason that warnings were given not to change the text of the covenant (Deut 4:2), and there were concerns about it being in the proper physical location (Ex 25:16). Mendenhall recognizes this reality: "To put it in the simplest terms, the treaty was a sacred act *and object*."[68]

We are now in a position to recognize the implications of this Old Testament pattern on the development of a new corpus of books. The earliest Christians were themselves immersed in the covenantal structure of the Old Testament and thus would have understood this critical connection between covenants and written texts. Of course, these similarities do not require early Christians to be directly aware of ancient Near Eastern/Hittite treaty structure; they were aware of this structure inasmuch as it was manifested in the Old Testament itself. As Kline observes, "These [NT] writers were well acquainted with the secular treaty structure in its embodiment in the Old Testament. However ignorant they were of the formal origins of the covenantal structure, they were fully familiar with the treaty form itself as they found it in their Scriptures."[69] Thus, if they believed that through Jesus Christ a *new* covenant had been inaugurated with Israel (Jer 31:31), it would have been entirely natural for them to expect new written documents to testify to the terms of that covenant.

In other words, this Old Testament covenantal background provides strong historical reason for thinking that early Christians would have had a predisposition toward written canonical documents and that such documents might have arisen naturally from the early Christian movement. At a minimum, the covenantal context of early Christianity suggests that the emergence of a new corpus of scriptural books, after the announcement of a new covenant, could not be regarded as entirely unexpected. Even Harnack, despite his proclivity toward the extrinsic model of canon, acknowledges the role played by the concept of covenant: "The conception of the 'New Covenant' necessarily suggested the need of something of *the nature of a document*; for what is a covenant without its document?"[70]

---

[68]George E. Mendenhall, "Covenant," in *ABD* 1:1181 (emphasis mine).

[69]Kline, *Structure of Biblical Authority*, p. 70.

[70]Harnack, *Origin of the New Testament*, p. 13 (emphasis his).

Our suspicions are confirmed when we examine the New Testament corpus in more detail and recognize that it too bears some of the characteristics of the ancient treaty-covenants:

1. The New Testament has its own "inscriptional curse" in Revelation 22:18-19: "I warn everyone who hears the words of the prophecy of this book: if anyone adds to them, God will add to him the plagues described in this book, and if anyone takes away from the words of the book of this prophecy, God will take away his share in the tree of life and in the holy city, which are described in this book."[71] While this no doubt applies most immediately to the book of Revelation itself, it is fitting that it comes at the very end of the entire New Testament corpus.

2. The New Testament has its own declarations that it should be read publicly. A number of Paul's epistles include commands that they be read at the gathering of the church (2 Cor 10:9; Col 4:16; 1 Thess 5:27). Likewise, the book of Revelation also anticipates that it will be read publicly when it pronounces a blessing on "the one who reads the words of this prophecy and . . . those who hear" (1:3).[72] Some scholars have suggested that the Gospels of Matthew and Mark were written with a liturgical structure that implied they were used for year-round public reading in worship, although other scholars have disputed this claim.[73]

3. The New Testament writings seem to perform the same covenantal functions as their Old Testament counterparts. Kline argues, for instance, that the canonical Gospels parallel the historical narratives of the Pentateuch, each functioning as the "historical prologue" where the great salvific acts of God are recited.[74] Vogels argues that the book of Acts fills the same

---

[71]For more on the inscriptional curse in early Christianity see Aune, *Revelation 17-22*, pp. 1208-16; and Michael J. Kruger, "Early Christian Attitudes Toward the Reproduction of Texts," in *The Early Text of the New Testament*, ed. Charles E. Hill and Michael J. Kruger (Oxford: Oxford University Press, 2012), pp. 63-80.

[72]Harry Y. Gamble, *Books and Readers in the Early Church* (New Haven, CT: Yale University Press, 1995), p. 206.

[73]George D. Kilpatrick, *The Origins of the Gospel According to St. Matthew* (Oxford: Clarendon, 1950), pp. 72-100; Michael D. Goulder, *Midrash and Lection in Matthew* (London: SPCK, 1974), pp. 182-83; Phillip Carrington, *The Primitive Christian Calendar: A Study in the Making of the Marcan Gospel* (Cambridge: Cambridge University Press, 1952). Of course, other scholars are not convinced that there is a lectionary structure to the Gospels; e.g., W. D. Davies and Dale C. Allison, *Gospel According to Saint Matthew*, pp. 60-61, argue there is no compelling evidence of this structure in Matthew.

[74]Kline, *Structure of Biblical Authority*, 172-203; see also idem, "The Old Testament Origins of

canonical function as the Old Testament Historical Books, since they both highlight the time the covenant people enter into new lands immediately after the death of the covenant mediator (Josh 1:2; Acts 1:8).[75] The New Testament Epistles fulfill a similar function as the Old Testament Prophetic Books in that they are designed to apply and uphold the terms of the covenant laid forth in the prior historical accounts[76] and also function as "covenant lawsuits" when the people of God reject the stipulations of the covenant and pursue false gods.[77] It is for these reasons that Christopher Seitz is able to declare, "In its formal and material givenness, the Law and the Prophets pattern has influenced the formal and material development of the NT canon."[78]

4. As Paul rehearses the pattern of Old Testament covenant-making in the book of Galatians, he reminds his readers of the general principle (echoing the inscriptional curse of Deut 4:2) that when it comes to covenants, "no one annuls it or adds to it once it has been ratified" (Gal 3:15).[79] Therefore, for Paul—and no doubt for early Christians influenced by Paul or who shared Paul's Jewish background—covenants not only had written documents, but those documents were not to be altered. We see this same principle again in 2 Corinthians 3:14 when Paul refers to the Jews who "read the old covenant."[80] Jensen notes that this is further evidence that Paul viewed covenants as having written texts: "For Paul, what you did with the

---

the Gospel Genre," *WTJ* 38 (1975): 1-27. Making a similar observation is Walter Vogels, "La structure symétrique de la Bible chrétienne," in *The Biblical Canons*, ed. J.-M. Auwers and H. J. de Jonge (Leuven: Leuven University Press, 2003), pp. 299.

[75]Vogels, "La structure symétrique de la Bible chrétienne," p. 300; Kline, *Structure of Biblical Authority*, pp. 72-73.

[76]Gerald T. Sheppard, "Canonization: Hearing the Voice of the Same God Through Historically Dissimilar Traditions," *Ex auditu* 1 (1985): 112.

[77]E.g., William L. Lane, "Covenant: The Key to Paul's Conflict with Corinth," *TynBul* 33 (1982): 3-29; Calvin Roetzel, "The Judgment Form in Paul's Letters," *JBL* 88 (1969): 305-12; and John L. White, "Introductory Formulae in the Body of the Pauline Letter," *JBL* 90 (1971): 91-97.

[78]Seitz, *Goodly Fellowship of the Prophets*, p. 103.

[79]For discussion of the term διαθήκη here in Gal 3:15, see Richard Longenecker, *Galatians* (Dallas: Word, 1990), pp. 126-30. Broader discussion of the term in early Christianity can be found in Willem C. van Unnik, "ἡ καινὴ Διαθήκη—A Problem in the Early History of the Canon," *Studia Patristica* 4 (1961): 212-27.

[80]Ralph P. Martin, *2 Corinthians* (WBC; Waco: Word, 1986), p. 69, argues that Paul coined this phrase. C. K. Barrett, *A Commentary on the Second Epistle to the Corinthians* (London: A & C Black, 1973), p. 121, argues that in this passage "old covenant" and "Old Testament" are virtually synonymous.

old covenant was *read* it."[81] If so, then the fact that Paul juxtaposes this "old covenant" with the "new covenant" in the same context (2 Cor 3:6) suggests the possibility that the latter may also have written texts.[82] As Jean Carmignac argues, "In order to use the expression 'Old Testament' he [Paul] must also be aware of the existence of a 'New Testament.'"[83] The likelihood of this possibility increases when we make the simple observation that Paul claims for himself and the other apostles a distinctive covenantal authority—as "ministers of the new covenant" (διακόνους καινῆς διαθήκης)—and makes this claim within a *written* letter to the Corinthians. If this letter functioned as a "covenant lawsuit" against the Corinthians, as some have argued,[84] then one could hardly fault them if they regarded the letter itself as bearing some sort of covenantal authority.

5. The fact that the new corpus of Christian Scripture eventually was called the "New Testament" or "new covenant" is indicative of the close relationship between the concepts of "covenant" and "canon." Early patristic writers often used the term διαθήκη ("covenant") to refer to canonical writings.[85] Melito of Sardis (ca. 180) appears to echo the language of Paul in 2 Corinthians 3:14 when he refers to τῆς παλαιᾶς διαθήκης βιβλία ("the books of the Old Covenant").[86] Such language shows again that early Christians viewed covenants as entities that are manifested in written documents ("books"). Moreover, if Melito is able to refer to an *old* covenant of books,

---

[81]Peter Jensen, *The Revelation of God* (Downers Grove, IL: IVP Academic, 2002), p. 81 (emphasis mine).

[82]For discussion of Paul's phrase "the letter kills" in 2 Cor 3:6, see chapter three below.

[83]Jean Carmignac, "II Corinthiens III. 6, 14 et le Début de la Formation du Noveau Testament," *NTS* 24 (1977): 384-86, at p. 385 (translation mine). Carmignac even goes further and suggests that this "New Testament" may have contained a number of books (even Gospels) in order for it to be parallel with the Old Testament (p. 386).

[84]Lane, "Covenant: The Key to Paul's Conflict with Corinth," pp. 3-29. Lane argues that Paul's letter takes the form of a "covenant lawsuit" where the representative of God's covenant prosecutes God's people when they are disobedient (pp. 15-18). E.g., note 2 Cor 5:20, "Therefore, we are ambassadors for Christ, God making his appeal through us." This same theme is evident in Kline, *Structure of Biblical Authority*, p. 73; Roetzel, "Judgment Form in Paul's Letters," pp. 305-12; and White, "Introductory Formulae in the Body of the Pauline Letter," pp. 91-97.

[85]Ferguson, "Covenant Idea," pp. 150-51; van Unnik, "ἡ καινὴ Διαθήκη—A Problem in the Early History of the Canon," pp. 212-27; Kinzig, "Title of the New Testament," pp. 519-44; and Duncan, "Covenant Idea in Melito of Sardis," p. 26.

[86]Eusebius, *Hist. eccl.* 4.26.14. J. N. D. Kelly, *Early Christian Doctrines* (San Francisco: Harper Collins, 1978), p. 56. The fact that Melito also refers to the Old Testament writings as "the *old* books" (τῶν παλαιῶν βιβλίων) provides further reason to think that he might have a set of "new books" in mind as well (*Hist. eccl.* 4.26.13).

this suggests the possibility that he has in mind a corresponding *new* covenant of books.[87] Also at the end of the second century, an anonymous anti-Montanist writer refers to the church's canonical books as τῷ τῆς τοῦ εὐαγγλίου καινῆς διαθήκης λόγῳ ("the word of the *new covenant* of the gospel"), erasing any doubts about whether the concepts of "canon" and "covenant" were closely linked in the minds of early Christians.[88] In fact, this author even applies an "inscriptional curse" to these new covenant writings when he says that they are writings "to which no one . . . can add and from which he cannot take away."[89] This clear echo of Deuteronomy 4:2 and Revelation 22:18-19 suggests not only that this writer views these new books as covenantal documents, but that this corpus of books cannot be changed or modified—they are fixed.[90]

It is interesting to note that Tertullian often translates the term διαθήκη with the Latin *instrumentum* (and sometimes *testamentum*), which were used in the Roman world to refer to written legal documents.[91] At one point he rejects the canonicity of the *Shepherd* and says it does not deserve a place in the *divino instrumento* ("the divine canon")—a clear reference to a new corpus of books.[92] Thus, by the time of Clement of Alexandria, the phrase *new covenant* was fully established as the official title of the church's canon.[93] Ferguson observes that for Clement, "'Covenant' meant or referred

---

[87]Duncan, "Covenant Idea in Melito of Sardis," pp. 25-26; Kinzig, "Title of the New Testament," pp. 527-28. I am not suggesting that Melito would view "new covenant" as a formal and official title for this new corpus of books. Rather, I am suggesting that there is such a close conceptual link between "covenant" and "canon" in the mind of Melito that he would naturally interchange the two ideas.

[88]*Hist. eccl.* 5.16.3. Van Unnik argues that this comment from the anti-Montanist writer only refers to the "message" of the new covenant and is not a reference to any writings ("ἡ καινὴ Διαθήκη," p. 218). However, the larger context of the quote makes it clear that writings are in view, because the author says he will not himself compose a written treatise against the Montanists "lest I might seem to some to be adding to the writings or injunctions of the word of the new covenant" (*Hist. eccl.* 5.16.3). Thus, Campenhausen argues that the anti-Montanist author "leaves no doubt that what he has in mind is the writing of the 'New Testament'" (*Formation*, p. 265). Bruce M. Metzger, *The Canon of the New Testament: Its Origin, Development, and Significance* (Oxford: Clarendon, 1987), p. 106, agrees that this a reference to a written corpus of books.

[89]*Hist. eccl.* 5.16.3.

[90]Willem C. van Unnik, "De la régle μήτε προσθεῖναι μήτε ἀφελεῖν dans l'histoire du canon," *VC* 3 (1949): 1-36.

[91]Ferguson, "Covenant Idea," p. 151; Metzger, *Canon of the New Testament*, p. 159. For further discussion of *instrumentum* in Tertullian, see Harnack, *Origin of the New Testament*, pp. 209-17.

[92]*Pud.* 10. See also *Marc.* 4.2; *Prax.* 15; 20; *Pud.* 1.

[93]E.g., *Strom.* 1.44.3; 3.71.3; 4.134.4; 5.85.1. See discussion in Kinzig, "Title of the New Testa-

to written documents."[94] Likewise, for Origen, Campenhausen argues that "*diatheke* in the sense of 'book' was a perfectly normal usage."[95] In fact, Origen used the word ἐνδιαθήκους—an obvious derivative of διαθήκη—to refer to the books that he regarded as "canonical."[96]

When all these factors are taken into account, it is not only clear that the early Christian movement was distinctively covenantal in its orientation, but that it would have shared the close connection between covenants and written texts so evident in the Old Testament/Jewish background out of which it was born. If so, then the emergence of a new corpus of covenantal books would not have been something entirely unexpected.

THE ROLE OF THE APOSTLES IN EARLY CHRISTIANITY

In addition to eschatological and covenantal beliefs, early Christians also had beliefs about the role and authority of the apostles that would have impacted the development of a new corpus of scriptural books. Our earliest Christian writings portray the apostles as having the very authority of Christ himself.[97] Jesus had commissioned his apostles "so that they might be with him and he might send them out to preach and have authority" (Mk 3:14-15). When Jesus sent out the Twelve, he reminds them that "it is not you who speak, but the Spirit of your Father speaking through you" (Mt 10:20). Thus, he is able to give a warning to those who reject the apostles' authority: "If anyone will not receive you or listen to your words, . . . it will be more bearable on the day of judgment for the land of Sodom and Gomorrah than for that town" (Mt 10:14). Likewise, John's Gospel describes Jesus' special promise to the apostles: "The Holy Spirit, whom the Father will send in my name, he will teach you all things and bring to your remembrance all that I have said to you" (Jn 14:26). In addition, Jesus indicates in his prayer to the Father that "I have given them [the apostles] the words that you gave me. . . . As you sent me into the world, so I have sent them into the world" (Jn 17:8,

---

ment," pp. 529-30; and Ferguson, "Covenant Idea," pp. 151-52.
[94]Ferguson, "Covenant Idea," p. 151.
[95]Campenhausen, *Formation*, p. 267.
[96]*Hist. eccl.* 6.25.1. Thanks to T. David Gordon for pointing out this particular reference.
[97]For further discussion, see C. F. D. Moule, *The Birth of the New Testament* (London: Adam & Charles Black, 1981), pp. 235-39; and Ralph P. Martin, "Authority in the Light of the Apostolate, Tradition and the Canon," *EvQ* 40 (1968): 66-82.

18). This same theme is picked up in the book of Acts as Peter testifies to the fact that the apostles were "chosen by God as witnesses . . . to preach to the people and to testify that [Christ] is the one appointed by God to be judge of the living and the dead" (Acts 10:41-42). Also, the book of 2 Peter makes it clear that the words of the apostles are the words of Jesus and are on par with the authority given to the Old Testament prophets: "You should remember the predictions of the holy prophets and the commandment of the Lord and Savior through your apostles" (2 Pet 3:2).

Early patristic writings indicate that this same conviction about the authority of the apostles was foundational for the early church. The book of *1 Clement* not only encourages its readers to "Take up the epistle of that blessed apostle, Paul,"[98] but also offers a clear reason why: "The Apostles received the Gospel for us from the Lord Jesus Christ, Jesus the Christ was sent from God. The Christ therefore is from God and the Apostles from the Christ."[99] In addition, the letter refers to the apostles as "the greatest and most righteous pillars of the Church."[100] Ignatius, bishop of Antioch, also recognizes the unique role of the apostles as the mouthpiece of Christ: "The Lord did nothing apart from the Father . . . neither on his own nor through the apostles."[101] Here Ignatius indicates that the apostles were a distinct historical group and the agents through which Christ worked. Thus, Ignatius goes out of his way to distinguish his own authority as a bishop from the authority of the apostles: "I am not enjoining [commanding] you as Peter and Paul did. They were apostles, I am condemned."[102]

Justin Martyr displays the same appreciation for the distinct authority of the apostles: "For from Jerusalem there went out into the world, men, twelve in number . . . by the power of God they proclaimed to every race of men that they were sent by Christ to teach to all the word of God."[103] Moreover, he views the Gospels as the written embodiment of apostolic

---

[98] *1 Clem.* 47:1-3. All English translations of the apostolic fathers, unless otherwise noted, are from Bart D. Ehrman, *The Apostolic Fathers*, 2 vols. (Cambridge, MA: Harvard University Press, 2003).

[99] *1 Clem.* 42:1-2.

[100] *1 Clem.* 5:2.

[101] Ign. *Magn.* 7:1.

[102] Ign. *Rom.* 4:4. For more on Ignatius's extensive discussion of apostolic authority, see Charles E. Hill, "Ignatius and the Apostolate," in *Studia Patristica* (vol. 36; Leuven: Peeters, 2001), pp. 226-48.

[103] *1 Apol.* 39. English translation from Alexander Roberts and James Donaldson, eds., *The Ante-Nicene Fathers* (Peabody, MA: Hendrickson, 1885).

tradition: "For the apostles, in the memoirs composed by them, which are called Gospels, have thus delivered unto us what was enjoined upon them."[104] Likewise, Irenaeus views all the New Testament Scriptures as the embodiment of apostolic teaching: "We have learned from none others the plan of our salvation, than from those through whom the Gospel has come down to us, which they did at one time proclaim in public, and, at a later period, by the will of God, handed down to us in the Scriptures, to be the ground and pillar of our faith."[105] Although this is only a sampling of patristic writers (and more could be added), the point is clear. The authoritative role of the apostles was woven into the fabric of Christianity from its very earliest stages. As C. F. D. Moule observed, "The Twelve evidently constituted the earliest Christian 'canon.'"[106]

Given this background, we come to the key question: what would happen if the early Christians believed that the authoritative message of the apostles were put in written form? How would such documents be viewed? Initially, of course, the apostles delivered their message orally through teaching and preaching.[107] But it was not long before they (and others) began to write their message down. And these apostolic documents told Christians to "stand firm and hold to the traditions you were taught by us, either by our spoken word *or by our letter*" (2 Thess 2:15). And again, "If anyone does not obey *what we say in this letter*, take note of that person and have nothing to do with him" (2 Thess 3:14).[108] It is here that we see the obvious connection

---

[104]*Apol.* 66.3.

[105]*Haer.* 3.1.1.

[106]Moule, *Birth of the New Testament*, p. 236.

[107]General treatments of oral tradition include: Samuel Byrskog, *Story as History—History as Story: The Gospel Tradition in the Context of Ancient Oral History* (Leiden: E. J. Brill, 2002); Richard Bauckham, *Jesus and the Eyewitnesses: The Gospels as Eyewitness Testimony* (Grand Rapids: Eerdmans, 2006); James D. G. Dunn, *Jesus Remembered* (Grand Rapids: Eerdmans, 2003); Henry Wansbrough, ed., *Jesus And the Oral Gospel Tradition* (Edinburgh: T & T Clark, 2004); Werner H. Kelber, *The Oral and the Written Gospel: The Hermeneutics of Speaking and Writing in the Synoptic Tradition, Mark, Paul, and Q* (Philadelphia: Fortress, 1983); Birger Gerhardsson, *Memory and Manuscript with Tradition and Transmission in Early Christianity*, rev. ed. (Grand Rapids: Eerdmans, 1998); Kenneth E. Bailey, "Informal Controlled Oral Tradition and the Synoptic Gospels," *Them* 20 (1995): 4-11; Jan M. Vansina, *Oral Tradition as History* (Madison, WI: University of Wisconsin Press, 1985); Richard A. Horsley, Jonathan A. Draper and John Miles Foley, eds., *Performing the Gospel: Orality, Memory, and Mark* (Minneapolis: Fortress, 2006); and, recently, Werner H. Kelber and Samuel Byrskog, eds., *Jesus in Memory: Traditions in Oral and Scribal Perspectives* (Waco, TX: Baylor University Press, 2009).

[108]The issue of whether certain New Testament books were pseudonymous (e.g., 2 Thessalonians,

between the role of the apostles and the beginnings of the canon. If apostles were viewed as the mouthpiece of Christ, and it was believed that they wrote down that apostolic message in books, then those books would be received as the very words of Christ himself. Such writings would not have to wait until second-, third- or fourth-century ecclesiastical decisions to be viewed as authoritative—instead they would be viewed as authoritative from almost the very start. For this reason, a written New Testament was not something the church formally "decided" to have at some later date, but was instead the natural outworking of the early church's view of the function of the apostles.

While apostolic texts would certainly have been authoritative, we are still left with the question of why the apostles (or their companions) would have written in the first place. Why not just stick with oral tradition? Although we will address the issue of orality (and textuality) more fully in the next chapter, here we can briefly explore a number of factors that may have naturally led to the textualization of early Christian tradition. For one, the disposition toward written covenantal texts (as discussed above) would have no doubt played a role. The heritage of the earliest Christians was one in which covenantal revelation from God was normally placed in written form. One is reminded of God's command to Moses: "Then the LORD said to Moses, 'Write this as a memorial in a book'" (Ex 17:14). Isaiah is given the same command, "And now, go, write it before them on a tablet and inscribe it in a book" (Is 30:8). Also, Jeremiah is exhorted: "'Thus says the LORD, the God of Israel: Write in a book all the words that I have spoken to you'" (Jer 30:2). And, again, we see this pattern in Habakkuk: "And the Lord answered me, 'Write the vision; make it plain on tablets'" (Hab 2:2). Thus, why should we be surprised when the New Testament authors do the same? Indeed,

---

1 and 2 Timothy) is not relevant to the point here. The point here is simply that (1) the earliest Christians viewed apostles as having authority and (2) they regarded certain books as having come from apostles—this alone is sufficient to explain the origins of a new canon. Whether or not the earliest Christians were mistaken about some of these beliefs does not affect our argument. Nor is our argument affected by books attributed to nonapostles (e.g., Mark, Luke, Hebrews). The reason these books were also deemed to be authoritative is that they were regarded as having apostolic *content* even if they were not written by the hand of an apostle. E.g., Justin is willing to call the Gospels "memoirs of the apostles" even though he knows two of them were not written by apostles (1 *Apol.* 66.3; *Dial.* 103); Tertullian describes Mark and Luke as "apostolic men" (*Marc.* 4.2).

John is given the same command: "'Write what you see in a book and send it to the seven churches'" (Rev 1:11). Luke tells us, "It seemed good to me also . . . to write" (Lk 1:3). Similarly, Jude says, "I was very eager to write to you about our common salvation" (Jude 3). Near the end of his Gospel, John says, "But these are written [in this book] so that you may believe that Jesus is the Christ" (Jn 20:31). It is here that we are faced with the possibility that Christians may have textualized their message as a way of identifying themselves with their Jewish heritage—a heritage in which God normally communicated in written form.[109]

Second, the textualization of the apostolic message would have occurred quite naturally as the apostles—the authoritative founders of the Christian movement (Eph 2:20)—began to die out. As time passed, it would have become clear that the message would need to be maintained in a more *permanent* form; that is, it would need to be written down. C. F. D. Moule observes:

> Where were the guarantees to be found for the authenticity of its [the church's] claims, after the accredited eye-witnesses had ceased to be available, and when even their immediate followers were growing scarce? The answer lay inevitably in written records. With the appeal to "the Lord and the Apostles" begins an *inevitable process of development leading to accredited writings.*[110]

Indeed, there is a parallel here with historiographical practices in the

---

[109]A number of scholars have begun to highlight the role physical manuscripts play as visual *identity markers* for a community: e.g., William A. Johnson, "Towards a Sociology of Reading in Classical Antiquity," *AJP* 121 (2000): 593-627; Larry W. Hurtado, "Manuscripts and the Sociology of Early Christian Reading," in *Early Text of the New Testament*, pp. 49-62; and Chris Keith, "Prolegomena on the Textualization of Mark's Gospel: Manuscript Culture, the Extended Situation, and the Emergence of Written Gospels," in *Keys and Frames: Memory and Identity in Ancient Judaism and Early Christianity*, ed. Tom Thatcher (Atlanta: Society of Biblical Literature, forthcoming), p. 24. If so, then we must consider the possibility that early Christians textualized their traditions as a means of visually expressing their Jewish/Old Testament identity. Of course, as we shall see in the next chapter, Christians were also keen to provide visual markers (such as the codex and *nomina sacra*) that would distinguish their books from Jewish books. But the fact that they used books at all (at least for their religious texts) may have been due to their desire to identify with the God of Israel. For more on the role of visual identity markers, see Jan Assmann, "Form as a Mnemonic Device: Cultural Texts and Cultural Memory," in *Performing the Gospel*, pp. 67-82.

[110]Moule, *Birth of the New Testament*, p. 239; cf. Martin, "Authority in Light of the Apostolate," p. 76.

broader Greco-Roman world.[111] While ancient historians clearly preferred to access historical events through the oral testimony of an eyewitness[112]— a "living voice"[113]—they were quite willing to put this testimony into written form as the eyewitnesses died out.[114] Samuel Byrskog comments on these ancient historians: "The writing down of an item meant that this piece of information was given a certain abiding character."[115] Thus, written records and oral/eyewitness testimony were not in opposition to one another; on the contrary, written accounts were simply a way to make oral/eyewitness testimony permanently accessible.

This need to textualize the oral tradition of founding members (or eye-witnesses) is a pattern that has also been recognized by scholars who study social and cultural memory theory.[116] In particular, the work of Jan Assmann has recognized that societies that experience an event that causes a *Traditionsbruch*—a "breakdown in tradition"—often turn to the written word to preserve the community memory for future generations.[117] The textualization of this tradition provides "a more enduring media capable of car-

---

[111]For an overview of the relationship between Greco-Roman historiography and the Gospels, see Craig S. Keener, *The Historical Jesus of the Gospels* (Grand Rapids: Eerdmans, 2009), pp. 71-125; Paul R. Eddy and Gregory A. Boyd, *The Jesus Legend: A Case for the Historical Reliability of the Synoptic Jesus Tradition* (Grand Rapids: Baker Academic, 2007), pp. 309-61. For particular discussion of historiography and Luke–Acts, see Loveday Alexander, *The Preface to Luke's Gospel: Literary Convention and Social Context in Luke 1:1-4 and Acts 1:1* (Cambridge: Cambridge University Press, 1993); and Joel B. Green and Michael C. McKeever, *Luke-Acts and New Testament Historiography* (Grand Rapids: Baker Academic, 1994).

[112]Polybius, *Histories* IV.2.1-2; Galen, *Temp. med.* 6 pref. (Kühn XI.796-97); Thucydides, I.22.1-2, V.26.5; Tacitus, *Hist.* 4.81, *Ann.* 3.16; Papias cited in Eusebius, *Hist. eccl.* 3.39.3-4. For discussion of Papias as a source see Byrskog, *Story as History*, pp. 272-92; Robert H. Gundry, *Matthew: A Commentary on His Handbook for a Mixed Church Under Persecution* (Grand Rapids: Eerdmans, 1994), pp. 1026-45; and Martin Hengel, *Studies in the Gospel of Mark* (London: SCM, 1985), pp. 47-53.

[113]For a general overview of the use of "living voice," see Loveday Alexander, "The Living Voice: Skepticism Toward the Written Word in Early Christian and Graeco-Roman Texts," in *The Bible in Three Dimensions*, ed. David J. A. Clines, Stephen E. Fowl and Stanley E. Porter (Sheffield: JSOT, 1990), pp. 221-47; and Bauckham, *Jesus and the Eyewitnesses*, pp. 21-29.

[114]E.g., Herodotus, 1.1; Thucydides, 1.22.4.

[115]Byrskog, *Story as History*, pp. 122-23.

[116]A helpful collection of essays that apply social/cultural memory theory to early Christianity can be found in: Alan Kirk and Tom Thatcher, eds., *Memory, Tradition, and Text: Uses of the Past in Early Christianity* (Atlanta: Society of Biblical Literature, 2005).

[117]Jan Assmann, *Das kulturelle Gedächtnis: Schrift, Erinnerung und politische Identität in frühen Hochkulteren* (Munich: C. H. Beck, 1992), p. 165; idem, *Religion and Cultural Memory*, trans. Rodney Livingstone (Stanford, CA: Stanford University Press, 2006), pp. 68-70.

rying memory in a vital manner across generations."[118] Events that might threaten a community's memory and cause a *Traditionsbruch* are varied, but for emerging communities, such a memory crisis is often caused by the death of the founding generation.[119] Assmann observes, "In such situations we find not only that new texts emerge, but also that already existing texts are given enhanced normative value. Where the contact with the living models is broken, people turn to the texts in their search for guidance."[120] Given the deep religious significance of the apostolic generation for the earliest Christians, these studies of social memory provide a compelling explanation for the explosion of early Christian literature in the second half of the first century.[121] In fact, it is worth observing that the textualization of tradition in these circumstances typically occurs within forty years of the community's founding—approximately the same amount of time between the death of Jesus and the production of Mark's Gospel.[122] This explanation also fits quite well with the patristic testimony, which suggests that Mark's Gospel was written to preserve the memory of Peter's teaching just before (or upon) his death.[123]

Another indication that early Christian literary production was (at least partly) motivated by the passing away of the apostles is the fact that many New Testament writings share elements of the "testamentary" genre.[124] This

---

[118]Alan Kirk, "Social and Cultural Memory," in *Memory, Tradition, and Text*, pp. 1-24, at p. 6.

[119]Assmann, *Das kulturelle Gedächtnis*, p. 218.

[120]Ibid., *Religion and Cultural Memory*, p. 69.

[121]Keith, in "Prolegomena to the Textualization of Mark's Gospel," p. 17, rightly recognizes that the *Traditionsbruch* does not inevitably and automatically lead to the textualization of the tradition; it can be preserved in other ways (such as ritual). While this is true, the *Traditionsbruch* caused by the absence of the apostles should be seen in light of the textual-covenantal disposition of Christianity's Jewish heritage. That disposition makes textualization the more likely option (this topic will be addressed more in the next chapter).

[122]The standard dating for Mark's Gospel is around A.D. 70; e.g., see arguments in Martin Hengel, *Studies in the Gospel of Mark*, pp. 28-30. But many scholars have argued for an earlier date, such as Bo Reicke, *The Roots of the Synoptic Gospels* (Philadelphia: Fortress, 1986), pp. 177-80; Christopher S. Mann, *Mark* (Anchor Bible; New York: Doubleday, 1986), pp. 72-83.

[123]There is widespread patristic evidence that the Gospel of Mark was viewed as the embodiment of Peter's teaching: e.g., Justin, *Dial.* 106; Irenaeus, *Haer.* 3.10.5; Tertullian, *Marc.* 4.5.3; Eusebius, *Hist. eccl.* 2.15; 6.14.6 (attributed to Clement of Alexandria). However, there are different patristic testimonies about whether Mark wrote before Peter died (Clement, Eusebius) or after Peter died (Irenaeus). Either way, it is clear that these patristic writers understood Mark's Gospel to be motivated by Peter's absence.

[124]For broad overviews of this genre, see Eckhard von Nordheim, *Die Lehre Der Alten. Vol 1, Das Testamente als Literaturgattung im Judentum der hellenistische-romischen Zeit* (Leiden: E. J.

genre (also known as a "farewell speech") was well known in the Second
Temple time period and purportedly records the final teachings of important individuals on the eve of their deaths.[125] The *raison d'être* behind a
testament/farewell speech is a very practical one: the critical teachings of a
key person must be put in permanent written form before that person dies.
This practical consideration is central to the book of 2 Peter as the apostle is
on the eve of his own death: "I think it right, as long as I am in this body, to
stir you up by way of reminder, since I know that the putting off of my body
will be soon, as our Lord Jesus Christ made clear to me. And I will make
every effort *so that after my departure you may be able at any time to recall
these things*" (2 Pet 1:13-15). Similar elements of the testament/farewell
speech occur in a number of other New Testament writings, including the
Pastoral Epistles, Jude, the Johannine letters, Revelation, and speeches in
the book of Acts (for example, Acts 20:17-35). Such features have led Charles
Hill to observe:

> A "testamentary aura" surrounds the writings of the NT, particularly the later
> ones. The apostles and their assistants are taking care to provide for the
> churches when the apostles depart from the scene. This is being done . . . by
> the preparation of written materials to function in an ongoing way for the life
> of the church.[126]

The presence of these testamentary elements within the New Testament
books confirms that among the earliest Christians there was already a motivation and an inclination to write. If so, then the emergence of apostolic
writings would not have been unnatural and unexpected among the earliest
Christians. On the contrary, it simply would have been a practical step as
the apostles began to die out.

Of course, some scholars have used such testamentary elements as evidence that these New Testament books (particularly 2 Peter) are formal
instances of the testamentary genre and therefore must be late pseudepi-

---

Brill, 1980); and Otto Knoch, *Die "Testamente" des Petrus und Paulus* (Stuttgart: KBW, 1973).
See also discussion in Richard Bauckham, *Jude, 2 Peter* (Waco, TX: Word, 1983), pp. 131-35,
158-62.
[125]E.g., *Testament of Moses, Testament of the Twelve Patriarchs, Testament of Job*. Parts/sections of
writings can also be considered testamental in nature: *1 Enoch* 91-107; *4 Ezra* 14:28-36; *2 Baruch* 77-86; *Jub* 21:1-23:7; Josephus, *Ant.* 4.309-319.
[126]Hill, "God's Speech in These Last Days," p. 242.

graphical works.[127] However, such a conclusion is unnecessary. A particular writing can share certain features of the testamentary genre without being a formal instance of that genre. Indeed, 2 Peter lacks certain key features that other testamentary literature possesses; namely, it does not record a "heavenly journey" of Peter (which was common in testamentary literature),[128] nor does it record the death of Peter or the response of his followers to his death.[129] More importantly, 2 Peter differs substantively from other testamentary literature in that it is in the form of a *letter*. This particular combination—testamentary features within an epistolary structure—is unprecedented prior to the book of 2 Peter.[130] For this reason, Green suggests that "If 2 Peter were conceived as a testament, could it not also be that the author 'created' this combination for use by a living and authentic author?"[131] Thus, even if we granted that 2 Peter was a formal instance of the testamentary genre, that still does not require that the book be pseudonymous.

While the imminent death of the apostles was no doubt a factor in the textualization of apostolic teaching, there is a third motivation that may have even been more fundamental. What is it that written texts could accomplish that oral tradition could not? We return again to the work of Assmann, who suggests that the answer lies in the fact that written texts provide access to an audience that is not co-present with the speaker.[132] Or, as Assmann put it, written texts are produced when there is "a need for transmission beyond the boundaries of an immediate situation."[133] It is the presence of an "extended situation" (*zerdehnte Situation*) that leads to the use of written texts—that is, a situation

---

[127]Richard Bauckham, "Pseudo-Apostolic Letters," *JBL* 107 (1988): 469-94.

[128]Anitra B. Kolenkow, "The Genre Testament and Forecasts of the Future in the Hellenistic Jewish Milieu," *JSJ* 6 (1975): 66-67.

[129]Peter H. Davids, *The Letters of 2 Peter and Jude* (PNTC; Grand Rapids: Eerdmans, 2006), p. 148.

[130]The book of 2 *Baruch* seems to share this combination, but it was written in the second century A.D. and could not have been the prototype for 2 Peter.

[131]Gene L. Green, *Jude and 2 Peter* (BECNT; Grand Rapids: Baker Academic, 2008), p. 167.

[132]Assmann, "Form as a Mnemonic Device," pp. 73-77; cf. Assmann, *Religion and Cultural Memory*, p. 103. On this point, see the excellent discussion (and interaction with Assmann) in Chris Keith, "A Performance of the Text: The Adulteress's Entrance into John's Gospel," in *The Fourth Gospel and Ancient Media Culture*, ed. Anthony LeDonne and Tom Thatcher (London: T & T Clark, 2011), pp. 49-69.

[133]Assmann, "Form as a Mnemonic Device," p. 76.

where "the speaker has to overcome distances in space and/or time in order to reach the listener."[134] Thus, written texts are employed by communities not as a means of rejecting oral tradition, but as a means of broadening and expanding its reach.[135]

When we consider the situation of the apostles in the first century it becomes immediately evident that they faced an "extended situation." Their mission was not just to those individuals that might be within their immediate hearing, but they also were called to bring their message to the entire world (Mt 28:18-20).[136] In other words, their audience was virtually infinite over time and space (and cultures). If they were to achieve their Christ-given mission, the apostles would have to employ a means of communication that extended beyond their personal presence. No doubt this goes a long way toward explaining why the apostles (and their companions) wrote letters—there was a need to communicate the apostolic message to an ever-expanding global church that they could not oversee in person.[137] Moreover, it suggests a plausible explanation for why the first two decades of Christianity, the 30s and 40s, produced hardly any letters while the 50s and 60s (and later) produced so many more. Perhaps the challenge of the global "extended situation" was not as apparent during the early years of the apostolic mission but became increasingly unavoidable as the church continued to expand. Regardless, the overall point should not be missed. It was the *mission* of the apostles which would have made writing—and the resulting collection of authoritative books—a virtual inevitability.

---

[134]Assmann, *Religion and Cultural Memory*, p. 103; cf. Assmann, "Form as a Mnemonic Device," p. 75. Assmann recognizes that oral tradition can also, to some extent, be used to create an "extended situation," but it still has significant limitations that writing does not have because it "must depend on time and place, on temporal reoccurrence" (p. 77).

[135]Keith, "A Performance of the Text," pp. 65-66.

[136]The global-universal focus of the apostolic mission is spread throughout the entire New Testament corpus, showing that it was entrenched part of early Christian understanding (e.g., Mk 13:10; Lk 24:47; Acts 1:7-8; Rom 1:5; 1 Cor 16:5-6; Gal 3:7-9; Eph 2:11-22; Col 1:7; 1 Tim 2:1-7; 3:16; 2 Tim 4:17; Rev 7:9; 14:6; 15:4).

[137]Hans-Josef Klauck, *Ancient Letters and the New Testament: A Guide to Context and Exegesis* (Waco, TX: Baylor University Press, 2006), pp. 188-93, surveys historical evidence that shows that ancient writers regarded epistles as a sufficient substitute for personal presence. See also Robert W. Funk, "The Apostolic Parousia: Form and Significance," in *Christian History and Interpretation: Studies Presented to John Knox*, ed. W. R. Farmer, C. F. D. Moule and Reinhold R. Niebuhr (Cambridge: Cambridge University Press, 1967), pp. 249-68.

CONCLUSION

In response to the extrinsic model's suggestion that there was nothing in early Christianity that might have led to a canon, this chapter has argued that the matrix of early Christian beliefs, when taken in tandem, would have created a favorable environment for the growth of a new revelational deposit. Those beliefs include the following:

1. Early Christians held eschatological beliefs that Israel's long-awaited redemption had occurred in Jesus of Nazareth. Given that the Old Testament itself testifies that the age of the Messiah will bring a new divine message and that new revelation often follows redemption (what Bovon calls the event-proclamation pattern), there are good reasons to think a new divine revelation would have emerged.

2. Early Christians held beliefs about covenants, namely that in Jesus Christ God had inaugurated a new covenant with Israel (Jer 31:31). Since the Old Testament witness suggests a tight relationship between covenants and written texts, it would be natural for the earliest Christians (who were Jews) to anticipate new covenant documents. Again, as Hillers has observed, when it comes to biblical covenants, "there is a written document in connection with it, the familiar 'text of the covenant.'"[138]

3. Early Christians held the belief that the apostles were Christ's authorized agents to deliver and transmit the new message of redemption. Although the apostles did this orally, they also began to write their message down (2 Thess 2:15). Thus, documents that were regarded as containing apostolic teaching would have been viewed as authoritative right from the beginning and would not have needed to wait for later ecclesiastical developments (2 Thess 3:14).

Given this first-century context, and the likely predispositions of early Christians, why should we attribute the emergence of a new collection of scriptural books solely to later ecclesiastical politics? Should we not at least consider the possibility that these scriptural books may have emerged because the first-century environment was conducive to the production of such books? If so, then we should be hesitant to suggest that the idea of a canon "was utterly remote from the minds of the first generations of Christian

---

[138]Hillers, *Covenant*, p. 145.

believers."[139] On the contrary, it seems that the minds of the first generations of Christian believers might have been focused on the very things that would have led to the development of a new corpus of sacred books. Paul Achtemeier sums it up: *"The formation of the canon represented the working out of forces that were already present in the primitive Christian community and that would have made some form of canon virtually inevitable."*[140]

---

[139]Gamble, *New Testament Canon*, p. 12.

[140]Paul J. Achtemeier, Joel B. Green and Marianne Meye Thompson, eds., *Introducing the New Testament and Its Literature* (Grand Rapids: Eerdmans, 2001), p. 589 (emphasis mine).

3

THE WRITING OF CANON

Were Early Christians Averse
to Written Documents?

There is more than a suggestion in the early
Church of a reluctance to write.

C. F. EVANS
"The New Testament in the Making,"
in *The Cambridge History of the Bible:*
From the Beginnings to Jerome

⚖

THROUGHOUT THIS VOLUME, WE HAVE BEEN arguing for more of an "intrinsic" model of canon, namely that the canon was not an artificial, ecclesiastical creation imposed on books written for another purpose, but was something that would have arisen naturally from the matrix of theological beliefs held by the earliest Christians. However, not all scholars are convinced that a corpus of authoritative writings would have emerged so naturally. The primary reason for this resistance is that some scholars view early Christianity as a predominantly, if not exclusively, *oral* religion that would have been hesitant to place value on written documents.[1]

---

[1] A key example of this approach is Werner Kelber, *The Oral and the Written Gospel: The Hermeneutics of Speaking and Writing in the Synoptic Tradition, Mark, Paul, and Q* (Philadelphia: Fortress, 1983). Kelber argues that the Gospel of Mark was a revolutionary document designed to

James Barr argues against an early emergence of a Christian corpus of
Scripture on precisely these grounds: "The cultural presupposition [of
early Christianity] suggested that committal to writing was an unworthy
mode of transmission of the profoundest truth."[2] Robert Funk uses this
same argument to push the emergence of the canon further back: "The
aversion to writing persisted in the early [Christian] movement well into
the second century."[3] Even when it comes to the apostle Paul, we are told
that he was "suspicious of texts" and only wrote letters because he was
"forced" to do so in response to false teachers.[4] This sort of argument—
that early Christians had an aversion to written texts, which would have
prevented the early emergence of a canon—constitutes the third major
tenet of the extrinsic model.[5]

As a result of this conviction, some scholars have offered a rather neg-

---

undercut the dominant orality of early Christianity and replace it with written texts. Other
general treatments of oral tradition in early Christianity (not necessarily sharing Kelber's ap-
proach) include: Samuel Byrskog, *Story as History—History as Story: The Gospel Tradition in the
Context of Ancient Oral History* (Leiden: E. J. Brill, 2002); Richard Bauckham, *Jesus and the Eye-
witnesses: The Gospels as Eyewitness Testimony* (Grand Rapids: Eerdmans, 2006); James D. G.
Dunn, *Jesus Remembered* (Grand Rapids: Eerdmans, 2003); Henry Wansbrough, ed., *Jesus and
The Oral Gospel Tradition* (Edinburgh: T & T Clark, 2004); Birger Gerhardsson, *Memory and
Manuscript with Tradition and Transmission in Early Christianity*, rev. ed. (Grand Rapids: Eerd-
mans, 1998); Kenneth E. Bailey, "Informal Controlled Oral Tradition and the Synoptic Gospels,"
Them 20 (1995): 4-11; Jan M. Vansina, *Oral Tradition as History* (Madison, WI: University of
Wisconsin Press, 1985); Richard A. Horsley, Jonathan A. Draper and John Miles Foley, eds.,
Performing the Gospel: Orality, Memory, and Mark (Minneapolis: Fortress, 2006); and, most recently, Werner Kelber and Samuel Byrskog, eds., *Jesus in Memory: Traditions in Oral and Scribal
Perspectives* (Waco, TX: Baylor University Press, 2009). For a helpful overview of recent research
on orality in early Christianity, see Kelly R. Iverson, "Orality and the Gospels: A Survey of Recent Research," *CBR* 8 (2009): 71-206.
[2]James Barr, *Holy Scripture: Canon, Authority and Criticism* (Philadelphia: Westminster, 1983), p.
12.
[3]Robert W. Funk, "The Once and Future New Testament," in *The Canon Debate*, ed. Lee M. Mc-
Donald and James A. Sanders (Peabody, MA: Hendrickson, 2002), p. 544.
[4]Tom Thatcher, "Beyond Texts and Traditions: Werner Kelber's Media History of Christian Origins," in *Jesus, the Voice, and the Text: Beyond the Oral and the Written Gospel*, ed. Tom Thatcher
(Waco, TX: Baylor University Press, 2008), p. 16. Thatcher is describing Werner Kelber's view in
this passage, so it is unclear whether he shares Kelber's view. For more on Paul's view of his letters, see Robert W. Funk, "The Apostolic Parousia: Form and Significance," in *Christian History
and Interpretation: Studies Presented to John Knox*, ed. W. R. Farmer, C. F. D. Moule and R. R.
Niebuhr (Cambridge: Cambridge University Press, 1967), pp. 249-68.
[5]For a summary of this approach, see C. F. Evans, "The New Testament in the Making," in *The
Cambridge History of the Bible: From the Beginnings to Jerome*, ed. P. R. Ackroyd and C. F. Evans
(Cambridge: Cambridge University Press, 1970), pp. 232-83, at pp. 233-34. See similar statements in Eric F. Osborn, "Teaching and Writing in the First Chapter of the *Stromateis* of Clement of Alexandria," *JTS* 10 (1959): 335-43.

ative portrayal of writing within the history of early Christianity. The act of writing is now receiving the blame for many of early Christianity's social ills. Not only are we told that it is responsible for making Christianity a "centralized" and "hierarchical" religion, but it is also characterized as a weapon of oppression used for the "marginalization of perceived deviant groups."[6] Writing is guilty of taking a "diversified" and "egalitarian" religion and corrupting it into a religion where the power was in the hands of a "small educated male elite."[7] Thus, it is now blamed for the suppression of women, discrimination against the poor, and the exclusion of the uneducated.[8] As a result, the written text is described as "dead,"[9] "despiritualized,"[10] "mute"[11] and "a move away from the free expression of the spirit."[12] In contrast, spoken/oral words are given a glowing appraisal, as we are told that they "breathe life," "carry a sense of presence and intensity" and are "endowed with a special quality of presentness and personal authority."[13]

Now, this idea that early Christianity was "a culture which tended to frown upon the writing of books"[14] can be largely traced back to the work of form critics (and their predecessors) in the late nineteenth and early twentieth centuries.[15] Particularly influential was the work of Franz Overbeck, who downplayed the value of early Christian writings as *Urliteratur* (preliterature) that lacked the artistry and sophistication of Greco-Roman writings.[16] Thus, he portrayed early Christianity as an inherently unliterary movement that would have placed no real value in texts. Ac-

---

[6]David M. Carr, *Writing on the Tablet of the Heart: Origins of Scripture and Literature* (Oxford: Oxford University Press, 2005), p. 283.

[7]Joanna Dewey, "Textuality in an Oral Culture: A Survey of the Pauline Traditions," in *Orality and Textuality in Early Christian Literature*, ed. Joanna Dewey (Atlanta: Scholars Press, 1995), pp. 37-65, at p. 60.

[8]Dewey, "Textuality in an Oral Culture," p. 59.

[9]F. C. Baur as cited in Hans von Campenhausen, *The Formation of the Christian Bible* (London: Adam & Charles Black, 1972), p. 135.

[10]Kelber, *Oral and the Written Gospel*, p. 158.

[11]Ibid.

[12]Funk, "Once and Future New Testament," p. 544.

[13]Kelber, *Oral and the Written Gospel*, pp. 18-20.

[14]Anthony E. Harvey, "Review of Midrash and Lection in Matthew by M. G. Goulder," *JTS* 27 (1976): 188-95, at p. 189.

[15]Harry Y. Gamble, *Books and Readers in the Early Church* (New Haven: Yale University Press, 1995), pp. 11-13.

[16]Franz Overbeck, "Über die Anfänge der partristischen Literatur," *Historische Zeitschrift* 48 (1882): 417-72.

cording to Overbeck, Christianity did not become a literary movement
until the mid-second century—only then would texts have begun to have
any real authority.[17] Early form critics were influenced greatly by Overbeck
and argued that earliest Christianity was a fundamentally oral culture that
would have been disinclined to put the message of Jesus in written form.[18]
Martin Dibelius is representative of this approach when he argues that
Christians were "an unlettered people which . . . had neither the capacity
nor the inclination for the production of books."[19]

However, the roots of this modern scholarly polemic against the written
word go beyond just the influence of form criticism. Francis Watson traces
it also to the existentialism of scholars such as Friedrich Schleiermacher
and Rudolf Bultmann, who insist that "the reality of religion can only be
immediately experienced"[20] and that "textuality is a barrier to immediacy."[21]
If true religion must always be an immediate spiritual encounter, then one
can see how written texts would be disparaged as obstacles to such en-
counters. Watson argues that the negative appraisal of writing among these
existential scholars is actually a neo-Marcionite rejection of Judaism: "Textuality is identified with Jewishness, the letter that kills by corrupting the
original purity of the gospel; and neo-Marcionism proposes to cleanse theology and church from the defilement of the Jewish letter."[22] Thus, it is no
surprise that Bultmann insists on interpreting the early Christian movement
apart from the Old Testament story of Israel—for him, it is not a religion
about the past but about the experience of the *kerygma* in the present.[23]

---

[17]Ibid., pp. 436-38.

[18]Gamble, *Books and Readers*, pp. 14-15. Even when the oral message was eventually put into
written form, the form critics still did not regard this as real literature (*Hochliteratur*) but as
popular literature (*Kleinliteratur*). Thus, according to form criticism, these were not writings
that would have borne any real authority.

[19]Martin Dibelius, *From Tradition to Gospel* (Cambridge: J. Clarke, 1971), p. 9. Overbeck's influence can be clearly seen in the first chapter, pp. 1-8.

[20]Francis Watson, *Text and Truth: Redefining Biblical Theology* (Grand Rapids: Eerdmans, 1997),
p. 130. The antitextual posture of the existentialists is not a new phenomenon. Even during the
Reformation, John Calvin recognized the tendency in his day to separate the Word from the
experience of the Spirit: "For of late, certain giddy men have arisen who, with great haughtiness
exalting the teaching office of the Spirit, despise all reading and laugh at the simplicity of those
who, as they express it, still follow the dead and killing letter" (*Institutes of the Christian Religion*,
ed. John T. McNeill, trans. Ford Lewis Battles [Philadelphia: Westminster, 1960], 1.9.1).

[21]Watson, *Text and Truth*, p. 135.

[22]Ibid.

[23]Rudolf Bultmann, "The Significance of the Old Testament for the Christian Faith," in *The Old*

His version of Christianity is largely cut off from its Jewish, and therefore its textual, roots.

Although the belief that early Christians had an aversion to written documents is certainly not unusual among some modern scholars, the question before us is whether that belief is entirely justified. Is it true that Christians were uninterested in books and placed no meaningful value on them until a much later time period? In this chapter we shall examine the three major arguments that have been used to support this belief: (1) the argument from sociohistorical background: early Christianity was an oral culture; (2) the argument from testimony: early Christians expressly stated their aversion to writing; and (3) the argument from eschatology: early Christians expected the imminent return of Christ.

THE ARGUMENT FROM SOCIOHISTORICAL BACKGROUND: EARLY CHRISTIANITY WAS AN ORAL CULTURE

For scholars who argue that Christians were averse to written documents, the most important consideration is the sociohistorical context of early Christianity. Contrary to our highly literate, post-Gutenberg society, we are reminded that the vast majority of the earliest Christians were poor, rural and illiterate, with neither the ability to read nor to write. The seminal study of William Harris argues that the average extent of literacy in the Greco-Roman world of the first century was ten to fifteen percent,[24] and some have suggested that for Jewish Palestine the rate was actually lower.[25] Sure, some Christians could read and write—particularly the bishops and other leaders[26]—but it still remained the case that most could not.[27] Even the

---

Testament and the Christian Faith: Essays by Rudolf Bultmann and Others, ed. Bernhard W. Anderson (London: SCM, 1964), pp. 8-35.

[24]William V. Harris, *Ancient Literacy* (Cambridge, MA: Harvard University Press, 1989). Harris's work rightly corrects some overly optimistic assessments of literacy in the ancient world: e.g., Colin H. Roberts, "Books in the Greco-Roman World and in the New Testament," in *Cambridge History of the Bible*, p. 48; and Oswyn Murray, *Early Greece* (London: Fontana, 1993), pp. 94-96.

[25]Meir Bar-Ilan, "Illiteracy in the Land of Israel in the First Centuries C.E.," in *Essays in the Social Scientific Study of Judaism and Jewish Society*, ed. Simcha Fishbane, Stuart Schoenfeld and Alain Goldschläger (Hoboken: KTAV, 1992), pp. 46-61; and Catherine Hezser, *Jewish Literacy in Roman Palestine* (Tübingen: Mohr Siebeck, 2001).

[26]Gamble, *Books and Readers*, pp. 9-10. Of course, this does not imply that all Christians outside of formal leadership were illiterate, nor does it imply that every church leader was literate without exception.

[27]Of course, it should be acknowledged that there are ranges of "literacy." A helpful overview of

early critics of Christianity, such as Lucian, Minucius Felix and Celsus, were quick to focus on this issue.[28] Celsus, writing in the second century, is particularly aggressive as he refers to Christians as "stupid," "ignorant," "bucolic yokels," "who had not even had a primary education."[29] Tim Cornell sums it up: "The ability to read and write never extended beyond a small proportion of the population."[30]

It is largely on this basis—the sociohistorical background of early Christianity—that scholars characterize early Christianity as an oral culture in which the written word would have been viewed with suspicion.[31] Kelber in particular uses this background to portray early Christianity not just as a movement that transmitted its traditions in an oral fashion, but as a movement that displayed "only tenuous connections with literate culture"[32] and was dominated by an "oral state of mind."[33] In other words, Kelber uses the broadly illiterate nature of early Christianity to establish not just the *medium* of transmission, but also the *mentality* (or disposition) of its culture. After determining that Christianity must have had this "oral mentality,"[34] Kelber leans on the work of scholars such as Walter Ong, Eric Havelock, Albert Lord and Milman Parry to determine what such a mentality would look like.[35] He argues that cultures with an oral state of mind

---

the different gradations of literacy can be found in Chris Keith, *Jesus' Literacy: Scribal Culture and the Teacher from Galilee* (London: T & T Clark, 2011), pp. 89-116.

[28]Lucian, *Peregr.* 11; Minucius Felix, *Oct.* 5.2-4; Origen, *Cels.* 3.44, 56. For more on pagan criticism of early Christianity, see Robert L. Wilken, "Pagan Criticism of Christianity: Greek Religions and Christian Faith," in *Early Christian Literature and the Classical Intellectual Tradition: In Honorem Robert M. Grant* (Paris: Editions Beauchesne, 1979), pp. 117-34; Stephen Benko, "Pagan Criticism of Christianity During the First Two Centuries A.D.," *ANRW* II.23.2 (1980): 1055-1118; Wayne C. Kannaday, *Apologetic Discourse and the Scribal Tradition: Evidence of the Influence of Apologetic Interests on the Text of the Canonical Gospels* (Atlanta: Society of Biblical Literature, 2004), esp. pp. 24-56.

[29]*Cels.* 3.44, 56; 1.62.

[30]Tim Cornell, "The Tyranny of the Evidence: A Discussion of the Possible Uses of Literacy in Etruria and Latium in the Archaic Age," in *Literacy in the Roman World*, ed. Mary Beard (Ann Arbor, MI: Journal of Roman Archaeology, 1991), p. 7.

[31]Stephen E. Young, *Jesus Tradition in the Apostolic Fathers* (Tübingen: Mohr Siebeck, 2011), p. 77.

[32]Kelber, *Oral and the Written Gospel*, p. 21.

[33]Ibid., p. 23.

[34]Ibid., p. 50.

[35]Walter J. Ong, *The Presence of the Word: Some Prolegomena for Cultural and Religious History* (New Haven, CT: Yale University Press, 1967); Eric Havelock, *Preface to Plato* (Cambridge, MA: Harvard University Press, 1963); Albert Lord, *The Singer of Tales* (Cambridge, MA: Harvard University Press, 1960); idem, "The Gospels as Oral Traditional Literature," in *The Relationships Among the Gospels: An Interdisciplinary Dialogue*, ed. William O. Walker Jr. (San Antonio: Trinity Uni-

would be "tenacious"[36] about the oral medium, and would thus regard writing as "questionable," "neither necessary nor desirable," and something that would cause "hermeneutical instabilities."[37] Thus, Kelber concludes that early Christians would have resisted writing out of fear that it "might compromise the Gospel."[38]

Before offering a response, we will want to acknowledge that much of this description of early Christian culture is accurate. We shall not challenge Harris's argument regarding the low literacy rate among early Christians (though aspects of his study have been rightly critiqued by some).[39] Even if the literacy rates were higher than Harris would allow, there is little doubt that the vast majority of the early Christian population was unable to read or write—though Celsus's rhetoric is certainly overstated.[40] In addition, no one today would dispute the fact that the Christian message was delivered orally (particularly in the earliest stages of Christianity). [41] The Gospels themselves provide ample evidence of this oral history, as form

---

versity Press, 1978), pp. 33-91. A collection of Parry's essays can be found in Adam M. Parry, ed., *The Making of Homeric Verse: The Collected Papers of Milman Parry* (Oxford: Clarendon, 1971).

[36]Kelber, *Oral and the Written Gospel*, p. 17.

[37]Ibid., p. 93. By way of clarification, this study will not be challenging the characteristics of oral cultures given by Kelber, Ong, Parry, Lord and others. The question before us is not whether oral cultures exhibit such characteristics (such as hostility to written texts), but whether early Christianity is just such a culture.

[38]Ibid.

[39]The main critiques of Harris can be found in Roger S. Bagnall, *Everyday Writing in the Graeco-Roman East* (Berkeley: University of California Press, 2011); H. Gregory Snyder, "Review of *Jewish Literacy in Roman Palestine*, by C. Hezser," *RBL* 8 (2002): 4 (Hezser's volume follows the methodology of Harris); Alan Millard, *Reading and Writing in the Time of Jesus* (New York: New York University Press, 2000), pp. 154-84; and the numerous essays in Mary Beard, ed., *Literacy in the Roman World*.

[40]Origen rightly responds to Celsus by agreeing that "many" Christians were uneducated (*Cels.* 3.44), but also reminds him that some Christians were educated (*Cels.* 3.48). In this way, the social makeup of Christianity was basically average—it was a mix of different classes and different levels of literacy. Thus, scholars overstate the situation when they describe the earliest followers of Christ as "simple peasants"; e.g., Bart D. Ehrman, *Misquoting Jesus* (San Francisco: HarperCollins, 2005), p. 39. For more on the social makeup of early Christianity, see Wayne A. Meeks, *The First Urban Christians: The Social World of the Apostle Paul* (New Haven, CT: Yale University Press, 1983); Abraham J. Malherbe, *Social Aspects of Early Christianity* (Philadelphia: Fortress, 1983); Edwin A. Judge, *The Social Pattern of Christian Groups in the First Century* (London: Tyndale, 1960); Robert M. Grant, *Early Christianity and Society: Seven Studies* (New York: Harper & Row, 1977); and Floyd V. Filson, "The Significance of the Early House Churches," *JBL* 58 (1939): 109-12.

[41]While there is wide agreement that at some point the Christian message was delivered orally, there is significant disagreement over the *way* it was delivered. For an assessment of competing theories, see the discussion in Bauckham, *Jesus and the Eyewitnesses*, 240-318; and Dunn, *Jesus Remembered*, 172-254.

critics have rightly observed for generations.[42] Traces of oral tradition are also evident throughout Paul's writings, which often speak with technical language about the "tradition" (παράδοσις)[43] which he both "received" (παραλαμβάνω) and "delivers" (παραδίδωμι).[44]

But—and this is the key question—is the largely illiterate nature of early Christianity, and its use of oral tradition, a sufficient basis to characterize it as having an "oral state of mind"[45] with an accompanying deep-seated opposition to writing? Does the existence of widespread illiteracy necessarily mean that a particular group has "only tenuous connections with literate culture"?[46] Not at all. We shall now argue that the lack of literacy does not necessarily mean the lack of *textuality*. Keith defines textuality as "the knowledge, usage, and appreciation of texts regardless of individual or majority ability to create or access them via literate skills."[47] This reminds us that

---

[42]Standard form-critical works include Rudolf Bultmann, *The History of the Synoptic Tradition* (Oxford: Blackwell, 1968); Dibelius, *From Tradition to Gospel*; and Karl Ludwig Schmidt, *Der Rahmen Der Geschichte Jesu: Literarkritische Untersuchungen Zur Ältesten Jesusüberlieferung* (Berlin: Trowitzsch, 1919). Although the oral transmission of Jesus tradition is not in doubt, many specifics of form criticism have come under scrutiny in recent years; see Christopher M. Tuckett, "Form Criticism," in *Jesus in Memory*, pp. 21-38; Bauckham, *Jesus and the Eyewitnesses*, pp. 240-63; Birger Gerhardsson, *The Reliability of Gospel Tradition* (Peabody, MA: Hendrickson, 2001); E. P. Sanders, *The Tendencies of the Synoptic Tradition* (Cambridge: Cambridge University Press, 1969); Graham N. Stanton, "Form Criticism Revisited," in *What About the New Testament?*, ed. Morna D. Hooker and Colin J. A. Hickling (London: SCM, 1975), pp. 13-27.

[43]1 Cor 11:2; 2 Thess 2:15; 3:6. Josephus also provides a similar example of this sort of tradition when he refers to the παράδοσιν he set down in writing (*C. Ap.* 1.49-50; cf. *Ant.* 13.297). For more on the role of tradition in early Christianity, see Oscar Cullmann, "The Tradition," in *The Early Church*, ed. A. J. B. Higgins (London: SCM, 1956), pp. 59-99; F. F. Bruce, *Tradition: Old and New* (Grand Rapids: Zondervan, 1970), pp. 29-38; idem, "Tradition and the Canon of Scripture," in *The Authoritative Word: Essays on the Nature of Scripture*, ed. D. K. McKim (Grand Rapids: Eerdmans, 1983), pp. 59-84; E. Earle Ellis, *The Making of the New Testament Documents* (Leiden: E. J. Brill, 2002), pp. 49-142; and G. W. H. Lampe, "Scripture and Tradition in the Early Church," in *Scripture and Tradition*, ed. Frederick W. Dillistone (London: Lutterworth Press, 1955), pp. 21-52.

[44]Rom 6:17; 1 Cor 11:23; 15:3-5; Gal 1:9; Phil 4:9; Col 2:6-8; 1 Thess 2:13; 2 Pet 2:21; Jude 3 (cf. 1 Tim 6:20; 2 Tim 1:14). The structure of 1 Cor 15:3-5 in particular suggests that Paul is passing along a standardized apostolic tradition about the resurrection of Jesus; see John S. Kloppenborg, "An Analysis of the Pre-Pauline Formula in 1 Cor 15:3b-5," *CBQ* 40 (1978): 351-67; Ulrich Wilckens, *Die Missionsreden der Apostelgeschichte*, 3rd ed. (Neukirchen-Vluyn: Neukirchener Verlag, 1974), pp. 190-223; and Hans Conzelmann, "On the Analysis of the Confessional Formula in 1 Cor 15:3-5," *Int* 20 (1966): 15-25. For discussion of Jesus tradition in Paul, see T. Holtz, "Paul and Oral Gospel Tradition," in *Jesus and the Oral Gospel Tradition*, pp. 380-93.

[45]Kelber, *Oral and the Written Gospel*, p. 23.

[46]Ibid., p. 21.

[47]Keith, *Jesus' Literacy*, p. 87. Vernon K. Robbins, "Interfaces of Orality and Literature in the Gospel of Mark," in *Performing the Gospel*, pp. 125-46, refers to this same type of culture as a "rhetorical" culture (p. 127).

a culture can appreciate and value written texts even though it is largely illiterate. Orality and textuality are not mutually exclusive. Mary Beard explains, "The character of a religious system can still be fundamentally determined by writing and by a 'literate mentality,' even in situations where very few of the practitioners of that religion are themselves literate. . . . Seen in this light, the number of literates within a religious community is a secondary issue."[48]

Orality and textuality—mutually exclusive? In our modern day, it is hard to imagine how a culture could place a high value on texts when most of the members of that culture are unable to read. But in the ancient world there was not necessarily a contradiction between these two things.[49] Even an illiterate individual could be intimately familiar with written texts, and thus participate in literacy, by hearing that text presented orally in public. This was certainly the case in the Greco-Roman world, as members of society were able to familiarize themselves with various sorts of texts (poetry, philosophical orations, official decrees and so on) through oral presentations, dramatic performances and public recitations.[50] In the same fashion, illiterate Christians could attain quite an impressive knowledge of early Christian texts as they were regularly read, preached and proclaimed. Paul himself calls for the public reading of his letters,[51] numerous arguments have been made that the Gospels were constructed for public reading,[52] and

---

[48]Mary Beard, "Writing and Religion: *Ancient Literacy* and the Function of the Written Word in Roman Religion," in *Literacy in the Roman World*, p. 39; see also John Halverson, "Oral and Written Gospel: A Critique of Werner Kelber," *NTS* 40 (1994): 182; Michael C. A. Macdonald, "Literacy in an Oral Environment," in *Writing and Ancient Near Eastern Society: Papers in Honour of Alan R. Millard*, ed. P. Bienkowski, C. B. Mee and A. E. Slater (London: T & T Clark, 2005), pp. 49-118, esp. p. 49; and Chris Keith, "A Performance of the Text: The Adulteress's Entrance into John's Gospel," in *The Fourth Gospel and Ancient Media Culture*, ed. Anthony LeDonne and Tom Thatcher (London: T & T Clark, 2011), pp. 49-69, esp. pp. 59-60.

[49]Gamble, *Books and Readers*, pp. 8-9.

[50]David E. Aune, "Prolegomena to the Study of Oral Tradition in the Hellenistic World," in *Jesus and the Oral Gospel Tradition*, pp. 59-196; Whitney Shiner, *Proclaiming the Gospel: First Century Performance of Mark* (Harrisburg, PA: Trinity Press International, 2003), pp. 39-40; and Eugene Bahn, "Interpretive Reading in Ancient Greece," *QJS* 18 (1932): 432-40.

[51]2 Cor 10:9; Col 4:16; 1 Thess 5:27; cf. Rev 1:3. For more on the public reading of Paul's letters, see Richard F. Ward, "Pauline Voice and Presence as Strategic Communication," in *Orality and Textuality in Early Christian Literature*, pp. 95-107.

[52]George D. Kilpatrick, *The Origins of the Gospel According to St. Matthew* (Oxford: Clarendon, 1950), pp. 72-100; Michael D. Goulder, *Midrash and Lection in Matthew* (London: SPCK, 1974), pp. 182-83; Phillip Carrington, *The Primitive Christian Calendar: A Study in the Making of the Marcan Gospel* (Cambridge: Cambridge University Press, 1952). See discussion of this phenomena in D. Moody Smith, "When Did the Gospels Become Scripture?," *JBL* 119 (2000): 3-20.

Justin Martyr provides evidence that Christians regularly engaged in such public reading.[53] Moreover, scriptural literacy (not the ability to read or write, but merely knowledge of the scriptural texts) would have also been promoted through liturgical and catechetical instruction.[54]

In light of such realities, it would be illegitimate to use widespread illiteracy as the basis for characterizing early Christianity as "unliterary"[55] and opposed to written texts. On the contrary, written texts may have even formed the basis for oral proclamations. Loveday Alexander rightly suggests that Gospel tradition may have been written down so that it could be *performed* orally—the written texts functioned as *aides-mémoire* for the oral proclamation of Gospel material.[56] As Shemaryahu Talmon observes, "A message which is transmitted as a written document at the same time would be proclaimed orally."[57] Likewise, the written Gospels, at least in part, are likely the result of oral proclamation and thus bear oral characteristics.[58] For instance, Joanna Dewey has shown that Mark may have been "a written transcription of oral narrative" or that "Mark is building on an oral storytelling tradition."[59] Thus, it appears that while the Christian

---

[53] *1 Apol.* 67.3. Harry Y. Gamble, "Literacy, Liturgy, and the Shaping of the New Testament Canon," in *The Earliest Gospels*, ed. Charles Horton (London: T & T Clark, 2004), refers to Justin's account of public reading and says "there is every reason to think that this sort of assembly for worship goes back to the very earliest days of the church" (p. 33).

[54] Nicholas Horsfall, "Statistics or States of Mind?," in *Literacy in the Roman World*, pp. 73-74.

[55] Dibelius, *From Tradition to Gospel*, pp. 37, 39.

[56] Loveday Alexander, "Memory and Tradition in the Hellenistic Schools," in *Jesus in Memory*, pp. 113-53. See also Shemaryahu Talmon, "Oral Tradition and Written Transmission, or the Heard and the Seen Word in Judaism of the Second Temple Period," in *Jesus and the Oral Gospel Tradition*, pp. 121-58; and Paul J. Achtemeier, "Omne Verbum Sonat: The New Testament and the Oral Environment of Late Western Antiquity," *JBL* 109 (1990): 3-27. It should be noted that one reason why written texts were performed orally is that they were not always readily available—they had to be recalled from memory. Performing texts from memory was a key part of the transmission process of early Christianity. For more on this point, see Alan Kirk, "Manuscript Tradition as a Tertium Quid: Orality and Memory in Scribal Practices," in *Jesus, the Voice, and the Text*, pp. 215-34.

[57] Talmon, "Oral Tradition and Written Transmission," p. 154.

[58] Written documents that are dependent on oral tradition are also common in the Greco-Roman world. See numerous examples in Aune, "Prolegomena to the Study of Oral Tradition in the Hellenistic World," pp. 59-196.

[59] Joanna Dewey, "Oral Methods of Structuring Narrative in Mark," *Int* 43 (1989): 32-44, at p. 43. See also Joanna Dewey, "The Gospel of Mark as Oral Hermeneutic," in *Jesus, the Voice, and the Text*, pp. 71-87. Similar arguments that Mark was an oral composition that was written down can be found in Whitney Shiner, "Memory Technology and the Composition of Mark," in *Performing the Gospel*, 147-65; and Pieter J. J. Botha, "Mark's Story as Oral Traditional Literature: Rethinking the Transmission of Some Traditions About Jesus," *Hervormde Teologiese Studies* 47 (1991): 304-31.

message was originally delivered orally, some of that oral material was soon embodied into written texts, and then those written texts were the basis for further oral performances—what we might call "secondary orality" (or reoralization).[60] Terence Mournet states: "Oral tradition served as sources for written texts. . . . In addition, texts were written to be vocalized and aurally received."[61] All of this suggests that orality and textuality in early Christianity should not be seen as mutually exclusive. They exist within a symbiotic and mutually reinforcing relationship.[62]

Of course, scholars who portray early Christianity as opposed to written texts often acknowledge this interplay between orality and textuality as written texts are performed in oral environments.[63] But this interplay is often construed as evidence that early Christians really put no value on written materials—they were *merely* aids to orality. Dewey makes this argument: "While texts were produced that later became very important within Christianity *as texts*, these texts began as aids to orality, and seemingly had little importance in themselves."[64] But, it is unclear why Dewey would conclude that these texts at an early stage must have had no importance. If the oral tradition bore authority, why would that authority cease when it was written down? That would only be the case if early Christianity was an oral religion with an aversion to written texts.[65] But that is the very

---

[60]Alexander, "Memory and Tradition," p. 149.

[61]Terence C. Mournet, "The Jesus Tradition as Oral Tradition," in *Jesus in Memory*, p. 51. See also Terence C. Mournet, *Oral Tradition and Literary Dependency* (Tübingen: Mohr Siebeck, 2005).

[62]Holly Hearon, "Implications of Orality for the Study of the Biblical Text," in *Performing the Gospel*, p. 9; Gerhardsson, *Reliability of Gospel Tradition*, pp. 110-23; James F. McGrath, "Written Islands in an Oral Stream: Gospel and Oral Traditions," in *Jesus and Paul: Global Perspectives in Honor of James D .G. Dunn* (London: T & T Clark, 2009), pp. 3-12; Alan Kirk, "Memory, Scribal Media, and the Synoptic Problem," in *New Studies in the Synoptic Problem: Oxford Conference, April 2008*, ed. Paul Foster et al. (Leuven: Peeters, 2011), pp. 459-82; and John Miles Foley, *Homer's Traditional Art* (University Park: Pennsylvania State University Press, 1999), p. 9.

[63]At points, Kelber seems to recognize that oral and written modes are not mutually exclusive (e.g., *Oral and the Written Gospel*, pp. 17, 23, 91), but this never seems to affect the sharp dichotomy he has created between orality and textuality. In more recent works, Kelber has backed away from this sharp dichotomy (what he calls the "Great Divide"); e.g., see the interview with Werner Kelber in Tom Thatcher, ed., *Jesus, the Voice, and the Text*, pp. 27-43.

[64]Joanna Dewey, "Textuality in an Oral Culture," p. 51 (emphasis in original).

[65]Øvivind Anderson, "Oral Tradition," in *Jesus and the Oral Gospel Tradition*, rightly observes that "in a largely oral culture you do not simply 'check' tradition by consulting the written text, for the written text is not yet considered a 'source'" (p. 51). But Anderson is careful to note that this only applies to a "largely oral culture" which lacks a "document-mindedness" (p. 52)—traits which do not accurately describe early Christianity (more on this below).

issue in question and should not simply be assumed. On the contrary, other scholars have suggested that the writing down of traditions can actually *increase* their normativity—what Assmann refers to as a *Verfestigung* ("hardening").[66] And this normativity can exist even if that written tradition continues to be performed orally. Alexander goes even further, not only arguing that orally performed texts can still be authoritative, but also that such texts are often performed *because* they are authoritative. She observes, "It is precisely because of their iconic status that certain texts and traditions are accorded the honor of constant reshaping and reperformance."[67]

The assumption that orally performed texts must have no value as texts is another example of how some scholars have confused a mode of transmission (oral) with a cultural disposition (oral state of mind). Or, as noted above, it assumes that widespread illiteracy means a culture has no interest in *textuality*. Parker is quite keen to correct this confusion: "Because this point has been misunderstood so often, it may be necessary to repeat that *[oral] performance is not the same as an oral culture.*"[68] To prove his point, Parker looks at the example of Roman poetry and shows that even though it was often performed publicly in various contexts, this does not mean that the oral was valued above the written. He argues, "I hope to show that the assumption that Rome can be considered an 'oral' society in any meaningful sense because of certain types of vocal performance of certain types of literary texts . . . is mistaken."[69] On the contrary, Parker demonstrates that Roman poets really valued the written word even though it was orally proclaimed. Indeed, Cicero states a position that is nearly the opposite of those who insist the oral is always preferred over the written: "One can derive much greater pleasure from reading lyric poetry than hearing it."[70] Similarly, Pliny states, "I don't want to be praised when I recite, but when I'm read."[71] Although these examples do not derive directly from an early

---

[66]Jan Assmann, *Das kulturelle Gedächtnis: Schrift, Erinnerung und politische Identität in frühen Hochkulteren* (Munich: C. H. Beck, 1992), p. 165.

[67]Alexander, "Memory and Tradition," p. 151.

[68]Holt N. Parker, "Books and Reading Latin Poetry," in *Ancient Literacies: The Culture of Reading in Greece and Rome*, ed. William H. Johnson and Holt N. Parker (Oxford: Oxford University Press, 2009), p. 194 (emphasis mine).

[69]Ibid.

[70]*Tusc.* 5.116.

[71]*Ep.* 7.17.7.

Christian context, they are still illustrative of the overall point: we should not be too quick to assume oral presentations of texts are necessarily indicative of a culture that despises texts.

Early Christianity as a culture of "textuality." Thus far we have argued that the broadly illiterate nature of early Christianity is not a sufficient basis on which to argue it was opposed to written texts. On the contrary, cultures that lack widespread literacy can still maintain a robust "textuality"—an interest in, knowledge of and appropriation of written texts. Oral and textual media should not be pitted against each other. But we still need to explore the literary culture of early Christianity further. What reasons do we have for thinking early Christianity had a culture of textuality? Let us review some of the main reasons for this characterization.

Early Christian writings. One obvious fact that should not be overlooked is that early Christians wrote books and wrote them quite early. Even critical scholars date the vast majority of the twenty-seven New Testament books to the first century, most of which were written between the 50s and the 90s.[72] Although there is inevitable disagreement over specifics, it appears that Christians were writing at least by the late 40s when Paul wrote Galatians (ca. 48),[73] and even earlier if one adopts an early date for James (ca. 45).[74] But it is not only the date of the New Testament writings that is noteworthy; it is also their quality. Contrary to the arguments of those such as Adolf Deissmann who suggest that the New Testament was written in

---

[72]A number of critical scholars are convinced that some New Testament writings are pseudonymous, including the Pastoral Epistles, Colossians, Ephesians, 2 Peter, Jude and others. As a result, some of these books are dated to the second century. For general discussions of the critical positions, see Robert A. Spivey and D. Moody Smith, *Anatomy of the New Testament* (New York: McMillan, 1989); and Bart D. Ehrman, *The New Testament: A Historical Introduction to the Early Christian Writings* (New York: Oxford University Press, 1997).

[73]There is debate over the precise dating of Galatians; e.g., Ronald Y. K. Fung, *The Epistle to the Galatians* (NICNT; Grand Rapids: Eerdmans, 1988), pp. 9-28, adopts the earlier date for Galatians (ca. 48), while John Drane, *Introducing the New Testament*, 3rd ed. (Minneapolis: Fortress, 2010), p. 288, adopts a later date (ca. 56-58).

[74]A number of scholars have suggested James is a late pseudonymous work; e.g., David R. Nienhuis, *Not by Paul Alone: The Formation of the Catholic Epistle Collection and the Christian Canon* (Waco: Baylor University Press, 2007); and Werner G. Kümmel, *Introduction to the New Testament* (London: SCM Press, 1975), pp. 411-14. However, an early date has been defended by others; e.g., Luke Timothy Johnson, *The Letter of James* (Anchor Biblical Commentary; New York: Doubleday, 1995), pp. 111-21; James B. Adamson, *James: The Man and His Message* (Grand Rapids: Eerdmans, 1989), pp. 3-52; and Joseph B. Mayor, *The Epistle of St. James* (London: Macmillan, 1892), pp. cxxi-cliii.

"vulgar" Greek,[75] recent scholarship has shown that it was written at a much more sophisticated level.[76] While not necessarily the artistic Greek of high literary culture, the Greek of the New Testament, generally speaking, can be classified as "professional prose."[77] High-quality Greek is particularly evident in books such as Luke–Acts, Hebrews, James and 1 & 2 Peter. In particular, Alexander has shown that the preface of Luke–Acts closely resembles the professional and technical writing of scholastic works in the ancient world, for example, handbooks on medicine, math, rhetoric or engineering.[78] But even beyond this, the New Testament authors demonstrate an impressive knowledge of the rhetorical conventions of the day.[79] Paul was particularly well-versed in rhetorical strategies and argumentation,[80] and we also see evidence of a high level of rhetorical sophistication in the Gospels,[81] Acts[82] and Hebrews.[83]

It is also important to recognize that the textual productivity of the earliest Christians was not limited to the writings of the New Testament. Not only did the New Testament authors compose a number of other written works that are now lost,[84] but we have good reasons to think that they knew and even drew upon even earlier Christian writings. Luke's preface tells us that "many" in his day had written gospels and that his work was by no means the first such production (Lk 1:1).[85] Most scholars today would

[75]Adolf Deissmann, *Light from the Ancient East* (New York: George H. Doran, 1927).

[76]Nigel Turner, "The Literary Charcter of New Testament Greek," *NTS* 20 (1974): 107-14; Gamble, *Books and Readers*, pp. 32-35.

[77]Gamble, *Books and Readers*, p. 34.

[78]Loveday Alexander, *The Preface to Luke's Gospel* (Cambridge: Cambridge University Press, 1993).

[79]George A. Kennedy, *A New Testament Interpretation Through Rhetorical Criticism* (Chapel Hill, NC: University of North Carolina, 1984); Burton L. Mack, *What Is Rhetorical Criticism?* (Minneapolis: Augsburg Fortress, 1990); Stanley E. Porter, *Handbook of Classical Rhetoric in the Hellenistic Period* (Leiden: E. J. Brill, 1997).

[80]Wilhelm Wuellner, "Greek Rhetoric and Pauline Argumentation," in *Early Christian Literature and the Classical Intellectual Tradition*, pp. 177-88.

[81]George A. Kennedy, "An Introduction to the Rhetoric of the Gospels," *Rhetoric* 1 (1983): 17-31.

[82]David A. deSilva, *An Introduction to the New Testament: Contexts, Methods, and Ministry Formation* (Downers Grove, IL: IVP Academic, 2004), pp. 380-85.

[83]deSilva, *Introduction to the New Testament*, pp. 781-87.

[84]E.g., 1 Cor 5:9; Phil 3:1; Col 4:16. On the latter text, J. B. Lightfoot, *St. Paul's Epistle to the Philippians* (Peabody, MA: Hendrickson, 1995), has a brief discussion on this passage titled, "Lost Epistle to the Philippians?," pp. 138-42.

[85]See discussion in Joel B. Green, *The Gospel of Luke* (NICNT; Grand Rapids: Eerdmans, 1997), pp. 37-38.

argue that the "Q" document (or something like it) was used by Matthew and Luke and was likely a written source known from a very early time period.[86] In addition, the earliest Christians might have written down Jesus tradition in "notebooks"—a precursor to their use of the codex.[87] Not only do Quintilian[88] and Martial[89] indicate that parchment notebooks were used in the Greco-Roman world during this time period, but such notebooks may be alluded to in 2 Tim 4:13: "When you come, bring the cloak that I left with Carpus at Troas, also the books (τὰ βιβλία), and above all the parchments" (τὰς μεμβράνας).[90] There is little doubt that τὰ βιβλία is a reference to books of the Old Testament, most likely on scrolls.[91] The term τὰς μεμβράνας is noteworthy because it is not a Greek word at all but a transliterated form of the Latin *membrana*—the same word used by Martial and Quintilian to refer to parchment notebooks. Thus, we have a suggestion here that such notebooks were used alongside the books of the Old Testament. What did these notebooks contain? There are a number of possi-

---

[86]For a general overview of Q, see John S. Kloppenborg, *The Formation of Q* (Philadelphia: Fortress, 1987). Although not opposed to Q per se, Dunn has argued that oral tradition should also be considered as an explanation of the similarities amongst the Synoptic gospels; see James D. G. Dunn, "Altering the Default Setting: Re-envisaging the Early Transmission of the Jesus Tradition," *NTS* 49 (2003): 139-75. Kelber, *Oral and the Written Gospel*, p. 201, avoids the implications of Q by insisting that it had an "oral disposition." However, even if Q does exhibit a structure dependent on oral discourse, one must still reckon with the fact that it is a written document; cf. Harry T. Fledderman, *Mark and Q: A Study of the Overlap Texts* (Leuven: Peeters, 1995), p. 20. The existence of Q is further evidence of how oral and written modes of discourse often overlapped.

[87]That such notebooks were used to record Jesus traditions has been argued by Colin H. Roberts and T. C. Skeat, *The Birth of the Codex* (London: Oxford University Press, 1987), p. 59; Saul Lieberman, *Hellenism in Jewish Palestine*, 2nd ed. (New York: Jewish Theological Seminary, 1962), p. 203; and Birger Gerhardsson, *Memory and Manuscript*, pp. 157-63.

[88]*Inst. Or.* 10.3.31-32. Quintilian states: *Scribi optime ceris, in quibus facillima est ratio delendi, nisi forte visus infirmior membranarum potius usum exiget.* The reference to the wax tablet (*ceris*) here makes it evident that the codex form is in question. Thus, the advice to use *membranarum* can mean nothing other than a vellum codex. See Roberts and Skeat, *Birth of the Codex*, p. 21, and Gamble, *Books and Readers*, p. 50.

[89]*Epigr.* 1.2: *quos arat brevibus membrana tabellis.* Full discussion in Roberts and Skeat, *Birth of the Codex*, pp. 24-29.

[90]T. C. Skeat, "'Especially the Parchments': A Note on 2 Timothy iv.13," *JTS* 30 (1979): 173-77, argues for an alternative translation of this verse where he equates the books and the parchments, but it has not been widely adopted.

[91]Gottlob Schrenk, "βίβλος, βιβλίον," *TDNT* 1:615-20; Luke 4:20; Galatians 3:10; Hebrews 9:19; Josephus, *Ant.* 3.74; *2 Clem.* 14:2; Graham N. Stanton, "Why Were Early Christians Addicted to the Codex?," in *Jesus and Gospel* (Cambridge: Cambridge University Press, 2004), p. 177.

bilities, such as excerpts of Jesus' teachings,[92] or early Christian *testimonia* (Old Testament prooftexts supporting Messianic claims about Jesus),[93] or even copies of Paul's own letters.[94]

All of this suggests that it would not have been unusual for the earliest Christians to have used such notebooks—even *prior* to the production of the earliest New Testament writing.

Use of the Old Testament. As much as early Christians were committed to producing and using their own writings, their interest in "textuality" did not begin there. It is all too frequently overlooked—in an oddly Marcionite fashion—that from the very beginning, Christians were committed to the books of the Hebrew Scriptures and saw them as paradigmatic for understanding the life and ministry of Jesus of Nazareth. Not only do our earliest Christian writings (for example, James and Paul's letters) exhibit extensive engagement with Old Testament texts, but this same interest in the Old Testament is evident throughout many other New Testament books such as Matthew, John and Hebrews.[95] These writers do more than simply quote the Old Testament; they regularly offer a developed and sophisticated exegetical interaction with these writings[96]—in a fashion not dissimilar to that of their contemporaries at Qumran.[97] Moreover, our earliest confessional and

---

[92]One must at least consider the possibility that Gospel material may have been contained within these codices. This early Christian practice would have parallels with rabbinic practices where various sorts of notebooks (wax, wood, papyrus) were used to facilitate knowledge of the oral torah (*m. Kelim* 24.7). See Gerhardsson, *Memory and Manuscript*, pp. 157-63; and Lieberman, *Hellenism in Jewish Palestine*, p. 203.

[93]Martin C. Albl, *And Scripture Cannot Be Broken: The Form and Function of the Early Christian Testimonia Collections* (Leiden: E. J. Brill, 1999). For further discussion, see Stanton, "Why Were Early Christians Addicted to the Codex?," pp. 182-85.

[94]E. Randolph Richards, "The Codex and the Early Collection of Paul's Letters," *BBR* 8 (1998): 151-66; David Trobisch, *Paul's Letter Collection: Tracing the Origins* (Minneapolis: Fortress, 1994); Gamble, *Books and Readers*, pp. 100-101.

[95]For a detailed examination of the way Paul engages deeply in the exegesis of Old Testament texts, see Francis Watson, *Paul and the Hermeneutics of Faith* (London: T & T Clark, 2004); and Richard B. Hays, *Echoes of Scripture in the Letters of Paul* (New Haven, CT: Yale University Press, 1989).

[96]Judith Lieu, *Christian Identity in the Jewish and Graeco-Roman World* (Oxford: Oxford University Press, 2004), pp. 36-37; Frances M. Young, *Biblical Exegesis and the Formation of Christian Culture* (Cambridge: Cambridge University Press, 1997).

[97]Millard, *Reading and Writing*, pp. 210-29, appeals to the Qumran community as an example of a first-century Jewish group with an ability and propensity to write, thus forming a possible parallel with the earliest Christian movement. Gamble, *Books and Readers*, p. 24, agrees that there is a similarity between the exegetical methods of Qumran and early Christianity.

creedal formulas embedded within the writings of the New Testament (and thus predating these writings) reveal a Christian message heavily dependent upon the Hebrew Scriptures.[98] Thus Harry Gamble concludes, "Although it need not be denied that there was a period, possibly a long one, during which some Christian traditions were orally transmitted, during that same period Christians were deeply and continuously engaged with texts. Christians were from the beginning assiduous students of Jewish scriptures."[99]

This Christian preoccupation with the Old Testament allows us to highlight again the possibility that the earliest believers may have written down selections from the Old Testament into *testimonia* notebooks designed to bolster the messianic claims of Jesus. Such extracts from the Old Testament would have been particularly useful to Christians in their early preaching, teaching and missionary activities.[100] Discoveries of these sorts of documents at Qumran have bolstered the likelihood that they were well known in the first century. Examples include 4QTestimonia, which catalogs five messianic texts,[101] 4QFlorilegium, which contains texts related to key eschatological figures,[102] and 4QTanhumim, which has various excerpts from the book of Isaiah.[103] We also possess a Christian example of a *testimonia* document in Papyrus Rylands Greek (PRG) 460, which contains a thematic linking of a number of Old Testament passages.[104] Although this particular document is likely a fourth-century one, it reminds us that these sorts of documents were not foreign to early Christians. Indeed, Martin Albl and Timothy Lim have argued that the manner in which the New Testament authors cite from the Old Testament suggests that they were drawing upon *testimonia* collections composed even earlier.[105]

All these considerations remind us that early Christianity was a textual culture even prior to the publication of their own books. They were a textual

---

[98]In particular, see discussions of the creedal formula in 1 Cor 15:3-4 noted above in n44.

[99]Gamble, *Books and Readers*, p. 24.

[100]Stanton, "Why Were Early Christians Addicted to the Codex?," p. 182.

[101]Joseph A. Fitzmyer, "'4Q Testimonia' and the New Testament," *TS* 18 (1957): 513-37.

[102]John M. Allegro, "Further Messianic References in Qumran Literature," *JBL* 75 (1956): 182-87.

[103]Christopher D. Stanley, "The Importance of 4QTanhumim (4Q176)," *RevQ* 60 (1992): 569-82.

[104]Colin H. Roberts, "Two Biblical Papyri in the John Rylands Library, Manchester," *BJRL* 20 (1936): 219-44, esp. pp. 241-44.

[105]Albl, *Scripture Cannot Be Broken*, p. 66; Timothy H. Lim, *Holy Scripture in the Qumran Commentaries and Pauline Letters* (Clarendon: Oxford University Press, 1997), p. 55.

culture because they inherited a Scripture from Judaism. It is this reality
that allows Watson to say, "Christian faith cannot dispense with writing. Its
reliance on written, scriptural texts is not accidental but of its essence."[106]

Christian book production. Our understanding of the "textuality" of early
Christians is determined not only by what (and when) they wrote, but *how*
they wrote; that is, the manner in which they constructed and copied their
own writings. While we have no manuscripts that date to the critical period
of the first century, the ones we do possess are still early enough to provide
an accurate glimpse into the literary culture of the earliest believers.[107] Contrary to the impression given by some that early Christians were inept when
it came to literary and scribal activity (no doubt due to their presumed oral
state of mind), the extant manuscripts we possess paint a very different
picture.[108] Loveday Alexander notes, "It is clear that we are dealing with a
group [early Christians] that used books intensively and professionally
from very early on in its existence. The evidence of the papyri from the
second century onwards suggests . . . the early development of a technically
sophisticated and distinctive book technology."[109]

Let us consider a few of the factors that demonstrate both the extent and
sophistication of early Christian literary activity. First, the sheer quantity of
Christian texts is noteworthy. While it is well known that the total number
of New Testament manuscripts far outpaces any other texts from antiquity,[110]

---

[106]Watson, *Text and Truth*, p. 128.

[107]New Testament manuscripts dated to the second century (or to ca. 200) include P^{52}, $P^{4-64-67}$, P^{66}, P^{77}, P^{75}, P^{90}, P^{103} and P^{104}.

[108]For more on book production within early Christianity, see Michael J. Kruger, "Manuscripts, Scribes, and Book Production within Early Christianity," in *Christian Origins and Classical Culture: Social and Literary Contexts for the New Testament*, ed. S. E. Porter and A. W. Pitts (Leiden: E. J. Brill, 2012), pp. 15-40; David Trobisch, *The First Edition of the New Testament* (Oxford: Oxford University Press, 2000); Kim Haines-Eitzen, *Guardians of Letters: Literacy, Power, and the Transmitters of Early Christian Literature* (Oxford: Oxford University Press, 2000); Larry W. Hurtado, *The Earliest Christian Artifacts: Manuscripts and Christian Origins* (Grand Rapids: Eerdmans, 2006); and Thomas J. Kraus and Tobias Nicklas, eds., *New Testament Manuscripts: Their Texts and Their World* (Leiden: E. J. Brill, 2006). Standard treatments of the Greco-Roman book include Wilhelm Schubart, *Das Buch bei den Griechen und Römern*, ed. E. Paul, 2nd ed. (Heidelberg: Schneider, 1962); Frederic G. Kenyon, *Books and Readers in Ancient Greece and Rome*, 2nd ed. (Oxford: Clarendon, 1932); and Horst Blanck, *Das Buch in der Antike* (Munich: Beck, 1992).

[109]Loveday Alexander, "Ancient Book Production and the Circulation of the Gospels," in *The Gospels for All Christians: Rethinking the Gospel Audiences*, ed. Richard Bauckham (Grand Rapids: Eerdmans, 1998), p. 85.

[110]Currently, there are over 5,500 New Testament manuscripts in Greek alone. The official num-

we also possess an impressive number from just the second and third centuries. Currently we have over sixty extant manuscripts (in whole or in part) of the New Testament from this time period, with most of our copies coming from Matthew, John, Luke, Acts, Romans, Hebrews and Revelation.[111] The Gospel of John proves to be the most popular of all, with eighteen manuscripts, a number of which may derive from the second century[112] (for example, P^{52}, P^{90}, P^{66}, P^{75}).[113] Matthew is not far behind, with twelve manuscripts; and some of these also have been dated to the second century[114] (for example, P$^{64-67}$, P^{77}, P^{103}, P^{104}).[115] Compared to other ancient

---

bers are kept at the *Institut für neutestamentliche Textforschung* (Institute for New Testament Textual Research) in Münster, Germany.

[111]Hurtado, *Earliest Christian Artifacts*, pp. 20-21. For the sake of this discussion, we will generally follow the dates indicated by Hurtado. Other listings of New Testament manuscripts can be found primarily in Kurt Aland, *Repertorium der griechischen christlichen Papyri, I, Biblische Papyri* (Berlin: de Gruyter, 1976); and Joseph van Haelst, *Catalogue des Papyrus Littéraires Juifs et Chrétiens* (Paris: Publications de la Sorbonne, 1976). Of course, some manuscripts, such as P^{46} (Paul's epistles), P^{45} (four Gospels plus Acts), and P^{75} (Luke and John), contain multiple books. Recently, Roger S. Bagnall, *Early Christian Books in Egypt* (Princeton, NJ: Princeton University Press, 2009) has challenged the early dating of some of these papyri. While such challenges are welcome, in a brief volume such as this we can only go with the general consensus of scholars up to this point.

[112]Hurtado, *Earliest Christian Artifacts*, p. 20, notes sixteen manuscripts of John, but two more from the third century have been discovered since then: P^{119} (P.Oxy. 4803) and P^{121} (P.Oxy. 4805). For an updated analysis of John's manuscripts (and text) see Juan Chapa, "The Early Text of the Gospel of John," in *The Early Text of the New Testament*, ed. Charles E. Hill and Michael J. Kruger (Oxford: Oxford University Press, 2012), pp. 140-56.

[113]On P^{52}, see Colin H. Roberts, "An Unpublished Fragment of the Fourth Gospel in the John Rylands Library," *BJRL* 20 (1936): 45-55. This early date for P^{52} has been challenged by Brent Nongbri, "The Use and Abuse of P52: Papyrological Pitfalls in the Dating of the Fourth Gospel," *HTR* 98 (2005): 23-48. An updated analysis of P^{90} can be found in Peter Rodgers, "The Text of the New Testament and Its Witnesses Before 200 A.D.: Observations on P90 (P.Oxy. 3523)," in *The New Testament Text in Early Christianity: Proceedings of the Lille Colloquium, July 2000*, ed. Christian-Bernard Amphoux and J. Keith Elliott (Lausanne: Éditions Du Zèbre, 2003), pp. 83-91. P^{66} is typically dated ca. 200. For a full-scale analysis of this manuscript, see Gordon D. Fee, *Papyrus Bodmer II (p66): Its Textual Relationships and Scribal Characteristics* (Salt Lake City: University of Utah Press, 1968). The original editors of P^{75} proposed a date between 175 and 225; see Victor Martin and Rodolphe Kasser, *Papyrus Bodmer XIV-XV* (Geneva: Bibliotheca Bodmeriana, 1961), 1:13.

[114]For more on Matthew's reception in early Christianity, see W.-D. Köhler, *Die Rezeption des Matthäusevangeliums in der Zeit vor Irenäus* (Tübingen: J. C. B. Mohr, 1987); and Massaux, *Influence de L'Évangile de Saint Matthieu sur la littérature chrétienne avant Saint Irénée*.

[115]On P$^{64-67}$, see Colin H. Roberts, "An Early Papyrus of the First Gospel," *HTR* 46 (1953): 233-37. P$^{64-67}$, and possibly P^4, are commonly dated ca. 200. Some have attempted an earlier date for these manuscripts; e.g., Carsten Peter Thiede, "Papyrus Magdalen Greek 17 (Gregory-Aland P64): A Reappraisal," *ZPE* 105 (1995): 13-20. But this has been rightly rejected in favor of Roberts's original dating; see Klaus Wachtel, "'P64/67: Fragmente des Matthäusevangeliums aus dem 1. Jahrhundert?," *ZPE* 107 (1995): 73-80. For discussion of P$^{4-64-67}$ as a possible four-

religious texts, the sheer quantity of these New Testament texts is impressive.[116] And this does not even include other Christian writings outside the New Testament such as the *Shepherd of Hermas*[117] or even apocryphal literature such as the *Gospel of Thomas*.[118] It is this sort of literary activity that led Gamble to observe, "No Greco-Roman religious group produced, used, or valued texts on a scale comparable to Judaism and Christianity."[119]

Second, we should consider the handwriting of these earliest manuscripts. Over the years, a number of scholars have argued that Christian texts are marked by a scribal hand more on the documentary end of the scale—what Colin Roberts would call "reformed documentary" or "informal uncial."[120] This informal handwriting has then been used as evidence that early Christian texts were more "second class" and utilitarian, indicating that they derived from a less sophisticated textual culture.[121]

Gospel codex, see T. C. Skeat, "The Oldest Manuscripts of the Four Gospels?," *NTS* 43 (1997): 1-34; Peter M. Head, "Is P4, P64, and P67 the Oldest Manuscript of the Four Gospels? A Response to T. C. Skeat," *NTS* 51 (2005): 450-57; Scott Charlesworth, "T. C. Skeat, P64+67 and P4, and the Problem of Fibre Orientation in Codicological Reconstruction," *NTS* (2007): 582-604; and Charles E. Hill, "Intersection of Jewish and Christian Scribal Culture: The Original Codex Containing P4, P64, and P67, and Its Implications," in *Among Jews, Gentiles, and Christians in Antiquity and the Middle Ages*, ed. Reidar Hvalvik and John Kaufman (Trondheim: Tapir Academic Press, 2011), pp. 75-91. It is possible that P77 (P.Oxy 2683 + P.Oxy. 4405) is part of the same codex as P103 (P.Oxy. 4403). On P103, see Eric W. Handley et al., eds., *The Oxyrhynchus Papyri* (London: Egypt Exploration Society, 1997), 64:5-7; discussion also in Peter M. Head, "Some Recently Published NT Papyri from Oxyrhynchus: An Overview and Preliminary Assessment," *TynBul* 51 (2000): 1-16, esp. p. 8. P104 (P.Oxy. 4404) is one of the earliest New Testament manuscripts we possess, dating to the middle or late second century; see again Thomas in *Oxyrynchus Papyri*, 64:7-9.

[116]Eldon Jay Epp, "Textual Criticism," in *The New Testament and Its Modern Interpreters*, ed. Eldon Jay Epp and George W. MacRae (Atlanta: Scholars Press, 1989), p. 91.

[117]We possess approximately eleven manuscripts of the *Shepherd* from the second and third centuries.

[118]We possess three manuscripts of *Thomas* from the second and third centuries: P.Oxy. 1, P.Oxy. 654, and P.Oxy. 655. For a general introduction to the Nag Hammadi material see Christopher M. Tuckett, *Nag Hammadi and the Gospel Tradition* (Edinburgh: T & T Clark, 1986). For recent discussions of *Thomas*, see April DeConick, *Recovering the Original Gospel of Thomas: A History of the Gospel and Its Growth* (London: T & T Clark, 2005); Mark S. Goodacre, *Thomas and the Gospels: The Case for Thomas's Familiarity with the Synoptics* (Grand Rapids: Eerdmans, 2012); and Simon Gathercole, *The Composition of the Gospel of Thomas: Original Language and Influences* (Cambridge: Cambridge University Press, 2012).

[119]Gamble, *Books and Readers*, p. 18. For arguments that Greco-Roman religions still valued the written text to some degree, see Beard, "Writing and Religion," pp. 35-58.

[120]Colin H. Roberts, *Manuscript, Society and Belief in Early Christian Egypt* (London: Oxford University Press, 1979), p. 14.

[121]Turner, *Typology*, p. 37; Roberts, *Manuscript*, p. 25; Bart D. Ehrman, "The Text as Window: New Testament Manuscripts and the Social History of Early Christianity," in *The Text of the*

However, this particular conclusion is open to question. Although some of
the earliest Christian papyri (second and third centuries) were not characterized by the formal bookhand that was common among Jewish scriptural books or Greco-Roman literary texts,[122] others were much closer to
the literary end of the scale than is often realized.[123] A number of early
Christian manuscripts contain an impressive amount of punctuation and
reader aids—rare even in literary papyri—which suggest that these early
Christian scribes were more in tune with professional book production
than is often supposed.[124] In addition, it cannot be overlooked that many
early Christian texts do exhibit a more refined hand and literary style, such
as a late second- or early third-century text of Irenaeus's *Against Heresies*
(P.Oxy. 405) which has a "handsome professional hand,"[125] a late second-
century text of Matthew (P[77]) which has an "elegant hand,"[126] a late second-
century copy of Paul's epistles (P[46]) which has a hand marked by "style and
elegance,"[127] a late second- or early third-century copy of Luke and Matthew
(P4–P64–P67) which has a "handsome script" which is "incontrovertibly
literary in style"[128] and a late second-century copy of John (P[66]) which has
calligraphy of "such high quality" that it may "indicate the work of a
scriptorium."[129] Such evidence led Stanton to declare, "The oft-repeated

---

New Testament in Contemporary Research: Essays on the Status Quaestionis, ed. Bart D. Ehrman
and Michael W. Holmes (Grand Rapids: Eerdmans, 1995), pp. 372-75.

[122]E.g., P[37], P[45], P[69], P[106], P[107].

[123]It is important to note that some *literary* papyri of classical works were also written in a rather
plain, unadorned and noncallographic hand (e.g., P.Oxy. 1809, 2076, 2288). However, E. G.
Turner does not necessarily consider this an indication of low scribal quality; indeed, he declares
that "'calligraphic' hands are suspect. . . . It is not uncommon for the finest looking hands to be
marred by gross carelessness in transcription" ("Scribes and Scholars," in *Oxyrhynchus: A City
and Its Texts*, ed. A. K. Bowman et al. [London: Egypt Exploration Society, 2007], pp. 258-59).

[124]E.g., P.Mich. 130 (*Shepherd of Hermas*; third century) and P.Ryl. 1.1 (Deuteronomy; third/
fourth century) contain a surprising number of accents and other lectional aids. Such features
indicate that many early Christian books were written for public reading; for more on this see
Gamble, *Books and Readers*, pp. 203-30; Scott Charlesworth, "Public and Private—Second-
and Third-Century Gospel Manuscripts," in *Jewish and Christian Scripture as Artifact and
Canon*, ed. Craig A. Evans and H. Daniel Zacharias (London: T & T Clark, 2009), pp. 148-75;
and Hill and Kruger, eds., *Early Text of the New Testament*, pp. 15-18.

[125]Roberts, *Manuscript*, p. 23.

[126]Ibid. Another fragment of this same page was discovered in 1997 (P.Oxy. 4405).

[127]F. G. Kenyon, *The Chester Beatty Biblical Papyri: Descriptions and Texts of Twelve Manuscripts on
Papyrus of the Greek Bible*, vol. 3/1 (London: Emery Walker, 1933), p. ix.

[128]Roberts, *Manuscript*, p. 23. For a discussion on dating these fragments see Skeat, "Oldest Manuscript of the Four Gospels," pp. 26-31.

[129]Fee, *Papyrus Bodmer II (p66)*, p. 82n20.

claim that the gospels were considered at first to be utilitarian handbooks needs to be modified."[130]

Third, early Christian literary culture was sufficiently developed to the point that it had its own distinctive literary technology and scribal practices. As far back as the evidence takes us, Christian book production was set apart by two specific traits, the adoption of the codex book format[131] and the use of the *nomina sacra*.[132] Although Christians did not invent the codex,[133] it was widely employed by them at least by the beginning of the second century, even in the face of a Greco-Roman and Jewish world that still vastly preferred the roll.[134] In fact, the earliest Christians were so com-

---

[130]Graham N. Stanton, "What Are the Gospels? New Evidence from Papyri," in *Jesus and Gospel*, p. 206. Of course, it should also be acknowledged that Christian manuscripts were often *intentionally* written in a more plain and less calligraphic fashion due to the diverse sociological makeup of its intended audience; see Larry W. Hurtado, "Manuscripts and the Sociology of Early Christian Reading," in *Early Text of the New Testament*, pp. 49-62.

[131]Relevant works on the codex include: Alain Blanchard, ed., *Les débuts du codex* (Turnhout: Brepols, 1989); Roberts and Skeat, *Birth of the Codex*; Eric G. Turner, *The Typology of the Early Codex* (Philadelphia: University of Pennsylvania Press, 1977); T. C. Skeat, "The Origin of the Christian Codex," *ZPE* 102 (1994): 263-68; Henry A. Sanders, "The Beginnings of the Modern Book," *University of Michigan Quarterly Review* 44, no. 15 (1938): 95-111; C. C. McCown, "Codex and Roll in the New Testament," *HTR* 34 (1941): 219-50; Larry W. Hurtado, "The Earliest Evidence of an Emerging Christian Material and Visual Culture: The Codex, the Nomina Sacra, and the Staurogram," in *Text and Artifact in the Religions of Mediterranean Antiquity: Essays in Honour of Peter Richardson*, ed. Stephen G. Wilson and Michael Desjardins (Waterloo: Wilfrid Laurier University Press, 2000), pp. 271-88; S. R. Llewelyn, "The Development of the Codex," in *New Documents Illustrating Early Christianity, Vol. 7: A Review of the Greek Inscriptions and Papyri Published in 1982-83*, ed. S. R. Llewelyn and R. A. Kearsley (North Ryde, NSW: Macquarie University Ancient History Documentary Research Center, 1994), pp. 249-56; Stanton, "Why Were Early Christians Addicted to the Codex?," pp. 165-91; Eldon J. Epp, "The Codex and Literacy in Early Christianity at Oxyrhynchus: Issues Raised by Harry Y. Gamble's *Books and Readers in the Early Church*," in *Critical Review of Books in Religion 1997*, ed. Charles Prebish (Atlanta: American Academy of Religion and Society of Biblical Literature, 1997), pp. 15-37.

[132]Studies on the *nomina sacra* include: Ludwig Traube, *Nomina Sacra: Versuch einer Geschichte der christlichen Kürzung* (Munich: Beck, 1907); A. H. R. E. Paap, *Nomina Sacra in the Greek Papyri of the First Five Centuries* (Leiden: E. J. Brill, 1959); Jose O'Callaghan, *Nomina Sacra in Papyrus Graecis Saeculi III Neotestamentariis* (Rome: Biblical Institute Press, 1970); Schuyler Brown, "Concerning the Origin of the *Nomina Sacra*," *SPap* 9 (1970): 7-19; George Howard, "The Tetragram and the New Testament," *JBL* 96 (1977): 63-83; Roberts, *Manuscript*, pp. 26-48; and Larry W. Hurtado, "The Origin of the *Nomina Sacra*: A Proposal," *JBL* 117 (1998): 655-73.

[133]Skeat, "Early Christian Book Production," p. 68. See discussion in McCown, "Codex and Roll in the New Testament," pp. 219-21. Of course, now it is well-accepted that the codex was likely a Roman invention (see Roberts and Skeat, *Birth of the Codex*, pp. 15-23).

[134]For statistics regarding the adoption of the codex by Christians and non-Christians, see Hurtado, *Earliest Christian Artifacts*, pp. 44-61. A helpful discussion of scrolls is found in Gam-

mitted to the codex that we can hardly find New Testament manuscripts that do not appear in this format.[135] The *nomina sacra*—the special abbreviation of words such as Ἰησοῦς, χριστός, κύριος and θεός[136]—not only appear in the very earliest of our Greek manuscripts, but also their appearance is remarkably widespread across regions and languages.[137] Indeed, so distinctive was the use of the *nomina sacra* that in many ways it identified a manuscript as being Christian in its origins.[138] When taken in conjunction with the unique, widespread and early use of the codex, T. C. Skeat argues that the *nomina sacra* "indicate a degree of organization, of conscious planning, and uniformity of practice among the Christian communities which we have hitherto had little reason to suspect."[139]

However, both the codex and the *nomina sacra* indicate more than just a developed book technology. They also show that early Christians valued these texts *as texts*, and not just repositories of oral tradition.[140] Both of these features have to do with the visual and physical form of the text—they show that these books had become valued as physical objects. In this way, they functioned to mark certain writings as distinctively Christian—it shows that the earliest Christians not only had a clear theological identity but a clear textual identity.[141] In regard to the *nomina sacra*, Barton suggests that these

---

ble, *Books and Readers*, pp. 43-48; and more recently in William A. Johnson, *Bookrolls and Scribes in Oxyrhynchus* (Toronto: University of Toronto Press, 2004).

[135]E.g., during the second century we have only the following Christian scriptural books not on codices: P.IFAO (Revelation); P.Oxy. 4443 (Esther); and P.Barc.inv. 2 (Psalms). However, it should be noted that the manuscript of Revelation is simply a reused roll (opisthograph) and therefore does not represent a conscious decision to use a roll. Moreover, it is uncertain whether the manuscripts of Esther and Psalms derive from a Christian or Jewish provenance. For more discussion see Hurtado, *Earliest Christian Artifacts*, pp. 54-56.

[136]Although these four words were abbreviated most consistently, scribes expanded the *nomina sacra* over time. For other examples of variants of *nomina sacra* see Aland, *Repertorium der griechischen christlichen Papyri*, pp. 420-28, and Bruce M. Metzger, *Manuscripts of the Bible: An Introduction to Greek Palaeography* (New York: Oxford University Press, 1981), pp. 36-37.

[137]*Nomina sacra* are found not only in Greek manuscripts, but also in Latin, Coptic, Slavonic and Armenian. The rare exceptions occur in private documents, magical texts (e.g., P.Oxy. 407), or from oversights of a careless scribe (e.g., P.Oxy. 656; Traube, *Nomina Sacra*, p. 90). For more detail see Roberts, *Manuscript*, p. 27.

[138]A. Luijendijk, *Greetings in the Lord: Early Christians in the Oxyrhynchus Papyri* (Cambridge, MA: Harvard University Press, 2008), pp. 57-78.

[139]Skeat, "Early Christian Book-Production," p. 73.

[140]John Barton, *The Spirit and the Letter: Studies in the Biblical Canon* (London: SPCK, 1997), p. 121.

[141]Hurtado, "Earliest Evidence of an Emerging Christian Material and Visual Culture: The Codex, the Nomina Sacra, and the Staurogram," pp. 271-88.

special abbreviations performed a function for New Testament manuscripts that was similar to the function the Tetragrammaton (special writing of the divine name[142]) performed for Old Testament manuscripts; namely, they indicated that a book was regarded as sacred.[143] In other words, they showed that physical *writings* themselves were valued. Barton comments, "The existence of the *nomina sacra* indicates that for Christians as for Jews there were features of the text as a physical object that were used to express its sacredness."[144] Indeed, Christian scribes also used the *nomina sacra* as they copied Old Testament texts, showing "that they had begun to treat Old and New Testament books as sacred texts in much the same sense—transferring special features of the New Testament back on to the Old."[145]

The fact that the codex and *nomina sacra* are such early features of Christian manuscripts (the latter probably within the first century[146]) raises

---

[142]For a discussion of the variety of ways that the divine name was abbreviated in the Old Testament, see Emanuel Tov, *Scribal Practices and Approaches Reflected in the Texts Found in the Judean Desert* (Leiden: E. J. Brill, 2004), pp. 218-19; and Emanuel Tov, "Scribal Features of Early Witnesses of Greek Scripture," in *The Old Greek Psalter: Studies in Honour of Albert Pietersma*, ed. Robert J. V. Hiebert, Claude E. Cox and Peter J. Gentry (Sheffield: Sheffield Academic Press, 2001), pp. 125-48.

[143]By suggesting that the *nomina sacra* and the *Tetragrammaton* performed similar functions, I am not suggesting that the latter is the explanation of the origins of the former (as originally argued by Traube, *Nomina Sacra*, p. 36). There are many competing theories for the specific form of the *nomina sacra*; for discussion see Hurtado, *Earliest Christian Artifacts*, pp. 95-134.

[144]Barton, *Spirit and the Letter*, p. 123. Barton's suggestion that the *nomina sacra* mark a book as sacred is not necessarily incompatible with the fact that the *nomina sacra* also occur in writings outside the New Testament; e.g., P.Egerton 2, *Gospel of Thomas*, P.Oxy. 840, and even amulets (see Campbell Bonner, *Studies in Magical Amulets* [Ann Arbor, MI: The University of Michigan Press, 1950], pp. 185, 223). For one, some early Christians may have regarded some of these apocryphal books as sacred. In addition, there are good reasons to think that apocryphal books were constructed to reflect the standard features of the Christian "Scripture" that was already being used by the church, and thereby would have included the *nomina sacra*.

[145]Barton, *Spirit and the Letter*, p. 123. Christopher M. Tuckett, "'Nomina Sacra': Yes and No?," in *The Biblical Canons*, ed. J.-M. Auwers and H. J. de Jonge (Leuven: Leuven University Press, 2003), pp. 431-58; Kurt Treu, "Die Bedeutung des Griechischen für die Juden im römischen Reich," *Kairos* 15 (1973): 123-44; and Robert A. Kraft, "The 'Textual Mechanics' of Early Jewish LXX/OG Papyri and Fragments," in *The Bible as Book: The Transmission of the Greek Text*, ed. Scot McKendrick and Orlaith O'Sullivan (London: British Library, 2003), pp. 51-72, have all argued that the *nomina sacra* might not be a Christian invention at all. See response from Hurtado, *Earliest Christian Artifacts*, pp. 99-110.

[146]Hurtado, "Origin of the *Nomina Sacra*," argues for a date "no later than the first century" (p. 660) and even suggests a pre-70 date is likely (p. 672). Roberts, *Manuscript*, p. 37, put its origins "at least the turn of the century," implying the date could be even earlier. The early date of the *nomina sacra* is confirmed by their inclusion in two manuscripts from the early second century, P52 (Gospel of John) and the Chester Beatty Numbers and Deuteronomy (P.Beatty VI). For the convention to be this widespread by the early second century suggests it likely

serious questions about whether the early Christian faith can be characterized as having a purely "oral state of mind."[147] Why would an oral culture, which supposedly resisted writing things down, exhibit such vivid, standardized and widespread textual practices? On the contrary, such practices suggest that we are dealing with a religious culture that is characterized, almost from the beginning, by a distinctive textual identity.

In sum, we have a number of solid historical reasons for thinking that the earliest Christians maintained a vibrant and relatively sophisticated literary culture. Even though most Christians were illiterate (as were most people in the ancient world during this time period), the Christian religion was certainly one that was characterized by *textuality*—an interest in, and dependence on, written texts. Scholars such as Kelber, Ong, Parry and Lord may be right about oral cultures having a resistance to written texts. The problem is that early Christianity was not such an oral culture. Therefore, to reconstruct the history of Christianity solely through the lens of orality is to significantly distort the history of Christianity. Talmon summarizes the problem with this whole approach:

> It would seem that the discovery of the psychodynamics of primary oral cultures produced in some Western intellectuals an orality bias. . . . One appropriates the concept of primary orality from cultures with no knowledge whatsoever of writing, and transfers it all too easily to biblical Israel and Qumran, early Christianity, and rabbinic Judaism, thus gratuitously introducing into these milieus the figment of a gaping dichotomy between oral tradition and written transmission. This procedure stands in need of revision.[148]

THE ARGUMENT FROM TESTIMONY: EARLY CHRISTIANS EXPRESSLY STATED THEIR AVERSION TO WRITING

In addition to the sociohistorical background of early Christianity, scholars

---

began even earlier. The inclusion of the *nomina sacra* in P[52] has been contested by Christopher M. Tuckett, "P52 and the Nomina Sacra," *NTS* 47 (2001): 544-48. See responses from Larry W. Hurtado, "P52 (P.Rylands Gk. 457) and the *Nomina Sacra*: Method and Probability," *TynBul* 54 (2003): 1-14; and Charles E. Hill, "Did the Scribe of P52 Use the *Nomina Sacra*? Another Look," *NTS* 48 (2002): 587-92.

[147]Kelber, *Oral and the Written Gospel*, p. 23.

[148]Talmon, "Oral Tradition and Written Transmission," p. 149. See also Andrew Gregory, "What Is Literary Dependence?," in *New Studies in the Synoptic Problem*, pp. 87-114, esp. p. 91.

have appealed to a second argument to show that the earliest believers devalued the written word. This argument is that some of the earliest Christians actually stated their opposition to written texts (ironically, in written texts) and said that they preferred oral tradition. The two most commonly offered examples of this purported phenomenon are Papias and Paul, so we will examine each in turn.[149]

Papias. Papias, writing around A.D. 125,[150] is frequently cited as an early Christian with an aversion to written texts.[151] Having just described his effort to learn the apostles' teachings through their companions, Papias provides a rationale for his actions: "I did not suppose that information from books would help me so much as the word of the living and surviving voice."[152] These words have been understood by many as reflective of a general Christian tendency to uplift oral tradition and disparage the value of the written word. F. C. Baur puts it bluntly when he declares that Papias preferred "the living word" as opposed to "the dead, transient written text."[153] Similar positions are advocated by Geoffrey Hahneman,[154] Lee

---

[149]Of course, scholars have suggested other (more subtle) examples; e.g., Philip F. Esler, "Collective Memory and Hebrews 11: Outlining a New Investigative Framework," in *Memory, Tradition, and Text: Uses of the Past in Early Christianity*, ed. Alan Kirk and Tom Thatcher (Atlanta: Society of Biblical Literature, 2005), pp. 151-71, makes an argument that the author of Hebrews is attempting to "detextualize" Old Testament traditions due to his oral environment. While Esler makes some helpful observations about how Hebrews would have been heard orally by its first-century audience, his argument that the author has a broad antitextual agenda seems unproven, particularly given the fact that the author is writing a book to make his point (!). In contrast to Esler, see David M. Allen, *Deuteronomy & Exhortation in Hebrews: A Study in Re-presentation* (Mohr Siebeck, 2008), who argues that Hebrews is being presented as a new Deuteronomy.

[150]Scholars are divided over the precise date when Papias wrote. Some have argued for a later date ca. 140; e.g., Brooke F. Westcott, *A General Survey of the History of the Canon of the New Testament* (London: Macmillan, 1889), p. 70; and J. B. Lightfoot, *Essays on the Work Entitled Supernatural Religion* (London: MacMillan & Co., 1889), pp. 147-50. Others argue for an even earlier date ca. 110; see J. Vernon Bartlet, "Papias's 'Exposition': Its Date and Contents," in *Amicitiae Corolla*, ed. H. G. Wood (London: University of London Press, 1933), pp. 16-22; Robert W. Yarbrough, "The Date of Papias: A Reassessment," *JETS* 26 (1983): 181-91.

[151]For discussion of Papias as a source see Samuel Byrskog, *Story as History*, pp. 272-92; Robert H. Gundry, *Matthew: A Commentary on His Handbook for a Mixed Church Under Persecution* (Grand Rapids: Eerdmans, 1994), pp. 609-22; Theo K. Heckel, *Vom Evangelium des Markus zum viergestaltigen Evangelium* (Tübingen: J. C. B. Mohr, 1999), pp. 219-22; W. D. Davies and Dale C. Allison, *The Gospel According to Saint Matthew* (ICC; Edinburgh: T & T Clark, 1997), pp. 7-17; Martin M. Hengel, *Studies in the Gospel of Mark* (London: SCM, 1985), pp. 47-53; and R. T. France, *Matthew: Evangelist and Teacher* (Grand Rapids: Zondervan, 1989), pp. 53-60.

[152]Eusebius, *Hist. eccl.* 3.39.4.

[153]As cited in Campenhausen, *Formation of the Christian Bible*, p. 135.

[154]Geoffrey M. Hahneman, *The Muratorian Fragment and the Development of the Canon* (Oxford: Clarendon, 1992), pp. 95-96.

McDonald,[155] Whitney Shiner,[156] Ron Cameron,[157] C. F. Evans[158] and Hans von Campenhausen.[159] The latter even argues that Papias's "enthusiasm for the oral tradition" is in fact "working in the opposite direction" of a written New Testament.[160] But is this approach the best interpretation of Papias's words? While most scholars assume that Papias's preference for the "living voice" is a preference for oral tradition (over against written traditions), Samuel Byrskog has argued that something very different is going on here.

Byrskog demonstrates that it was standard practice among ancient historians (for example, Herodotus, Polybius, Thucydides) to establish the veracity of a particular event on the basis of eyewitness testimony.[161] Ideally, the historian would record an event which he himself had seen (what Byrskog call "autopsy"), but he would also be content with the testimony of others who had seen the event ("indirect autopsy").[162] Either way, eyewitness testimony was a central component of a credible historical account. Ancient historians were often criticized if they relied too heavily on other written sources—their historical accounts needed to be built on the "living voice" of an actual eyewitness.[163]

Papias provides a number of indications that he is functioning according to standard historiographical practices: (1) he mentions that he "inquired" (ἀνεκρίνον)[164] into the words of the elders, the same language Polybius uses to describe the "interrogation" of eyewitnesses;[165] (2) he claims to have carefully "remembered" (ἐμνημόνευσα)[166] what he learned from the elders, a phrase that Bauckham understands as "making the notes" to aid memory and which matches the historiographical practices

---

[155]Lee M. McDonald, *The Biblical Canon: Its Origin, Transmission, and Authority* (Peabody, MA: Hendrickson, 2007), pp. 246-47.

[156]Shiner, *Proclaiming the Gospel*, pp. 18-19.

[157]Ron Cameron, *Sayings Traditions in the Apocryphon of James* (Philadelphia: Fortress, 1984), pp. 93-100.

[158]Evans, "New Testament in the Making," p. 234.

[159]Campenhausen, *Formation of the Christian Bible*, p. 135.

[160]Ibid., p. 134.

[161]Byrskog, *Story as History*, pp. 48-65.

[162]Ibid., p. 60.

[163]E.g., Polybius criticized Timaeus for relying too much on written sources (12.27.1-3).

[164]*Hist. eccl.* 3.39.4.

[165]12.27.3 (Polybius uses the noun form of this word); cf. Lucian, *Hist. Conscr.* 47.

[166]*Hist. eccl.* 3.39.3.

of Lucian;[167] and (3) he "certifies" (διαβεβαιούμενος)[168] the truth of these things to the reader, which is again a common historigraphical convention.[169] Thus, it is within this context of ancient historiography that Papias's words must be understood. With such a backdrop in mind, it is clear that Papias's preference for the "living voice" is not speaking of a preference for oral tradition at all, but rather his desire to hear from eyewitnesses of Jesus while they are still alive. Put differently, he is not concerned with oral tradition, but *oral history*.[170] Bauckham sums it up: "When Papias speaks of 'a living and surviving voice,' he is not speaking metaphorically of the 'voice' of oral tradition, as many scholars have supposed. He speaks quite literally of the voice of an informant."[171]

Once Papias's intent is understood, then this explains why he was busy composing his own written collection of Jesus tradition, *The Exposition of the Lord's Oracles*.[172] Rather than seeing such a written composition as paradoxical in light of Papias's supposed preference for oral tradition (as many scholars must do), we can now see that it is the natural outcome of a historian's investigation. Although historians were keen to establish the truth of events through direct (or indirect) autopsy, they were also quite willing to put these testimonies into written form once their investigations were complete.[173] Herodotus explains his reasons for writing, namely so that "the memory of the past may not be blotted out from among men by time."[174] Similarly, Thucydides confesses that his *History* has been written so that it will not just "be heard for the moment" but so that it will be "a possession for all time."[175] These examples remind us that a historian's desire to acquire

---

[167]Lucian, *Hist. Conscr.* 47; see Bauckham, *Jesus and the Eyewitnesses*, p. 26.

[168]*Hist. eccl.* 3.39.3. The term "certifies" comes from Bart D. Ehrman, *The Apostolic Fathers* (2 vols.; Cambridge, MA: Harvard University Press, 2003), 2:99.

[169]Lucian, *Hist. Conscr.* 39–40.

[170]Byrskog, *Story as History*, pp. 26–40.

[171]Bauckham, *Jesus and the Eyewitnesses*, p. 27; cf. Gamble, *Books and Readers*, pp. 30–31.

[172]*Hist. eccl.* 3.39.1.

[173]Byrskog, *Story as History*, pp. 122-23. Charles E. Hill, "What Papias Said About John (and Luke): A New Papias Fragment," *JTS* 49 (1998): 582-629, at pp. 622-24, helpfully reminds us that Papias was not collecting sayings of Jesus to compete with the canonical Gospels, but as aid to interpreting the canonical Gospels. Cf. Lightfoot, *Supernatural Religion*, pp. 158-60.

[174]Herodotus, 1.1. English translation from Alfred D. Godley, *Herodotus* (Loeb; Cambridge, MA: Harvard University Press, 1920).

[175]Thucydides, 1.22.4. English translation from Charles Foster Smith, *Thucydides* (Loeb; Cambridge, MA: Harvard University Press, 1980).

direct oral testimony should not be taken as a desire to only transmit such testimony orally; these two desires should not be confused with one another. On the contrary, eyewitness oral testimony is often the very foundation for written historical accounts—the former naturally leads to the latter as the eyewitnesses die out.[176] Once again, orality and textuality are not antithetical but complementary.

Of course, there are contexts other than a historiographical one in which ancient authors express a preference for a "living voice" over the written word.[177] On this basis, scholars are quick to proclaim that an antipathy towards writing was widespread throughout the ancient world.[178] And to some extent this is true.[179] However, upon closer examination, these other instances also do not indicate a pure commitment to orality over textuality. As Byrskog reminds us, writing in the ancient world "was not deplored and rejected *as such*; there was usually a rationale behind that attitude."[180] For example, those who taught the art of ancient rhetoric (that is, public speaking) were keen to downplay the effectiveness of written speeches over against that of the "living voice" of public performances.[181] But this sort of criticism is hardly surprising given that public proclamation is inherently oral and therefore, as Alexander has observed, surely does not constitute a "wholesale prohibition against writing."[182] How else would one learn the art of rhetoric except by watching the teacher in action? A similar downplaying of the written word occurs in ancient discussions of how to teach various crafts, whether scientific, mechanical or medical.[183] Galen argues that when it comes to such skills, it is best to learn "from a teacher" who can demonstrate those skills rather than trying "to

---

[176]Byrskog, *Story as History*, p. 245.
[177]Loveday Alexander, "The Living Voice: Skepticism Toward the Written Word in Early Christian and Graeco-Roman Texts," in *The Bible in Three Dimensions*, ed. David J. A. Clines, Stephen E. Fowl and Stanley E. Porter (Sheffield: JSOT, 1990), pp. 226-37.
[178]Gerhardsson, *Memory and Manuscript*, p. 157.
[179]Pieter J. J. Botha, "Living Voice and Lifeless Letters: Reserve Towards Writing in the Graeco-Roman World," *HvTSt* 49 (1993): 742-59.
[180]Byrskog, *Story as History*, p. 109 (emphasis mine).
[181]E.g., Quintilian, *Inst.* 2.2.8; Pliny, *Ep.* 2.3.
[182]Alexander, "Living Voice," p. 227. See further discussion of how rhetoric interplays with written texts in Simon Goldhill, "The Anecdote: Exploring Boundaries Between Oral and Literate Performances in the Second Sophistic," in *Ancient Literacies*, pp. 96-113, esp. p. 98.
[183]Alexander, "Living Voice," pp. 228-29.

navigate out of a book."[184] But, again, such sentiments are hardly evidence that there was a widespread prejudice against writing. Surely even in the modern day we would be reticent to use a doctor who had learned how to perform surgery solely out of books (!).

The only other plausible historical context (besides ancient historiography) in which to understand Papias's words would be that of the ancient philosophical schools. When it comes to learning philosophy, Seneca is representative of these schools in his insistence that "you will gain more from the living voice and from sharing someone's daily life than from any treatise."[185] Alexander argues that Papias should be understood precisely against this background—and she may well be correct.[186] However, even if she is, it does not demonstrate that early Christians (or even early philosophical schools) had an inherent aversion to writing. Several considerations: (1) Seneca's point is not that books are to be avoided, but simply that philosophical learning is *more effective* when one has a live teacher ("the living voice").[187] This is a commonsense idea that no doubt many would share today.[188] (2) Seneca does not use the phrase "living voice" as a reference to anonymous oral tradition, but to an actual person. (3) There are indications that philosophical schools often used written documents as supplements to their oral teaching—that the two were used together.[189] This fact simply reinforces what was discussed above, namely that written and oral

---

[184]Galen, *De libr. propr.* 5, Kühn 19.33.

[185]*Ep.* 6.5; cf. Galen, *De venae sect.* 5, Kühn 11.221. Another well-known example of such concerns among philosophers is Plato's complaint about writing in *Phaedrus*, 274c-275c. However, it seems that Plato is not opposed to writing in principle, but that "Plato's real concern is with the difference between oral and written *teaching*" (Botha, "Living Voice," p. 749; emphasis his). Botha notes again: "What Plato is rejecting is the belief that a book can be a passport to a kind of 'instant' skill" (p. 750). While at times Plato's criticism of writing seems more fundamental (*Seventh Letter* 342-43), at other times Plato seems quite positive toward writing. Similarly, the comments on writing by Clement of Alexandria in the first chapter of his *Stromateis* (1.1) should also be understood within the context of Hellenistic philosophical schools (which have a bent toward secrecy and, for that reason, keep certain teachings oral). Clement was not opposed to the written word in principle, as is seen by his robust commitment to the written books of the New Testament (see discussion below in chapter five). For more discussion of Clement, see Osborn, "Teaching and Writing," pp. 335-43; Botha, "Living Voice and Lifeless Letters," pp. 753-55; and Gamble, *Books and Readers*, pp. 32, 259n109.

[186]Alexander, "Living Voice," pp. 230-37.

[187]Ironically, Seneca actually downplays the importance of the living voice in other places (*Ep.* 33.9).

[188]Millard, *Reading and Writing*, p. 203.

[189]Alexander, "Living Voice," p. 231.

modes of delivery are not mutually exclusive but are often complementary.

Regardless of which background is most appropriate for understanding Papias's appeal to the "living voice," we are left with few reasons to think that his statement constitutes evidence that early Christians had a prejudice against the written word.[190] Even if others in the Greco-Roman world had an antipathy to written texts, this does not thereby prove that Papias (or other Christians) shared these sentiments. Indeed, early Christianity was distinct from the surrounding culture precisely in its commitment to the written word (the Old Testament) as the basis for its religious commitments.[191] Moreover, Papias informs us of other written texts that he knows and values, namely Matthew, Mark, 1 Peter, 1 John and even Revelation.[192] He feels no need to choose between these written books and the "living voice," because he believes these books *already* have the "living voice" behind them—for example, he defends the authority of Mark on the basis of its connections to the eyewitness testimony of Peter.[193] This demonstrates that for Papias the "living voice" is not antithetical to written texts, but often the foundation for them.

Paul. In addition to Papias, some scholars have appealed to 2 Corinthians 3:6 to maintain their sharp dichotomy between oral and written modes of transmission: "[God] has made us competent to be ministers of a new covenant, not of the letter but of the Spirit. For the letter kills, but the Spirit gives life."[194] For instance, when Werner Kelber interprets these words of Paul, he cannot help but see it as another example of how early Christians disparaged the written word in favor of oral tradition. He argues, "Paul's concern, we observed, is the grammatological nature of the Law. The principal antithesis not between Spirit versus works, but between Spirit

---

[190]See also Andrew F. Walls, "Papias and Oral Tradition," *VC* 21 (1967): 137-40.

[191]Roberts, "Books in the Greco-Roman World and in the New Testament," p. 51.

[192]Eusebius, *Hist. eccl.* 3.39.15-17; Andrew of Caesarea, *On the Apocalypse* 34.12. For Papias's opinion of these documents, see further discussion below in chapter five.

[193]Walls, "Papias and Oral Tradition," pp. 138-39.

[194]E.g., Barr, *Holy Scripture*, p. 12; Kelber, *Oral and the Written Gospel*, pp. 155-59; Robert P. Carroll, "Inscribing the Covenant: Writing and the Written in Jeremiah," in *Understanding Poets and Prophets: Essays in Honour of George Wishart Anderson*, ed. A. Graeme Auld (Sheffield: Sheffield Academic Press, 1993), pp. 61-76; and Mark D. Given, "Paul and Writing," in *As It Is Written: Studying Paul's Use of Scripture*, ed. Stanley E. Porter and Christopher D. Stanley (Atlanta: Society of Biblical Literature, 2008), pp. 237-59.

versus the Written."[195] Thus, according to Kelber, 2 Corinthians 3:6 is really
a polemic against "the written medium."[196]

However, are we to think that the Paul's contrast between letter and
Spirit here is primarily concerned with the medium of revelation? A closer
examination of the passage suggests Paul is making a very different point.
Paul's contrast between these two mediums is really a contrast between two
covenants—that is, he is contrasting the Mosaic covenant focused on law
(γράμματος) with the new covenant focused on the heart (πνεύματος).[197] It
is for this reason that Paul refers to himself as one of the διακόνους καινῆς
διαθήκης ("ministers of the new covenant"); as an apostle he has a divine
call to usher in a new age of forgiveness and grace.[198] This understanding is
confirmed by the immediate context where Paul in 2 Corinthians 3:3 contrasts πλαξὶν λιθίναις ("tablets of stone") with πλαξὶν καρδίαις σαρκίναις
("tablets of human hearts"). The former is a clear reference to the Mosaic
covenant, in which Moses received the "tablets of stone" on the mountaintop (Ex 31:18), and the latter is a clear reference to the new covenant in
which God promised "to write [the law] on their hearts" (Jer 31:33; compare
Ezek 11:19).[199] Just a few verses later Paul makes the same point again using
slightly different terminology; he calls the old covenant the "ministry of
condemnation" (2 Cor 3:9) and contrasts it with the new covenant as a
"ministry of the Spirit" (2 Cor 3:8). The point of each of these contrasts is *not*

---

[195]Kelber, *Oral and the Written Gospel*, p. 158.

[196]Ibid.

[197]For a full-length work on this passage, see Scott J. Hafemann, *Paul, Moses, and the History of Israel:
The Letter/Spirit Contrast and the Argument from Scripture in 2 Corinthians 3* (Tübingen: J. C. B.
Mohr, 1995). Sigurd Grindheim, "The Law Kills but the Gospel Gives Life: The Letter-Spirit
Dualism in 2 Cor 3:5-18," *JSNT* 84 (2001): pp. 97-115, agrees with Hafemann that the text con-
trasts two covenants but disagrees about the nature of the contrast. Bernardin Schneider, "The
Meaning of St. Paul's Antithesis 'The Letter and the Spirit,'" *CBQ* 15 (1953): 163-207, provides a
helpful survey of the historical views of this passage and demonstrates that the most common
view is that Paul is contrasting the old and new covenants (though, again, there are minor disagreements about the nature of that contrast). For a survey of modern views, see Randall C.
Gleason, "Paul's Covenantal Contrasts in 2 Corinthians 3:1-11," *BSac* 154 (1997): 61-79.

[198]It is noteworthy that in the immediate context Paul describes his own role/calling in similar
terms to that of Moses (2 Cor 2:16; cf. Ex 4:10). For more on Paul and Moses, see Karl Olav
Sandnes, *Paul—One of the Prophets? A Contribution to the Apostle's Self-Understanding* (Tübin-
gen: J. C. B. Mohr, 1997); and Peter R. Jones, "The Apostle Paul: Second Moses to the New
Covenant Community. A Study in Pauline Apostolic Authority," in *God's Inerrant Word*, ed.
John Warwick Montgomery (Minneapolis: Bethany Fellowship, 1974), pp. 219-41.

[199]Philip E. Hughes, *Paul's Second Epistle to the Corinthians* (Grand Rapids: Eerdmans, 1962), pp.
89-90.

that one covenant liked to write things down and the other preferred to keep things oral. Rather, as Hafemann has argued, "The 'letter/Spirit' contrast encapsulates this distinction between the role of the law within the Sinai covenant, in which it effects and pronounces judgment on Israel, and its new role within the new covenant in Christ, in which it is kept by the power of the Spirit."[200] Many other biblical texts make this same sort of contrast between the two covenants (Ezek 36:26; Jn 1:17; Rom 2:29; 7:6; 8:2; Gal 3:17-18; 4:24-26).[201]

Once this overall contrast is understood, then we can appreciate the significance of the statement that "the letter kills, but the Spirit gives life." Paul uses the term γράμμα ("letter") not as a reference to the physical act of writing, but as a way of highlighting the *external* nature of the law when it is considered apart from the Spirit—it is a law "*merely* expressed in writing."[202] Without the Spirit, God's law remains only words on a page, and there is no power to keep it. And thus the law leads to death. In the age of the new covenant, however, God has poured out his Spirit in a fuller and richer way, and thus God's people are no longer condemned by the law but are able to keep it. The law has now become internalized. As God declares in Jeremiah 31:33, "I will put my law *within* them, and I will write it on their hearts." The problem with the Sinai covenant, then, was not with the law itself (nor with writing).[203] The problem was a hard-hearted people who lacked the Spirit.[204]

---

[200]Scott J. Hafemann, *2 Corinthians* (NIVAC; Grand Rapids: Zondervan, 2000), pp. 132-33.

[201]For more, see Herman Ridderbos, *Paul: An Outline of His Theology* (Grand Rapids: Eerdmans, 1975), pp. 218-19.

[202]Hafemann, *Paul, Moses and the History of Israel*, p. 168 (emphasis his); cf. Hughes, *The Second Epistle to the Corinthians*, pp. 99-100; and Thomas Schreiner, *Paul: Apostle of God's Glory in Christ* (Downers Grove, IL: IVP Academic, 2001), pp. 134-35. Hays, *Echoes of Scripture in the Letters of Paul*, p. 131, appears to affirm Kelber's interpretation when he declares, "for Paul the problem with the old covenant lies precisely in its character as a written thing." However, at a later point he clarifies by saying, "The problem with this old covenant is precisely that it is (*only*) written, lacking the power to effect the obedience that it demands" (p. 131; emphasis mine). Thus, Hays offers a view similar to the one we are advocating here.

[203]Gottlob Schrenk, "γράφω," *TDNT* 1:768, makes it clear that "the antithesis [between letter and Spirit] is not directed absolutely against γραφή as such. We have seen that Paul affirms the lasting significance of Scripture and he does not intend in any way to weaken its authority." He goes on to say that Paul's contrast "is not meant in such a way that the supersession of the γράμμα involves that of the γραφή. On the contrary, the latter becomes an authority regulated by Christ and His Spirit."

[204]Of course, the believing remnant within Old Testament Israel would have had the Spirit in

Given Paul's argument, we would not expect him (or early Christians in general) to have some aversion to new written Scriptures from God. Paul is not opposed to the written law of the old covenant, and we have no reason to think he would be opposed to a written law in the new covenant. Being in the age of the Spirit is not the same as being in the age of orality. After all, Paul is communicating these covenant truths in a written letter (!). Indeed, one might even make the opposite argument from Kelber. Now that the Spirit has come in fullness, and God's people are empowered to keep the law, there would be even *less* resistance to the written word.

THE ARGUMENT FROM ESCHATOLOGY: EARLY CHRISTIANS EXPECTED THE IMMINENT RETURN OF CHRIST

The third and final argument that has been adduced to show that early Christians avoided the written word is that early Christians believed that the apocalyptic end of the world would happen in their own lifetime, and thus they would have seen no need for a new corpus of books. This sentiment has been most often expressed by those in the form-critical camp. Martin Dibelius described the earliest Christians as a "company of unlettered people which expected the end of the world any day" and therefore "had neither the capacity nor the inclination for the production of books."[205] William Barclay makes a similar claim: "There remains one reason why the gospel story was not committed to writing and it may have well been the dominating reason. In the early days the Christians expected the Parousia, the Second Coming, the return of Jesus in glory, at any moment."[206] And, again, Evans argues: "The eschatological urgency of the [early Christian] message and mission to 'this generation' required as its instrument the

---

some measure. Thus the contrast between the covenant at Sinai and the new covenant is not absolute.
[205]Dibelius, *From Tradition to Gospel*, p. 9.
[206]William Barclay, *The First Three Gospels* (London: SCM, 1966), p. 45. Other scholars who have made similar statements include: Raymond E. Brown, *An Introduction to the New Testament* (New York: Doubleday, 1997), p. 5; and Willi Marxsen, *Introduction to the New Testament: An Approach to Its Problems* (Philadelphia: Westminster, 1968), p. 23. Harry Y. Gamble, "Christianity: Scripture and Canon," in *The Holy Book in Comparative Perspective*, ed. Frederick M. Denny and Rodney L. Taylor (Columbia: University of South Carolina Press, 1985), p. 56n6, argues that the eschatological nature of Christianity "militated against the composition of Christian literature." However, he says nearly the opposite in *Books and Readers*, p. 20. So, it appears his position may have changed.

short prophetic utterance, and almost precluded the more impersonal and protracted medium of writing."[207]

In response to such claims, we shall consider two questions: (1) did early Christians really expect Jesus to return in their own lifetime?; and (2) even if they did, would such a belief have constituted an obstacle to literary production?

Did early Christians expect Jesus to return in their lifetime? One of the most repeated ideas about the earliest Christians is that they believed that the kingdom of God would come (apocalyptically) within their own lifetime. In fact Schweitzer famously argued that Jesus *himself* thought the world would end in his own lifetime; of course the world didn't end, and Jesus died disillusioned on the cross, saying, "My God, my God, why have you forsaken me?" (Mk 15:34).[208] Others have appealed to apocalyptic passages such as Mark 13:30 // Matthew 24:34 // Luke 21:32, kingdom of God passages such as Matthew 16:28 // Mark 9:1 // Luke 9:27 and Matthew 10:23, and Pauline statements such as 1 Thessalonians 4:15-17, to argue that the earliest disciples would have expected Jesus to return within their own lifetime.[209] However, despite these claims, other scholars have repeatedly shown that these passages in no way necessitate that Christ predicted his own return within the first generation of Christianity.[210] Generally speaking, two types of mistakes have led to a misunderstanding of these passages.

First, there is often a misunderstanding of the way apocalyptic imagery functions in these texts. N. T. Wright observes that the Schweitzer-like understanding of these passages is a "devastating misreading of apocalyptic language," particularly as it pertains to the destruction of the temple in A.D. 70.[211] But secondly, and more importantly, such an interpretation of Jesus' teaching fails to understand the distinctive two-stage, already-but-not-yet nature of the kingdom of God.[212] In a very real sense, the kingdom of God

---

[207]Evans, "New Testament in the Making," p. 233.

[208]Albert Schweitzer, *The Quest of the Historical Jesus* (New York: Macmillan, 1968), pp. 358-77.

[209]Bart D. Ehrman, *Jesus: Apocalyptic Prophet of the New Millennium* (New York: Oxford University Press, 1999). Ehrman's approach to the historical Jesus is quite similar to that of Schweitzer.

[210]For a helpful rebuttal of such claims see discussion in Thomas Schreiner, *New Testament Theology: Magnifying God in Christ* (Grand Rapids: Baker Academic, 2008), pp. 803-16; N. T. Wright, *Jesus and the Victory of God* (Minneapolis: Fortress, 1996), pp. 329-65; and Ben Witherington III, *Jesus, Paul and the End of the World* (Downers Grove, IL: IVP Academic, 1992), pp. 23-44.

[211]Wright, *Jesus and the Victory of God*, p. 365.

[212]For fuller discussion on this point, see again George Eldon Ladd, *Jesus and the Kingdom: The*

did come in the lifetime of the disciples (Mt 12:28; Lk 4:21; 17:20-21); but in
another (apocalyptic) sense, it is still yet to come when Jesus returns to
judge the world (Mt 7:21; 8:11; Mk 14:25; 15:43). Failure to make this careful
distinction leads to an all-or-nothing approach to the coming of the
kingdom of God and thus creates the impression that Jesus was mistaken
about his own return.[213]

In addition to these considerations, one must ask how these teachings
of Jesus would have maintained any credibility past the first generation of
Christians if they were widely believed to teach that he promised to return
within that time frame. Either Jesus himself would have been rejected as a
false prophet, or the Synoptic accounts would have been rejected as misleading and corrupt.[214] Indeed, we might have expected some major crisis
around this issue in the early church—but that is not what we find.[215] As
Richard Bauckham observes, "The question of the delay of the Parousia
was very rarely raised in the second century."[216] Sure, the earliest Christians no doubt believed that Jesus *could* return in their own lifetime (Lk
12:39-40; 1 Thess 4:15-17; 5:2), and this led some to wonder why it appeared
to take so long (2 Pet 3:4-10),[217] but there is no indication that they widely
believed that Jesus *must* return in their own lifetime.[218] Thomas Schreiner
comments, "The continued use of the Synoptics and the persistent hope
for a return of Jesus in the life of the early church suggest that from the

---

Eschatology of Biblical Realism (New York: Harper & Row, 1964); and Schreiner, *New Testament Theology*, pp. 41-79.

[213]Richard Bauckham, "The Delay of the Parousia," *TynBul* 31 (1980): 3-36, demonstrates that the struggle with God's delay was not a uniquely Christian phenomenon but one that also existed within the Jewish apocalyptic background of the first century.

[214]Dale C. Allison, *Constructing Jesus: Memory, Imagination, and History* (Grand Rapids: Baker Academic, 2010), pp. 144-53, argues that even if Jesus were mistaken about his return, we would not necessarily expect early Christians to abandon their faith. Allison raises some good points, but if Jesus were mistaken surely we would expect a larger amount of "eschatological disillusionment" in early Christianity than we actually find.

[215]Leslie W. Barnard, "Justin Martyr's Eschatology," *VC* 19 (1965): 86-98. Barnard observes that if the church had anxiety over the delay of the parousia, "[It] seems to have left little trace in early Christian literature" (p. 89).

[216]Richard Bauckham, *Jude, 2 Peter* (Waco, TX: Word, 1983), p. 293.

[217]The issue of eschatological delay is present in only a few other early texts (*1 Clem.* 23:2-5; *2 Clem.* 11:1-7; Herm. *Vis.* 3.4.3; 3.5.1; 3.8.9) and does not present itself as a significant crisis in early Christianity.

[218]Witherington, *Jesus, Paul and the End of the World*, pp. 23-24, argues that the New Testament uses the language of imminence to speak of the second coming, but this does not require that Jesus return in the first generation.

beginning the words of Jesus [about the second coming] were interpreted as not being in error."[219]

Did the expectations of Jesus' return inhibit literary production? For the sake of argument, let us imagine that the earliest Christians *did* believe that Jesus would return within their own generation. Would such a belief necessarily mean they would have resisted producing and using authoritative written documents? There appears to be little reason to think so. Ironically, Paul is put forth as one who believed that Jesus would return in his own lifetime (as supposedly indicated by texts such as 1 Thess 4:15-17), but yet we only know about this belief because Paul wrote it down in a letter.[220] And Paul viewed this letter, as all his letters, as authoritative (1 Thess 2:13) and to be read publicly to the church (1 Thess 5:27).[221] Such a scenario indicates that apocalyptic beliefs are not necessarily incompatible with the production of written, authoritative texts.

Even more than this, we have another example of a group during the first century that was decidedly apocalyptic and, at the same time, a prolific producer of texts: the Qumran community.[222] The apocalyptic nature of the Qumran community is well known.[223] They believed that they were on the edge of God's special eschatological inbreaking in which he would return and establish his kingdom, throwing off the rule of the Gentiles.[224] And they believed this imminent eschaton would begin with their own community,

---

[219]Schreiner, *New Testament Theology*, p. 805.

[220]Ernest Best, *A Commentary on the First and Second Epistles to the Thessalonians* (New York: Harper & Row, 1972), pp. 194-96. For a response to Best's understanding of this passage, see G. K. Beale, *1-2 Thessalonians* (IVPNTC; Downers Grove, IL: IVP Academic, 2003), pp. 140-41.

[221]For more on Paul's understanding of his writings, see chapter four.

[222]E. Earle Ellis, "New Directions in the History of Early Christianity," in *Ancient History in a Modern University: Early Christianity, Late Antiquity and Beyond*, ed. T. W. Hillard, et al. (Grand Rapids: Eerdmans, 1997), 1:75-76.

[223]John J. Collins, *Apocalypticism in the Dead Sea Scrolls* (London: Routledge, 1997); James C. VanderKam, "Apocalyptic Tradition in the Dead Sea Scrolls and the Religion of Qumran," in *Religion in the Dead Sea Scrolls*, ed. John J. Collins and Robert A. Kulger (Grand Rapids: Eerdmans, 2000), pp. 113-34; Emile Puech, "Messianism, Resurrection, and Eschatology at Qumran and in the New Testament," in *The Community of the Renewed Covenant: The Notre Dame Symposium on the Dead Sea Scrolls*, ed. Eugene Ulrich and James C. VanderKam (Notre Dame: University of Notre Dame Press, 1994), pp. 235-56; James H. Charlesworth, Hermann Lichtenberger and Gerbern S. Oegema, eds., *Qumran-Messianism: Studies on the Messianic Expectations in the Dead Sea Scrolls* (Tübingen: Mohr Siebeck, 1998); Israel Knohl, *The Messiah Before Jesus: The Suffering Servant of the Dead Sea Scrolls* (Berkeley: University of California Press, 2000).

[224]E. P. Sanders, *Judaism: Practice and Belief 63BCE–66CE* (London: SCM, 1992), pp. 368-69; cf. 1QM and 11QT^a.

which explains the emphasis on rigorous discipline and purity so evident in their writings.[225] In many ways, the eschatology of the Qumran community was similar to that of early Christianity—particularly the conception of the "the last days" as including the present as well as future events.[226] Even though they believed God's redemption was near, the Qumran community continued to concern themselves with everyday activities; they saw no contradiction between these things. And one of the major activities of the Qumran community was the production of religious texts. Not only were many of their writings committed to careful exegetical interaction with Old Testament texts,[227] but they also composed new treatises which no doubt would have had a quasi-scriptural status.[228] As noted above, the early Christian communities performed these same two functions: they interacted with the text of the Old Testament and also produced new authoritative texts. Thus, it appears that eschatological communities that produce scriptural texts were not an unusual occurrence in the first century.

In light of these considerations, David Meade makes the opposite point from the form critics, namely that apocalypticism in the early Christian communities, far from preventing literary activity, actually "provides the ideological basis for the *extension* of Scripture."[229] Gerd Theissen agrees:

---

[225]E.g., 1QS 6.2-8; 1QSa 2.3-10; 1QM 7.4-6; 11QT^a 45.12-14. For more on purity at Qumran, see Michael Newton, *The Concept of Purity at Qumran and in the Letters of Paul* (Cambridge: Cambridge University Press, 1985); Jacob Neusner, "History and Purity in First-Century Judaism," *HR* 18 (1978): 1-17; Lawrence H. Schiffman, "Communal Meals at Qumran," *RQ* 10 (1979–81): 45-56.

[226]Annette Steudel, "אחרית הימים in the Texts from Qumran," *RevQ* 16 (1993): 225-46; cf. Albert I. Baumgarten, *The Flourishing of Jewish Sects in the Maccabean Era: An Interpretation* (Leiden: E. J. Brill, 1997), pp. 176-77; and John J. Collins, "Teacher and Messiah? The One Who Will Teach Righteousness at the End of Days," in *Community of the Renewed Covenant*, pp. 193-210. Puech, "Messianism," p. 246, declares, "We find in both the Qumran literature and the NT very similar messianic ideas."

[227]1QS 6.6-7; CD 9.8. For more on Qumran exegesis, see F. F. Bruce, *Biblical Exegesis in the Qumran Texts* (London: Tyndale, 1959).

[228]CD^a 10.10-14; 10.21–12.2; 4QMMT; see discussion in Talmon, "Oral Tradition and Written Transmission," pp. 146-47. Talmon also points out that the Qumran community would have likely recorded in writing the words of the Teacher of Righteousness "almost simultaneously with their oral delivery" (p. 158). This is at least suggestive that the earliest Christians may have done something similar with the teachings of Jesus.

[229]David Meade, "Ancient Near Eastern Apocalypticism and the Origins of the New Testament Canon of Scripture," in *The Bible as a Human Witness: Hearing the Word of God Through Historically Dissimilar Traditions*, ed. Randall Heskett and Brian Irwin (London: T & T Clark, 2010), pp. 302-21, at p. 308 (emphasis his).

"The thesis about the imminent expectation of the end as a factor impeding literary creation is false. Jewish apocalyptic writing is full of imminent expectations and yet attests to a flourishing literary production."[230]

CONCLUSION

It has been our purpose in this chapter to address the third major tenet of the extrinsic model, namely that the earliest Christians were reticent to use written documents and that therefore the idea of a NT canon would have been a decidedly late phenomenon. This particular argument has taken a number of forms. First, and most prominently, scholars have made a socio-historical argument—the fact that most Christians were illiterate must mean that they had an aversion to written texts. However, we have observed that this argument suffers from a number of problems. Most fundamentally, it assumes that the absence of literacy must mean the absence of textuality; it assumes only highly literate cultures are interested in books. But, as we noted, Christianity exhibited a deep interest in texts, despite the fact that most of its adherents could not read. In addition, the sociohistorical argument overlooks the fluid and symbiotic nature of oral and written modes of delivery. These modes were not mutually exclusive and often interfaced with and complemented one another. Second, scholars have used the argument from testimony, namely the early Christians actually *expressed* their resistance to written texts. However, there are only two substantive instances where this is a possibility—Papias and Paul—and upon closer examination there are few reasons to think that they exhibit a prejudice against writing per se. On the contrary, both of these authors seem quite comfortable with written documents and are even producing Christian writings themselves. Third, scholars have made an eschatological argument that early Christians would have resisted the written medium due to their belief in the imminent return of Christ. Why bother writing if the end is near? However, as we just argued, we have an example of an eschatologically oriented group from this time period that also believed the end was near and were quite keen to write, namely the Qumran community. So, again, there are no reasons to think these two characteristics are mutually exclusive.

---

[230]Gerd Theissen, *The New Testament: A Literary History* (Minneapolis: Fortress, 2012), p. 10.

Once these misconceptions are addressed, then we can more clearly see that early Christianity was quite a "bookish" religion from the very start. Christians found their identity in books (the Old Testament), they quickly produced their own books, they preached and taught from these books, and were keen to copy and reproduce these books for generations to come. Sure, this was not their only means of communication—the earliest believers still leaned heavily on oral proclamation. And in many instances, Christians may have even preferred oral modes of communication over the written. But, this is not the same as a prejudice *against* writing. One can use oral modes without being, in principle, opposed to written modes. Books were a substantial part of the DNA of the early Christian religion even if they were not always used by any particular individual. All of this suggests that the development of a new corpus of scriptural writings should not be regarded as entirely unexpected. Indeed, one might say that it could have developed quite naturally.

4

THE AUTHORS OF CANON

Were the New Testament Authors Unaware
of Their Own Authority?

*[Paul] apparently was unaware of the divinely
inspired status of his own advice.*

LEE MCDONALD, *The Biblical Canon*

⚖

D. MOODY SMITH, IN HIS 2000 PRESIDENTIAL ADDRESS at the Society of Biblical Literature, declared: "The presumption of a historical distance, and consequent difference of purpose, between the composition of the NT writings and their incorporation into the canon of Scripture is representative of our discipline."[1] Moody has rightly recognized the fourth major tenet of modern canonical studies, namely that the New Testament authors wrote unaware of their own authority and without any intention that their writings would be "Scripture."[2] Their writings, we are told, were designed only as "occasional documents" to address immediate problems

---

[1]D. Moody Smith, "When Did the Gospels Become Scripture?," *JBL* 119 (2000): 3.
[2]E.g., Hans Hübner, *Biblische Theologie des Neuen Testaments. Vol. 1: Prolegomena* (Göttingen: Vandenhoeck & Ruprecht, 1990), pp. 38-43; William Wrede, *The Origin of the New Testament*, trans. James S. Hill (London and New York: Harper and Brothers, 1909), p. 10; Lee M. McDonald, *The Biblical Canon: Its Origin, Transmission, and Authority* (Peabody, MA: Hendrickson, 2007), pp. 32-33, 248-49; Werner G. Kümmel, *Introduction to the New Testament* (Nashville: Abingdon, 1973), p. 476; and Gottlob Schrenk, "γραφω," *TDNT* 1:745.

or issues, and it was only when the later church began to value these writings that they began to acquire authoritative status.[3] Mark Allan Powell, in his recent New Testament introduction, affirms this view plainly: "The authors of our New Testament books did not know that they were writing scripture."[4] Schneemelcher takes this same approach: "The Gospels were not written as 'canonical' books, which were intended to be a norm as a 'new scripture' or to claim authority."[5]

Of course, it should be acknowledged that this particular understanding of the New Testament authors is correct on a number of important points. No one would suggest that these authors would have been able to foresee the full shape of the future canon (and their precise place within it)—that is not something that they could have anticipated.[6] And it is also true that many documents within the New Testament have "occasional" dimensions to them, meaning that they were seeking (at least in part) to address particular situations within the first-century church.[7] However, do these con-

---

[3]Harry Y. Gamble, "Christianity: Scripture and Canon," in *The Holy Book in Comparative Perspective*, ed. Frederick M. Denny and Rodney L. Taylor (Columbia, SC: University of South Carolina Press, 1985), p. 41; see also Helmut Koester, *From Jesus to the Gospels: Interpreting the New Testament in Its Context* (Minneapolis: Fortress, 2007), pp. 64-65; and John Goldingay, *Models for Scripture* (Grand Rapids: Eerdmans, 1994), pp. 152-53. Elsewhere, Gamble seems more open to the possibility that the Gospels were not written for a narrow audience but would have been intended for wider distribution; see Harry Y. Gamble, *Books and Readers in the Early Church* (New Haven, CT: Yale University Press, 1995), pp. 102-3.

[4]Mark Allan Powell, *Introducing the New Testament: A Historical, Literary, and Theological Survey* (Grand Rapids: Baker Academic, 2009), p. 50. See also McDonald, *Biblical Canon*, p. 249; and William R. Farmer and Denis M. Farkasfalvy, *The Formation of the New Testament Canon* (New York: Paulist, 1976), p. 54.

[5]Wilhelm Schneemelcher, ed., *New Testament Apocrypha*, trans. Robert McLachlan Wilson (Louisville: Westminster John Knox, 1991), 1:17. For a very similar view, see Harry Y. Gamble, *The New Testament Canon: Its Making and Meaning* (Philadelphia: Fortress, 1985), p. 18; Morton S. Enslin, "Along Highways and Byways," *HTR* 44 (1951): 67-92; and C. F. Evans, "The New Testament in the Making," in *The Cambridge History of the Bible: From the Beginnings to Jerome*, ed. P. R. Ackroyd and C. F. Evans (Cambridge: Cambridge University Press, 1970), pp. 232-83, at p. 237.

[6]Powell, *Introducing the New Testament*, p. 50.

[7]While the New Testament documents had occasional dimensions to them, we should also note that they were still intended for wider distribution. For instance, scholars have long considered the Gospels to be occasional documents—written only for specific groups—but this has rightly been challenged in recent years. In particular, see Richard Bauckham, ed., *The Gospel for All Christians: Rethinking the Gospel Audiences* (Grand Rapids: Eerdmans, 1998). Luke Timothy Johnson, *The Writings of the New Testament*, 3rd ed. (Minneapolis: Fortress, 2010), pp. 527-29, points out that Paul's letters, while certainly occasional, also bear indications that they were intended for wider distribution; e.g., Paul commands that letters written to one church be shared with other churches (Col 4:16).

siderations necessarily mean that the New Testament authors had no sense of their own authority and wrote with no intention that their documents would somehow govern the life of the church? Although such claims about the New Testament authors might be widespread and oft-repeated, some scholars have begun to question their validity. This has not only been done by Smith[8] (as noted above), but also by John Barton[9] and N. T. Wright.[10] Taking a cue from such studies, this chapter will continue to challenge the notion that the New Testament authors wrote with no awareness of their own authority. Our thesis is a simple one: the New Testament authors, generally speaking, demonstrate awareness that their writings passed down authentic apostolic tradition and therefore bore supreme authority in the life of the church.[11] Or, as Wright puts it, these authors "were conscious of a unique vocation to write Jesus-shaped, Spirit-led, church-shaping books, as part of their strange first-generation calling."[12]

Whether or not we should use the term *Scripture* to describe how the New Testament writers understood their books is sure to generate debate and disagreement—some are comfortable with this terminology, and others less so. But, the particular terminology is really beside the point. Robert Spivey and Smith, for instance, are unwilling to acknowledge Paul is writing "Scripture" but are quite willing to say "[Paul] was consciously asserting his apostolic authority."[13] What Spivey and Smith never explain, however, is what material difference there is between these two kinds of authority. If apostolic authority allows one, by the Holy Spirit, to write (or speak) the very Word of God, then how is this qualitatively dif-

---

[8]Smith, "When Did the Gospels Become Scripture?," pp. 3-20. In this article, Smith appears to be backing off his earlier position in which he affirmed that "The Apostle Paul . . . did not think he was writing holy scripture" (Robert A. Spivey and D. Moody Smith, *Anatomy of the New Testament* [New York: McMillan, 1989], p. 450).

[9]John Barton, *The Spirit and the Letter: Studies in the Biblical Canon* (London: SPCK, 1997), p. 25.

[10]N. T. Wright, *The Last Word: Beyond the Bible Wars to a New Understanding of the Authority of Scripture* (San Francisco: HarperSanFrancisco, 2005), p. 51.

[11]For discussion of the authority of the apostles and the role of apostolic tradition, see chapter two above.

[12]Wright, *Last Word*, p. 52.

[13]Spivey and Smith, *Anatomy of the New Testament*, p. 450. Kümmel, *Introduction to the New Testament*, p. 478, seems to make a similar (unexplained) distinction. He argues that the authority of an apostle was "like that of the Lord, a living authority" and "not the authority of Scripture." But if a person writes with the authority of the Lord himself, how is this meaningfully different than what we call Scripture?

ferent from Scripture? For this reason, Barton is correct to remind us that specific terminology is, to some extent, irrelevant. The fact that New Testament books, in the earliest stages, were not called Scripture as often as we might expect is not due to their lack of authority, he argues, but is more likely due to the fact that "Scripture" was generally conceived as something old and ancient—something these new writings clearly were not.[14] Barton comments:

> It scarcely seems to matter very much whether or not we say that they were "Scripture": their status as the most important books in the world was assured. If they were not *graphē*, then *graphē* had been surpassed by them; phenomenologically, they were Scripture, having the kind of authority and standing for Christians that holy books do have.[15]

The key issue, then, is not what language the New Testament writers might have used to describe their own books (though on occasion they called them "Scripture"; compare 2 Pet 3:16; 1 Tim 5:18), or even what we would like to call these books, but whether these writers consciously wrote books that they understood to contain the new apostolic revelation about Jesus Christ and therefore to have supreme authority in the church.[16]

We shall proceed through an exegetical analysis of key passages in various portions of the New Testament, including the Pauline letters, the Gospels and some of the other New Testament writings. Space prohibits us from examining passages from each of the twenty-seven New Testament books, but a sampling of texts should be sufficient to establish the general point.

---

[14]Barton, *Spirit and the Letter*, pp. 67-68.
[15]Ibid., p. 25.
[16]Of course, a New Testament writer could understand his book to be "apostolic" in the sense that the book is passing down authoritative apostolic tradition even if he himself is not an apostle but had direct and immediate access to an apostle (e.g., Mark passing down the teachings of Peter). For this reason, early Christians were resistant to books that were written after the apostolic time period. For instance, the Muratorian fragment rejects the *Shepherd of Hermas* on the grounds that it was written "very recently, in our own times" (line 74). The meaning of this phrase has recently been disputed by Geoffrey M. Hahneman, *The Muratorian Fragment and the Development of the Canon* (Oxford: Clarendon, 1992), pp. 34-72. See response from Charles E. Hill, "The Debate over the Muratorian Fragment and the Development of the Canon," *WTJ* 57 (1995): 437-52.

THE PAULINE LETTERS

Given that the apostle Paul is the author of the most individual books of the New Testament, it seems appropriate to begin our discussions with his writings.

Galatians 1:1. When it comes to express declarations of Paul's apostolic authority, perhaps no book is clearer than Galatians. As F. F. Bruce has observed, Paul begins this letter by "emphasizing the divine source of his apostolic commission."[17] Such emphatic language no doubt indicates that Paul's apostolic credentials had been questioned by some in Galatia[18]— something he intended to correct at the very outset of his letter. Thus, in Galatians 1:1 Paul goes out of his way to assure his readers that his apostolic commission was not grounded in human authority, for it came "not from men nor through man" (οὐκ ἀπ' ἀνθρώπων οὐδὲ δι' ἀνθρώπου). Such a statement would clarify that Paul's calling was not dependent on the other apostles (compare Gal 1:17-20) nor did it come through any other human intermediary.[19] On the contrary, it came directly "through Jesus Christ and God the Father" (διὰ Ἰησοῦ Χριστοῦ καὶ θεοῦ πατρὸς), a likely reference to his Damascus road experience (Acts 9:1-9). Once Paul establishes his unique authority to speak as an apostle of Jesus Christ, he applies this authority to the situation at hand. Galatians 1:6 indicates that the Galatians (or at least some of them) have begun to desert the gospel of grace and have turned to "a different gospel" (ἕτερον εὐαγγέλιον). Thus, Paul reassures them that "the gospel that was preached *by me* is not man's gospel. For . . . I

---

[17]F. F. Bruce, *The Epistle to the Galatians: A Commentary on the Greek Text* (Grand Rapids: Eerdmans, 1982), p. 71.

[18]Bruce, *Galatians*, p. 72. A helpful overview of the various theories about the identity of Paul's opponents can be found in Ronald Y. K. Fung, *The Epistle to the Galatians* (Grand Rapids: Eerdmans, 1988), pp. 3-9; John C. Hurd, "Reflections Concerning Paul's 'Opponents' in Galatia," in *Paul and His Opponents*, ed. Stanley E. Porter (Leiden: E. J. Brill, 2005), pp. 129-48; and Martin C. De Boer, "The New Preachers in Galatia," in *Jesus, Paul, and Early Christianity*, ed. Margaret M. Mitchell and David P. Moessner (Leiden: E. J. Brill, 2008), pp. 39-60.

[19]Jack T. Sanders, "Paul's 'Autobiographical' Statements in Galatians 1–2," *JBL* 85 (1966): 335-43, and other scholars, have argued that Paul's claims in Galatians about receiving revelation directly from Christ are contradictory to claims in places such as 1 Corinthians 11:23; 15:3, where he is dependent on tradition passed down from the other apostles. For a response, see Bruce, *Galatians*, pp. 88-89; Ronald Y. K. Fung, "Revelation and Tradition: The Origin of Paul's Gospel," *EvQ* 57 (1985): 23-41; Philippe H. Menoud, "Revelation and Tradition: The Influence of Paul's Conversion on His Theology," *Int* 7 (1953): 131-41; William R. Baird, "What Is the Kerygma: A Study of 1 Corinthians 15:3-8 and Galatians 1:11-17," *JBL* 76, no. 3 (1957): 181-91; and Knox Chamblin, "Revelation and Tradition in the Pauline Euangelion," *WTJ* 48 (1986): 1-16.

received it through a revelation of Jesus Christ" (Gal 1:11-12) and therefore it is not to be abandoned.[20] Indeed, Paul pronounces divine judgment in 1:8 (ἀνάθεμα) on any who deny that the gospel he preaches is the true gospel. All of this leaves the Galatian readers with the unmistakable impression that Paul's letter comes to them with the authority of Christ himself and is designed to correct their false thinking about the gospel message. As Ronald Fung observes, "According to Paul, the gospel which came to him as a result of God's revelation of Christ . . . is the same as that which he was still preaching at the time of writing and to which *he is now in his letter calling the readers to return*."[21] Whether they would have called such a letter Scripture is beside the point—it bore the highest possible authority that a document could bear.

1 Thessalonians 2:13. In perhaps Paul's earliest letter, he is explicit once again about his own authority as an apostle of Jesus Christ when he reminds the Thessalonians, "When you received the word of God, which you heard from us, you accepted it not as the word of men but as what it really is, the word of God" (1 Thess 2:13).[22] By the phrase "word of God" (λόγον θεοῦ), Paul is no doubt referring to the authoritative "apostolic tradition"[23] which they had already passed to the Thessalonians through their oral

---

[20]In these verses (Gal 1:11-12), Paul does two things to place himself in continuity with Old Testament prophets as a messenger of God: (1) By using the verb εὐαγγελισθὲν ("was preached") in Galatians 1:11, especially in conjunction with the noun εὐαγγέλιον ("gospel"), Paul links himself with Isaianic texts that anticipated the proclamation of the gospel message in the age of the Messiah (e.g., Is 40:9; 52:7; 61:1). Most noteworthy is Isaiah 61:1, where the speaker declares, "The Spirit of the Lord GOD is upon me, because the LORD has anointed me to bring good news (εὐαγγελίσασθαι)"—a passage also referenced in Luke 4:17-19. (2) Paul uses the term "revelation" (ἀποκαλύψεως) to describe his prophetic message. Michael Pahl, "The 'Gospel' and the 'Word': Exploring Some Early Christian Patterns," *JSNT* 29 (2006): 224, observes that ἀποκάλυψις, along with μυστήριον, "are found in Jewish and Christian writings with reference to prophetic revelation."

[21]Fung, "Revelation and Tradition," p. 24.

[22]Of course, some scholars doubt the authenticity of 1 Thessalonians, or argue that 1 Thessalonians 2:13-16 is a deutero-Pauline interpolation. On the latter point, see Birger A. Pearson, "1 Thessalonians 2:13-16: A Deutero-Pauline Interpolation," *HTR* 64 (1971): 79-94; Hendrikus Boers, "The Form-Critical Study of Paul's Letters: I Thessalonians as a Case Study," *NTS* 22 (1976): 140-58; and Daryl Schmidt, "1 Thess. 2.13-16: Linguistic Evidence for Interpolation," *JBL* 102 (1983): 269-79. For a response, see Jon A. Weatherly, "The Authenticity of 1 Thessalonians 2:13-16: Additional Evidence," *JSNT* 42 (1991): 79-98.

[23]G. K. Beale, *1-2 Thessalonians* (IVPNTC; Downers Grove, IL: IVP Academic, 2003), p. 79; Gordon D. Fee, *The First and Second Letter to the Thessalonians* (NICNT; Grand Rapids: Eerdmans, 2009), p. 87. On the use the phrase "word of God" for the authoritative apostolic message, see Pahl, "The 'Gospel' and the 'Word,'" pp. 211-27.

teaching and preaching.[24] This is confirmed by Paul's use of παραλαβόντες ("received") which was a common term used to denote the reception of apostolic tradition (for example, 1 Cor 11:23; 15:1-3; Gal 1:9; Col 2:6-8; 2 Thess 3:6). Moreover, the phrase "word of God" is used elsewhere by Paul to refer to such authoritative divine teaching (for example, 1 Cor 14:36; Col 1:25; 2 Tim 2:9).[25] Thus, commenting on 1 Thessalonians 2:13, Ernest Best is able to say, "Paul makes here the daring claim which identifies his words with God's words."[26] But, if Paul's apostolic instruction bears divine authority, are we to think that the instruction contained in 1 Thessalonians itself does *not*? Is this letter somehow exempt from that very authority? Three factors make this seem quite unlikely: (1) In 1 Thessalonians 4:2-8 Paul expressly states that he is reiterating his apostolic teaching about personal holiness that he previously delivered to them—teaching that came "through the Lord Jesus" (διὰ τοῦ κυρίου Ἰησου)[27] and therefore could be regarded as "the will of God" (θέλημα τοῦ θεοῦ).[28] Thus, 1 Thessalonians, a written letter, clearly presents itself as containing divine instruction. So much so that, after Paul finishes his instructions about holiness, he warns the Thessalonians that whoever disregards this instruction, "disregards not man but God" (1 Thess 4:8). Or, as Gordon Fee puts it, "To reject Paul's teaching is to reject God himself."[29] (2) Paul acknowledges elsewhere that

---

[24]Treatments of apostolic tradition include: Oscar Cullmann, "Tradition," in *The Early Church*, ed. A. J. B. Higgins (London: SCM, 1956), pp. 59-99; F. F. Bruce, *Tradition: Old and New* (Grand Rapids: Zondervan, 1970), pp. 29-38; idem, "Tradition and the Canon of Scripture," in *The Authoritative Word: Essays on the Nature of Scripture*, ed. Donald K. McKim (Grand Rapids: Eerdmans, 1983), pp. 59-84; and G. W. H. Lampe, "Scripture and Tradition in the Early Church," in *Scripture and Tradition*, ed. Frederick W. Dillistone (London: Lutterworth, 1955), pp. 21-52.

[25]The "word of God" also refers to divine teaching outside Paul's writings: Luke 3:2; 5:1; Acts 4:31; 6:2; 8:14; 11:1; Hebrews 13:7. The authority of "the word of God" is evident by the fact that the phrase is also used to refer to Scripture itself (e.g., Mt 15:6; Mk 7:13; Rom 9:6; Heb 4:12).

[26]Ernest Best, *A Commentary on the First and Second Epistles to the Thessalonians* (New York: Harper & Row, 1972), p. 111.

[27]The NIV rightly captures the sense of 1 Thessalonians 4:2 as follows: "For you know what instructions we gave you *by the authority of the Lord Jesus*." For more discussion, see Beale, *1-2 Thessalonians*, pp. 114-15; and F. F. Bruce, *1 & 2 Thessalonians* (Waco: Word, 1982), pp. 79-80.

[28]1 Thessalonians 4:3. Michael W. Holmes, *1 & 2 Thessalonians* (Grand Rapids: Zondervan, 1998), p. 124, comments on this verse: "Paul views the instructions he passed on to the Thessalonians (4:2) not merely as precepts to be followed but rather as nothing less than the expression of 'God's will' for them (4:3)."

[29]Fee, *Thessalonians*, p. 153.

the mode of delivery for his apostolic instruction is secondary: "So then, brothers, stand firm and hold to the traditions (παραδόσεις[30]) that you were taught by us, either by our spoken word *or by our letter*" (2 Thess 2:15). Indeed, at other points Paul indicates that his letters are more powerful than even his personal presence (2 Cor 10:10).[31] (3) Paul ends his letter by exhorting the Thessalonians—with an oath before the Lord—to make sure this letter was read publicly to the church (1 Thess 5:27; compare 2 Cor 10:9; Col 4:16; Rev 1:3). Scholars have recognized that such a practice parallels the Jewish practice of reading portions of the Old Testament Scripture aloud in the public worship of the synagogue (Lk 4:17-20; Acts 13:15; 15:21).[32] Of course, we have examples in the early church of letters being publicly read that did not bear such authority.[33] However, Paul's insistence that 1 Thessalonians be publicly read is coupled with his own overt claims to apostolic authority contained in the letter itself; this combination provides good reasons to think he viewed (and his audience would have viewed) this letter as bearing divine authority.[34]

1 Corinthians 14:37-38. As we continue to sample key texts where Paul states his apostolic authority, we come to one of the most explicit: "If anyone thinks that he is a prophet, or spiritual, he should acknowledge that the things I am writing to you are a command of the Lord. If anyone does not recognize this, he is not recognized" (1 Cor 14:37-38). Most noteworthy about this passage is that Paul directly addresses the precise nature of his writings and declares that they are a "command of the Lord" (κυρίου

---

[30]This term is also indicative of apostolic tradition (e.g., 1 Cor 11:2; 2 Thess 3:6).

[31]In terms of the authenticity of 2 Thessalonians, please see note 43 below.

[32]Gamble, *Books and Readers*, pp. 209-11; Bruce N. Fisk, "Synagogue Influence and Scriptural Knowledge Among the Christians of Rome," in *As It Is Written: Studying Paul's Use of Scripture*, ed. Stanley E. Porter and Christopher D. Stanley (Atlanta: Society of Biblical Literature, 2008), pp. 157-85; Lee I. Levine, "The Second Temple Synagogue: The Formative Years," in *The Synagogue in Late Antiquity*, ed. Lee I. Levine (Philadelphia: ASOR, 1987), pp. 7-31; and Claude E. Cox, "The Reading of the Personal Letter as the Background for the Reading of Scriptures in the Early Church," in *The Early Church in Its Context: Essays in Honor of Everett Ferguson*, ed. Abraham J. Malherbe, Frederick W. Norris and James W. Thompson (Leiden: E. J. Brill, 1998), pp. 74-91.

[33]*Hist. eccl.* 6.12.2; 3.3.6; 4.23.11; Canon 36 of the Council of Carthage.

[34]By the time of Justin Martyr in the second century, New Testament writings were regularly being read in public as Scripture alongside the Old Tesament: "And on the day called Sunday, all who live in cities or in the country gather together to one place, and the memoirs of the apostles or the writings of the prophets are read, as long as time permits; then, when the reader has ceased, the president verbally instructs, and exhorts to the imitation of these good things" (*1 Apol.* 67.3).

ἐντολή). Such a phrase is common throughout the Old Testament as a reference to either the commands that come directly from God himself or to the commands he had given to Moses.[35] Indeed, the very similar ἐντολῶν θεοῦ ("commandments of God") is used by Paul earlier in this same letter to refer to authoritative instructions that come from God himself (1 Cor 7:19).[36] Such constructions stand in contrast to other Pauline passages such as Titus 1:14 that refer to the ἐντολαῖς ἀνθρώπων ("commandments of people"). Thus, it seems clear that in 1 Corinthians 14:37-38 Paul is equating "the things I am writing (γράφω)" with the very words of God himself.[37] So confident is Paul of his authority to speak for the Lord that he declares that anyone who does not recognize the authority of his writings is himself "not recognized" (ἀγνοεῖται[38]). Fee calls such a pronouncement a "prophetic

---

[35]E.g., Lev 4:13; 5:17; 27:34; Num 15:39; Deut 4:2; 6:17; 8:6, 11:28; 30:16; Josh 22:3; Judg 3:4; Ezra 7:11; Neh 10:29; Ps 19:8.

[36]The word ἐντολή itself is also used frequently by Paul to refer to the teachings of the Scriptures (e.g., Rom 7:8-13; 13:9; Eph 2:15; 6:2). It is worth noting here that when Paul issues commands by saying "I, not the Lord" in 1 Corinthians 7:12 (and surrounding passages), it is not an attempt to contrast his lower authority with Christ's higher authority. On the contrary, Paul's statement simply means that he has no direct command from Jesus on this particular subject and therefore must speak "on his own authority" (Gordon D. Fee, *The First Epistle to the Corinthians* [Grand Rapids: Eerdmans, 1987], p. 292). But, both commands—whether from Jesus or Paul—have the same level of authority. For more discussion, see Wayne Grudem, "Scripture's Self-Attestation and the Problem of Formulating a Doctrine of Scripture," in *Scripture and Truth*, ed. D. A. Carson and John D. Woodbridge (Grand Rapids: Baker, 1992), p. 47; Herman N. Ridderbos, *Redemptive History and the New Testament Scripture* (Phillipsburg, NJ: P & R, 1988), p. 21; Leon Morris, *The First Epistle of Paul to the Corinthians* (Grand Rapids: Eerdmans, 1975), p. 109; John Murray, "The Attestation of Scripture," in *The Infallible Word* (Philadelphia: P & R, 1946), p. 38; and Cullmann, "Tradition," p. 74.

[37]Christian Stettler, "The 'Command of the Lord' in 1 Cor 14:37—A Saying of Jesus?," *Bib* 87 (2006): 42-51, suggests that when Paul refers to a "commandment of the Lord" he is not referring to his own authority to speak for Christ but is merely passing along a tradition from the *earthly* Jesus. However, this suggestion runs into numerous problems, the most obvious of which is that there is nothing in the immediate context that could be construed as a saying of Jesus. When Paul passes along Jesus tradition elsewhere in this letter, it is usually quite clear what he is referring to (e.g., 1 Cor 11:23-25). In addition, Stettler argues that Paul would never refer to his own teaching as a "command of the Lord" because Paul's "opinion . . . is not of the same authority" as that of Jesus (p. 43). But Paul is quite clear elsewhere that he speaks with the very authority of Jesus (Gal 1:1) and even refers to his teachings as the "word of God" (1 Thess 2:13), a phrase which is not meaningfully different from the "command of the Lord" in terms of authority. It is for these reasons (among others) that the vast majority of commentators rightly understand this passage as Paul speaking with the authority of the risen Christ.

[38]Although some early manuscripts favor the imperative ἀγνοείτω (P46, ℵ, Ac, B, D²), the UBS committee is quite confident that ἀγνοεῖται is original (ℵ*, A*vid, Dgr*, 33, 1379, Origen). See Bruce M. Metzger, *A Textual Commentary on the Greek New Testament* (Stuttgart: German Bible Society, 1994), p. 501.

sentence of judgment on those who fail to heed this letter."[39] In a similar fashion, Raymond Collins argues that Paul is offering "a warning of eschatological disaster" for all who reject his letter.[40] As noted in the prior chapter, this language once again reflects Paul's role as a minister of the new covenant (2 Cor 3:6) as he threatens a "covenant lawsuit" against any members of the covenant who refuse to submit to his God-given authority.[41] Archibald Robertson and Alfred Plummer sum up this entire passage: "[Paul] is conscious that what he says does not come from himself; he is the mouthpiece of Christ."[42]

2 Thessalonians 3:6, 14. As we have just observed in 1 Corinthians 14:37-38, Paul is very insistent that his own commands and teachings be obeyed—and is willing to pronounce judgment on those who refuse to do so. This trend is evident elsewhere in Paul's writings, particularly 2 Thessalonians 3:6 and 14.[43] Paul declares, "Now we command you (παραγγέλλομεν), brothers, in the name of our Lord Jesus Christ, that you keep away from any brother who is walking . . . not in accord with the tradition (παράδοσιν) that you received (παρελάβοσαν) from us" (2 Thess 3:6). As noted above, the "tradition" Paul is referring to here is no doubt the authoritative apostolic teaching that he has passed down to the Thessalonians—something that is confirmed by the use of key terminology such as παράδοσιν and παρελάβοσαν.[44] For this reason, Paul once again

---

[39]Fee, *First Epistle to the Corinthians*, p. 712.

[40]Raymond F. Collins, *First Corinthians* (Collegeville, MN: Liturgical Press, 1999), p. 517.

[41]William L. Lane, "Covenant: The Key to Paul's Conflict with Corinth," *TynBul* 33 (1982): 3-29.

[42]Archibald Robertson and Alfred Plummer, *The First Epistle of St. Paul to the Corinthians* (ICC; Edinburgh: T & T Clark, 1961), p. 327.

[43]Of course, a number of modern scholars question the authenticity of 2 Thessalonians. However, such concerns are not relevant for our argument here. Our point is simply that the author of 2 Thessalonians (even if he is just purporting to be Paul) is claiming authority for this writing. Moreover, there are a number of scholars who have challenged these criticisms of 2 Thessalonians; e.g., Abraham J. Malherbe, *The Letters to the Thessalonians* (New York: Doubleday, 2000), pp. 364-74; Robert K. Jewett, *The Thessalonian Correspondence: Pauline Rhetoric and Millenarian Piety* (Philadelphia: Fortress, 1986), pp. 3-18; I. Howard Marshall, *1&2 Thessalonians* (NCBC; Grand Rapids: Eerdmans, 1983), pp. 28-45; Best, *Thessalonians*, pp. 37-59; and, most recently, Paul Foster, "Who Wrote 2 Thessalonians? A Fresh Look at an Old Problem," *JSNT* 35 (2012): 150-75.

[44]The specific issue Paul is addressing is those members of the church who have become "idle" (ἀτάκτως). For more on this topic, see Bruce W. Winter, "'If a Man Does Not Wish to Work . . .' A Cultural and Historical Setting for 2 Thessalonians 3:6-16," *TynBul* 40 (1989): 303-15; and Ronald Russell, "The Idle in 2 Thess 3:6-12: An Eschatological or a Social Problem?," *NTS* 34 (1988): 105-19.

declares a type of prophetic judgment against those who disobey such apostolic teaching.[45] In this case, Paul asks the Thessalonians to "keep away from" (στέλλεσθαι) the disobedient brother, certainly a reference to some sort of church discipline, perhaps ostracism or even excommunication (though we cannot be sure).[46] But it is not just Paul's *past* teaching that has authoritative status, but also Paul's *present* commands contained in this very letter. Indeed, Paul makes it clear that the very words he is writing in 2 Thessalonians 3:6 constitute a "command" (παραγγέλλομεν) that is being issued "in the name of the Lord Jesus Christ." Leon Morris observes that this construction makes the command "as authoritative as it can possibly be."[47] Thus we have here yet another example where divine authority is attached directly to Paul's written words. Paul reiterates this point in 2 Thessalonians 3:14 when he offers a related warning: "If anyone does not obey *what we say in this letter*, take note of that person, and have nothing to do with him." Not only does Paul expect his written letter to be obeyed (ὑπακούει), but insists again on church discipline for the one who disobeys, exhorting his listeners to "have nothing to do with him" (μὴ συναναμίγνυσθαι αὐτῷ).[48] Charles Wanamaker is more direct: "Paul calls for their excommunication."[49]

By now, we can see a trend among many of these Pauline passages. On quite a regular basis Paul (1) affirms his own apostolic authority to speak for Christ, (2) makes it clear that this apostolic authority not only applies to his

---

[45]Charles A. Wanamaker, *The Epistles to the Thessalonians* (NIGTC; Grand Rapids: Eerdmans, 1990), p. 281.

[46]Beale, *1-2 Thessalonians*, pp. 254, 260-63, suggests that 2 Thessalonians 3:6 may be a lesser penalty than excommunication, designed to keep the Thessalonians from being influenced by such a person (cf. 1 Cor 15:33). But he does acknowledge that excommunication is a possibility in 2 Thessalonians 3:14 and that there is a clear connection between 3:6 and 3:14. See also Judy Skeen, "Not as Enemies, but Kin: Discipline in the Family of God—2 Thessalonians 3:6-10," *RevExp* 96 (1999): 287-94. E. J. Bicknell, *The First and Second Epistles to the Thessalonians* (London: Methuen and Co., 1932), p. 93, refers to the punishment as "social ostracism."

[47]Leon Morris, *The Epistles of Paul to the Thessalonians* (TNTC; Grand Rapids: Eerdmans, 1974), p. 144.

[48]The same word (συναναμίγνυσθαι) is used in 1 Corinthians 5:9-11 where the Corinthians are told not to "associate with" a brother who is committing sexual immorality and refuses to repent—a clear instance of excommunication language. Bruce, *Thessalonians*, p. 210, acknowledges this connection but still suggests that the punishment in 2 Thessalonians 3:14 was less severe than 1 Corinthians 5:9-11. For a similar view, see Morris, *Thessalonians*, p. 149.

[49]Wanamaker, *Thessalonians*, p. 289. In agreement is Charles J. Bumgardner, "'As a Brother': 2 Thessalonians 3:6-15 and Ecclesiastical Separation," *DBSJ* 14 (2009): 55-97.

oral teaching, but is being employed in the very letters that he is writing, and (3) indicates that anyone who rejects his teachings (oral or written) is thereby rejecting the commands of Christ and subject to prophetic condemnation or excommunication. Such a scenario makes it difficult to accept McDonald's claim that Paul "apparently was unaware of the divinely inspired status of his own advice."[50]

THE GOSPELS

Given that the Gospels are a very different genre than the Epistles, and are "formally anonymous" in the body of the texts themselves, we would not expect the authors to provide the same type of direct and explicit statements about their own authority as Paul does in his letters.[51] Indeed, the Gospel authors are decidedly behind the scenes and only rarely make appearances within the flow of the story.[52] However, the formal anonymity of the Gospels need not be taken as evidence that their authors did not view these texts as bearing authority. Armin Baum has argued that the historical books of the New Testament (Gospels and Acts) were *intentionally* written as anonymous works in order to reflect the practice of the Old Testament Historical Books, which were themselves anonymous (as opposed to other Old Testament writings, such as the Prophets, which included the identity of the author).[53] This makes the Gospels and Acts distinctive from most Greco-Roman biographies, which often included the author's name (though not always).[54] Such a stylistic device allowed the authors of the Gospels to "disappear" and to give "highest priority to their subject matter."[55] Thus, the anonymity of the Gospels, far from diminishing their scriptural authority, actually served to increase it by consciously placing

---

[50]McDonald, *Biblical Canon*, p. 32.

[51]For an up-to-date discussion of Gospel genre, see Craig S. Keener, *The Historical Jesus of the Gospels* (Grand Rapids: Eerdmans, 2009), pp. 73-84. The traditional view that the Gospels are Greco-Roman biographies is defended by Richard A. Burridge, *What Are the Gospels?* (Cambridge: Cambridge University Press, 1992).

[52]Some exceptions include Mark 7:19; 13:14; Luke 1:1-4; John 2:22; 21:24.

[53]Armin D. Baum, "The Anonymity of the New Testament History Books: A Stylistic Device in the Context of Greco-Roman and Ancient Near Eastern Literature," *NovT* 50 (2008): 120-42.

[54]Examples of biographies that were formally anonymous include Lucian's *Life of Demonax*, *Secundus the Silent Philosopher* and *Lives of the Prophets*, Arrian's *Anabasis*, and Sulpicious Severus's *Life of St. Martin*.

[55]Baum, "Anonymity," p. 139.

the Gospels "in the tradition of Old Testament historiography."[56]

In addition to Baum's argument, there are also other ways we can assess the degree to which the Gospel authors were aware of their own authority. Despite the fact that these Gospels are formally anonymous, there are still indications within the texts themselves—albeit more subtle than those in the Epistles—that provide indications about the identity of the authors and, more importantly, about their intention to pass along authoritative apostolic tradition about the person of Jesus of Nazareth.

Mark 1:1. As Robert Guelich has observed, the opening line of Mark's[57] Gospel "has spawned endless debates over the meaning of each word."[58] However, regardless of whether one considers "The beginning of the gospel (εὐαγγελίου) of Jesus Christ" to be the title of the book itself[59] or connected to the verses that immediately follow,[60] Robert Stein is correct to remind us that the opening line still informs the reader "that the entire work is to be understood as the good news about Jesus Christ."[61] Mark's deliberate use of the term εὐαγγελίον[62] is most noteworthy, for that term was not originally used among early Christians to refer to written texts, but rather was a reference to the authoritative message of the apostolic preaching.[63] Thus, from

---

[56]Ibid.

[57]Whether the canonical Gospels are really authored by the names in their titles is not relevant for the argument here. We are simply arguing that the Gospels *present* themselves as apostolic—whether they actually were is another question entirely. For simplicity, we will refer to the authors of these Gospels by the names in their titles.

[58]Robert Guelich, "The Gospel Genre," in *Das Evangelium und die Evangelien* (Tübingen: J. C. B. Mohr, 1983), p. 204. Summaries of the various views on this verse can be found in Allen Paul Wikgren, "ΑΡΧΗ ΤΟΥ ΕΥΑΓΓΕΛΙΟΥ," *JBL* 61 (1942): 11-20; and C. E. B. Cranfield, *The Gospel According to St. Mark* (Cambridge: Cambridge University Press, 1959), pp. 34-35.

[59]E.g., M. Eugène Boring, "Mark 1:1-15 and the Beginning of the Gospel," *Sem* 52 (1990): 43-81; Joel Marcus, *Mark 1-8* (New York: Doubleday, 1999), pp. 143-45; and Vincent Taylor, *The Gospel According to St. Mark* (Grand Rapids: Baker, 1981), p. 152.

[60]E.g., William L. Lane, *The Gospel According to St. Mark* (Grand Rapids: Eerdmans, 1974), pp. 39-62; Morna D. Hooker, *The Gospel According to St. Mark* (London: A & C Black, 1991), pp. 31-52; and Guelich, "Gospel Genre," pp. 204-16.

[61]Robert H. Stein, *Mark* (BECNT; Grand Rapids: Baker Academic, 2008), p. 39. In agreement is Guelich, "Gospel Genre," pp. 204-16, who also denies that Mark 1:1 is a title, but still affirms that "the evangelist applies εὐαγγελίον in 1:1 to his literary work" (p. 206). See also R. T. France, *The Gospel of Mark* (Grand Rapids: Eerdmans, 2002), pp. 50-51.

[62]For an account of the origins of this term within Christianity, see Graham N. Stanton, *Jesus and Gospel* (Cambridge: Cambridge University Press, 2004), pp. 9-62; and William Horbury, "'Gospel' in Herodian Judea," in *The Written Gospel*, ed. Markus Bockmuehl and Donald A. Hagner (Cambridge: Cambridge University Press, 2005), pp. 7-30.

[63]Robert H. Gundry, "ΕΥΑΓΓΕΛΙΟΝ: How Soon a Book?," *JBL* 115 (1996): 321-25; Helmut Koes-

the very beginning, the author of Mark makes it clear that his account is to be understood as the embodiment of that foundational apostolic message. The fact that the term εὐαγγελίον also occurs toward the end of the Gospel in Mark 14:9, creating an obvious literary *inclusio*, further reinforces the idea that the entire work is to be construed as a summary of the gospel message.[64] This has led John Roberts and Andreas du Toit to observe that "we have here [in Mark 1:1] a really tremendous claim to authority."[65] Likewise, Martin Hengel argues that Mark's Gospel presents itself as the "saving message" of Jesus Christ and therefore it "meets the requirement of the sufficiency of Holy Scripture."[66] But, there are even further lines of evidence that support this understanding of Mark's Gospel:

1. The opening line of Mark's Gospel matches language from the opening of some Old Testament prophetic books. For instance, Hosea 1:2 uses a similar formula: "The beginning (ἀρχὴ) of the words of the Lord to Hosea."[67] Gerd Theissen comments on Mark's use of this formula, "The readers and hearers of Mark's Gospel were familiar with such prophetic writings, which began with word of God coming to a human being."[68] By placing his own writings in the context of the Old Testament prophetic books, the author of Mark indicates that he too is bringing a message from the Lord.

2. The fact that Mark presents his Gospel as the embodiment of apostolic tradition is confirmed by the fact that it essentially follows the outline of

---

ter, "From the Kerygma Gospel to the Written Gospels," *NTS* 35 (1989): 361-81. However, Gundry and Koester's conclusions have been rightly balanced out by James A. Kelhoffer, "'How Soon a Book' Revisited: ΕΥΑΓΓΕΛΙΟΝ as a Reference to 'Gospel' Materials in the First Half of the Second Century," *ZNW* 95 (2004): 1-34.

[64]In addition, Mark uses the term more often than the other Gospels (Mk 1:1, 14, 15; 8:35; 10:29; 13:10; 14:29), compared to only four times in Matthew and none in Luke and John.

[65]John H. Roberts and Andreas B. Du Toit, *Preamble to New Testament Study: The Canon of the New Testament*, Guide to the New Testament vol. 1 (Pretoria: N. G. Kerkboekhandel Transvaal, 1979), 1:127.

[66]Martin Hengel, *The Four Gospels and the One Gospel of Jesus Christ* (Harrisburg, PA: Trinity Press International, 2000), p. 90.

[67]N. Clayton Croy, "Where the Gospel Text Begins: A Non-Theological Interpretation of Mark 1:1," *NovT* 43 (2001): 123-24, defends the close connection between Mark 1:1 and Hosea 1:2 and even points out that introductory phrases using ἀρχὴ were added to the manuscripts of many LXX writings. However, Croy's argument that Mark 1:1 is a later scribal gloss is not a necessary conclusion from this data. One need only suggest that Mark wrote with awareness of LXX manuscripts that contained this type of language.

[68]Gerd Theissen, *The New Testament: A Literary History* (Minneapolis: Fortress, 2012), p. 54.

Peter's sermon in Acts 10:34-43,[69] considered by many scholars today to be pre-Lukan tradition and therefore likely one of the earliest expressions of the church's "gospel" message.[70] Both Mark's Gospel and Acts 10:34-43 begin with gospel terminology,[71] speak of Jesus as the Messiah ("Christ"),[72] draw connections to an Isaianic/Old Testament context,[73] place the "beginning" of the ministry in Galilee,[74] discuss John the Baptist's role,[75] and, of course, highlight Jesus' redemptive ministry, death and resurrection.[76] These parallels indicate that Mark's Gospel would have been perceived as the embodiment of traditional apostolic material (particularly material connected to Peter).[77] Guelich comments, "If the basic *framework* of Mark's Gospel and the Scriptural context for his calling it the 'gospel of Jesus Messiah' corresponds to what one finds in the tradition behind Acts 10:34-43, the traditional character of Mark's *material* used in writing the Gospel is even more apparent."[78]

3. The fact that Mark presents his Gospel as containing the apostolic message is also confirmed by internal indications that the material originates with the witness of the apostle Peter himself. Aside from the fact

---

[69]These connections were originally noted by C. H. Dodd, "The Framework of the Gospel Narrative," *ExpT* 43, no. 32 (1931): 396-400; idem, *The Apostolic Preaching and Its Developments* (New York: Harper, 1949), pp. 46-52; and Martin Dibelius, *From Tradition to Gospel* (Cambridge: J. Clarke, 1971), p. 25.

[70]For a defense of the pre-Lukan nature of Acts 10:34-43, see Peter Stuhlmacher, *Das Paulinische Evangelium* (Göttingen: Vandenhoeck & Ruprecht, 1968), p. 279n1; Graham N. Stanton, *Jesus of Nazareth in New Testament Preaching* (SNTSMS 27; Cambridge: Cambridge University Press, 1974), pp. 70-81; and Michael Bird, "Mark: Interpreter of Peter and Disciple of Paul," in *Paul and the Gospels: Christologies, Conflicts, and Convergences*, ed. Michael Bird and Joel Willitts (London: T & T Clark, 2011), pp. 37-38.

[71]Mark 1:1 uses εὐαγγελίον, Acts 10:36 uses εὐαγγελιζόμενος (cf. Is 52:7).

[72]Mark 1:1: "The gospel of Jesus Christ"; Acts 10:36: "Preaching good news of peace through Jesus Christ."

[73]Mark 1:3 cites Isaiah 40:3; Acts 10:36 references "Israel" and alludes to Isaiah 52:7; Acts 10:38 alludes to Isaiah 61:1. See discussion in F. F. Bruce, *The Book of the Acts* (Grand Rapids: Eerdmans, 1988), pp. 212-13.

[74]Mark 1:1 uses ἀρχή; Acts 10:37 uses ἀρξάμενος.

[75]Mark 1:4-8 discusses John the Baptist; Acts 10:37: "Beginning from Galilee after the baptism that John proclaimed."

[76]Acts 10:38: "[Jesus] went about doing good and healing" parallels Mark 1–14; Acts 10:39-40, "They put him to death . . . but God raised him on the third day," parallels Mark 15–16.

[77]Samuel Byrskog, *Story as History—History as Story: The Gospel Tradition in the Context of Ancient Oral History* (Leiden: E. J. Brill, 2002), pp. 284-88, surveys evidence that Acts 10:34-43 is connected to Peter himself.

[78]Guelich, "Gospel Genre," p. 212 (emphasis his).

that Mark's connection to Peter was well known among the early church fathers[79] and is attested by other parts of the New Testament (1 Pet 5:13; Acts 12:12-17),[80] the Gospel of Mark itself draws connections to Peter by forming another literary *inclusio* that centers on Peter himself—the first disciple mentioned in Mark is Peter (Mk 1:16) and the last disciple mentioned is Peter (Mk 16:7).[81] Moreover, both of these mentions of Peter are quite emphatic—Mark goes out of his way to bring Peter to the forefront of each passage.[82] This Petrine *inclusio*, combined with the inordinately high number of times the name Peter occurs in the Gospel[83] and the manner in which Peter dominates the narratives of the disciples,[84] makes it clear that Peter was to be understood as the "main eyewitness source behind Mark's gospel."[85] Hengel observes, "Simon Peter is as a disciple named first and last in the Gospel to show that it is based on his tradition and therefore his authority."[86]

4. Another notable factor is the way that the author of Mark connects the story of Jesus with the story of Israel—something that all the Synoptics do to one degree or another.[87] For Mark, the "beginning" of the gospel is

---

[79]E.g., Papias cited in Eusebius, *Hist. eccl.* 3.39.14-15; Justin, *Dial.* 106; and Irenaeus, *Haer.* 3.10.5. For further connections between Mark and Peter, see Richard Bauckham, *Jesus and the Eyewitnesses: The Gospels as Eyewitness Testimony* (Grand Rapids: Eerdmans, 2006), pp. 205-7; Ulrich H. J. Körtner, "Markus der Mitarbeiter des Petrus," *ZNW* 71 (1980): 160-73; Hengel, *Four Gospels*, pp. 78-89; Everett Kalin, "Early Traditions About Mark's Gospel: Canonical Status Emerges, the Story Grows," *CurTM* 2 (1975): 333-41; and Cuthbert H. Turner, "Marcan Usage: Notes Critical and Exegetical on the Second Gospel V. The Movements of Jesus and His Disciples and the Crowd," *JTS* 26 (1925): 225-40.

[80]David Trobisch, *The First Edition of the New Testament* (Oxford: Oxford University Press, 2000), pp. 47-49.

[81]The practice of using an *inclusio* to identify an eyewitness source can be found in Greco-Roman works such as Lucian's *Alexander* and Porphyry's *Life of Plotinus*. See discussion in Bauckham, *Jesus and the Eyewitnesses*, pp. 132-45.

[82]In Mark 1:16 we read that Jesus saw "Simon and Andrew, the brother of Simon" (Σίμωνα καὶ Ἀνδρέαν τὸν ἀδελφὸν Σίμωνος). Robert A. Guelich, *Mark 1–8:26* (Dallas: Word Books, 1989), p. 50, observes, "The double reference to Simon most likely indicates his relative stature in Mark's Gospel." In Mark 16:7, the angel says, "But go, tell his disciples *and Peter* (καὶ τῷ Πέτρῳ)." The redundancy of Peter's name here is once again indicative of added emphasis.

[83]The name Peter occurs nineteen times, and the name Simon occurs seven times, which is proportionately much more than the other three Gospels. See Hengel, *Four Gospels*, p. 82.

[84]See discussion of Peter's heightened role in Bird, "Mark: Interpreter of Peter and Disciple of Paul," pp. 35-36.

[85]Bauckham, *Jesus and the Eyewitnesses*, p. 125.

[86]Hengel, *Four Gospels*, p. 82.

[87]Smith, "When Did the Gospels Become Scripture?," pp. 3-20.

not the birth of Jesus or even his public ministry, but the messianic expectations and longings of Israel as displayed in various Old Testament passages.[88] In particular, Mark 1:2 portrays Jesus as the fulfillment of Yahweh's promise to visit his people in Malachi 3:1 (compare Ex 23:20), even changing the original "the way before me" to "your way."[89] Likewise, Mark 1:3 cites Isaiah 40:3, where the people are to prepare the "way of the LORD"— again an indication that Jesus is the realization of Yahweh's coming to his people Israel. Moreover, the heavenly voice and giving of the Spirit in Mark 1:10-11 indicate that Jesus is the Spirit-equipped servant of Isaiah 42:1 (compare Is 52:7; 61:1).[90] While such Old Testament connections do not necessarily constitute an explicit claim by Mark to be writing with divine authority, they do constitute an effort by Mark to present his Gospel as the continuation of the biblical narrative.[91] And this was no doubt recognized by those who read it. As N. T. Wright has observed, "The Jews of the period did not simply think of the biblical traditions atomistically, but were able to conceive of the story as a whole, and to be regularly looking for its proper conclusion."[92]

John 21:24. Unlike the Synoptics, John's Gospel is more explicit about the identity of its author. In John 21:24 we are told: "This is the disciple who is bearing witness (μαρτυρῶν) about these things, and who has written (γράψας) these things."[93] Of course, the identity of this mysterious "beloved disciple" has engendered much academic debate, and there are

---

[88]Robert A. Guelich, "'The Beginning of the Gospel': Mark 1:1-15," *BR* 27 (1982): 5-15.

[89]See discussion in Robert H. Gundry, *Mark: A Commentary on His Apology for the Cross* (Grand Rapids: Eerdmans, 1993), pp. 34-35.

[90]Guelich, "Gospel Genre," pp. 206-7.

[91]Regarding apocryphal gospels such as *Thomas*, Smith observes, "Thomas is not a narrative; it could not, I think by intention, be construed as continuing the biblical story" ("When Did the Gospels Become Scripture?," p. 13).

[92]N. T. Wright, *The New Testament and the People of God* (Minneapolis: Fortress, 1992), p. 218.

[93]John H. Bernard, *A Critical and Exegetical Commentary on the Gospel According to St. John* (Edinburgh: T & T Clark, 1928), and a number of other scholars depending on his work, have suggested that John 21:24 only means that John is a "source" behind the Gospel, but not that he actually wrote it. However, Bauckham makes a compelling argument that γράψας cannot mean that John was a "source" but must mean that the author has directly written it, or dictated it to a secretary (*Jesus and the Eyewitnesses*, pp. 358-62). Others have suggested that John 21:24 only means that the beloved disciple has written the immediately preceding verses. However, even Rudolf Bultmann, *The Gospel of John* (Philadelphia: Westminster, 1971), p. 717n4, acknowledges that John 21:24 "looks back to the gospel" itself. See also Rudolf Schnackenburg, *The Gospel According to St. John* (London: Burns and Oates, 1982), p. 373.

various suggestions about who he might be.[94] However, regardless of which
suggestion one finds most compelling, it is quite clear that this individual is
presented as being part of the inner apostolic circle. He was one of the first
disciples called (Jn 1:35-40[95]), present at the Last Supper (Jn 13:23), present
at the crucifixion (Jn 19:26, 35), and was with Peter and Jesus at the very end
of the Gospel (Jn 21:20). Indeed, the beloved disciple forms an *"inclusio* of
eyewitness testimony" by appearing at the very beginning (Jn 1:35-40) and
very end (Jn 21:20) of the Gospel, very much like Peter functions in the
Gospel of Mark.[96] Bauckham concludes that "the Gospel [of John] presents
the Beloved Disciple as the disciple whose eyewitness reports are the most
important source of the Gospel's historical narrative."[97] Thus, at a minimum,
John 21:24 makes it clear to the reader that the Gospel of John contains apostolic eyewitness testimony (μαρτυρῶν) from someone directly connected
to Jesus' inner circle.[98] But there is more. The beloved disciple's status as an
authoritative "witness" (μαρτυρῶν) who has been there from the beginning
also finds a striking parallel in John 15:27, when Jesus declares to his disciples, "You will also bear witness (μαρτυρεῖτε), because you have been
with me from the beginning (ἀπ' ἀρχῆς)."[99] And the power of this witness

---

[94]For a survey of different positions on the authorship of John (twenty-three of them!), see James
H. Charlesworth, *The Beloved Disciple: Whose Witness Validates the Gospel of John?* (Valley Forge,
PA: Trinity, 1995), pp. 127-224. The traditional view that the beloved disciple was John the
apostle, son of Zebedee, is still held by a number of scholars: Craig S. Keener, *The Gospel of
John* (Peabody, MA: Hendrickson, 2003), 1:83-104; Leon Morris, *The Gospel According to
John* (Grand Rapids: Eerdmans, 1995), pp. 775-77; D. A. Carson, *The Gospel According to John*
(Grand Rapids: Eerdmans, 1991), pp. 682-85; Andreas J. Köstenberger, *John* (BECNT; Grand
Rapids: Baker, 2004), pp. 603-6; and Craig Blomberg, *The Historical Reliability of John's Gospel:
Issues and Commentary* (Downers Grove, IL: IVP Academic, 2001).

[95]Although the phrase "beloved disciple" does not occur here, Bauckham makes a compelling
argument that the parallels between John 1:35-40 and John 21 confirm that the "beloved disciple" is in view in both passages (*Jesus and the Eyewitness*, pp. 390-93).

[96]Ibid., pp. 390-93.

[97]Ibid., p. 393.

[98]Andrew T. Lincoln, "The Beloved Disciple as Eyewitness and the Fourth Gospel as Witness,"
JSNT 85 (2002): 3-26, has challenged the eyewitness role of the beloved disciple and has argued
it is merely a "literary device." For a response, see Bauckham, *Jesus and the Eyewitness*, pp. 386-
88. Benjamin W. Bacon, "The Motivation of John 21:15-25," *JBL* 50 (1931): 71-80, agrees that
John 21:24 is making a claim that the Gospel of John is apostolic but simply denies the historical authenticity of this claim. However, the purpose of this chapter is not to prove that the claim
of John 21:24 is historically accurate—that is another matter entirely. Our concern here is simply to show that the writers of these books *claimed* apostolic authority and that their readers
would have understood that claim.

[99]Bauckham, *Jesus and the Eyewitness*, pp. 389-90.

comes from the Holy Spirit whom Jesus just promised to his disciples in the prior verse (Jn 15:26).[100] It is helpful to see these two verses side by side:

> You will also bear witness (μαρτυρεῖτε) because you have been with me from the beginning. (Jn 15:27)

> This is the disciple who is bearing witness (μαρτυρῶν) about these things, and who has written these things. (Jn 21:24)

Thus, it seems that John 21:24 is a declaration to the reader that Jesus' promise in 15:26-27 to send authoritative witnesses has been fulfilled—*the very book they are reading is the authoritative testimony of Jesus' Spirit-filled disciples.*[101] On the basis of all these connections, Jean Zumstein is able to declare that the Gospel of John "claims to have a status comparable to that which is ordinarily assigned to Scripture."[102] Likewise, Ridderbos sees John 21:24 as evidence that "the beloved disciple has written down his testimony and made it into Scripture."[103]

This conclusion is confirmed when we read John 21:24 alongside John 20:30-31.[104] In the latter passage, the author acknowledges that while not everything is "written in this book" (γεγραμμένα ἐν τῷ βιβλίῳ τούτῳ), that which is written allows a person to "have life in his [Jesus'] name." It is worth noting that this precise phrase γεγραμμένα ἐν τῷ βιβλίῳ τούτῳ occurs in a number of key Old Testament passages clearly referring to the Scriptures themselves:

- Deut 28:58: "careful to do all the words of this law that are written in this book (γεγραμμένα ἐν τῷ βιβλίῳ τούτῳ)"

- 2 Chron 34:21: "do according to all that is written in this book (γεγραμμένα ἐν τῷ βιβλίῳ τούτῳ)"

---

[100]Bultmann, *Gospel of John*, p. 554, declares, "It is perfectly clear that their [the disciples'] witness and that of the Spirit are identical."

[101]Judith Lieu, "How John Writes," in *Written Gospel*, pp. 173-74, makes a very similar point. She argues that John 2:17-22 and John 12:14-16—both passages that speak of the disciples understanding events more clearly at a later point by the help of the Spirit—show the reader that John 15:26-27 is being fulfilled in the very book they are reading.

[102]Jean Zumstein, "La naissance de la notion d'Écriture dans la littérature johannique," in *The Biblical Canons*, ed. J.-M. Auwers and H. J. de Jonge (Leuven: Leuven University Press, 2003), p. 377; translation mine.

[103]Herman Ridderbos, *The Gospel of John* (Grand Rapids: Eerdmans, 1997), p. 671.

[104]For a discussion of the literary connection between John 21:24-25 and John 20:30-31, see Fernando F. Segovia, "The Final Farewell of Jesus: A Reading of John 20:30-21:25," *Sem* 53 (1991): 167-90.

- Jer 25:13: "I will bring upon that land . . . everything written in this book (γεγραμμένα ἐν τῷ βιβλίῳ τούτῳ)"

In addition, this precise phrase occurs in the book of Revelation, which is widely considered to be written consciously as "Scripture."[105] In Revelation 22:18, the author offers an "inscriptional curse"[106] on his writing, warning that it is not to be altered lest one suffer the plagues "described in this book (γεγραμμένας ἐν τῷ βιβλίῳ τούτῳ)." Although such parallels are not definitive,[107] they are at least suggestive that the author of the Gospel of John saw himself in a *prophetic* role—like that of the Old Testament prophets—and therefore was concerned to write down the very words that would allow the reader to "have life in his name" (Jn 20:31). Thus, Keener concludes that John 20:30-31 indicates that "the author of the Fourth gospel may quietly suggest that his work belongs in the same category with the Scriptures of old."[108]

Luke 1:1-4. In a very similar manner to John's Gospel, Luke also makes express claims to be passing down apostolic tradition. In the prologue,[109]

---

[105]McDonald, *Biblical Canon*, p. 31.

[106]See discussion of inscriptional curses in chapter two above.

[107]We can see parallel phrases in Greco-Roman writings on occasion; e.g., Aristides uses the phrase γεγραμμένα ἐν τῷ βιβλίῳ (*Orationes* 26); Plutarch has the similar phrase γράφοντες ἐν τῷ βιβλίῳ τούτῳ (*Demosthenes* 3). So it is possible that it is merely coincidental that John's use of this phrase in John 20:30 is in accord with Old Testament practice. However, given John's Jewish roots, and given the implications already noted regarding John 21:24, the fact that it is a coincidence seems to be less likely. There is also as similar phrase in Ecclesiasticus 50:27, ἐχάραξεν ἐν τῷ βιβλίῳ τούτῳ, but this no doubt reflects the very Old Testament usage we are observing.

[108]Keener, *Gospel of John*, 2:1215. Keener also notes that John 20:31 uses the perfect γέγραπται to refer to his own writing, a term which normally is used by John throughout his Gospel to refer to Scripture (Jn 2:17; 6:31, 45; 8:17; 10:34; 12:14, 16; 15:25). Gottlob Schrenk, "γραφω," *TDNT* 1:745, makes this same observation: "When speaking of the aim of his own writing, i.e., to awaken faith, he can use a word which elsewhere he reserves for OT Scripture, γέγραπται."

[109]Some central works on the prologue of Luke include: Loveday Alexander, *The Preface to Luke's Gospel* (Cambridge: Cambridge University Press, 1993); Vernon K. Robbins, "The Claims of the Prologues and Greco-Roman Rhetoric: the Prefaces to Luke and Acts in Light of Greco-Roman Rhetorical Strategies," in *Jesus and the Heritage of Israel*, ed. David P. Moessner (Harrisburg: Trinity, 1999), pp. 63-83; Schuyler Brown, "The Role of the Prologues in Determining the Purpose of Luke-Acts," in *Perspectives on Luke-Acts*, ed. Charles H. Talbert (Edinburgh: T & T Clark, 1978), pp. 99-111; David E. Aune, "Luke 1:1-4: Historical or Scientific Prooimion?," in *Paul, Luke and the Graeco-Roman World*, ed. Alf Christopherson, et al. (Sheffield: Sheffield Academic Press, 2002), pp. 138-48. For more bibliographical references, see Joel B. Green and Michael C. McKeever, *Luke-Acts and New Testament Historiography* (Grand Rapids: Baker, 1994).

the author claims that the traditions included in his Gospel have been "delivered" (παρέδοσαν) to him by those "who from the beginning were eyewitnesses and ministers of the word" (οἱ ἀπ᾽ ἀρχῆς αὐτόπται καὶ ὑπηρέται γενόμενοι τοῦ λόγου).[110] Some have suggested that this is a reference to two groups, first the "eyewitness" and then later the "ministers of the word," thus making Luke himself a third-generation Christian.[111] However, the fact that the singular article οἱ is used for both terms suggests that they refer to a single group.[112] For this reason, most scholars view the "eyewitnesses and ministers of the word" as a clear reference to the apostles.[113] This conclusion is supported by the fact that elsewhere the ministry of the apostles is described with very similar language:

1. Although Luke uses the rare word "eyewitnesses" (αὐτόπται) in the prologue, Joel Green argues that he probably did this in deference to historiographical concerns and has in mind the general concept of "witnesses" (μάρτυρες), which he uses so commonly elsewhere to describe the role of the apostles.[114] Luke–Acts is filled with references to the apostles as God's foundational "witnesses" to his mighty acts in Christ (Acts 1:8; 3:15; 5:32; 10:39-41; 26:16). Particularly noteworthy is that Luke 24:48, the very end of the Gospel, also describes the apostles as "witnesses" (μάρτυρες), thus

---

[110]Darrell L. Bock, *Luke: Volume 1: 1:9–9:50* (Grand Rapids: Baker, 1994), rightly points out that the structure of Luke 1:1-2 may indicate that the earlier gospel accounts mentioned by Luke were also dependent upon these "eyewitnesses and ministers of the Word" (p. 57). But such an observation does not mean that Luke himself was not dependent on such sources. I. Howard Marshall, *The Gospel of Luke* (Grand Rapids: Eerdmans, 1978), argues that the ἡμῖν in Luke 1:2 "has a narrower reference to Luke and his contemporaries who were dependent on eyewitnesses for their knowledge of the earthly life of Jesus" (p. 41).

[111]Roger Balducelli, "Professor Riesenfeld on Synoptic Tradition," *CBQ* 22 (1960): 416-21. Joseph A. Fitzmyer, *The Gospel According to Luke* (New York: Doubleday, 1985), p. 294, agrees that Luke is third generation, but does not sharply divide the two groups; instead he argues that the first group (the eyewitnesses) later *became* the second group (ministers of the word). For a similar view, see Richard J. Dillon, "Previewing Luke's Project from His Prologue (Luke 1:1-4)," *CBQ* 43 (1981): 205-27.

[112]Bock, *Luke*, p. 58.

[113]Allison Trites, *The New Testament Concept of Witness* (Cambridge: Cambridge University Press, 1977), pp. 136-39. However, Joel B. Green, *The Gospel of Luke* (Grand Rapids: Eerdmans, 1997), p. 42, reminds us that this phrase would have also included those such as Paul and Barnabas who were not part of the original Twelve. Marshall says it well: "They are to be identified with the apostles, although not exclusively with the Twelve" (*Gospel of Luke*, p. 42).

[114]Green, *Gospel of Luke*, p. 41; Bauckham, *Jesus and the Eyewitnesses*, pp. 389-90. John Nolland, *Luke 1:1–9:20* (WBC; Dallas, TX: Word Publishing, 1989), p. 7, links the two concepts together: "Being present as an eyewitness is the basis for becoming a witness."

forming an impressive literary *inclusio* around the whole book. This *inclusio* is strengthened by the fact that in both the beginning and the end of Luke the apostles are witnesses to the same thing: how the Scriptures have been "fulfilled" in the ministry of Christ. In Luke 1:1-2 we are told that apostles were (eye)witnesses to the things which have been "fulfilled" (πεπληροφορημένων) in their midst,[115] and in Luke 24:44 we are told that the apostles were witnesses to things that have been "fulfilled" (πληρωθῆναι) in their midst (compare Lk 24:48). Such an *inclusio* suggests that Luke intends his Gospel to be taken as an apostolic witness to how the Old Testament Scriptures have been realized and completed by the ministry of Jesus Christ. In this sense, Luke's writings could be conceived as a "sequel" to the historical narrative of the Old Testament. As Marshall observes, "[Luke] regarded his work as depicting the continuation of the history recorded in the Old Testament."[116] Craig Evans makes the same point: "[Luke] intends his writing to be read alongside of the biblical story; indeed he believes it has become part of the story."[117]

2. Acts 1:22 describes the two main characteristics of apostles—namely that they must be present from the "beginning" (ἀρξάμενος) and must be foundational "witnesses" (μάρτυρα) to the resurrection. This forms a striking parallel with those "who from the beginning were eyewitnesses" in Luke 1:2 (compare Acts 10:37). Additionally, this same combination occurs in John 15:27, when Jesus describes his disciples, "And you also will bear witness (μαρτυρεῖτε), because you have been with me from the beginning (ἀπ᾽ ἀρχῆς)."[118]

3. As Luke describes the commission that Jesus gave to the apostle Paul in Acts 26:16, he describes Paul as a "minister and witness" (NASB; ὑπηρέτην καὶ μάρτυρα), quite similar to the "eyewitnesses and ministers" (αὐτόπται καὶ ὑπηρέται) in Luke 1:2.

4. Acts 6:4 refers to the apostles as those devoted to "the ministry of the word" (τῇ διακονίᾳ τοῦ λόγου), a phrase strikingly similar to that of Luke

---

[115]Bock, *Luke*, p. 57; Marshall, *Gospel of Luke*, p. 41; Fitzmyer, *Gospel According to Luke*, p. 293.

[116]I. Howard Marshall, *Luke: Historian and Theologian* (Grand Rapids: Zondervan, 1970), p. 56.

[117]Craig A. Evans, "Luke and the Rewritten Bible: Aspects of Lukan Hagiography," in *The Pseudepigrapha and Early Biblical Interpretation*, ed. James H. Charlesworth and Craig A. Evans (Sheffield: JSOT Press, 1993), p. 200.

[118]Bauckham, *Jesus and the Eyewitness*, pp. 389-90.

1:2 where they are described as "ministers of the word" (ὑπηρέται τοῦ λόγου). Indeed, as noted above in our discussion of 1 Thessalonians 2:13, the "word" is typically used throughout the New Testament to describe the authoritative apostolic message.[119] Fitzmyer comments on the use of this phrase in Luke 1:2: "Even though 'the word' may be intended here merely as a 'general term applicable to the story of Christian origins' . . . The use which the absolute form *ho logos* acquires in Acts (for example, [Acts] 8:4; 10:36; 11:19; 14:25; compare Lk 8:12-15) gives it the significant overtone of the 'word of God.'"[120] It should be observed that, in Acts 1:1, Luke looks back and describes his own Gospel account with this same term (τὸν λόγον).

5. As also observed in the discussion of 1 Thessalonians 2:13 above, such language like παρέδοσαν ("delivered") in Luke 1:2 is used widely throughout the New Testament to speak of the passing along or handing down of apostolic tradition.[121]

All these considerations suggest that Luke is presenting his Gospel as the embodiment of the authoritative apostolic "word" that had been delivered and entrusted to him. Of course, Luke acknowledges that he is constructing his own account of this tradition[122]—he is offering an "orderly" (καθεξῆς) arrangement.[123] Even so, Luke does not write as a third-generation outsider, but as one who has received his material directly from the apostles. David Moessner makes the point that the word παρηκολουθηκότι is not so much an indication that Luke "investigated" these things but

---

[119]Pahl, "The 'Gospel' and the 'Word,'" pp. 211-27.

[120]Fitzmyer, *Gospel According to Luke*, p. 295.

[121]E.g., Acts 16:4; 1 Corinthians 11:2, 23; 15:3; 2 Peter 2:21; Jude 3.

[122]Evans, "Luke and the Rewritten Bible," pp. 170-201, argues that Luke is intentionally rewriting the "sacred tradition" that he has received in imitation of the technique of the author of Chronicles (and other hagiographa). When such sacred tradition is rewritten, it is normal for the author to edit, expand and modify material according to theological needs of his audience. Thus, Luke's rewriting of the tradition should not be taken as evidence that Luke regarded that tradition as insufficient or problematic. Similarly, Nolland, *Luke 1:1-9:20*, pp. 6-12, argues rightly against the notion that Luke's decision to write is somehow driven by his belief that prior accounts were somehow deficient or flawed. Luke gives no indication of criticism of those who came before him but only that it seemed good "to me also" (κἀμοί). See further discussion in Alexander, *Preface*, pp. 201-2.

[123]Michael D. Goulder, *The Evangelist's Calendar: A Lectionary Explanation of the Development of Scripture* (London: SPCK, 1978), pp. 8-13, suggests that Luke's intention to produce an "orderly" (καθεξῆς) arrangement is best understood as Luke producing a gospel that can be read in the proper liturgical order in public worship. If so, then this is an additional indicator that Luke was intentionally written as a "scriptural" sort of document.

rather that he is "one who 'has been steeped' or 'trained' in those particular traditions."[124] Thus, Luke presents himself as having been instructed in "all" (πᾶσιν) these traditions "for some time" (ἄνωθεν)—most likely from the apostle Paul (and perhaps others).[125] In this way, Luke gives the reader the "distinguishing credential"[126] for why he should be trusted. He speaks with an apostolic voice.

It is particularly revelant for Luke to produce these apostolic credentials if he is to accomplish the *purpose* for which he is writing, namely that Theophilus might have "certainty" (ἀσφάλειαν) concerning the "things you have been taught" (κατηχήθης λόγων). Bock argues that such language indicates that Theophilus is a believer (perhaps newly converted) who needs reassurance about the "teaching he had previously received."[127] Similarly, Marshall argues that Theophilus likely was the recipient of formal Christian catechetical (κατηχήθης) instruction.[128] If so, then Luke is not writing simply to restate raw historical facts, but is writing with a

---

[124]David P. Moessner, "How Luke Writes," in *Written Gospel*, p. 165. See also idem, "'Eyewitnesses,' 'Informed Contemporaries,' and 'Unknowing Inquirers': Josephus' Criteria for Authentic Historiography and the Meaning of ΠΑΡΑΚΟΛΟΥΘΕΩ," *NovT* 38 (1996): 105-22. In agreement is Alexander, *Preface*, pp. 34-41; and Bauckham, *Jesus and the Eyewitnesses*, p. 123. Bock, *Luke*, p. 60; and Fitzmyer, *Gospel According to Luke*, pp. 296-97, disagree and argue that παρηκολουθηκότι means "investigate." However, these different views may not be as far apart as some think. Bock agrees that the term can mean that Luke "followed along" or "studied" these things (p. 60). That is quite similar to the view we are advocating here, namely that Luke presents himself as a student or studier of these traditions (under the tutelage of the apostles). In other words, Luke was "trained." While the term "investigate" captures some of these same ideas, it gives the impression that Luke was "discovering" or maybe "uncovering" the story of Jesus on his own, whereas the prologue makes it clear that Luke clearly "received" (παρέδοσαν) his core information from the apostles. In addition, the term ἀκριβῶς ("carefully") is not as decisive as some suggest. It is quite possible to understand Luke as saying that he "studied/ followed all these things *carefully* from the start."

[125]Moessner, "How Luke Writes," p. 166, suggests that Luke may have Paul in mind in Luke 1:2 because he uses the phrase ὑπηρέται ("servant"), which he later applies to Paul in Acts 26:16.

[126]Ibid., p. 165.

[127]Bock, *Luke*, p. 66. Although some older commentators have suggested that Theophilus is a Roman official (e.g, J. Norval Geldenhuys, *Commentary on the Gospel of Luke* [London: Marshall, Morgan & Scott, 1950], p. 53) it should be noted that Theophilus is a common name among Jews and Greeks and that the title κράτιστε ("most excellent") could simply be an honorary address to someone important, not necessarily a Roman official (Josephus, *Life* 430; *Ag. Ap.* 1.1).

[128]Marshall, *Gospel of Luke*, p. 43. Green, *Gospel of Luke*, pp. 45-46, disagrees and argues that formal catechetical instruction could not be dated so early. However, Marshall recognizes that the instruction that Theophilus received was not "the rigorous catechumenate of a later age"; even so, "new converts were doubtless given careful training in the faith" (*Gospel of Luke*, p. 43).

"theological intention."[129] Luke is presenting his Gospel as an apostolic
source for encouraging and reassuring Christians about the good news
they have believed—that is, it was a book written for the church. It was not
just history, but *salvation-history*.[130] As Fitzmyer observes, Luke's Gospel
"is not that of a secular Hellenistic historian . . . [but] far more in the mode
of OT biblical history."[131]

All of these considerations suggest Luke is presenting his Gospel as an
apostolic document designed to show how Christ completes the story of
the Old Testament and thereby to bolster confidence in foundational
Christian truths. Evans sums it up: "Luke does not see himself primarily as
a biographer, nor even a historian. The Lukan evangelist is a writer of
Scripture, a hagiographer who is proclaiming what God has 'accomplished
among us.'"[132]

Matthew 1. Unlike the other three Gospels, Matthew contains fewer
internal clues that it is passing along apostolic tradition (Mt 9:9; 10:3).[133]
Nevertheless, there are still indications that this Gospel was written with
the intention of completing the Old Testament story.[134] Most notable in
this regard is the unique way that Matthew begins his Gospel, with an

---

[129]Fitzmyer, *Gospel According to Luke*, p. 290.

[130]I do not use the term "salvation history" in the manner made popular by Hans Conzelmann,
Theology of St. Luke (New York: Harper & Row, 1960). Instead, I am using it to refer to the
Gospel as the bearer of the salvific message—i.e., the Gospel of Luke is *both* history and theol-
ogy. For more on this issue, see Marshall, *Luke: Historian and Theologian*; and Oscar Cullmann,
Salvation in History (London: SCM, 1967).

[131]Fitzmyer, *Gospel According to Luke*, p. 290.

[132]Evans, "Luke and the Rewritten Bible," p. 201. It is worth noting that there is some evidence
Luke was regarded as "Scripture" quite early. 1 Timothy 5:18 cites "The laborer deserves his
wages" and introduces it with "For the Scripture says." Although it's possible that 1 Timothy
5:18 may be citing some apocryphal source, the only known match for this citation is Luke
10:7. One must at least consider the possibility that 1 Timothy is citing Luke's Gospel as Scripture. See discussion in John P. Meier, "The Inspiration of Scripture: But What Counts as Scripture?," *Mid-Stream* 38 (1999): 71-78. On an additional note, C. K. Barrett, "The First New
Testament?," *NovT* 38 (1996): 94-104, seems to share the notion that Luke–Acts was written as
a Scripture of sorts when he declares that "the author accepts the Old Testament, and provides,
to accompany it, an *explanatory and interpretative parallel book*—we may call it, though Luke
did not, a New Testament" (p. 102, emphasis mine).

[133]For a discussion of the authorship of Matthew, see R. T. France, *Matthew: Evangelist and
Teacher* (Grand Rapids: Zondervan, 1989), pp. 50-80; and Ned B. Stonehouse, *The Origins of
the Synoptic Gospels* (Grand Rapids: Baker, 1963), pp. 1-47.

[134]Smith, "When Did the Gospels Become Scripture?," pp. 7-8. For more on Matthew's Scripture-
like style, see E. P. Sanders and Margaret Davies, *Studying the Synoptic Gospels* (London: SCM,
1989), pp. 258-65.

opening "title" (Mt 1:1) followed by a genealogy (Mt 1:2-17). Davies and
Allison argue that Matthew's very first phrase, Βίβλος γενέσεως, is not so
much a reference to the genealogy that follows but to the book as a
whole.[135] This is the way the phrase is used in Genesis 2:4 and 5:1; it does
not refer to a genealogy per se but to the primeval history of God's
people.[136] In addition, argue Davies and Allison, the term γενέσεως
would naturally lead the reader to think of the LXX title of the book of
Genesis, Γένεσις. They comment, "Genesis was a Βίβλος, and its name
was Γένεσις. One is therefore led to ask whether the introductory use of
Βίβλος γενέσεως would not have caused Matthew's readers to think of
the Torah's first book and to anticipate that some sort of 'new genesis,' a
genesis of Jesus Christ, would follow."[137] Thus, the opening phrase of
Matthew is best understood as "Book of the New Genesis wrought by
Jesus Christ."[138] Such a beginning suggests that Matthew is intentionally
writing in a scriptural style—he viewed his book, and wanted his au-
dience to view his book, as continuing the biblical story. Thus Willi
Marxsen is able to declare, "By means of this phrase therefore the work
[Matthew] is presented almost as 'Holy Scripture'—by analogy with the
Old Testament."[139]

The fact that Matthew appears to be molding his Gospel after the pattern
of Old Testament books is confirmed by the fact that he turns immediately
to a genealogy, placing the Jesus story into the story of Israel, with a special
emphasis on David.[140] The genealogy, of course, is a well-known Old Testament genre that is frequently used to demonstrate the historical un-

---

[135]W. D. Davies and Dale C. Allison, *The Gospel According to Saint Matthew* (ICC; Edinburgh: T
& T Clark, 1997), pp. 150-53. In agreement is Leon Morris, *The Gospel According to Matthew*
(Grand Rapids: Eerdmans, 1992), pp. 18-19.

[136]Davies and Allison, *Matthew*, p. 150. Even though Genesis 5:1 is followed by a genealogy, Davies and Allison point out that (1) this is more of a history than a genealogy; and (2) it is a list
of descendants as opposed to a list of ancestors like in Matthew.

[137]Ibid., p. 151.

[138]Ibid., p. 153. R. T. France, *The Gospel of Matthew* (NICNT; Grand Rapids: Eerdmans, 2007),
translates this phrase as "book of genesis" (p. 28); however, he does not view it as a title for the
Gospel as a whole.

[139]Willi Marxsen, *Introduction to the New Testament: An Approach to Its Problems* (Philadelphia:
Westminster, 1968), p. 151.

[140]The focus on the number fourteen in the genealogy may be an instance of *gematria*, as the letters of the name "David" add up to fourteen. In addition, David is the fourteenth name on the
list. See discussion in Davies and Allison, *Matthew*, pp. 161-65.

folding of God's redemptive activities among his people.[141] In this regard, Matthew's closest parallel is the book of Chronicles, which also begins with a genealogy that has an emphasis on the Davidic line.[142] If by the first century Chronicles was regarded as the final book in the Hebrew canon, as some scholars have argued,[143] then Matthew's Gospel would certainly be a fitting sequel. An Old Testament canon ending with Chronicles would have served as a reminder to the Jews that Israel's return from exile documented in Ezra–Nehemiah is not the full story—it is only a physical return, not a spiritual one. The hearts of the people still needed to be changed. Israel remained in spiritual exile.[144] Such an ending would have placed Israel in an eschatological posture, looking ahead to the time when the Messiah, the son of David, would come to Jerusalem and bring full deliverance to his people.[145]

If so, then Matthew's opening chapter would be a clear indication that he is intending to finish this story. He is picking up where the Old Testament ended, with a focus on David and the deliverance of Israel. Moreover, the Great Commission at the very end of Matthew's Gospel (Mt 28:18-20) is a vivid echo of the end of 2 Chronicles (2 Chron 36:23), leading Greg Beale to argue that "Matthew constructs his Gospel partly to reflect the beginning and ending of Chronicles."[146] Regardless of whether one accepts that Chron-

---

[141]Of course, there are also examples of genealogies in nonbiblical literature. For more, see Gerard Mussies, "Parallels to Matthew's Version of the Pedigree of Jesus," *NovT* 28 (1986): 32-47; and Marshall D. Johnson, *The Purpose of Biblical Genealogies, with Special Reference to the Setting of the Genealogies of Jesus* (Cambridge: Cambridge University Press, 1969).

[142]Robert H. Gundry, *Matthew: A Commentary on His Handbook for a Mixed Church Under Persecution* (Grand Rapids: Eerdmans, 1994), pp. 13-19, argues that much of Matthew's genealogy is dependent on Chronicles 1-3.

[143]As mentioned on p. 50n12, there are good reasons to think a threefold division of the canon was in place by the first century; Luke 24:44; Sir 39:1; 4QMMT (95–96); Philo, *Contempl. Life* 25.

[144]For discussion of Israel as still in exile, see N. T. Wright, *New Testament and the People of God*, pp. 268-79; Craig Evans, "Aspects of Exile and Restoration in the Proclamation of Jesus and the Gospels," in *Exile: Old Testament, Jewish, and Christian Conceptions*, ed. James M. Scott (Leiden: E. J. Brill, 1997), pp. 299-328; Craig A. Evans, "Jesus and the Continuing Exile of Israel," in *Jesus & the Restoration of Israel: A Critical Assessment of N. T. Wright's Jesus & the Victory of God*, ed. Carey C. Newman (Downers Grove, IL: IVP Academic, 1999), pp. 77-100; and Stephen G. Dempster, *Dominion and Dynasty: A Biblical Theology of the Hebrew Bible* (Downers Grove, IL: IVP Academic, 2003), pp. 224-27.

[145]Nahum Sarna, "Bible," in *Encyclopedia Judaica* III:832.

[146]G. K. Beale, *The Temple and the Church's Mission: A Biblical Theology of the Dwelling Place of God* (Downers Grove, IL: IVP Academic, 2004), p. 177. The connection to 2 Chronicles 36:23 is disputed by Davies and Allison, *Matthew*, p. 679.

icles was the final book in the Hebrew canon, the close connections between Matthew and Chronicles remain. Indeed, on this basis, Davies and Allison conclude that Matthew "thought of his gospel as a continuation of the biblical history—and also, perhaps, that he conceived of his work as belonging to the same literary category as the scriptural cycles treating of OT figures."[147]

If indeed Matthew is intending to record God's long-awaited deliverance of his people Israel—a second exodus, if you will—then it should come as little surprise that Matthew is so keen to portray Jesus as a second Moses. Such Moses typology in the Gospel of Matthew is well-documented; for example, Jesus' life is threatened as a baby and yet he is rescued (Ex 2:1-10; Mt 2:1-18); Jesus recapitulates the original exodus from Egypt (Hos 11:1; Mt 2:15); Jesus has a time of hidden preparation prior to public ministry (Ex 3:1; Mt 2:23; 3:13); Jesus launches his ministry by passing through waters of baptism in the desert (Ex 14; Mt 3:13-17; compare 1 Cor 10:2); Jesus performs miracles and feeds the people in the wilderness (Ex 16; Num 11; Mt 14:13-20), and so on.[148] It is particularly noteworthy that in Matthew 5:1 Jesus delivers his "law" after ἀνέβη εἰς τὸ ὄρος καὶ καθίσαντος ("he went up on the mountain, and . . . sat down"). With this same language, Moses is regularly portrayed as going up to the mountain to receive God's law (Ex 19:3, 12-13; 24:12, 13, 18; 34:2; Num 27:12; Deut 1:24, 41, 43; 5:5; 9:9), and even is described as having sat down there (Deut 9:9; compare b. Meg. 21a; b. Soṭah 49a).[149] Such imagery surely has implications for how the teachings of Jesus in the Gospel of Matthew (and the Gospel as a whole) are to be received. Jesus is presented as the new (and ultimate) deliverer with a new and authoritative law from God. This has even led Smith and others to reconsider the possibility that Matthew divides up his Gospel into five main teaching discourses in order to parallel the five books of Moses, thereby presenting his Gospel as the "definitive revelation" of Jesus.[150]

---

[147]Davies and Allison, Matthew, p. 187.
[148]For more on Moses typology, see Dale C. Allison, The New Moses: A Matthean Typology (Edinburgh: T & T Clark, 1993); Vern S. Poythress, The Shadow of Christ in the Law of Moses (Phillipsburg, NJ: P & R, 1991); Sanders and Davies, Studying the Synoptic Gospels, pp. 260-61; and Meredith G. Kline, "The Old Testament Origins of the Gospel Genre," WTJ 38 (1975): 1-27. For a broader look at images of Moses in the New Testament, see John Lierman, The New Testament Moses (Tübingen: Mohr Siebeck, 2004).
[149]Davies and Allison, Matthew, pp. 423-24.
[150]Smith, "When Did the Gospels Become Scripture?," p. 8. The thesis that Matthew is a new

OTHER NEW TESTAMENT WRITINGS

Although there is not enough space available to treat every remaining book in the New Testament corpus, we shall highlight a few more places where the author seems aware of the apostolic authority of his own writing.

Hebrews 2:1-4. When it comes to the book of Hebrews, the identity of the author has dominated scholarly discussions.[151] Rather than following Origen's wise conclusion that "But who wrote the epistle, in truth God knows,"[152] scholars have continued to make suggestions ranging from Apollos[153] to Priscilla[154] to Luke.[155] Unfortunately, such a limited focus has led many to overlook a far more important fact about the author, namely that he presents himself as directly dependent upon apostolic tradition. When referring to the "great salvation" that his letter explores, the author indicates that this message of salvation "was declared at first by the Lord, and it was attested (ἐβεβαιώθη) to us (εἰς ἡμᾶς) by those who heard, while God also bore witness by signs and wonders and various miracles and by gifts of the Holy Spirit" (Heb 2:3-4). There is little doubt that "those who heard" directly from Jesus is a reference to the apostles themselves, whose own ministry was accompanied by signs, wonders and manifestations of the Spirit (Acts 2:43; 4:30; 5:12; 6:8; 14:3; 15:12; Rom 15:19; 2 Cor 12:12; compare Lk 1:2).[156] The use of the term ἐβεβαιώθη ("attested") highlights the authority of these individuals; they did not simply speak the message to our

---

Pentateuch was originally suggested by Benjamin W. Bacon, "The Five Books of Matthew Against the Jews," *Exp* 15 (1918): 56-66. For a fuller analysis of Bacon's view, see France, *Matthew: Evangelist and Teacher*, pp. 142-45. One need not accept Bacon's thesis in order to recognize that Matthew is presenting the teachings of Jesus (and therefore his Gospel) as new revelation from God.

[151]For a survey of the authorship issue, see F. F. Bruce, *The Epistle to the Hebrews* (Grand Rapids: Eerdmans, 1990), pp. 14-20; Philip E. Hughes, *A Commentary on the Epistle to the Hebrews* (Grand Rapids: Eerdmans, 1990), pp. 19-30; Paul Ellingworth, *The Epistle to the Hebrews* (NICNT; Grand Rapids: Eerdmans, 1993), p. 320; and Craig R. Koester, *Hebrews* (The Anchor Bible; New York: Doubleday, 2001), pp. 42-46.

[152]*Hist. eccl.* 6.25.14.

[153]Ellingworth, *Hebrews*, p. 21.

[154]Adolf von Harnack, "Probabilia über die Addresse und den Verfasser des Hebräerbriefes," *ZNW* 1 (1900): 16-41.

[155]David L. Allen, *Lukan Authorship of Hebrews* (Nashville: B & H Academic, 2010).

[156]Bruce, *Hebrews*, pp. 68-69; George W. Buchanan, *To the Hebrews* (The Anchor Bible; New York: Doubleday, 1981), p. 25; Pamela M. Eisenbaum, "Locating Hebrews Within the Literary Landscape of Christian Origins," in *Hebrews: Contemporary Methods, New Insights*, ed. Gabriella Gelardini (Leiden: E. J. Brill, 2005), pp. 227-28.

author, but they "confirmed"[157] or "validated"[158] or "guaranteed"[159] the message to him. The phrase "to us" (εἰς ἡμᾶς) need not imply that the author received this apostolic tradition together with his audience; the same plural language is used in Luke 1:2 and 1 John 1:2 and does not require the inclusion of the audience.[160]

Thus, the author portrays himself as being in a very similar position to that of Mark or Luke—authoritative apostolic testimony has been entrusted to him and he is now passing it along to his readers. As Donald Hagner observes, "In this regard he [the author of Hebrews] may be likened to Luke."[161] Likewise, George Buchanan observes that the author was delivering what "he had received directly from the apostles themselves."[162] The connection between our author and the apostolic circle is confirmed by the fact that his traveling companion is none other than Timothy (Heb 13:23), likely to be the Timothy who knew and travelled with Paul and Silas (Acts 16:3; 17:14; Rom 16:21; 1 Cor 4:17; 2 Cor 1:19).[163] If so, then our author, although not a direct eyewitness to Jesus, presents himself as an apostolic coworker who participated directly in the apostolic mission. This stands in contrast to writers such as Ignatius[164] and Clement of Rome,[165] who sharply distinguish between the apostolic time period and their own time period. They look back to the ministry of the apostles and do not present themselves as having participated in it. Thus we should not be surprised if the earliest Christians would have received Hebrews as an apostolic book. Indeed, Origen understood the book in precisely this way when he suggested it was written by someone who was part of the apostolic circle, likely a companion and disciple of Paul himself.[166] This would explain why He-

---

[157]The NASB and NIV translate ἐβεβαιώθη as "confirmed."

[158]Heinrich Schlier, "βέβαιος, βεβαιόω" in TDNT 1:600-603.

[159]William L. Lane, Hebrews 1–8 (WBC; Waco, TX: Word, 1991), p. 39, translates ἐβεβαιώθη as "guaranteed."

[160]Hughes, Hebrews, pp. 77-78. Marshall argues that the ἡμῖν in Luke 1:2 "has a narrower reference to Luke and his contemporaries who were dependent on eyewitnesses for their knowledge of the earthly life of Jesus" (Gospel of Luke, p. 41). For discussion of 1 John 1:2, see next section below.

[161]Donald A. Hagner, Hebrews (NIBC; Peabody, MA: Hendrickson, 1993), p. 41.

[162]Buchanan, To the Hebrews, p. 25.

[163]Hughes, Hebrews, pp. 592-93.

[164]Ign. Rom. 4:4.

[165]1 Clem. 42:1-2.

[166]Hist. eccl. 6.25.13.

brews was so closely associated with the apostle within early Christianity.[167] In addition to the authorial claims of this book, it should also be observed that the author actually presents the terms of the new covenant (through Christ) in the same mode and manner as the terms of the old covenant (through Moses) were presented in the book of Deuteronomy.[168] In his recent study, David Allen not only demonstrates that Hebrews is dependent on the text and motifs of Deuteronomy, but he also shows that the entire structure of Deuteronomy—and its call for God's people to choose between life and death—is "re-presented" in Hebrews with a Christocentric purpose.[169] As a result, Allen concludes that Hebrews "does not just use Deuteronomy, it becomes a new Deuteronomy."[170] In essence, the book of Hebrews reworks Deuteronomy and reshapes the story of Israel for a new generation, thereby becoming a new torah.[171]

2 Peter 3:2. An oft-overlooked text in the discussion of the canon is 2 Peter 3:2, in which the reader is asked to submit to "the predictions of the holy prophets and the commandment of the Lord and Savior through your apostles." The manner in which the author[172] juxtaposes "prophets" of the old covenant and the "apostles" of the new covenant shows that he views

---

[167]For an analysis of Hebrews's journey into the canon, and its association with Paul, see William H. P. Hatch, "The Position of Hebrews in the Canon of the New Testament," *HTR* 29 (1936): 133-51. On connections with Paul, see also Dieter Georgi, "Hebrews and the Heritage of Paul," in *Hebrews: Contemporary Methods, New Insights*, ed. Gabriella Gelardini (Leiden: E. J. Brill, 2005), pp. 241-44. If Luke were the author of Hebrews, then this would explain the Pauline connections; see Allen, *Lukan Authorship of Hebrews*.

[168]David M. Allen, *Deuteronomy & Exhortation in Hebrews: A Study in Re-presentation* (Tübingen: Mohr Siebeck, 2008).

[169]Ibid., pp. 214-16.

[170]Ibid., p. 225.

[171]Ibid., p. 213.

[172]The debate over the authorship of 2 Peter is not relevant to our immediate point here because we are only discussing whether the author presents his writings as authoritative or not. For the various positions on this issue, see Richard Bauckham, *Jude, 2 Peter* (Waco, TX: Word, 1983), p. 158; Bo Reicke, *The Epistles of James, Peter, and Jude* (The Anchor Bible; New York: Doubleday, 1964); J. N. D. Kelly, *A Commentary on the Epistles of Peter and of Jude* (New York: Harper & Row, 1969), p. 237; C. E. B. Cranfield, *I & II Peter and Jude: Introduction and Commentary* (London: SCM, 1960), p. 149; Joseph B. Mayor, *The Epistle of St. Jude and the Second Epistle of St. Peter* (London: Macmillan, 1907), p. cxxvii; Daniel J. Harrington, *Jude and 2 Peter* (Collegeville, MN: Liturgical Press, 2003), p. 237; Michael J. Kruger, "The Authenticity of 2 Peter," *JETS* 42 (1999): 645-71; E. M. B. Green, *2 Peter Reconsidered* (London: Tyndale, 1960); and Donald Guthrie, *New Testament Introduction* (Downers Grove, IL: IVP Academic, 1990), p. 805-42.

them as two equal sources of divine authority.[173] This suggests that 2 Peter understands divine revelation to be in two distinct phases or epochs— perhaps an allusion to the beginnings of a bicovenantal canon.[174] Given that the "predictions of the holy prophets" is a clear reference to written texts (Old Testament Prophets),[175] we must at least consider the possibility that the "commandment of the Lord (ἐντολῆς τοῦ κυρίου) . . . through your apostles" might be a reference (at least in part) to written texts.[176] The immediate context lends support to this possibility when just a few verses later the author refers to *written apostolic texts*, namely Paul's letters, and even regards them as Scripture (2 Pet 3:16).[177] In fact, the phrase ἐντολῆς τοῦ κυρίου finds a notable parallel in Paul: "If anyone thinks that he is a prophet, or spiritual, he should acknowledge that the things I am writing to you are a *command of the Lord* (κυρίου ἐντολή)" (1 Cor 14:37).

In addition, just one verse earlier, our author refers to another written apostolic text, namely his own prior letter (2 Pet 3:1; compare 1 Pet 1:1).[178] Now, if the author of 2 Peter regards written apostolic texts as authoritative Scripture (2 Pet 3:16), and he believes that his readers should submit to the commands of the apostles (2 Pet 3:2), then that has implications for his *own* writings given that he explicitly refers to himself as an apostle (2 Pet 1:1) and recounts his eyewitness apostolic credentials (2 Pet 1:16-18). Are we to think that the author of 2 Peter intended Paul's letters to be regarded as authoritative but not his own? Would the readers of 2 Peter have regarded Paul's apostolic writings as authoritative but disregarded the authority of the very

---

[173]Bauckham, *Jude, 2 Peter*, p. 288.

[174]Denis M. Farkasfalvy, "'Prophets and Apostles': The Conjunction of the Two Terms Before Irenaeus," in *Texts and Testaments: Critical Essays on the Bible and the Early Church Fathers*, ed. W. Eugene March (San Antonio: Trinity University Press, 1980), p. 120, argues that this text "appears to sketch a theology of the Canon, or, as I prefer to call it, a theology of the 'pre-Canon' or 'proto-Canon.'"

[175]Attempts to make "prophets" here refer to New Testament prophets has been roundly rejected; see Bauckham, *Jude, 2 Peter*, p. 287.

[176]The reference in 2 Peter 3:2 to the singular "commandment" of the apostles has confused some. Harrington, *Jude and 2 Peter*, sums it up well when he declares, "[The command] refers not so much to one commandment (e.g., the love command) but rather to the substance of the Christian faith proclaimed by the apostles" (pp. 281-82).

[177]For more discussion of this passage as it pertains to the development of the canon, see Michael J. Kruger, *Canon Revisited: Establishing the Origins and Authority of the New Testament Books* (Wheaton, IL: Crossway, 2012), pp. 204-5.

[178]This prior letter was most likely 1 Peter, but it does not matter for our point here. For a survey of different opinions on this question, see Bauckham, *Jude, 2 Peter*, pp. 285-86.

apostolic writing they were reading (especially given Peter's status in early Christianity)? No, all these factors indicate that the author of 2 Peter not only regarded Paul's writings as supremely authoritative, but would have regarded his own writings with the same authority.

1 John 1:1-4. The apostolic authority of John's first epistle is evident from the opening verses:

> That which was from the beginning, which we have heard, which we have seen with our eyes, which we have looked at and have touched with our hands, concerning the Word of life—the life was made manifest, and we have seen it, and testify (μαρτυροῦμεν) to it and proclaim (ἀπαγγέλλομεν) to you the eternal life (1 Jn 1:1-2).

A number of aspects of these verses support the fact that the author is putting forth his apostolic credentials: (1) The epistle employs vivid eye-witness language—hearing, seeing, even touching—confirming the fact that the author was present to witness the ministry of Jesus from the be-ginning (ἀρχῆς[179]) and thus fits the criteria of an apostle (compare Lk 1:2; 24:48; Acts 1:21-22; 4:20).[180] Marshall observes, "There cannot be any real doubt that the writer claims to have been an eyewitness of the earthly min-istry of Jesus."[181] (2) As an eyewitness, the author is able to do something else that is central to the apostolic office, namely to "testify" or to be a "witness" (μαρτυροῦμεν) to what he has seen and heard. As noted above, the New Testament is filled with references to the apostles as Christ's foun-dational witnesses (Lk 24:48; Acts 1:8; 1:22; 3:15; 5:32; 10:39-41; 26:16). Par-ticularly noteworthy is that John's Gospel—to which this letter clearly al-ludes in these opening verses[182]—portrays the apostles as witnesses (Jn 15:27; 21:24). (3) The apostolic identity of the author is further confirmed by

---

[179]F. F. Bruce, *The Epistles of John: Introduction, Exposition and Notes* (Grand Rapids: Eerdmans, 1984), pp. 34-35, observes that although the ἀρχῆς of 1 John 1:1 obviously connects the reader back to John 1:1, the two words are used differently. The former is used for the beginning of Jesus' earthly ministry, whereas the latter marks the beginning of creation. Thus, there is a strong connection between 1 John 1:1 and Luke 1:2, as both refer to apostles as those who were with Christ "from the beginning." Rudolf Bultmann, *The Johannine Epistles* (Hermenia; Phila-delphia: Fortress, 1973), p. 8, agrees and adds the observation that John 1:1 has "in the begin-ning" (ἐν ἀρχῇ) whereas 1 John 1:1 has "from the beginning" (ἀπ' ἀρχῆς).

[180]Gary M. Burge, *The Letters of John* (NIVAC; Grand Rapids: Zondervan, 1996), p. 54.

[181]I. Howard Marshall, *The Epistles of John* (Grand Rapids: Eerdmans, 1978), p. 106.

[182]Marshall, *Epistles of John*, p. 100. The fact that 1 John uses the word ἀρχή in the very first verse would no doubt draw a connection to John 1:1.

the fact that he does not only testify/witness, but also takes on the more authoritative task of "proclaiming" (ἀπαγγέλλομεν). Stott notes, "In order to testify, the apostles must have seen and heard Christ for themselves; in order to proclaim they must have received a commission from him."[183] (4) The author describes his message as τοῦ λόγου τῆς ζωῆς ("the word of life").[184] As noted above, the *word* is typically used throughout the New Testament to describe the authoritative apostolic message (Lk 1:2; Acts 6:4; 1 Thess 2:13).[185] No doubt the "word of life" is also an allusion to Jesus himself (John 1:1); but there is no need to choose between these options for "the message and the person are ultimately identical."[186] (5) The author uses the collective "we"—a reference to the fact that he is speaking not simply as an individual, but as part of a distinctive group that has been commissioned to "witness" and "proclaim" the "word of life."[187] Again, it is difficult to avoid the implication that the apostles are in view here. F. F. Bruce comments, "The language John uses is the language of apostolic witness."[188] (6) The authority of the author's message is bolstered in 1 John 1:5 when he states that he received his message directly from Jesus himself: "This is the message *we have heard from him* and proclaim to you." In other words, the author wants to make it clear that his message is actually Christ's message and therefore bears his authority.

When taken as a whole, all these considerations suggest that the author is plainly putting forth his apostolic credentials. With that foundation laid, he is then able to declare, "And we are writing (γράφομεν) these things so that our joy may be complete" (1 Jn 1:4). Thus, we have a clear example again of the apostolic message being put into *written* form (compare Jn 20:31; 21:24) which would have been received by its readers as authoritative as the apostles themselves. Such language led Bultmann to affirm, "The author of

---

[183]John R. W. Stott, *The Letters of John* (Grand Rapids: Eerdmans, 1996), p. 67.

[184]Bultmann, *Johannine Epistles*, p. 8, points out that the neuter relative pronoun ὅ in 1:3 indicates that the message/good news is primarily in view.

[185]Pahl, "The 'Gospel' and the 'Word,'" pp. 211-27.

[186]Marshall, *Epistles of John*, p. 102. For more on the debate about the meaning of *word* in 1 John's prologue, see J. Emmette Weir, "The Identity of the Logos in the First Epistle of John," *ExpT* 86 (1974/1975): 118-20; and K. Grayston, "'Logos' in 1 John 1:1," *ExpT* 86 (1974/1975): 279.

[187]Bruce, *Epistles of John*, pp. 35-38; Robert W. Yarbrough, *1-3 John* (BECNT; Grand Rapids: Baker Academic, 2008), pp. 33-34.

[188]Bruce, *Epistles of John*, p. 35.

this epistle is conscious of himself as having a personal authority, that is, as being a representative of the bearers of the tradition."[189]

Revelation 1:1-3. The most explicit claim for a book's authority no doubt comes from the author of Revelation. The opening line of the book directly claims that it is the inspired prophecy of Jesus Christ delivered to John by an angel (Rev 1:1). Consequently, there is a divine blessing attached with this book: "Blessed is the one who reads aloud the words of this prophecy, and blessed are those who hear, and who keep what is *written* in it, for the time is near" (Rev 1:3). Moreover, as discussed in chapter two above, the authority of this book is heightened by the inclusion of an inscriptional curse at the end, warning the reader to neither add to nor take away from this document lest they suffer divine judgment (Rev 22:18-19). On the basis of these explicit statements, even McDonald is willing to acknowledge that Revelation "claims for itself such a lofty position that [it] would come close to the notion of inspiration and Scripture."[190]

CONCLUSION

The purpose of this chapter has been to address the oft-repeated claim that the New Testament authors were unaware of their own authority and were only concerned to write occasional documents, and that it was only at a later time that such documents began to take on a "scriptural" authority in the church (even though the original authors had no such intentions). In contrast to such claims, this chapter has argued that there are a number of instances where the New Testament authors are quite aware of their own authority. Indeed, they expressly understood their writings to be *apostolic* in nature— that is, they were consciously passing down the authoritative apostolic message. Given the authoritative role of the apostles in early Christianity, and the manner in which they were commissioned to speak for Christ, an apostolic writing would bear the highest possible authority. Indeed, it would bear Christ's authority. Thus, it matters not whether the New Testament authors specifically used the term "Scripture" when speaking of their own books. When Paul says "the things I am writing to you are a command of the Lord" (1 Cor 14:37), it would have functionally been the same as Scripture. As Barton

---

[189]Bultmann, *Johannine Epistles*, p. 11.
[190]McDonald, *Biblical Canon*, p. 31.

observes, "phenomenologically, they were Scripture, having the kind of authority and standing for Christians that holy books do have."[191]

Of course, the narrow purpose of this chapter must be kept in mind. Our argument here is simply that the New Testament writings, generally speaking, were intended to be documents with an authority equivalent to that of Scripture. This does not constitute an argument that these books were, in fact, Scripture—that would be a separate (and far lengthier) discussion. We have dealt only with the intentions/self-awareness of the New Testament authors, not whether their self-awareness was accurate. After all, authors of other writings during this general time frame may have also viewed themselves as writing Scripture (for example, Maccabees, *Shepherd of Hermas*). Nevertheless, the self-awareness of the New Testament authors does have important implications for how we understand the development of the New Testament canon. Throughout this volume we have argued for an "intrinsic" model of canon, namely that the idea of a New Testament was not a later ecclesiastical development but something driven by forces already inherent to first-century Christianity. If the New Testament writers were aware of their own authority, then this gives further confirmation to the intrinsic model. Although they could not have foreseen that the church would be guided by exactly twenty-seven books, they did intend to write books that would guide the church. Thus, the existence of a new covenantal deposit of books was not due simply to Marcion's heresies or to later church politics, but to the intentional activities of the New Testament writers themselves.

---

[191]Barton, *Spirit and the Letter*, p. 25.

5

THE DATE OF CANON

Were the New Testament Books
First Regarded as Scripture at the
End of the Second Century?

[Irenaeus] essentially created the core of the
New Testament canon of Holy Scripture.

ARTHUR BELLINZONI
"The Gospel of Luke in the Apostolic Fathers:
An Overview," in *Trajectories Through the
New Testament and the Apostolic Fathers*

⚱

F<small>EW ISSUES IN THE STUDY OF THE</small> N<small>EW</small> T<small>ESTAMENT</small> <small>CANON</small> have generated more discussion than that of the canon's *date*.[1] When did New Testament writings first begin to be viewed as Scripture?[2] For those who argue that the New Testament books were not written with any intention of being authoritative documents, there seems to be an ever-growing gap

---

[1]The classic example is the disagreement between Theodor Zahn and Adolf van Harnack. See Theodor Zahn, *Geschichte des neutestamentlichen Kanons*, 2 vols. (Erlangen: A. Deichert, 1888); and Adolf von Harnack, *Origin of the New Testament and the Most Important Consequences of a New Creation* (London: Williams & Northgate, 1925). Ironically, even Harnack's later date is earlier than the modern "consensus" that we will discuss below.

[2]Obviously this question presumes the *functional* definition of canon. On this definition, the "date" of canon is determined by when these books were used as Scripture in the life of the church. See chapter one for more discussion.

between the time of their production and the time they were regarded as scriptural. Indeed, the former belief is often the foundation for the latter— if these books were not written to be Scripture, then we should not expect to see them used as Scripture until a much later time in the life of the church. The date of the canon, as a result, has been pushed further and further back. Many modern scholars have now settled on the end of the second century (ca. 200) as the point at which much of this transition took place. Helmut Koester is quite clear: "In the later period, the Gospels were considered holy scripture; no such respect was accorded them in the earliest period [before the year 200 c.e.]."[3] Lee McDonald holds the same view: "[New Testament] documents were not generally recognized as Scripture until the end of the second century c.e."[4] Similar positions can be found in Hans von Campenhausen,[5] Dimitris Kyrtatus,[6] Kenneth Carroll[7] and a number of other scholars. Thus, we come to the fifth (and final) major tenet of the extrinsic model, namely that the end of the second century was the decisive period when these documents attained a scriptural status.

The reason for this focus on the end of the second century is not hard to find. It is at this point that the major figure Irenaeus, bishop of Lyons, offers some of the clearest and most comprehensive statements on the canon to

---

[3]Helmut Koester, "The Text of the Synoptic Gospels in the Second Century," in *Gospel Traditions in the Second Century: Origins, Recensions, Text, and Transmission*, ed. William L. Petersen (Notre Dame: University of Notre Dame Press, 1989), p. 19. Koester appeals to the New Testament's lack of scriptural status as a reason it was so readily changed by scribes during this early period. Thus, argues Koester, we cannot trust that the New Testament text was transmitted with fidelity during this precanonical phase. Similar arguments can be found in Geoffrey M. Hahneman, *The Muratorian Fragment and the Development of the Canon* (Oxford: Clarendon, 1992), p. 96; Donald W. Riddle, "Textual Criticism as a Historical Discipline," *ATR* 18 (1936): 227; and David Parker, *The Living Text of the Gospels* (Cambridge: Cambridge University Press, 1997), pp. 202-5. For further reflection on this issue, see Michael J. Kruger, "Early Christian Attitudes Toward the Reproduction of Texts," in *The Early Text of the New Testament*, ed. Charles E. Hill and Michael J. Kruger (Oxford: Oxford University Press, 2012), pp. 63-80.
[4]Lee M. McDonald, *The Biblical Canon: Its Origin, Transmission, and Authority* (Peabody, MA: Hendrickson, 2007), p. 359.
[5]Hans von Campenhausen, *The Formation of the Christian Bible* (London: Adam & Charles Black, 1972), pp. 103, 182, 186.
[6]Dimitris Kyrtatus, "Historical Aspects of the Formation of the New Testament Canon," in *Canon and Canonicity: The Formation and Use of Scripture*, ed. Einar Thomassen (Copenhagen: Museum Tusculanum Press, 2010), pp. 29-44.
[7]Kenneth L. Carroll, "The Earliest New Testament," *BJRL* 38 (1955): 45-57.

date.[8] Most notable is his affirmation that the four Gospels were so certain that their existence is entrenched in the very structure of creation: "It is not possible that the gospels can be either more or fewer than the number they are. For, since there are four zones of the world in which we live and four principle winds . . . [and] the cherubim, too, were four-faced."[9] But it is not just the Gospels that Irenaeus affirms. He quotes other New Testament books extensively, even more than the Old Testament, and clearly regards them as Scripture.[10] These include the entire Pauline corpus (minus Philemon), Acts, Hebrews, James, 1 Peter, 1 and 2 John, and Revelation—over one thousand New Testament passages in total.[11] It is for these reasons that Elaine Pagels regards Irenaeus as the "principal architect"[12] of the canon, that Arthur Bellinzoni says that Irenaeus "essentially created the core of the New Testament canon of Holy Scripture,"[13] and that others regard everything prior to Irenaeus as simply the "prehistory" of the canon.[14] In the opinion of these scholars, Irenaeus is an innovator.[15] His actions were a "radical departure from traditional Christian practice."[16] In an effort to defend the church against what he regarded as aberrant views (primarily Marcion's), Irenaeus imposed a new set of Scriptures on a church that, up to that point, was quite content with oral tradition.[17]

To be sure, there is much in this account of the canon's origins that is correct. It is quite reasonable for scholars to gravitate to the end of the

---

[8]A general introduction to Irenaeus can be found in Robert M. Grant, *Irenaeus of Lyons* (London: Routledge, 1997); and Eric Osborn, *Irenaeus of Lyons* (Cambridge: Cambridge University Press, 2001).

[9]*Haer.* 3.11.8.

[10]E.g., *Haer.* 1.3.6; 2.27.2; 3.11.8; 3.12.12; 3.12.9; 5.5.2. See discussion in Graham Stanton, *Jesus and Gospel* (Cambridge: Cambridge University Press, 2004), pp. 105-6; and Bruce M. Metzger, *The Canon of the New Testament: Its Origin, Development, and Significance* (Oxford: Clarendon, 1987), pp. 154-55.

[11]Irenaeus may also have considered the *Shepherd of Hermas* to be Scripture (*Haer.* 4.20.2).

[12]Elaine Pagels, *Beyond Belief: The Secret Gospel of Thomas* (New York: Random House, 2003), p. 111.

[13]Arthur J. Bellinzoni, "The Gospel of Luke in the Apostolic Fathers: An Overview," in *Trajectories Through the New Testament and the Apostolic Fathers*, ed. Andrew Gregory and Christopher M. Tuckett (Oxford: Oxford University Press, 2005), p. 49n17.

[14]Wilhelm Schneemelcher, ed., *New Testament Apocrypha*, trans. Robert McLachlan Wilson (Louisville: Westminster John Knox, 1991), p. 18. See also Campenhausen, *Formation of the Christian Bible*, pp. 103-46.

[15]Hahneman, *Muratorian Fragment*, p. 101.

[16]Kyrtatus, "Historical Aspects of the Formation of the New Testament Canon," p. 35.

[17]Campenhausen, *Formation of the Christian Bible*, p. 147.

second century given that the extant sources related to canon are more abundant (and more explicit) during this time period. Thus we are able to draw more certain conclusions about the state of the canon at the end of the second century, as opposed to the beginning of that century, when the historical waters are more murky. Moreover, as Larry Hurtado has observed, the latter half of the second century brings certain advantages in the way books are cited: "Christian writers of the decades prior to ca. 150 CE do not characteristically cite texts explicitly in the way that texts are cited much more frequently in subsequent times."[18] Nevertheless, we still must ask whether the existence of a new scriptural corpus of books can really be laid so fully at the feet of Irenaeus. Is it historically plausible to think that such an authoritative corpus popped into existence so quickly? A catalyst for such a seismic shift does not appear readily at hand. While prior generations of scholars might have appealed to Marcion as the catalyst, recent research has suggested that Marcion's influence was not nearly as great as supposed.[19] If so, then the Irenaeus-as-innovator approach, and the late date for the canon that it implies, warrants a reevaluation. This chapter will probe deeper into the early stages of the second century and will argue that, while the evidence is limited, there are still indications that books were received as Scripture prior to the time of Irenaeus. Such evidence indicates that the origin of a new corpus of scriptural books should not be conceived of as a "big bang" type of event, extrinsically imposed on the church, but as something that grew gradually over time with roots that extend further back in the history of the church than previously allowed.

---

[18]Larry W. Hurtado, "The New Testament in the Second Century: Texts, Collections, and Canon," in *Transmission and Reception: New Testament Text-Critical and Exegetical Studies*, ed. Jeff W. Childers and D. C. Parker (Piscataway, NJ: Gorgias, 2006), p. 27. Even though Hurtado agrees that citation patterns change at the end of the second century, he does not attribute that change to a newly found "text consciousness" (as some maintain) but to an emergent "author consciousness" where texts are seen more as the works of authors and cited as such (pp. 26-27).

[19]For a helpful overview of recent approaches to Marcion, see John Barton, "Marcion Revisited," in *The Canon Debate*, ed. Lee M. McDonald and James A. Sanders (Peabody, MA: Hendrickson, 2002), pp. 341-54; John Barton, *The Spirit and the Letter: Studies in the Biblical Canon* (London: SPCK, 1997), pp. 35-62; R. Joseph Hoffmann, *Marcion: On the Restitution of Christianity: An Essay on the Development of Radical Paulinist Theology in the Second Century* (Chico, CA: Scholars Press, 1984); and David L. Balás, "Marcion Revisited: A 'Post-Harnack' Perspective," in *Texts and Testaments: Critical Essays on the Bible and the Early Church Fathers*, ed. W. Eugene March (San Antonio: Trinity University Press, 1980), pp. 95-107.

UNDERSTANDING IRENAEUS

We must begin our discussion by first looking more closely at Irenaeus's own declarations. Does he provide indications that he is the innovator and architect of a new corpus of scriptural books? Are there hints that he is peddling a new idea to the church that would be unknown and unfamiliar? When we take a closer look at *Against Heresies*, this does not appear to be the case at all. Throughout this treatise Irenaeus is content to use and cite a wide variety of New Testament books as Scripture and presumes his audience is familiar with them. He appeals to these books quite naturally and unapologetically, cites them by name, and provides no indication that this audience might be unaware of their existence or surprised by their authoritative role in the life of the church. In fact, as Charles E. Hill has observed, "It is only in Book 3 that [Irenaeus] pauses to say anything specific about the authoritative Scriptural sources that he had been using without apology up to that point."[20] Thus, Irenaeus does not write like a person advocating the scriptural status of these books for the first time.

But what about Irenaeus's rather esoteric argument that the Fourfold Gospel is reflective of the fourfold creatures around the throne? Does this not indicate that Irenaeus is on the defensive and in a desperate search for some basis for his new beliefs? Some scholars would say yes. Geoffrey Hahneman insists that Irenaeus's reasoning "suggests that this must have been something of an innovation, for if a Fourfold Gospel had been established and generally acknowledged, then Irenaeus would not have offered such a tortured insistence on its numerical legitimacy."[21] However, several factors suggest otherwise. First, even if Irenaeus's reasoning implies he is in a defensive posture against contemporary challenges (presumably Marcion), this does not necessarily mean that his beliefs are innovative. The existence of opposition to a belief should not be taken as evidence that a belief is new

---

[20]Charles E. Hill, *Who Chose the Gospels? Probing the Great Gospel Conspiracy* (Oxford: Oxford University Press, 2010), p. 40.

[21]Hahneman, *Muratorian Fragment*, p. 101 (Hahneman's statement is almost a word-for-word quote from Harry Y. Gamble, *The New Testament Canon: Its Making and Meaning* [Philadelphia: Fortress, 1985], p. 31, though he does not indicate he is quoting another source). Oscar Cullmann, "The Plurality of the Gospels as a Theological Problem in Antiquity," in *The Early Church*, ed. A. J. B. Higgins (London: SCM, 1956), pp. 51-53, is also critical of Irenaeus's reasoning, calling it "theologically valueless speculation" (p. 53). However, Cullmann still affirms an earlier date for the Fourfold Gospel itself.

and unestablished—as some scholars seem prone to do.[22] Irenaeus could simply be defending the church's long-held beliefs against the challenges that have arisen in his own time.[23] Indeed, this is Irenaeus' *own* view of the matter (which surely must bear some weight). He believed that the message of salvation was "handed down to us in the Scriptures" which the apostles themselves (and their companions) had written.[24] Thus, he sees the concept of a Christian corpus of Scriptures as something that dates back to the apostolic era, something the church has possessed long before his own time (and Marcion's). Given that Irenaeus was a disciple of Polycarp, who knew the apostle John personally, his testimony about the origins of the Scriptures cannot be dismissed lightly.[25]

Second, while Irenaeus's appeal to the four creatures around the throne may appear to be a "tortured" argument to our modern ears—and therefore evidence of his desperateness—it would not have been viewed this way in the ancient world. Early Christians (and Jews) would have regarded numbers as having substantial symbolic significance.[26] Regarding the number four, G. K. Beale notes that it is "a number of completeness, especially connoting something of universal or worldwide scope."[27] Not only is the number four used this way in Revelation[28]—the very book to which

---

[22]E.g., Hahneman, *Muratorian Fragment*, p. 102, appeals to the "Alogi" and their rejection of the Gospel of John as evidence there was no Fourfold Gospel established at the end of the second century (thus making Irenaeus an isolated anomaly). Instead, he argues that the Alogi were "protesting against the *introduction* [of John's Gospel] into the church's usage" (p. 102, emphasis mine). But why should the disagreement of the Alogi necessarily be taken as evidence that there was no Fourfold Gospel? Does the establishment of the Fourfold Gospel require zero disagreement? For more discussion on this issue see, Michael J. Kruger, *Canon Revisited: Establishing the Origins and Authority of the New Testament Books* (Wheaton, IL: Crossway, 2012), pp. 261-66.

[23]Martin Hengel, *The Four Gospels and the One Gospel of Jesus Christ* (Harrisburg, PA: Trinity Press International, 2000), p. 10.

[24]*Haer* 3.1.1.

[25]*Haer* 3.3.4; *Hist. eccl.* 5.20.4-8. It is clear that Irenaeus had more than a mere acquaintance with Polycarp and regularly sat under his teaching; see discussion in Charles E. Hill, *The Johannine Corpus in the Early Church* (Oxford: Oxford University Press, 2004), pp. 351-59.

[26]Richard Bauckham, *The Climax of Prophecy: Studies in the Book of Revelation* (Edinburgh: T & T Clark, 1993), pp. 29-37; G. K. Beale, *The Book of Revelation* (Grand Rapids: Eerdmans, 1999), pp. 58-64; Adela Yarbro Collins, "Numerical Symbolism in Jewish and Early Christian Apocalyptic Literature," *ANRW* 2.21.2 (1984): 1221-87.

[27]Beale, *Revelation*, p. 59.

[28]In addition to the four creatures around the throne (Rev 4:6-8), there are four angels (Rev 7:1; 9:14-15), four winds (Rev 7:1), four directions (Rev 7:1; 20:8), the fourfold formula "every tribe, tongue, people, and nation," and the repeated formula of thunder, rumblings and lightning occurs four times (Rev 4:5; 8:5; 11:19; 16:18).

Irenaeus alludes[29]—but it also used this way in earlier Jewish writings. For instance, the *Sibylline Oracles* comment on Adam in a similar fashion: "It is God himself who fashioned Adam of *four* letters, the first-formed man, fulfilling by his name east, west, south, and north."[30] This background helps us understand the *kind* of argument that Irenaeus is making. Like the author of the *Sibylline Oracles*, Irenaeus can look back on what God has done, observe its symbolic balance and proportion, and conclude that it is precisely what we might expect God to do. As Hill reminds us, "Irenaeus's argument is not one of logical necessity but of aesthetic necessity, of harmony, beauty or proportion."[31] Thus, Irenaeus's appeal to the number four should not be viewed as an awkward, artificial argument that betrays a brand-new approach to the canon. Indeed, it is more likely to indicate the opposite—Irenaeus is simply offering a retrospective theological explanation for a longstanding church tradition.

Third, T. C. Skeat has argued that the tradition linking the Fourfold Gospel with the four creatures around God's throne was one that *preceded* Irenaeus and thus derives from an earlier point in the second century.[32] While Irenaeus clearly appeals to the order of the creatures in Revelation, Skeat demonstrates that a number of features of Irenaeus's description of these creatures actually derives from Ezekiel's account.[33] The best explanation for this phenomenon, he argues, is that Irenaeus took over an earlier tradition concerning the Fourfold Gospel that appealed to the fourfold creatures in Ezekiel, and then he made a similar argument based on the four creatures in Revelation.[34] Thus, Irenaeus's conception of a Fourfold

---

[29]In *Haer.* 3.11.8, Irenaeus not only alludes to the four creatures around the throne (Rev 4:6-8), but also alludes to the four winds and four directions (Rev 7:1).

[30]*Sib. Or.* 4.24-26 (emphasis mine); see also *2 En.* 30:13. As another mark of completeness, ancient writers often divided up history into four epochs or four kingdoms; e.g., Daniel 2; *1 Enoch* 83–90; *2 Baruch* 39; *Apoc. Ab.* 28. Irenaeus does something very similar when he divides all of biblical history into four covenants (*Haer.* 3.11.8).

[31]Hill, *Who Chose the Gospels?*, p. 37. See also Osborn, *Irenaeus*, pp. 175-76.

[32]T. C. Skeat, "Irenaeus and the Four-Gospel Canon," *NovT* 34 (1992): 194-99.

[33]E.g., Irenaeus describes the creatures as "cherubim" (Ezek 10:20); he describes God as seated on the cherubim (Ezek 1:22; 10:1); and he describes the creatures as "four-faced" (Ezek 1:6).

[34]That the argument for a Fourfold Gospel was originally based on Ezekiel is supported by the fact that the order of the creatures in Ezekiel's account provides an order for the Gospels which is quite old: Matthew (Man), John (Lion), Luke (Ox), Mark (Eagle). This is the so-called Western order. The order of the creatures in Revelation provides no recognizable order: John (Lion), Luke (Ox), Matthew (Man), Mark (Eagle). See Skeat, "Irenaeus and the Four-Gospel Canon," pp. 196-97.

Gospel is actually based on much older church tradition.

All of these factors indicate that there are no reasons to regard Irenaeus's most controversial claim—that the church receives four and only four Gospels—to be a new idea in his day. Graham Stanton sums it up: "By the time Irenaeus wrote in about 180 AD, the fourfold Gospel was *very well established*. Irenaeus is not defending an innovation, but explaining why, unlike the heretics, the church has four gospels, no more, no less."[35]

CONTEMPORARIES OF IRENAEUS

Now that we have examined Irenaeus himself, we need to ask next whether there were others in his general time frame that shared his views about the scriptural status of these books. While Irenaeus is often portrayed as the lone voice for a new scriptural canon, we shall see below that he is far from alone in his beliefs. Indeed, the fact that a number of other historical sources from this time period reflect similar beliefs suggests that the scriptural status of New Testament books has a much older pedigree.

The Muratorian Fragment. Written at almost the same time as Irenaeus, the Muratorian fragment is our earliest canonical list (ca. 180).[36] The list confirms the scriptural status of twenty-two of the twenty-seven New Testament books, including all four Gospels, Acts, the thirteen epistles of Paul, Jude, 1 and 2 John (and possibly 3 John[37]), and Revelation. Hebrews, James, and 1 and 2 Peter are not mentioned, though it is unclear why.[38] In addition, the list appears to include two apocryphal books, namely the *Apocalypse of Peter* and the Wisdom of Solomon.[39] However, the inclusion of these apoc-

---

[35]Graham N. Stanton, "The Fourfold Gospel," *NTS* 43 (1997): 322 (emphasis mine).

[36]The fragment itself is an eighth-century Latin text that was originally composed in Greek at the end of the second century (see below for discussion of dating). Basic introductory details (author, provenance, etc.) are discussed in the standard works on canon: Gamble, *New Testament Canon*, pp. 32-33; McDonald, *Biblical Canon*, pp. 369-79; Campenhausen, *Formation*, pp. 243-61; Metzger, *Canon of the New Testament*, pp. 191-201.

[37]Since the fragment cites 1 John at an earlier point (lines 29-31), it is reasonable to think that the other two epistles mentioned in lines 68-69 are 2 and 3 John. For more on this possibility, see the arguments of Peter Katz, "The Johannine Epistles in the Muratorian Canon," *JTS* 8 (1957): 273-74.

[38]The poor quality and fragmentary nature of the Muratorian fragment have led Zahn and others to suggest that the omission of books such as 1 Peter may have been due to scribal error; see Zahn, *Geschichte des neutestamentlichen Kanons*, 2:143.

[39]Although the *Apocalypse of Peter* is mentioned, its disputed status is quickly acknowledged: "though some of us are not willing for the latter to be read in church" (line 72). The mention of

ryphal writings does not affect its relevance for our discussion here. The question before us is whether Christians possessed a corpus of written Scriptures prior to the end of the second century, not whether there was complete unity about which books. We should not use lack of *agreement* over the edges of the canon as evidence for the lack of the *existence* of a canon. When one compares Irenaeus and the Muratorian fragment, there is remarkable unity on the core, namely the four Gospels, the Pauline epistles, Acts, and a few of the smaller books.

For those who insist that Irenaeus is the "principal architect"[40] of the canon, the existence of the Muratorian fragment is problematic. It not only indicates that others beyond Irenaeus already regarded these books as having a scriptural status, but it also indicates that early Christians had already begun to do what some would regard as unthinkable: draw boundaries around these books by placing them in a defined list. Such an act of restriction and limitation suggests that by the end of the second century the canon is at a fairly mature stage—a reality that is at odds with the "big bang" approach to canon.[41] For these reasons, the date of the Muratorian fragment has been challenged by some. Most notable is the work of Albert C. Sundberg, who argued that the fragment has been wrongly dated and is a better fit within the fourth century.[42] Sundberg's work has been followed and expanded by Hahneman.[43] Although this fourth-century date has

---

the Wisdom of Solomon is particularly perplexing because it would be more fitting under an *Old* Testament list. One possible explanation has been suggested by William Horbury, namely that there was a widespread practice in the church of first listing the received books of both Old and New Testaments and then, at the end, mentioning the "disputed" books from both testaments that were useful for the church but not necessarily regarded as canonical. See William Horbury, "The Wisdom of Solomon in the Muratorian Fragment," *JTS* 45 (1994): 149-59.

[40]Pagels, *Beyond Belief*, p. 111.

[41]Even if the Muratorian fragment was written in reaction to Montanism or Marcionism (Campenhausen, *Formation*, pp. 243-61), there are no reasons to think that this list represents the first time these books are regarded as scriptural. As Metzger argues, "It is nearer to the truth to regard Marcion's canon as accelerating the process of fixing the Church's canon, a process that had *already begun* in the first half of the second century" (*Canon of the New Testament*, p. 99; emphasis mine).

[42]Albert C. Sundberg, "Canon Muratori: A Fourth-Century List," *HTR* 66 (1973): 1-41; idem, "Towards a Revised History of the New Testament Canon," *Studia Evangelica* 4 (1968): 452-61; idem, "The Biblical Canon and the Christian Doctrine of Inspiration," *Int* 29 (1975): 352-71; idem, "The Making of the New Testament Canon," in *The Interpreter's One-Volume Commentary on the Bible*, ed. Charles M. Laymon (Nashville: Abingdon, 1971), pp. 1216-24.

[43]Hahneman, *Muratorian Fragment and the Development of the Canon*; and idem, "Muratorian Fragment and the Origins of the New Testament Canon," in *Canon Debate*, pp. 405-15.

been adopted by some scholars,[44] the second-century date has been thoroughly defended and remains the dominant view.[45] Joseph Verheyden sums it up well: "None of the arguments put forward by Sundberg and Hahneman in favour of a fourth-century, eastern origin of the Fragment are convincing."[46]

Theophilus of Antioch. Theophilus was bishop of Antioch and wrote his only surviving work, *To Autolycus*, around A.D. 177.[47] At one point in this apologetic treatise, Theophilus tries to persuade Autolycus that Christian writings had the same level of integrity and authority as Old Testament writings, despite the fact that they were not as ancient. To accomplish this goal, Theophilus argues that Christian writings, while newer than the Old Testament, share the same level of inspiration by the Holy Spirit: "Concerning the righteousness which the law enjoined, confirmatory utterances are found both with the prophets and in the Gospels, because they all spoke inspired by one Spirit of God."[48] It is noteworthy that in this passage Theophilus places the "Gospels" on the same level of inspiration and authority as the Old Testament Prophets. While written at different times, they have the same integrity because God is the author of both. Which Gospels did he have in mind? In the next few sentences, Theophilus proceeds to give examples of the "Prophets" by quoting from Isaiah, Jeremiah, Hosea, Zechariah and Proverbs.[49] He then proceeds to give an example of the "Gospels"

---

[44]McDonald, *Biblical Canon*, pp. 369-78; Helmut Koester, *Ancient Christian Gospels: Their History and Development* (London: SCM Press, 1990), p. 243; Harry Y. Gamble, "Canon, New Testament," in *The Anchor Bible Dictionary*, ed. David N. Freedman (New York: Doubleday, 1992), 1:856 (though Gamble is more cautious).

[45]See responses to Sundberg/Hahneman from Philippe Henne, "La Datation du canon de Muratori," *RB* 100 (1993): 54-75; Charles E. Hill, "The Debate over the Muratorian Fragment and the Development of the Canon," *WTJ* 57 (1995): 437-52; Everett Ferguson, "Review of Geoffrey Mark Hahneman, *The Muratorian Fragment and the Development of the Canon*," *JTS* 44 (1993): 691-97; Theo K. Heckel, *Vom Evangelium des Markus zum viergestaltigen Evangelium* (Tübingen: J. C. B. Mohr, 1999), pp. 339-54; and Joseph Verheyden, "The Canon Muratori: A Matter of Dispute," in *The Biblical Canons*, ed. J.-M. Auwers and H. J. de Jonge (Leuven: Leuven University Press, 2003), pp. 487-556.

[46]Verheyden, "Canon Muratori," p. 556.

[47]For introduction, see Robert M. Grant, *Theophilus of Antioch: Ad Autolycum* (Oxford: Oxford University Press, 1970). For further discussion of the dating issue, see Hill, *Johannine Corpus in the Early Church*, p. 79.

[48]*Autol.* 3.12.

[49]Robert M. Grant, "The Bible of Theophilus of Antioch," *JBL* 66 (1947): 187, argues that Theophilus only sees the Gospels as on par with the "Writings" of the Old Testament, meaning the third (and less authoritative) section of the Hebrew canon. However, the manner in which

by citing Matthew four times (Mt 5:28, 32, 44; 6:3).[50] Elsewhere he plainly affirms the scriptural status of John, even mentioning him by name: "And hence the holy writings teach us, and all the spirit-bearing [inspired] men, one of whom, John, says, 'In the beginning was the Word, and the Word was with God.'"[51] Theophilus also appears to cite Luke 18:27 and places it alongside citations from Genesis and Isaiah, all of which are designed to show the might and power of God in creation.[52] Although Theophilus does not mention Mark's Gospel in this short treatise, his knowledge of all four Gospels is likely given the fact that Jerome informs us that Theophilus composed a harmony of Matthew, Mark, Luke and John.[53] In this manner, he was like Tatian, who composed his famous Gospel harmony, the *Diatesseron*, about the same time period.[54] Tatian also based his harmony on the four

---

Theophilus juxtaposes the Gospels with books such as Isaiah and Jeremiah suggests that he views them as fully authoritative.

[50]*Autol.* 3.13-14. In the preface to his *Commentary of Matthew*, Jerome informs us that Theophilus wrote his own commentary on Matthew many years earlier—confirming that Theophilus regarded it as Scripture.

[51]*Autol.* 2.22.

[52]*Autol.* 2.13. Although Luke 18:27 has parallels in the other Synoptics (Mt 19:26; Mk 10:7), the form of the citation here only matches Luke. See Grant, "Bible of Theophilus," p. 186.

[53]*Epist.* 121.6.15. Apparently, Theophilus might also have written a commentary on the four Gospels, but Jerome indicates that this is disputed. For discussion, see William Sanday, "A Commentary on the Gospels Attributed to Theophilus of Antioch," in *Studia Biblica et Ecclesiastica* (Oxford: Clarendon, 1885), pp. 89-101.

[54]For a general introduction to the *Diatesseron*, see William L. Petersen, *Tatian's Diatesseron: Its Creation, Dissemination, Significance, and History in Scholarship* (Leiden: E. J. Brill, 1994); and Bruce M. Metzger, *Early Versions of the New Testament: Their Origin, Transmission and Limitations* (Oxford: Clarendon, 1977), pp. 10-36. Theophilus demonstrates that an author can hold to the scriptural status of the individual Gospels and, at the same time, produce a Gospel harmony. Therefore the production of a Gospel harmony should not be taken as an indication that an author is *opposed* to the Fourfold Gospel or trying to supplant it, contrary to some who have argued this must have been Tatian's intent; e.g., William L. Petersen, "The Diatesseron and the Fourfold Gospel," in *Earliest Gospels*, ed. Charles Horton (London and New York: T & T Clark International, 2004), pp. 50-68; Gamble, *New Testament Canon*, pp. 30-31. Moreover, the very concept of a harmony, rather than demonstrating that these books lack authoritative status, implies the very opposite, namely that the author regards them as having the kind of authoritative status that would be threatened if they disagreed with one another. Why even try to harmonize nonauthoritative books? If they are nonauthoritative there is no reason to be concerned about their lack of agreement. Metzger states it plainly: "The Diatesseron supplies proof that all four Gospels were regarded as authoritative, otherwise it is unlikely that Tatian would have dared to combine them into one gospel account" (*New Testament Canon*, p. 115). In fact, Kenneth L. Carroll, "Tatian's Influence on the Developing New Testament," in *Studies in the History and Text of the New Testament in Honor of Kenneth Willis Clark*, ed. Boyd L. Daniels and M. Jack Suggs (Salt Lake City: University of Utah Press, 1967), pp. 59-70, argues that Tatian was not opposed to the Fourfold Gospel but the creator of it (!).

canonical Gospels; indeed, the term *Diatesseron* means "through four."[55]

In regard to whether Theophilus knew other New Testament writings, Robert M. Grant catalogs an impressive number of Pauline phrases which "show that Theophilus was acquainted with a collection of Pauline letters, probably including the Pastoral Epistles."[56] As for whether Theophilus regarded these letters as Scripture, he cites Titus 3:1, 1 Timothy 2:1-2 and Romans 3:7 and plainly refers to them as "the divine word" (θεῖος λόγος).[57] Again, Grant observes, "The divine word from the Pauline epistles is on approximately the same level as prophet and gospel quoted before."[58] Also, after exhorting the reader to look to the "prophetic Scriptures," Theophilus proceeds to cite Romans 2:7-9, likely indicating that he viewed the book of Romans as part of these Scriptures.[59] As for other New Testament books, Eusebius informs us that Theophilus used the book of Revelation to refute the heretic Hermogenes (suggesting the possibility that Theophilus viewed it as Scripture),[60] but we have no certain evidence about his view of the Catholic Epistles.[61] Of course, this should not be taken as an indication that Theophilus did not consider the Catholic Epistles to be scriptural— silence about a book is not evidence for the rejection of that book (particularly given that we only possess this single surviving work). In the final analysis, the core of Theophilus's collection of scriptural books is basically

---

[55]The *Diatesseron* has some odd textual variants that are not found in our canonical Gospels; see discussion in Petersen, "Diatesseron and the Fourfold Gospel," pp. 50-68. But the existence of textual variants is categorically different than Tatian using another gospel beyond the canonical four. We have evidence elsewhere that oral Jesus tradition affected the transmission of the Gospel texts in certain instances (e.g., Lk 22:44; Jn 5:4; Jn 7:53–8:11), so we should not be so surprised by the fact that it happens in the *Diatesseron*.

[56]Grant, "Bible of Theophilus," p. 182.

[57]*Autol.* 3.14. Adolf von Harnack, "Theophilus von Antiochia und das Neue Testament," *ZKG* 11 (1889–1890): 1-21, argues that the Pauline letters were not regarded as Scripture. For a rebuttal, see Grant, "Bible of Theophilus," pp. 183-84.

[58]Grant, "Bible of Theophilus," p. 184.

[59]*Autol.* 1.14. McDonald, *Biblical Canon*, p. 279, argues that Theophilus viewed Romans as part of the "prophetic Scripture."

[60]*Hist. eccl.* 4.24.1. That Tertullian also drew from Revelation in his attack on Hermogenes has led some to suggest Tertullian was dependent on Theophilus; see J. Hendrik Waszink, *Tertullian: The Treatise Against Hermogenes* (New York: Newman Press, 1956), p. 89; and Hill, *Johannine Corpus*, p. 80. Given that Tertullian saw Revelation as Scripture (*Marc.* 4.5), there are good reasons to think that Theophilus also saw Revelation as Scripture.

[61]Grant, "Bible of Theophilus," p. 185, does point out some echoes of 1 and 2 Peter in 2.34 (1 Pet 4:3), 2.13 (2 Pet 1:19), and 2.9 (2 Pet 1:21), and some possible allusions to Hebrews in 2.25 (Heb 5:12; 12:9), and 1.3 (Heb 12:29).

the same as that of Irenaeus; it included the four Gospels, the Pauline letters, and likely a few other books.

Clement of Alexandria. Writing only slightly later than Irenaeus (ca. 198), Clement of Alexandria provides yet another critical glimpse into the state of the canon at the end of the second century. As the head of the catechetical school of Alexandria, Clement was an intellectual giant and well-read in both biblical and extrabiblical literature—the latter of which he would employ quite often in his own theological writings. Thus, Clement felt free to use a variety of apocryphal writings, such as *Preaching of Peter*,[62] the *Gospel of the Egyptians*[63] and the *Gospel of the Hebrews*.[64] However, his mere use of these writings, contrary to the claims of some scholars, is not an indication that he regarded them as scriptural.[65] Nor was it an indication that the scriptural status of New Testament books was in doubt during his time period. Clement, like others in his day, was quite willing to employ extracanonical writings while, at the same time, clearly distinguishing them from the books he regarded as scriptural. In his mind, there was nothing inconsistent about this practice. For instance, when it comes to gospel writings, he expressly affirms that there are four, and only four "traditional" Gospels that the church receives: Matthew, Mark, Luke and John.[66] At one point, while using a saying from the *Gospel of the Egyptians*, he intentionally downplays its authority by noting that the saying does not occur in our canonical four.[67] Thus, Martin Hengel reminds us, "Clement's relative generosity towards 'apocryphal' texts and traditions, which is connected with the unique spiritual milieu in Alexandria and his constant controversies with many kinds of discussion partners . . . should not obscure

---

[62]*Strom.* 1.29; 6.5-7.

[63]*Strom.* 3.6-13.

[64]*Strom.* 2.9; 5.14.

[65]Referring to Clement of Alexandria's use of apocryphal gospels, Hahneman draws an unexpected conclusion: "This would seem unlikely if the Fourfold Gospel canon had already been established" (*Muratorian Fragment*, p. 94). But Hahneman never explains why this would be the case. Does the mere *use* of apocryphal material mean there could not be a Fourfold Gospel? Particularly strange about this conclusion is that Hahneman already reminded the reader not to confuse "acquaintance with the four gospels and the Fourfold Gospel canon" (p. 94). If so, then we should also not confuse mere acquaintance with apocryphal gospels and the acceptance of them as Scripture.

[66]Eusebius, *Hist. eccl.* 6.14.5-7.

[67]*Strom.* 3.13.

the fact that even for him the apostolic origin and special church authority of the four gospels was already unassailable."[68]

Of course, Clement affirmed more books as scriptural beyond the four Gospels. He received all thirteen Epistles of Paul, Hebrews, Acts, 1 Peter, 1 and 2 John, Jude and Revelation.[69] And again, there are neither any indications that Clement viewed the scriptural status of these books as an innovation, nor does he appear to have received his information from Irenaeus. On the contrary, like Irenaeus, he viewed these books as having an ancient pedigree within the Christian church. These were the ones that were "handed down" to the church from the apostles themselves.[70] Clement's commitment to the New Testament books, over and above the apocryphal literature or other Christian writings, is also borne out in the degree of frequency with which he cites them. James Brooks has observed that Clement cites the canonical books "about sixteen times more often than apocryphal and patristic writings."[71] This disparity is thrown into sharper relief when we consider just the four Gospels. According to the work of Bernard Mutschler, Clement references Matthew 757 times, Luke 402 times, John 331 times and Mark 182 times.[72] Comparatively, Clement cites apocryphal gospels only 16 times.[73] Apparently, Clement was not in doubt about which books he regarded as canonical.

---

[68]Hengel, *Four Gospels*, pp. 18-19.

[69]Metzger, *Canon of the New Testament*, p. 135. James A. Brooks, "Clement of Alexandria as a Witness to the Development of the Canon," *SecCent* 9 (1992): 41-55, differs from Metzger in that he includes Jude and 2 John but leaves out Philemon. Given that Eusebius informs us that Clement wrote commentaries on all the "Catholic Epistles," there is good reason to think he would have also included James, 2 Peter and 3 John. It is also possible that Clement regarded other books as Scripture, such as the *Epistle of Barnabas* (Eusebius, *Hist. eccl.*, 6.14.1; *Strom.* 2.6.31; 2.7.35; 2.20.116; 5.10.63). Clement's high opinion of *Barnabas* was no doubt driven by his apparent belief that the author was the first-century companion of Paul (*Strom.* 2.20.116). Whether Clement regarded *Barnabas* as Scripture is not germane to our point here, because we are concerned about the *existence* of a canon, not whether there was full *agreement* on the canon.

[70]*Strom.* 3.13.93.

[71]Brooks, "Clement of Alexandria," p. 48. Brooks draws his statistics from the work of Otto Stählin, *Clemens Alexandrinus* (4 vols.; Leipzig: J. C. Hinrichs, 1905). Stählin catalogs 3,279 total references to the New Testament in Clement of Alexandria, as opposed to just 71 to the New Testament Apocrypha.

[72]Bernard Mutschler, *Irenäus als johanneischer Theologe* (Tübingen: Mohr Siebeck, 2004), p. 101. For discussion of Mutschler, see Hill, *Who Chose the Gospels?*, pp. 71-72.

[73]Brooks, "Clement of Alexandria," p. 44.

Thus, we see a clear pattern emerging. At the end of the second century, it appears that Irenaeus was not alone. According to the Muratorian fragment, Theophilus of Antioch and Clement of Alexandria (not to mention Tatian)—influential and geographically diverse sources at the end of the second century—there was a core collection of scriptural books in place that the church fathers themselves did not view as newly established. Such a widespread belief cannot be explained solely by the "big bang" theory of canonization centered on Irenaeus. It must have roots that predate the end of the second century.

PREDECESSORS TO IRENAEUS

If Irenaeus was not the canonical innovator he is often made out to be, then he must have received his canonical traditions from those who preceded him. So we turn our attention to the middle and early parts of the second century. However, as noted above, this will not be a simple task. The further back we journey into this century, the murkier the historical waters become. And due to the different patterns of citation during this time, we should not expect the same level of clarity and certainty as afforded by writers such as Irenaeus, Clement and Theophilus. Nevertheless, if the New Testament canon did not pop into existence overnight, then we should expect to find some remnants of its existence during this earlier time period.

Justin Martyr. If we are searching for a historical precedent for the widespread beliefs about canon at the end of the second century, then Justin Martyr (writing ca. 150–160) is a promising candidate.[74] For one, we should remember that he was the teacher and mentor of Tatian himself.[75] Thus, if Tatian clearly knew the four canonical Gospels, we have good historical grounds for thinking he would have received this information from Justin. When we look more closely into Justin's writings, our suspicions are confirmed. He refers to plural "gospels"[76] and at one point provides an indication of how many he has in mind when he describes these gospels as "drawn up by His apostles and those who followed them."[77]

---

[74]For a helpful overview of Justin, see Sara Parvis and Paul Foster, eds., *Justin Martyr and His Worlds* (Minneapolis: Fortress, 2007).
[75]Ireaneus, *Haer.* 1.28.1; Eusebius, *Hist. eccl.* 4.29.1.
[76]*1 Apol.* 66.3.
[77]*Dial.* 103.

Since such language indicates (at least) two gospels written by apostles, and (at least) two written by apostolic companions, it is most naturally understood as reference to our four canonical Gospels.[78] This finds support in the fact that Justin cites from all three Synoptic Gospels,[79] and even refers to Mark's Gospel as "[Peter's] Memoirs,"[80] showing that he was not only familiar with these three Gospels but also the earlier church tradition about their origins.[81]

Although some deny that Justin knew John's Gospel,[82] there are good reasons to think that he did.[83] After all, Justin clearly knew other Johannine literature, such as the book of Revelation, which he regarded as written by the apostle John.[84] No doubt his familiarity with Johannine tradition is connected to the fact that during his dialogue with Trypho he lived in John's former residence of Ephesus.[85] Moreover, Justin is quite familiar with Johannine terminology such as *logos*,[86] as well as a number of themes distinctive to John's Gospel,[87] and even seems to cite the Gospel of John directly: "For Christ also said, 'Except ye be born again, ye shall not enter into the kingdom of heaven'" (compare Jn 3:3).[88] All these considerations, combined with the fact that Justin's disciple Tatian used the Gospel of John as

---

[78]Graham N. Stanton, "Fourfold Gospel," pp. 317-46.

[79]E.g., *Dial* 100.1; 103.8; 106.3-4. Koester, *Ancient Christian Gospels*, p. 38, declares that the citations in Justin "derive from written gospels, usually from Matthew and Luke, in one instance from Mark."

[80]*Dial.* 106.

[81]The connection between Mark's Gospel and Peter was widespread in early Christianity; e.g., Justin, *Dial.* 106; Irenaeus, *Haer.* 3.10.5; Tertullian, *Marc.* 4.5.3; Eusebius, *Hist. eccl.* 2.15; 6.14.6 (attributed to Clement of Alexandria). For more on this point, see Everett Kalin, "Early Traditions About Mark's Gospel: Canonical Status Emerges as the Story Grows," *CurTM* 2 (1975): 332-41.

[82]Koester, *Ancient Christian Gospels*, p. 246; Gamble, *New Testament Canon*, p. 28. Others argue that Justin knew John but did not regard it as authoritative; e.g., John W. Pryor, "Justin Martyr and the Fourth Gospel," *SecCent* 9 (1992): 153-67; and Leslie W. Barnard, *Justin Martyr* (Cambridge: Cambridge University Press, 1967), p. 63.

[83]Further argument for Justin's reception of John can be found in Charles E. Hill, "Was John's Gospel Among Justin's Apostolic Memoirs?," in *Justin Martyr and His Worlds*, pp. 88-94.

[84]*Dial.* 81.4.

[85]*Hist. eccl.* 4.18.6.

[86]*1 Apol.* 46.2; cf. *Dial.* 88.7. Kenneth L. Carroll, "The Creation of the Fourfold Gospel," *BJRL* 37 (1954–1955): 68-77, is not persuaded by the appearance of *logos* and argues it can be explained by general awareness of the teachings of Philo (p. 70).

[87]E.g., Jesus as μονογενὴς (*Dial.* 105.1; cf. Jn 1:18; 3:16); piercing Jesus' hands and feet with nails (*1 Apol.* 35.7; cf. Jn 20:25, 27).

[88]*1 Apol.* 61.4.

the chronological backbone of his *Diatesseron,* and that Justin claims to know *more* than just three gospels,[89] makes it difficult to believe that John was not included in Justin's gospel collection.

Even if Justin had a Fourfold Gospel collection, there is still the question of whether he regarded these writings as Scripture. In this regard, much has been made of the fact that Justin does not refer to these Gospels by name but regularly calls them the "memoirs of the apostles" (ἀπομνημονεύματα τῶν ἀποστόλων), suggesting that "he values them chiefly as historical records, not as inspired Scripture."[90] However, this may be reading too much into Justin's language. The fact that Justin does not explicitly name the Gospel authors, but instead uses the classical Greek term "memoirs,"[91] is likely due to the apologetic context in which he writes—unbelieving Jews and Gentiles would have recognized the latter but would have had little interest in the former.[92] In addition, it appears that Justin probably derived the "memoirs" language from his own predecessor Papias (whom we will discuss below).[93] If we want to know Justin's opinion of these memoirs, we

---

[89]*Dial.* 103. This issue receives far too little attention. Although some scholars argue that Justin only knew the three Synoptics, they rarely explain what Justin's fourth gospel must have been if it weren't John. Since Justin explicitly states he knows (at least) four core gospels, this issue must be addressed.

[90]Gamble, *New Testament Canon,* p. 29. See also Koester, *Ancient Christian Gospels,* p. 41.

[91]The term ἀπομνημονεύματα ("memoirs") was used in classical literature, such as Xenophon's *Memorabilia* concerning Socrates. The fact that Justin twice compares Jesus with Socrates (*1 Apol* 5.3; *2 Apol* 10.5), is a further indication that Justin likely used the "memoirs" language for apologetic purposes to persuade his unbelieving audience. Koester, *Ancient Christian Gospels,* pp. 38-39, objects to these claims, arguing that the term ἀπομνημονεύματα did not have connections to Xenophon's works in Justin's day.

[92]J. B. Lightfoot, *Essays on the Work Entitled Supernatural Religion* (London: MacMillan & Co., 1889), p. 33; Oskar Skarsaune, "Justin and His Bible," in *Justin Martyr and His Worlds,* pp. 53-76, esp. pp. 71-73; Graham N. Stanton, "Jesus Traditions and Gospels in Justin Martryr and Irenaeus," in *Biblical Canons,* pp. 353-70, esp. p. 355; Barnard, *Justin Martyr,* p. 63. Dibelius understood the use of "memoirs" as an apologetic by Justin to ensure that the Gospels "would be classified as literature proper" (Martin Dibelius, *From Tradition to Gospel* [Cambridge: J. Clarke, 1971], p. 40). Charles H. Cosgrove, "Justin Martyr and the Emerging Christian Canon: Observations on the Purpose and Destination of the Dialogue with Trypho," *VC* 36 (1982): 209-32, disagrees with these sentiments and argues that there is no reason to think that Justin is writing to a pagan audience with apologetic motives. Thus, he concludes that Justin uses the term "memoirs" to describe the Gospels because "he conceives of them as purely historical documents and not as authorities" (p. 223).

[93]*Hist. eccl.* 3.39.15. Papias refers to Mark writing down what Peter "remembered" (ἐμνημόνευσεν). For more on this point, see Richard Heard, "The [ΑΠΟΜΝΗΜΟΝΕΥΜΑΤΑ] in Papias, Justin, and Irenaeus," *NTS* 1 (1954–1955): 122-33. Loveday Alexander, "Memory and Tradition in the Hellenistic Schools," in *Jesus in Memory: Traditions in Oral and Scribal Perspectives,* ed. Werner

will do better to look in other places. In particular, we should consider Justin's understanding of their role in worship:

> And on the day called Sunday, all who live in cities or in the country gather together to one place, and the memoirs of the apostles or the writings of the prophets are read, as long as time permits; then, when the reader has ceased, the president verbally instructs, and exhorts to the imitation of these good things.[94]

This passage is particularly instructive because it informs us that Justin regarded these "memoirs" as on par with the Old Testament Prophets. Martin Hengel comments on this passage, "It is striking that the reading of the Gospels is mentioned before the prophets; to some extent it has taken over the significance of the Jewish reading of the Torah."[95] It is no surprise, then, that when Justin draws upon the canonical Gospels, he often uses "it is written," the *formula citandi* for introducing scriptural books.[96] He even cites the canonical Gospels alongside Old Testament texts, "with the clear implication that they have the same status."[97]

It is worth noting that Justin's testimony about Christian books being read in public worship finds confirmation in the physical features of New Testament manuscripts from this time period. While it is not always easy to determine whether a manuscript is designed for public or private use—these are not absolute categories that can be entirely separated from one another—a number of our earliest New Testament manuscripts exhibit features that suggest they were designed for public reading.[98] Although it may come as a surprise to us in the modern day, most ancient books were not

---

Kelber and Samuel Byrskog (Waco, TX: Baylor University Press, 2009), pp. 113-53, takes a different approach and argues that Justin may have borrowed the term from second-century Hellenistic schools.

[94]*1 Apol.* 67.3.

[95]Martin Hengel, "The Titles of the Gospels and the Gospel of Mark," in *Studies in the Gospel of Mark* (London: SCM, 1985), p. 76.

[96]E.g., *Dial* 100.1; 103.6-8; 104.1; 105.6; 106.3-4; and 107.1. Koester, *Ancient Christian Gospels*, p. 41, plays down the implications of this language by claiming it does not mean Justin regarded the Gospels as "Scripture" but instead Justin merely meant these things were "recorded in a written document."

[97]Stanton, "Jesus Traditions," p. 358. *1 Apol* 61.3-8 has sayings of Jesus set alongside quotes from Isaiah.

[98]For a broad overview of public reading in early Christianity, see Harry Y. Gamble, *Books and Readers in the Early Church* (New Haven, CT: Yale University Press, 1995), pp. 205-31.

designed to make the reading task an easy one. Colin Roberts observed that, "As a rule Greek manuscripts make very few concessions to the reader."[99] However, Scott Charlesworth has shown that it is precisely in this area that our New Testament manuscripts, even as early as the second century, are distinctive.[100] Not only do they often contain a number of reading aids (for example, sense breaks, diaeresis, rough breathing marks, punctuation points, accents),[101] but they often have much fewer lines per page when compared to other Greco-Roman texts.[102] Such features suggests that these manuscripts were designed "to ease the task of [public] reading aloud."[103] If so, then we have further confirmation that by the middle of the second century, these writings were functioning as Scripture in the context of Christian worship.

Of course, some scholars have doubted Justin's commitment to a Fourfold Gospel on the grounds that his Gospel citations are often harmonized and thus must be from *another* source beside the canonical four.[104]

---

[99]Colin H. Roberts, "Two Biblical Papyri in the John Rylands Library, Manchester," *BJRL* 20 (1936): 227. William A. Johnson, "Towards a Sociology of Reading in Classical Antiquity," *AJP* 121 (2000): 593-627, demonstrates this very point when he discusses how many books in the ancient world were designed more as status symbols to be looked at than as something that might be regularly read. See also Larry W. Hurtado, "Manuscripts and the Sociology of Early Christian Reading," in *Early Text of the New Testament*, pp. 49-62.

[100]Scott Charlesworth, "Public and Private—Second- and Third-Century Gospel Manuscripts," in *Jewish and Christian Scripture as Artifact and Canon*, ed. Craig A. Evans and H. Daniel Zacharias (London: T & T Clark, 2009), pp. 148-75. Second-century examples of such "public" texts include P[103], P[77], P[90], P[104], P[64+67], P[52].

[101]For the lack of such lectional aides in Greek literary texts, see Eric G. Turner, *Greek Manuscripts of the Ancient World* (London: Institute of Classical Studies, 1987), pp. 7-12.

[102]Eric G. Turner, *The Typology of the Early Codex* (Philadelphia: University of Pennsylvania Press, 1977), pp. 85-87; Larry W. Hurtado, *The Earliest Christian Artifacts: Manuscripts and Christian Origins* (Grand Rapids: Eerdmans, 2006), pp. 173-74. Turner notes that while classical literary texts can have upwards of fifty lines per page, some Christian texts of the same size average far fewer lines (and letters per line). A noteworthy example of this trend is P[46], which is estimated to have about twenty-five to twenty-eight lines per page (at least in the earliest portions), whereas P.Oxy. 2537 (Lysias) is approximately the same size and averages forty-five or more lines per page.

[103]Turner, *Typology of the Early Codex*, p. 85.

[104]E.g., Wilhelm Bousset, *Die Evangeliencitate Justins Des Märtyrers in Ihrem Wert Für Die Evangelienkritik* (Göttingen: Vandenhoeck & Ruprecht, 1891), pp. 114-16, argues that Justin was using traditions earlier than the Synoptics; Adolf Hilgenfeld, *Kritische Untersuchungen Über Die Evangelien Justin's, Der Clementinischen Homilien und Marcion's* (Halle: C. A. Schwetschke, 1850), pp. 101-304, argues that Justin is dependent on an apocryphal gospel; Donald A. Hagner, "The Sayings of Jesus in the Apostolic Fathers and Justin Martyr," in *Gospel Perspectives: The Jesus Tradition Outside the Gospels*, ed. David Wenham (Sheffield: JSOT Press, 1985), pp. 233-68, argues Justin is more likely dependent on oral tradition. For an argument that Justin

Koester even suggests that Justin was producing a new Gospel harmony—
"the one inclusive new Gospel"—which would make all the other gospels
"obsolete."[105] William Petersen argues that Justin's harmony was actually
the precursor to Tatian's harmony, the latter being dependent on the
former.[106] While Koester and Petersen are correct that Justin, at times,[107]
cites from the Gospels in a harmonized fashion, there are no indications
that he wrote a full-scale harmony designed to be a new super-Gospel.[108]
Indeed, the high degree of authority he attributes to apostolic Gospels (as
noted above) would make such an intention quite unlikely. A better solution, suggested by Graham Stanton, Oskar Skarsaune and others, is that
Justin is probably drawing from a collection of Jesus sayings that had been
extracted from the Gospels for catechetical instruction.[109] Such "testimony
books" were not unusual during this time period,[110] and authors would
often harmonize or conflate the material drawn from the main source.[111]

---

was using Matthew, see Édouard Massaux, "Le texte du Sermon sur la Montagne de Matthieu
utilisé par Saint Justin," *ETL* 28 (1952): 411-48.

[105]Koester, "Text of the Synoptic Gospels in the Second Century," p. 30.

[106]William L. Petersen, "Textual Evidence of Tatian's Dependence upon Justin's
ΑΠΟΜΝΗΜΟΝΕΥΜΑΤΑ," *NTS* 36 (1990): 512-34.

[107]It should be noted that Justin does not always cite the Gospels in a harmonized form. This
most often occurs in the *Apology*, whereas there are numerous Gospel citations in the *Dialogue*
that seem to be drawn directly from the canonical gospels (especially 97-107).

[108]Koester and Petersen seem to have confused a Gospel *harmony* with Gospel *harmonizations*.
While Tatian was no doubt influenced by some of Justin's harmonized traditions, the two
works are very different. Sharon L. Mattila, "A Question Too Often Neglected," *NTS* 41 (1995):
199-217, argues that Tatian tends to form his harmony in large blocks, drawing from one
Gospel (quite faithfully) for a period of time before switching to another one and then doing
the same. In contrast, Justin's text is often paraphrased and tends to harmonize single passages
by drawing material from a variety of chapters and contexts. Mattila summarizes, "Whatever
compositional methods might lie behind Justin's ἀπομνημονεύματα, they do not resemble
those evident in the Diatesseron" (p. 206).

[109]The most thorough analysis of Justin's extracts from the Gospels is Arthur J. Bellinzoni, *The
Sayings of Jesus in the Writings of Justin Martyr* (Leiden: E. J. Brill, 1967). See also Leslie L. Kline,
"Harmonized Sayings of Jesus in the Pseudo-Clementine Homilies and Justin Martyr," *ZNW*
66 (1975): 223-41.

[110]E.g., Pliny the Younger, *Ep.* 3.5; Eusebius, *Hist. eccl.* 4.26.12; Clement of Alexandria, *Exc.* For
more on how such *testimonia* books were used for collecting excerpts from the Old Testament,
see James Rendel Harris, *Testimonies* (Cambridge: Cambridge University Press, 1916); Joseph
A. Fitzmyer, "'4Q Testimonia' and the New Testament," *TS* 18 (1957): 513-37; and, more recently, Martin C. Albl, *And Scripture Cannot Be Broken: The Form and Function of the Early
Christian Testimonia Collections* (Leiden: E. J. Brill, 1999).

[111]John Whittaker, "The Value of Indirect Tradition in the Establishment of Greek Philosophical
Texts or the Art of Misquotation," in *Editing Greek and Latin Texts. Papers Given at the Twenty-
Third Annual Conference on Editorial Problems, University of Toronto 6-7 November 1987*, ed.

Thus, rather than suggesting that Justin is trying to supersede the canonical Gospels, we should just recognize that he cites them in two different ways; sometimes he does so directly (most often in the *Dialogue*), and other times, he draws from his collection of harmonized Jesus sayings (most often in the *Apology*).[112]

As for other New Testament books, the evidence is much less clear. Paul Foster sees little evidence that Justin was aware of Paul's letters.[113] He argues that "in the surviving writings of Justin there is no obvious sign of Paul or his writings."[114] In contrast, Skarsaune argues that Justin shows "extensive" use of Paul's letters, particularly Romans, Galatians and Ephesians,[115] and Barnard even argues that Justin knew all of Paul's letters (minus the Pastorals).[116] Such scholarly disagreements are difficult to resolve. However, it is reasonable to think that Justin might have known Paul's letters given his interactions with Marcion. In regard to what sort of authority Justin might have attributed to Paul's letters (if he knew them), we can only deduce his views based on his general opinion of the apostles.[117] For Justin, the apostles

John Grant (New York: AMS, 1989), pp. 63-95, at pp. 86-90; Bruce M. Metzger, "Patristic Evidence and the Textual Criticism of the New Testament," in *New Testament Studies: Philological, Versional, and Patristic* (Leiden: E. J. Brill, 1980), pp. 167-88, esp. 186. As an example, see Clement of Alexandria's *Excerpts of Theodotus*.

[112]Of course, we should acknowledge that even when Justin cites the Gospels "directly" and not from a collection of Jesus sayings, he sometimes still shapes them (and harmonizes them) according to his own needs and purpose. For this reason, some scholars suggest that Justin's Gospel citations can be explained simply by his free use of the Synoptic Gospels themselves; see W.-D. Köhler, *Die Rezeption des Matthäusevangeliums in der Zeit vor Irenäus* (Tübingen: J. C. B. Mohr, 1987), pp. 161-265; Joseph Verheyden, "Assessing Gospel Quotations in Justin Martyr," in *New Testament Textual Criticism and Exegesis, Festschrift J. Delobel*, ed. Adelbert Denaux (Leuven: Peeters, 2002), pp. 361-78. This latter article is a response to William L. Petersen, "What Text Can New Testament Textual Criticism Ultimately Reach?," in *New Testament Textual Criticism, Exegesis, and Early Church History: A Discussion of Methods*, ed. Barbara Aland and Joël Delobel (Kampen, Netherlands: Kok Pharos, 1994), pp. 136-52.

[113]Paul Foster, "Justin and Paul," in *Paul and the Second Century*, ed. Michael Bird and Joseph R. Dodson (London: T & T Clark, 2011), pp. 108-25.

[114]Foster, "Justin and Paul," p. 124.

[115]Skarsaune, "Justin and His Bible," pp. 74, 187n95; see also Andreas Lindemann, *Paulus im ältesten Christentum: Das Bild des Apostels und die Rezeption der paulinischen Theologie in der frühchristlichen Literatur bis Marcion* (Tübingen: J. C. B. Mohr, 1979), 353-67.

[116]Barnard, *Justin Martyr*, pp. 62, 74. His reticence to use Paul more explicitly than he does may have again simply been due to his apologetic context; for more, see C. E. Hill, "Justin and the New Testament Writings," in *Studia Patristica*, ed. E. Livingstone (Leuven: Peeters, 1997), pp. 42-48.

[117]Skarsaune, "Justin and His Bible," pp. 68-71; Hill, "Justin and the New Testament Writings," pp. 46-48.

were proclaimers of "the word of God,"[118] in fulfillment of God's promises to
send new prophets,[119] and it was Christ himself who spoke "through the
apostles."[120] Thus, if he knew Paul's letters, we have good reasons to think he
would have held Paul's letters (and writings of other apostles) in the highest
regard. In addition to Paul, Justin also seems to show knowledge of Acts, 1
Peter, Hebrews and Revelation.[121] Although the scriptural status of the first
three is unclear, Justin seems to place a high value on Revelation. He affirms
Revelation's apostolic character[122] and even refers to it as one of "our
writings" in contradistinction to the Old Testament books.[123]

The apostolic fathers. There has been much scholarly discussion on the
role of the apostolic fathers in tracing the origins of the New Testament writings.[124] Some scholars have been quite skeptical about whether the apostolic
fathers reveal much of anything about the development of the canon, arguing
that most of the Jesus tradition we find in these writings was likely drawn
from other sources, whether oral or written.[125] After all, it is argued, the shape
of the Jesus tradition found in these writers is often different from what we
find in the canonical Gospels.[126] And the skepticism of some scholars goes
even further. William Petersen has argued that even if a citation in the apostolic fathers is an *exact match* with a known New Testament writing we still

---

[118]*1 Apol.* 39.3.

[119]*1 Apol.* 39.3; *Dial.* 109.1; *Dial.* 110.2.

[120]*1 Apol.* 42; cf. *Dial.* 42.1.

[121]Eric Francis Osborn, *Justin Martyr* (Tübingen: Mohr Siebeck, 1973), p. 135.

[122]*Dial.* 81.4.

[123]*1 Apol.* 28.1.

[124]For more on this enormous subject see Andrew Gregory and Christopher M. Tuckett, eds., *The Reception of the New Testament in the Apostolic Fathers* (Oxford: Oxford University Press, 2005); idem, eds., *Trajectories Through the New Testament and the Apostolic Fathers*; Donald A. Hagner, *The Use of the Old and New Testaments in Clement of Rome* (Leiden: E. J. Brill, 1973); idem, "Say-ings of Jesus in the Apostolic Fathers and Justin Martyr," pp. 233-68; and A Committee of the Oxford Society of Historical Theology, ed., *The New Testament in the Apostolic Fathers* (Oxford: Clarendon, 1905).

[125]For the argument that the apostolic fathers are drawing almost entirely on oral sources, see Stephen E. Young, *Jesus Tradition in the Apostolic Fathers* (Tübingen: Mohr Siebeck, 2011). Paul Foster, "The Text of the New Testament in the Apostolic Fathers," in *Early Text of the New Testa-ment*, pp. 282-301, argues cogently that the apostolic fathers are not able to aid us in tracing the development of the New Testament text, due to the difficulty of identifying citations and the loose citation practices. But the question of whether the apostolic fathers help us trace the *text* of the New Testament is a different question from whether it helps us trace the *canon* of the New Testament.

[126]Helmut Koester, *Synoptische Überlieferung bei den apostlischen Vätern* (Berlin: Akademie-Ver-lag, 1957).

cannot be absolutely sure the author is quoting that writing because the text of the New Testament was continually in flux during this time period.[127] Similar arguments have been made by other scholars, who remind us that many other sources were available to early Christians that might have contained Jesus tradition with the same wording as our New Testament Gospels (for example, the Q source).[128] In light of such considerations, Koester makes it clear where he thinks the burden of proof should be: "Unless it can be proven otherwise, it must be assumed that authors who referred to and quoted such materials [Jesus tradition] were dependent upon these life situations of the church and did not quote from written documents."[129]

No doubt these scholars are correct that the writings of the apostolic fathers present sticky situations—it is not always easy to determine the source of their citations.[130] The work of Koester, Petersen and others has rightly corrected prior studies that have been overly confident that the New Testament writings are (usually) the best explanation.[131] Surely the apostolic fathers did continue to draw on oral tradition (and other sources) well into the second century. Thus, it is important that we be appropriately cautious and careful. However, does this mean that the apostolic fathers cannot inform our understanding of the development of the canon? And does it

---

[127]William L. Petersen, "Textual Traditions Examined: What the Text of the Apostolic Fathers Tells Us About the Text of the New Testament in the Second Century," in *Reception of the New Testament in the Apostolic Fathers*, pp. 29-46.

[128]Christopher M. Tuckett, "The Synoptic Tradition in the Didache," in *The New Testament in Early Christianity: La réception des écrits néotestamentaires dans le christianisme primitif*, ed. J.-M. Sevrin (Leuven: Leuven University Press, 1989), pp. 197-230; Andrew Gregory, *The Reception of Luke and Acts in the Period Before Irenaeus* (Tübingen: Mohr Siebeck, 2003), pp. 5-20; and Andrew Gregory and Christopher M. Tuckett, "Reflections on Method: What Constitutes the Use of the Writings That Later Formed the New Testament in the Apostolic Fathers?," in *Reception of the New Testament in the Apostolic Fathers*, pp. 61-82.

[129]Helmut Koester, "Written Gospels or Oral Tradition?," *JBL* 113 (1994): 297.

[130]For more on analyzing patristic citations, see Metzger, "Patristic Evidence and the Textual Criticism of the New Testament," 167-88; Bart D. Ehrman, "The Use and Significance of Patristic Evidence for NT Textual Criticism," in *New Testament Text Criticism, Exegesis, and Early Church History*, ed. Barbara Aland and Joël Delobel (Kampen, Netherlands: Kok Pharos, 1994), pp. 118-35; M. Jack Suggs, "The Use of Patristic Evidence in the Search for a Primitive New Testament Text," *NTS* 4 (1958-1957): 139-47; Gordon D. Fee, "The Text of John in Origen and Cyril of Alexandria: A Contribution to Methodology in the Recovery and Analysis of Patristic Citations," *Bib* 52 (1971): 357-73; and Richard Glover, "The Didache's Quotations and the Synoptic Gospels," *NTS* 5 (1958): 12-29.

[131]More of a "maximalist" position has been taken by Édouard Massaux, *Influence de L'Évangile de Saint Matthieu sur la littérature chrétienne avant Saint Irénée* (Lueven: Lueven University Press, 1986); and W.-D. Köhler, *Die Rezeption des Matthäusevangeliums in der Zeit vor Irenäus*.

mean that our default position must be that the apostolic fathers were using oral tradition unless it can be proved otherwise? Although we cannot fully resolve this debate here, several considerations suggest that we have grounds for being a little more optimistic:

1. Those like Koester who insist that oral tradition is the best explanation of Jesus tradition in the apostolic fathers often presuppose the standard form-critical model where the earliest Christians had an aversion to written texts and preferred (almost exclusively) oral tradition well into the second century. But, as observed in chapter three above, this entire model is seriously in doubt.[132] Earliest Christianity was a religion of *textuality*—even if large numbers of its followers were unable to read. Not only are written and oral methods of transmission not opposed to each other, but they can, and often do, exist side by side and complement one another.[133] If so, then there is no reason to think the burden of proof must lie in only one direction. We can agree with James Kelhoffer when he argues that "the burden of proof for ascertaining literary dependence should not necessarily rest with those who tend to argue either in favor or against literary dependence . . . [witnesses] must be considered on a case by case basis."[134]

2. If early Christianity as a whole was characterized by textuality, then we would expect this to be particularly true for the apostolic fathers themselves who (obviously) were quite literate, not only composing their own texts, but often interacting with the writings of others.[135] Thus, we have

---

[132]Most recently, see Richard Bauckham, *Jesus and the Eyewitnesses: The Gospels as Eyewitness Testimony* (Grand Rapids: Eerdmans, 2006), pp. 240-63. Earlier than Bauckham, others challenged some central tenets of form criticism: e.g., Birger Gerhardsson, *Memory and Manuscript with Tradition and Transmission in Early Christianity*, rev. ed. (Grand Rapids: Eerdmans, 1998); E. P. Sanders, *The Tendencies of the Synoptic Tradition* (Cambridge: Cambridge University Press, 1969); Graham N. Stanton, "Form Criticism Revisited," in *What About the New Testament?*, ed. Morna D. Hooker and Colin J. A. Hickling (London: SCM, 1975), pp. 13-27.

[133]Holly Hearon, "Implications of Orality for the Study of the Biblical Text," in *Performing the Gospel: Orality, Memory and Mark*, ed. Richard A. Horsley, Jonathan A. Draper and John Miles Foley (Minneapolis: Fortress, 2006), p. 9; and Gamble, *Books and Readers*, pp. 28-32.

[134]James A. Kelhoffer, "'How Soon a Book' Revisited: ΕΥΑΓΓΕΛΙΟΝ as a Reference to 'Gospel' Materials in the First Half of the Second Century," *ZNW* 95 (2004): 9-10.

[135]By way of example, we see much textual interchange in Polycarp's letter to the Philippians. Several examples: (1) The Philippians sent a letter to Polycarp asking for copies of Ignatius's letters (*Phil* 13.1-2); (2) Polycarp collected the letters of Ignatius and had them copied; (3) Polycarp sent his letter back to the Philippians with Ignatius's letters attached; and (4) Polycarp forwarded a letter from the Philippians onto Antioch. This array of literary traffic simply shows that the apostolic fathers were quite willing to interact with, cite and copy written texts. For

good reasons to think that the apostolic fathers, more than average Christians, would have been aware of, and influenced by, written texts. If so, then the key question is as follows: If we know early Christianity in general was textually oriented, and if we know that the apostolic fathers in particular were quite willing to interact with other Christian writings, then why should we presume that they "did not quote from written documents"[136] when it comes to the material that sounds like it comes from the New Testament? There appears to be little reason to do so. Once again, scholars should be *equally* open to the possibility of oral or written sources.

3. While the apostolic fathers wrote (for the most part) in the first half of the second century, we have even earlier (first-century) examples where authors were already drawing on *written* gospel material. The two most common solutions to the Synoptic problem—the two-source hypothesis and the Griesbach hypothesis—both agree that there was *literary* dependence between the authors of the earliest gospels; either Matthew and Luke copied Mark and Q (two-source), or Mark copied from Matthew and Luke (Griesbach). And even if one acknowledges that oral tradition also played a key role in this complex matrix,[137] few doubt that there was at least *some* textual dependence between these various authors.[138] If a substantive level of textual dependency is happening in the first century, why would we think that it is not a likely scenario in the second century among the apostolic fathers when these texts are even more well known?

4. It is certainly correct that even if a citation in the apostolic fathers is an exact match with a known New Testament writing, we still cannot be absolutely sure that it is a citation from that book. But why must the only goal of our historical analysis be the production of absolutely certain results?[139] It seems that such a "minimalist" approach sets the bar so high

---

more, see Michael J. Kruger, "Manuscripts, Scribes, and Book Production Within Early Christianity," in *Christian Origins and Classical Culture: Social and Literary Contexts for the New Testament*, ed. Stanley E. Porter and Andrew W. Pitts (Leiden: E. J. Brill, 2012), pp. 15-40.

[136]Koester, "Written Gospels or Oral Tradition?," p. 297.

[137]For more on the role of oral tradition in the solution to the Synoptic problem, see James D. G. Dunn, "Altering the Default Setting: Re-envisaging the Early Transmission of the Jesus Tradition," *NTS* 49 (2003): 139-75; and Terence C. Mournet, *Oral Tradition and Literary Dependency* (Tübingen: Mohr Siebeck, 2005).

[138]Andrew Gregory, "What Is Literary Dependence?," in *New Studies in the Synoptic Problem: Oxford Conference, April 2008*, ed. Paul Foster, et al. (Leuven: Peeters, 2011), pp. 87-114.

[139]E.g., Gregory affirms the goal of his methodology: "a small sample of quite secure evidence

for what counts as a reference to a New Testament book that no reasonable level of historical evidence could meet it.[140] It should be no surprise, then, if very few instances are found where the apostolic fathers actually cite New Testament books—that conclusion was already determined by the method.[141] As an alternative, we might consider that the goal of historical analysis is not to produce absolutely certain results (lest we are left with no results), but results that are reasonable and probable. For this reason, other scholars have suggested that when we have a match, it is reasonable to explain the data on the basis of *known* sources, rather than conjectural ones.[142]

5. We do well to remember Larry Hurtado's observation above that earlier writers in the second century tend to quote books without identifying their sources—but this does not mean they did not know and use these books. He asks,

> Is the practice of the post-150 CE period indicative of an emergent "text consciousness" or is it more correct to see an emergent *author-consciousness*? That is, I suggest that what changes in the post-150 CE period is a greater tendency to see texts as the *works of authors* and so to cite them as such, rather than simply appropriating the contents of texts.[143]

---

may be of more value than a larger sample of less secure evidence" (*Reception of Luke and Acts*, p. 13).

[140]E.g., even if one of the apostolic fathers expressly stated, "For it is written in the Gospel of Luke . . . ," one could still object that we cannot be absolutely sure that it is the same Luke we possess. After all, some scholars have suggested that these early Christians used a proto-Luke which eventually was enlarged into our current, larger version of Luke; e.g., John Knox, *Marcion and the New Testament: An Essay in the Early History of the Canon* (Chicago: University of Chicago Press, 1942). Other scholars have suggested we can have certain results when the citation includes the redactional work of the evangelist; e.g., Tuckett, "Synoptic Tradition," p. 95 (relying on Koester, *Synoptische Überlieferung*). However, this does not even provide certain results given that (1) redactional features may have been independently added by two different redactors; and (2) we cannot even be sure about which features of the Gospels are actually redactional (Tuckett himself acknowledges these limitations).

[141]Young, *Jesus Tradition*, p. 26, argues against the works of Massaux and Köhler on the grounds that their "method largely predetermines the outcome." However, the same thing could be said of Young's view (and others who have a more minimalist approach to the apostolic fathers).

[142]Édouard Massaux, *The Influence of the Gospel of Saint Matthew on Christian Literature Before Saint Irenaeus*, trans. Norman J. Belval and Suzanne Hecht (Macon, GA: Mercer University Press, 1994), 2:32, states, "I do not see the need to multiply hypotheses unnecessarily since the text of Mt. was within reach. . . . Why then turn to an oral tradition or to a parent document of the gospels, whose existence is hypothetical?" Massaux's methodology was refined further by Köhler, *Die Rezeption des Matthäusevangeliums in der Zeit vor Irenäus*. For a similar approach to Massaux on this issue, see Metzger, *Canon of the New Testament*, p. 73n47.

[143]Hurtado, "New Testament in the Second Century," p. 27 (emphasis his).

In fact, even Irenaeus often cites the "words of the Lord" without identifying his sources, even though it is clear he is drawing on the written Gospels.[144]

6. The fact that the textual form of the citations in the apostolic fathers is, at times, different than what we find in our New Testament should also not be used as evidence that these authors were unaware of the New Testament books (or that they were necessarily drawing from other sources). Written texts were encountered by most people in the ancient world primarily in *oral* forms (public readings, recitations and retelling of stories, and so on) due to the fact that society was largely nonliterate.[145] Thus, as people would make oral *use* of the Gospel texts, then it would be quite natural for some citations to be paraphrased or conflated.[146] Such loose citations were also common in Greco-Roman literature.[147] E. G. Turner notes that the need for exact citations "is a presupposition of scholarship we take for granted, but it was not part of the tradition of classical Greece. Used to the cut and thrust of oral dialectic, the Greeks tended to be careless of exact quotation or copying and of precise chronology, undisturbed by anachronisms."[148]

Although these considerations are not sufficient to answer all our questions, they at least give us reason to think that the apostolic fathers may have more to show us about the development of the New Testament canon than some have supposed. Therefore, let us now turn our attention to a few examples.

---

[144]William R. Farmer and Denis M. Farkasfalvy, *The Formation of the New Testament Canon* (New York: Paulist, 1976), p. 50.

[145]The standard work on literacy in the ancient world is William V. Harris, *Ancient Literacy* (Cambridge, MA: Harvard University Press, 1989). Although Harris is generally accepted among scholars, it is balanced by Alan Millard, *Reading and Writing in the Time of Jesus* (New York: New York University Press, 2000).

[146]Christopher D. Stanley, *Paul and the Language of Scripture: Citation Technique in the Pauline Epistles and Contemporary Literature* (Cambridge: Cambridge University Press, 1992); Charles E. Hill, "'In These Very Words': Methods and Standards of Literary Borrowing in the Second Century," in *Early Text of the New Testament*, pp. 261-81; and F. Gerald Downing, "Writers' Use or Abuse of Written Sources," in *New Studies in the Synoptic Problem*, pp. 523-48. Petersen, "Textual Traditions Examined," objects to this explanation on the grounds that "many of the 'deviating' readings found in the Apostolic Fathers have parallels in other Fathers or documents" (p. 42). However, as noted above, this can be explained by the fact that early Christians often used "testimony books" composed of sayings of Jesus that were used for catechetical instruction. Bellinzoni, *Sayings of Jesus in the Writings of Justin Martyr*, made this argument in regard to Justin's text of the Gospels.

[147]E.g., Whittaker, "Art of Misquotation," pp. 63-95.

[148]Eric G. Turner, *Greek Papyri: An Introduction* (Oxford: Clarendon Press, 1968), pp. 106-7.

Papias. One of the most significant figures during this time period is Papias, bishop of Hierapolis, who wrote around A.D. 125.[149] Although the historical value of Papias's testimony has been disputed by some scholars,[150] his credibility as a source has been defended by others.[151] What makes Papias particularly noteworthy is the fact that he was historically positioned to have credible knowledge about the New Testament writings—according to Irenaeus, he was a friend of Polycarp and had heard the apostle John preach.[152] Eusebius also points out that he knew the daughters of Philip the Evangelist (Acts 21:8-9).[153] Moreover, Papias plainly declares that the source of his information is "the Elder"[154] who is likely to be "John the Elder," whom Papias refers to elsewhere as a disciple and eyewitness of Jesus himself.[155] This means that even though Papias wrote around A.D. 125, he received this information about the Gospels directly from one of Jesus' dis-

---

[149]Scholars are divided over the precise date when Papias wrote. Some have argued for a later date ca. 140; e.g., Brooke F. Westcott, *A General Survey of the History of the Canon of the New Testament* (London: Macmillan, 1889), p. 70; and Lightfoot, *Essays on the Work Entitled Supernatural Religion*, pp. 147-50. Others argue for an even earlier date ca. 110; see J. Vernon Bartlet, "Papias's 'Exposition': Its Date and Contents," in *Amicitiae Corolla*, ed. H. G. Wood (London: University of London Press, 1933), pp. 16-22; Robert W. Yarbrough, "The Date of Papias: A Reassessment," *JETS* 26 (1983): 181-91; and Rupert Annand, "Papias and the Four Gospels," *SJT* 9 (1956): 46-62.

[150]Eusebius himself was critical of Papias, calling him "a man of very little intelligence" (*Hist. eccl.* 3.39.13). But, as Gundry points out, Eusebius was no doubt critical of Papias because he did not share his view of the book of Revelation (*Matthew*, p. 615).

[151]For discussion of Papias as a source, see Samuel S. Byrskog, *Story as History—History as Story: The Gospel Tradition in the Context of Ancient Oral History* (Leiden: E. J. Brill, 2002), pp. 272-92; Robert H. Gundry, *Matthew*, pp. 609-22; Heckel, *Vom Evangelium des Markus zum viergestaltigen Evangelium*, pp. 219-22; W. D. Davies and Dale C. Allison, *The Gospel According to Saint Matthew* (ICC; Edinburgh: T & T Clark, 1997), pp. 7-17; Hengel, *Studies in the Gospel of Mark*, pp. 47-53; and R. T. France, *Matthew: Evangelist and Teacher* (Grand Rapids: Zondervan, 1989), pp. 53-60.

[152]Irenaeus, *Haer.* 5.33.4.

[153]Eusebius, *Hist. eccl.* 3.39.9.

[154]Eusebius, *Hist. eccl.* 3.39.15-16.

[155]*Hist. eccl.* 3.39.3-4; Martin Hengel, *Die Johanneische Frage: Ein Lösungversuch mit einem Beitrag zur Apolalyse von Jörg Frey* (Tübingen: Mohr Siebeck, 1993), pp. 75-95. The identity of this particular John is much disputed in modern scholarship, with some scholars suggesting it was not the apostle John, the son of Zebedee, but a different John who was also a disciple of Jesus (and the author of the Johannine epistles and the Gospel of John). See Martin Hengel, *Four Gospels*, pp. 67-68; and Bauckham, *Jesus and the Eyewitnesses*, pp. 412-37. Others suggest that John the Elder is just a reference to John the apostle (cf. Irenaeus, *Haer.* 5.33.4). See Gundry, *Matthew*, pp. 611-12; D. A. Carson, *The Gospel According to John* (Grand Rapids: Eerdmans, 1991), pp. 69-70; Craig S. Keener, *The Gospel of John* (Peabody, MA: Hendrickson, 2003), pp. 95-98; and, more extensively, John Chapman, *John the Presbyter and the Fourth Gospel* (Oxford: Clarendon Press, 1911).

ciples at the end of the first century (ca. 90–100).[156] This makes Papias's testimony one of the most critical for understanding how early Christians viewed these books.

Papias provides information about a number of New Testament writings, but he speaks most plainly about the origins of the canonical Gospels:

> The Elder used to say: Mark became Peter's interpreter and wrote accurately all that he [Peter[157]] remembered (ἐμνημόνευσεν). . . . For he was intent on just one purpose: to leave nothing out that he heard or to include any falsehood among them. . . . Matthew collected the oracles (τὰ λόγια) in the Hebrew language (Ἑβραΐδι διαλέκτῳ), and each interpreted them as best he could.[158]

Papias indicates that Mark's Gospel was received on the basis of its connections with the apostle Peter—a very old tradition within early Christianity.[159] This fits well with the observation made by Richard Bauckham that Mark's Gospel forms an impressive literary inclusio centered on the person of Peter.[160] Moreover, Papias assures the reader of the reliability of Mark's account when he says that Mark made sure "to leave nothing out that he

---

[156]Richard Bauckham, *Jesus and the Eyewitnesses*, pp. 202-39. There is ongoing discussion about whether Papias only received his information from those who *followed* (παρηκολουθηκώς) the elders described in *Hist. eccl.* 3.39.3-4, or directly from the elders themselves (particularly John the Elder). Eusebius seems to indicate he received information in *both* ways (*Hist. eccl.* 3.39.7) and actually heard from John directly. Irenaeus also indicated Papias heard from "John" directly (*Haer.* 5.33.4). However, it is possible that both Eusebius and Irenaeus are mistaken and misunderstood Papias.

[157]The verb ἐμνημόνευσεν could go with either Peter or with Mark; Alexander, "Memory and Tradition," p. 118, opts for Peter.

[158]Eusebius, *Hist. eccl.* 3.39.15-16.

[159]E.g., Justin, *Dial.* 106; and Irenaeus, *Haer.* 3.10.5; Tertullian, *Marc.* 4.5.3; Eusebius, *Hist. eccl.* 2.15; 6.14.6 (attributed to Clement of Alexandria); for more on this point, see Kalin, "Early Traditions About Mark's Gospel," pp. 332-41. Kurt Niederwimmer, "Johannes Markus un die Frage nach dem Verfasser des zweiten Evangeliums," *ZNW* 58 (1967): 172-88, has argued that Papias's statements about Peter are untrustworthy and likely fabricated to bolster Mark's Gospel over against Gnostic works that were also claiming connections with Peter (e.g., Clement of Alexandria, *Strom.* 7.106.4, speaks of how the Valentinians claimed "Glaucias" was the interpreter of Peter). However, while we can never be absolutely sure Papias is truthful, we have little reason to think he is fabricating these connections to Peter, particularly given the lack of any obvious anti-Gnostic polemic. It is as likely that the Valentinians copied these earlier claims about Mark rather than the other way around (Byrskog, *Story as History*, p. 273). Other scholars disagree and have suggested that Papias is anti-Gnostic: e.g., Ron Cameron, *Sayings Traditions in the Apocryphon of James* (Philadelphia: Fortress, 1984), pp. 98-99; and Walter Bauer, *Orthodoxy and Heresy in Earliest Christianity* (Philadelphia: Fortress, 1971), pp. 184-88.

[160]Bauckham, *Jesus and the Eyewitnesses*, pp. 124-26, 155-82.

heard or to include any falsehood among them"—a standard "integrity formula" reflective of Deuteronomy 4:2.[161] If Papias received Mark's Gospel on the basis of its apostolic (and eyewitness) credentials, no doubt he would have regarded it as having substantial authority.[162] This also likely explains Papias's reception of Matthew's Gospel—he viewed it too as an early apostolic witness.[163] Indeed, Cameron argues that Papias's entire discussion is designed to show that Mark and Matthew are a "reliable, authoritative witness" and derive "from the earliest stage of transmission."[164] In other words, according to Papias, the reliability of Mark and Matthew is "guaranteed by authoritative remembrances."[165] In this regard, there is a striking parallel between the way Papias describes the canonical Gospels as something "remembered" (ἐμνημόνευσεν) by the apostles,[166] and the way Justin Martyr describes the Gospels as the "memoirs" (ἀπομνημονεύματα) of the apostles.[167] This shows an impressive amount of continuity in early gospel traditions—apparently Justin was simply following a well-established pattern, already present in Papias's time, of describing the canonical Gospels as the "memoirs of the apostles."

Of course, some scholars have argued that the "Matthew" mentioned by Papias is not really a reference to our canonical Matthew but probably to an

---

[161]For more on this "integrity formula" in early Christianity, see David E. Aune, *Revelation 17-22* (WBC; Nashville: Thomas Nelson, 1998), pp. 1208-16; and Michael J. Kruger, "Early Christian Attitudes Toward the Reproduction of Texts," in *Early Text of the New Testament*, pp. 63-80. Not only is this formula present in other Jewish literature outside the Old Testament (e.g., *Aristeas* 310-311; *1 En.* 104:9-10; 1 Macc 8:30; Josephus, *Ag. Ap.* 1.42; 11QT^a 54.5-7; *b. Meg.* 14a), but it is also reflected in Greco-Roman writers such as Artemidorus (*Oneirocritica* 2.70), Aristides (*Orations* 30.20), Chariton (*Chaereas and Callirhoe* 3.1.5), Cicero (*De oratore* 3.8.29), Dionysius of Halicarnassus (*Antiquitates Romanae* 5.8), and Lucian (*Hist. Conscr.* 47).

[162]We should be reminded here that the point of this whole chapter is simply to evaluate when early Christians viewed New Testament books as authoritative, not whether their assessments of these books were accurate. Thus it matters not whether Papias was, in fact, correct about the authorship of Mark. Rather, the point here is that Papias received it as authoritative based on his beliefs about its authorship.

[163]Papias's testimony that Matthew was received as authoritative at an early point is consistent with the fact that Matthew was one of the most (if not *the* most) popular gospels in earliest Christianity. This is borne out by the early textual witnesses to Matthew; see Tommy Wasserman, "The Early Text of Matthew," in *Early Text of the New Testament*, pp. 83-107.

[164]Cameron, *Sayings Traditions*, p. 110.

[165]Ibid., p. 112. See also Andrew F. Walls, "Papias and Oral Tradition," *VC* 21 (1967): 137-40.

[166]*Hist. eccl.* 3.39.15.

[167]*Dial.* 106.3.

early Aramaic sayings source, perhaps similar to Q.[168] This argument is based on the following: (1) Papias's Matthew was originally written in Hebrew and we know that the canonical Matthew was not;[169] and (2) Papias's Matthew is called τὰ λόγια ("the oracles"), which is not a normal term for the Gospels and again suggests a sayings source like Q. But neither of these is a compelling reason to think something other than the canonical Matthew is meant. The odd statement that Matthew originally wrote in Ἑβραΐδι διαλέκτῳ can be understood as indicating that Matthew wrote in a Hebraic *style*,[170] or that Papias was simply confused on this particular point,[171] but neither requires that Papias is referring to a Q-like source. As for τὰ λόγια, the phrase is also used by Papias to describe the Gospel of Mark, which is clearly not just a sayings source because Papias said it included "things said or *done* by the Lord."[172]

---

[168]John Nolland, *The Gospel of Matthew: A Commentary on the Greek Text* (NIGTC; Grand Rapids: Eerdmans, 2005), p. 3; Thomas W. Manson, "The Gospel of St. Matthew," in *Studies in the Gospels and Epistles*, ed. Matthew Black (Edinburgh: T & T Clark, 1962), pp. 68-104; Annand, "Papias and the Four Gospels"; and Matthew Black, "The Use of Rhetorical Terminology in Papias on Mark and Matthew," *JSNT* 37 (1989): 31-41.

[169]We have no reason to think Matthew was originally written in Hebrew; see Josef Kürzinger, *Papias Von Hierapolis Und Die Evangelien Des Neuen Testaments* (Regensburg: F. Pustet, 1983), pp. 9-32; and Albertus F. J. Klijn, *Jewish-Christian Gospel Tradition* (Leiden: E. J. Brill, 1992), p. 11. However, some have suggested the theory that there was an early form of Matthew in Hebrew (a proto-Matthew) that was later expanded into our current Greek Matthew; see Malcolm Lowe and David Flusser, "Evidence Corroborating a Modified Proto-Matthean Synoptic Theory," *NTS* 29 (1983): 25-47.

[170]Kürzinger, *Papias Von Hierapolis Und Die Evangelien Des Neuen Testaments*, pp. 9-32; Gundry, *Matthew*, pp. 619-20. Others have disagreed with Kürzinger's hypothesis, including Hengel, *Four Gospels*, p. 71; and Davies and Allison, *Matthew*, p. 16.

[171]Jewish-Christian gospels (some which were purported to be originally in Hebrew) have a complicated history in early Christianity. For an introduction to Jewish Christian gospels, see Klijn, *Jewish-Christian Gospel Tradition*, pp. 3-43; and Philipp Vielhauer and Georg Strecker, "Jewish-Christian Gospels," in *New Testament Apocrypha*, vol. 1, pp. 134-78. Since Matthew was well known as a Jewish gospel, it is not difficult to see how Papias and others might get confused on its original language. Such confusion on this issue, however, would not necessitate that Papias is confused on other issues; see France, *Matthew*, pp. 64-66.

[172]*Hist. eccl.* 3.39.15. Moreover, τά λόγια is also used for Old Testament Scripture (e.g., Acts 7:38; Rom 3:2), and for the title of Papias's own work, Λογίων κυριακῶν ἐξηγήσεος, which clearly refers to more than just sayings of Jesus. For more on the meaning of τά λόγια, see Dieter Lührmann, "Q: Sayings of Jesus or Logia?," in *The Gospels Behind the Gospels: Current Studies on Q*, ed. Ronald A. Piper (Leiden: E. J. Brill, 1995), pp. 97-116. Lührmann makes a compelling argument that Papias's use of λόγια rather than λόγοι is noteworthy because the former means not just "words" but "inspired divine utterances from the past" (p. 108). If so, then Papias's use of this word for Mark and Matthew is an indication that he viewed them as being, in some sense, authoritative divine speech.

As for other New Testament writings, it appears that Papias also knew 1 John,[173] 1 Peter,[174] Revelation[175] and also some Pauline epistles.[176] Given that Papias knew Johannine writings, and also sat under John's preaching, we have good grounds for thinking he would have known John's Gospel.[177] This possibility is given further credence when we recognize that the list of disciples given by Papias matches the order in which they appear in John's Gospel.[178] Thus, Bauckham declares, "There should be no doubt that Papias knew the Fourth Gospel."[179] There are also good reasons to think that Papias knew Luke, but we cannot be sure.[180] But, if he did, then this suggests a Fourfold Gospel in the first half of the second century—something also suggested by a number of other scholars.[181]

---

[173]*Hist. eccl.* 3.39.17.

[174]Ibid.

[175]Andrew of Caesarea, *On the Apocalypse* 34.12.

[176]Richard Heard, "Papias' Quotations from the New Testament," *NTS* 1 (1954): 130-34, argues that Papias likely used a number of Paul's epistles (particularly 1 and 2 Corinthians).

[177]Hill, *Johannine Corpus in the Early Church*, pp. 385-96. Richard Bauckham, "Papias and Poly-crates on the Origin of the Fourth Gospel," *JTS* 44 (1993): 24-69, makes a compelling case that if Papias appealed to 1 Peter in order to explain the origin of Mark's Gospel, then Papias prob-ably mentioned 1 John in order to explain the origin of John's Gospel (*Hist. eccl.* 3.39.17).

[178]*Hist. eccl.* 3.39.3-4. For a statistical study of this list, see Jake H. O'Connell, "A Note on Papias's Knowledge of the Fourth Gospel," *JBL* 129 (2010): 793-94. But not all are convinced that the order of Papias's list is a decisive consideration; see Gerd Theissen, *The New Testament: A Liter-ary History* (Minneapolis: Fortress, 2012), p. 215. The so-called anti-Marcionite prologues de-scribe Papias as a disciple of John and even the amanuensis of John's Gospel. While these connections are consistent with the other evidence we have seen, the date and reliability of these prologues is too uncertain to put much weight on them.

[179]Bauckham, "Papias and Polycrates," p. 44.

[180]Andrew of Caesarea, in his commentary on Revelation, tells us that Papias declared, "I saw Satan fallen from heaven"—a saying of Jesus found only in Luke 10:18 (translation from Hill, *Who Chose the Gospels?*, p. 214). For more on Papias's knowledge of Luke, see Charles E. Hill, "What Papias Said About John (and Luke): A New Papias Fragment," *JTS* 49 (1998): 625-29. Denis M. Farkasfalvy, "The Papias Fragments on Mark and Matthew and Their Relationship to Luke's Prologue: An Essay on the Pre-History of the Synoptic Problem," in *The Early Church in Its Context: Essays in Honor of Everett Ferguson*, ed. Abraham J. Malherbe, Frederick W. Norris and James W. Thompson (Leiden: E. J. Brill, 1998), pp. 92-106.

[181]A date for the Fourfold Gospel in the first half of the second century is also affirmed by: Christian-Bernard Amphoux, "La finale longue de Marc: un épilogue des quatre évangiles," in *The Synoptic Gospels: Source Criticism and the New Literary Criticism*, ed. Camille Focant (Leuven: Leuven Uni-versity Press, 1993), pp. 548-55 (early second century); T. C. Skeat, "The Origin of the Christian Codex," *ZPE* 102 (1994): 263-68 (early second century); Stanton, "Fourfold Gospel," pp. 317-46 (ca. A.D. 150); and James A. Kelhoffer, *Miracle and Mission: The Authentication of Missionaries and Their Message in the Longer Ending of Mark* (Tübingen: Mohr Siebeck, 2000). Older works affirm-ing an early date for the Fourfold Gospel include Theodor Zahn, *Geschichte des neutestamentlichen Kanons*; Harnack, *Origin of the New Testament*, pp. 68-83; and Edgar J. Goodspeed, *The Formation of the New Testament* (Chicago: University of Chicago Press, 1926), pp. 33-41.

In light of the methodological skepticism often displayed toward the apostolic fathers (discussed above), this testimony from Papias is particularly stunning. While some scholars have argued that the citations in the apostolic fathers ought to be explained solely on the basis of oral tradition, Papias reminds us that early Christians (even by the end of the first century) were already thinking of Jesus tradition in light of *written* documents—two of which were named Matthew and Mark. This fact alone should provide doubts about whether oral tradition (or apocryphal sources) should be viewed as the primary source for Jesus tradition during this time period.[182]

The Epistle of Barnabas. Written sometime in the early second century (ca. 130), the *Epistle of Barnabas* was quite popular with early Christians.[183] It is a theological treatise that argues, among other things, that Christians are the rightful heirs and interpreters of the Old Testament.[184] At one point it appears to cite a New Testament book: ὡς γέγραπται πολλοὶ κλητοὶ ὀλίγοι δὲ ἐκλεκτοὶ εὑρεθῶμεν ("As it is written, 'Many are called, but few are chosen'").[185] The fact that the only parallel for this citation is Matthew 22:14 has led a number of scholars, including Köhler and Carleton Paget, to suggest that Matthew is the most likely source.[186] The standard attempt to explain such citations by appealing to oral tradition is not possible in this case due to the introductory phrase γέγραπται[187]—a written source is surely required.[188] And while we certainly cannot rule out the possibility that

---

[182]Of course Papias is quite willing to draw on the "living voice" (*Hist. eccl.* 3.39.4) in addition to written gospels. But this does not indicate, as so many suppose, that oral tradition is the *only* or *primary* source of his information (see discussion on this often misunderstood statement in chapter three above).

[183]For a broad overview, see J. Carleton Paget, *The Epistle of Barnabas: Outlook and Background* (Tübingen: Mohr Siebeck, 1994).

[184]For discussion of the purpose and theology of *Barnabas*, see Carleton Paget, *Epistle of Barnabas*, pp. 46-70.

[185]*Barn.* 4:14.

[186]Köhler, *Die Rezeption des Matthäusevangeliums in der Zeit vor Irenäus*, p. 113; James Carleton Paget, "The *Epistle of Barnabas* and the Writings That Later Formed the New Testament," in *Reception of the New Testament in the Apostolic Fathers*, pp. 229-49.

[187]The same word appears in *Barn.* 5:2; 14:6; 15:1; and 16:6.

[188]Even if *Barnabas* is quoting from a written source, this does not mean that the phrase had no oral history. It is interesting to note that this same phrase appears as a textual variant at Matthew 20:16 according to some manuscripts (C D W Θ *f*¹ *f*¹³). J. Vernon Bartlet, "The Epistle of Barnabas," in *New Testament in the Apostolic Fathers*, p. 18, suggests this is evidence that this phrase had an oral history. However, Bruce M. Metzger, *A Textual Commentary on the Greek New Testament* (Stuttgart: German Bible Society, 1994), p. 41, suggests this textual variation is more likely due to a scribe who was harmonizing the text with Matthew 22:14.

Barnabas is drawing upon another written gospel besides Matthew, it seems
unreasonable to insist that such an unknown gospel is the *better* explanation of the data. After all, we know that Matthew was a very popular
writing during this time period and was certainly regarded as Scripture by
others (including Justin Martyr and probably Papias). Moreover, Pier Beatrice has argued that both Matthew and *Barnabas* introduce the citation in
a very similar theological context—a polemic against the Jews combined
with a warning against the new people of God—making it even more likely
that the latter is directly citing the former.[189]

Some have still insisted that *Barnabas* is not citing Matthew by suggesting that (1) the author of *Barnabas* mistakenly believed the passage
came from the Old Testament, or that (2) the author is drawing on a similar
text in 4 Ezra 8:3: "many are created but few are saved."[190] However, not only
is there no evidence that Barnabas made a mistake (that is pure conjecture),
but there is minimal verbal overlap between *Barnabas* 4:14 and 4 Ezra 8:3.
Why should we prefer 4 Ezra as a source when the match with Matthew is
nearly identical? Moreover, if we are trying to trace relationships between
these texts, then it is more likely that Matthew 22:14 was itself a modifi-
cation/extrapolation of 4 Ezra 8:3, which was then quoted later by the
author of *Barnabas*.[191] In fact, a number of scholars have argued Matthew
22:14 is a redactional addition of Matthew.[192] And if *Barnabas* reflects
knowledge of a Matthean redaction, then this increases the likelihood that
it was actually drawing on Matthew's Gospel.[193] Carleton Paget concludes:

---

[189]Pier F. Beatrice, "Une citation de l'Évangile de Matthieu dans l'Épître de Barnabé," in *New Testament in Early Christianity*, pp. 231-45.

[190]Young, *Jesus Tradition*, p. 27; Hagner, "Sayings of Jesus," p. 242. Similar phrases are found in 2 *Bar.* 44:15; and Plato, *Phaedo* 69c.

[191]That Matthew 22:14 is a modified/redacted version of earlier Jewish sources has been argued by Daniel C. Olson, "Matthew 22:1-14 as Midrash," *CBQ* 67 (2005): 435-53, esp. p. 437. Simi-larly, see Ben F. Meyer, "Many (=All) Are Called, But Few (=Not All) Are Chosen," *NTS* 36 (1990): 89-97, esp. pp. 96-97.

[192]Gundry, *Matthew*, pp. 169-70; Joachim Jeremias, *The Parables of Jesus* (New York: Scribner, 1955), p. 38; Eta Linnemann, *Parables of Jesus: Introduction and Exposition* (London: SPCK, 1975), pp. 93-94; and Bernard B. Scott, *Hear Then the Parable: A Commentary on the Parables of Jesus* (Minneapolis: Fortress, 1989), p. 162. Also, most scholars do not consider Matthew 22:14 to be part of Q, but a redaction of an earlier version of this parable (which Luke 14:16-24 re-produces most closely). See James M. Robinson, Paul Hoffmann and John S. Kloppenborg, eds., *The Critical Edition of Q* (Minneapolis: Fortress, 2000), p. 448.

[193]Koester, *Synoptische Überlieferung*, p. 3, has argued that we can only be certain an author is draw-ing on a written gospel when it shows familiarity with redactional portions of those gospels.

But in spite of all these arguments, it still remains the case that the closest existing text to *Barn* 4.14 in all known literature is Matt 22.14, and one senses that attempts to argue for independence from Matthew are partly motivated by a desire to avoid the implications of the *formula citandi* ["it is written"] which introduces the relevant words: namely, that the author of *Barnabas* regarded Matthew as scriptural.[194]

If we are correct that *Barnabas* is citing the Gospel of Matthew as Scripture, then we might be more open to considering the possibility that he does so elsewhere in his treatise.[195] In addition, it tells us something critical about this time period; it tells us that early Christians were not, in principle, opposed to (or unfamiliar with) the idea that a written New Testament text could be considered "Scripture" on par with the Old.[196]

Ignatius. Ignatius is a particularly useful source for analyzing the early reception of New Testament writings not only because he was an influential bishop in a major metropolitan city (Antioch), but also because he wrote numerous epistles at the turn of the century en route to his martyrdom in Rome (ca. A.D. 110).[197] Most noteworthy is that Ignatius appears to have known and used quite an extensive collection of Paul's letters. Paul Foster is quite confident that Ignatius knew at least four of these—1 Corinthians, Ephesians, and 1 and 2 Timothy.[198] This is confirmed not only by Ignatius's citation of these books,[199] but also by a statement in his epistle to the Ephe-

---

[194]Carleton Paget, *"Epistle of Barnabas,"* p. 233.

[195]E.g., 5.9 reads ὅτι οὐκ ἦλθεν καλέσαι δικαίους ἀλλὰ ἁμαρτωλούς ("for he did not come to call the righteous, but sinners") and is nearly identical to Matthew 9:13.

[196]Again, the fact that *Barnabas* cites other literature outside the Old and New Testaments as "Scripture" (e.g., 16.5 cites *1 En.* 89 with "For Scripture says") is beside the point being made here. The question is not whether there was agreement among early Christians on the extent of "Scripture," but simply whether early Christians understood that new scriptural books had been given under the administration of the new covenant.

[197]For a helpful introduction to Ignatius and his writings, see Paul Foster, *The Writings of the Apostolic Fathers* (London: T & T Clark, 2007), pp. 81-107 (though he takes a later date for the letters, ca. 125-150); William R. Schoedel, *Ignatius of Antioch* (Philadelphia: Fortress, 1985); and, most recently, Thomas A. Robinson, *Ignatius of Antioch and the Parting of the Ways: Early Jewish-Christian Relations* (Grand Rapids: Baker Academic, 2009).

[198]Paul Foster, "The Epistles of Ignatius of Antioch and the Writings That Later Formed the New Testament," in *Reception of the New Testament in the Apostolic Fathers*, pp. 159-86, at p. 172. A similar conclusion is found in William R. Inge, "Ignatius," in *New Testament and the Apostolic Fathers*, pp. 61-83. Schoedel, *Ignatius*, p. 9, is willing to say that Ignatius only has "certain" knowledge of 1 Corinthians (despite the fact that Ignatius clearly knew multiple letters of Paul).

[199]E.g., Ign. *Eph.* 14:1; 16:1; 18.1; Ign. *Magn.* 8:1; 10:2; Ign. *Rom.* 5:1; 9:2; Ign. *Pol.* 5:1.

sians: "Paul, who was sanctified, who gained a good report, who was right blessed, in whose footsteps may I be found when I shall attain to God, who in *every epistle* makes mention of you in Christ Jesus."[200] It is clear that Ignatius possesses a Pauline letter collection which would have been composed of at least the Pauline letters that expressly mention the Ephesian church, namely 1 Corinthians, Ephesians, and 1 and 2 Timothy.[201] But some have suggested that we need not take Ignatius's statement as an indication that he possessed *only* these four letters—his language may simply indicate that he remembered (or prayed for) the Ephesians even as he wrote other letters,[202] or his language might simply be "a polite exaggeration."[203] The fact that Ignatius also appears to know Romans, Philippians and Galatians suggests his Pauline letter collection might have been quite extensive.[204] Regardless, the key point is that Ignatius not only has a Pauline letter collection, but mentions it to the Ephesian church with full expectation that they are also aware of it. The fact that Ignatius does not introduce, defend, or elaborate on Paul's collection suggests that it is well known not only to Ignatius himself but also to his audience.

As for the authority Ignatius attached to the Pauline letters, the citation above already indicates that he had a high view of Paul's office, describing him as one "blessed in whose footsteps may I be found."[205] Elsewhere, Ignatius acknowledges the full apostolic authority of Paul (and other apostles) and views it as categorically different from his own: "I am not enjoining [commanding] you as Peter and Paul did. They were apostles, I am condemned."[206]

---

[200]Ign. *Eph.* 12:2 (emphasis added).

[201]1 Corinthians 15:32; 16:8; Ephesians 1:1 (though ἐν Ἐφέσῳ is omitted in P⁴⁶, ℵ* and B); 1 Timothy 1:3; 2 Timothy 1:18; 4:12; and possibly Romans 16:5. For more on the critical and central role of Ephesus in early Christianity, see Paul R. Trebilco, *The Early Christians in Ephesus from Paul to Ignatius* (Tübingen: Mohr Siebeck, 2004); and Eugene E. Lemcio, "Ephesus and the New Testament Canon," *BJRL* 69 (1986): 210-34.

[202]Heinrich Rathke, *Ignatius von Antiochien und die Paulusbriefe* (Berlin: Akademie-Verlag, 1967), pp. 21-22. It is worth noting that the English "makes mention" may not be the best translation of μνημονεύει (Ign. *Eph.* 12:2). Instead it is possible (and maybe even preferable) to render this verb as "to remember" or "to think of."

[203]Daniel Hoffman, "The Authority of Scripture and Apostolic Doctrine in Ignatius of Antioch," *JETS* 28 (1985): 75. See also J. B. Lightfoot, *The Apostolic Fathers* (2 vols.; London: MacMillan, 1889), 2:65-66; and Schoedel, *Ignatius*, 73n7.

[204]Lightfoot, *Apostolic Fathers*, 2:65-66; Schoedel, *Ignatius*, p. 73; Metzger, *Canon of the New Testament*, p. 49.

[205]Ign. *Eph.* 12:2.

[206]Ign. *Rom.* 4:4.

And again he says, "I have not thought that I, a condemned man, should give you orders like an apostle."[207] Throughout his writings, Ignatius offers repeated and overt references to the absolute and unparalleled authority of the apostles.[208] Hill draws the natural implications from such a fact when he notes that any apostolic texts known by Ignatius would have "held an extremely if not supremely high standing with him."[209] Similarly, Robert Grant argues that Ignatius regarded apostolic doctrine as supreme and "it makes little difference to him whether the doctrine has been transmitted in oral or in written form."[210] Thus, whether or not Ignatius explicitly uses the term "Scripture" in reference to Paul's letters is beside the point—his opinion of apostolic texts would have already been clear to the reader.[211]

But, Ignatius did not receive apostolic instruction only from Paul. At numerous points he exhorts his readers to follow the "decrees" (δόγμασιν) and "ordinances" (διαταγμάτων) of the apostles.[212] The fact that he uses the plural "apostles" suggests that he is thinking of a larger deposit of apostolic material beyond Paul, perhaps including Peter, John and others. But what is the source of this apostolic instruction now that the apostles themselves are gone? Certainly it is possible that he is just referring to the

---

[207]Ign. *Trall.* 3:3.

[208]Charles E. Hill, "Ignatius and the Apostolate," in *Studia Patristica*, vol. 36 (Leuven: Peeters, 2001), pp. 226-48.

[209]Hill, "Ignatius and the Apostolate," p. 234.

[210]Robert M. Grant, "Scripture and Tradition in St. Ignatius of Antioch," *CBQ* 25 (1963): 327.

[211]Sundberg, "Biblical Canon and the Christian Doctrine of Inspiration," pp. 352-71, has argued that Ignatius, and other church fathers, viewed themselves as "inspired" with the same level of authority as the apostles (e.g., Ign. *Trall.* 4:1; Ign. *Rom.* 8:3; Ign. *Phld.* 7:1-2). Others have made similar arguments; e.g., Everett Kalin, "The Inspired Community: A Glance at Canon History," *CTM* 42 (1971): 205-8; Craig D. Allert, *A High View of Scripture? The Authority of the Bible and the Formation of the New Testament Canon* (Grand Rapids: Baker Academic, 2007), pp. 58-66. However, it is not at all clear that these passages in Ignatius necessarily indicate that he viewed his authority as equal to the apostles. Sundberg does not seem to recognize that similar language can sometimes be used to speak of both ecclesiastical authority and apostolic authority. When the larger context of Ignatius's writings are taken into consideration, there is little doubt that he sees the authority of the apostles as unique and unparalleled (Hill, "Ignatius and the Apostolate," pp. 226-48.). The same is true of other church fathers. While Irenaeus makes occasional statements that indicate the Holy Spirit is at work in the church of his own day (*Haer.* 5.6.1), there are no grounds for pressing this to mean that he would accept modern-day writings as equivalent to the writings of the apostles—on the contrary, Irenaeus is very clear that the apostles are behind the authoritative books he receives (*Haer.* 3.1.1). For more this subject, see Frank Thielman, "The New Testament Canon: Its Basis for Authority," *WTJ* 45 (1983): 400-410.

[212]E.g., Ign. *Magn.* 13:1; Ign. *Trall.* 7:1.

oral tradition circulating around the churches during this time period. However, several considerations suggest that Ignatius may be referring to written apostolic instruction: (1) Ignatius and his audience *already* viewed apostolic "decrees" as something that existed in written form because they knew and used Paul's letters. Thus, it would be natural for them to understand these "decrees" and "ordinances" as referring to written texts. (2) The terms "decrees" (δόγμασιν) and "ordinances" (διαταγμάτων) were often used during this time period to refer to *written* texts, and even to the Old Testament itself.[213] (3) When Ignatius exhorts the churches to follow the decrees of the apostles, sometimes he is specific about *which* apostles he is referring to; for example, in *Rom* 4.3 he mentions that the churches have received commands from both Paul and Peter. But if Ignatius's audience is able to distinguish between Paul's commands and Peter's commands, then this suggests that some of their apostolic sources have Paul's name attached, and others have Peter's name attached. A natural explanation of this phenomenon is that they possessed distinctive written documents, some attributed to Peter and others to Paul. (4) One of the most overlooked aspects of Ignatius's exhortations to follow the "decrees" of the apostles is that his exhortations presume (quite naturally) that the recipients have access to the *same* apostolic teaching he does. This presumption that all these churches have a common, fixed source for apostolic teaching is explained well by the fact that they all possessed the same apostolic documents. (5) Our inclinations are supported by the fact that, according to a number of scholars, Ignatius appears to know other apostolic writings, particularly the Gospels of Matthew and John, and possibly Luke.[214]

---

[213]See examples in Hill, "Ignatius and the Apostolate," pp. 235-39.

[214]E.g., Ign. *Smyrn.* 6:1 (Mt 19:12); Ign. *Smyrn.* 1:1 (Mt 3:15); Ign. *Magn.* 8:2 (Jn 1:14; 17:16); Ign. *Phld.* 7:1 (Jn 3:8); Ign. *Smyrn* 3:2 (Lk 24:39). For more, see Inge, "Ignatius," pp. 63-83 (who argues on p. 83 that it is "highly probable" that Ignatius used John); Charles E. Hill, "Ignatius, 'The Gospel,' and the Gospels," in *Trajectories Through the New Testament and the Apostolic Fathers*, pp. 267-85; Hill, *Johannine Corpus*, argues that "Ignatius' knowledge of John can be taken as proved" (p. 442); Foster, "Epistles of Ignatius of Antioch," p. 180, argues that there is one "certain" place where Ignatius cites Matthew's Gospel (e.g., Ign. *Smyrn.* 1:1); Grant, "Scripture and Tradition," pp. 325-27, argues that Ignatius knew Matthew and John; Metzger, *Canon of the New Testament*, pp. 44-49. An argument that Ignatius did not know Matthew can be found in J. Smit Sibinga, "Ignatius and Matthew," *NovT* 8 (1966): 263-83. For an overall assessment of the relationship between Matthew and Ignatius, see Christine Trevett, "Approaching Matthew from the Second Century: The Under-Used Ignatian Correspondence," *JSNT* 20 (1984): 59-67.

Michael Goulder and Charles Hill even argue that Ignatius often uses the term "gospel" not to refer to oral preaching as is so often claimed,[215] but as a reference to the written Gospels.[216]

Ignatius, then, not only stands as a witness to the high authority early Christians attributed to the apostles and their teachings—an authority that would be functionally indistinguishable from Scripture—but also demonstrates that Christians were using written documents as a source for this apostolic teaching. And these written documents are many of the same written documents found in our New Testament: 1 Corinthians, Ephesians, 1 and 2 Timothy (possibly Romans, Philippians and Galatians), Matthew and John (and possibly Luke). Of course, we should remember that this does not mean that Ignatius was unaware of other New Testament documents (he may have known and used more than these), but it simply means that the extant writings of Ignatius give no indication either way.

Polycarp. Polycarp was a central figure in the earliest stages of Christianity.[217] Not only was he the bishop of Smyrna at the turn of the century, but he apparently knew the apostle John personally.[218] Moreover, he was said to have been a companion of Papias and also the teacher/mentor of Irenaeus himself.[219] It is no surprise, then, that Polycarp is aware of apostolic writings and values them highly. He mentions Paul several times,[220] acknowledges that he is an apostle,[221] and distinguishes Paul's authority from his own authority as a bishop: "For neither I nor anyone like me is able to replicate the wisdom of the blessed and glorious Paul."[222] Moreover, he is aware of a Pauline letter collection[223] and exhorts his audience to read

---

[215]Koester, *Ancient Christian Gospels*, pp. 7-8.

[216]Michael D. Goulder, "Ignatius' 'Docetists,'" *VC* 53 (1999): 16-30; Hill, "Ignatius, 'The Gospel,' and the Gospels," pp. 271-74.

[217]For a brief introduction to Polycarp, see Michael W. Holmes, "Polycarp of Smyrna, Epistle to the Philippians," in *The Writings of the Apostolic Fathers*, ed. Paul Foster (London: T & T Clark, 2007), pp. 108-25.

[218]*Hist. eccl.* 5.20.4-7.

[219]*Hist. eccl.* 5.33.4.

[220]*Phil.* 3.2; 9.1; 11.2, 3.

[221]*Phil.* 9.1.

[222]*Phil.* 3.2.

[223]Polycarp refers to Paul's "letters" (*Phil.* 3.2). Since Polycarp is writing to the Philippians, some have questioned whether he implied Paul wrote more than one letter to the Philippians, or whether the plural here could refer to a single letter; e.g., J. B. Lightfoot, *St. Paul's Epistle to the*

Paul's letters: "If you carefully peer into them, you will be able to be built up in the faith that was given to you."[224] Although Polycarp does not indicate the precise scope of his Pauline letter collection, we can achieve a broad outline of it by observing which letters he cites/uses. Scholars generally agree that Polycarp knew Romans, 1 Corinthians, Galatians, Ephesians, Philippians, and 1 and 2 Timothy.[225] Again, Polycarp may have known *more* letters of Paul than these, but he simply doesn't use them in his letter to the Philippians.

As for the authority that Polycarp attributes to Paul's letters, we should not forget the way Polycarp shows honor to Paul as an apostle—and acknowledges that Paul's apostolic authority is notably different from his own authority as a bishop.[226] In fact, in *Phil.* 6.3 Polycarp places the "apostles" alongside the "prophets" as equal authorities, showing that he sees revelation as delivered in two distinct epochs.[227] Denis Farkasfalvy observes that this prophet-apostle structure in Polycarp—what he calls a theology of the "proto-Canon"—is also well attested throughout other early Christian texts, including New Testament books, the apostolic fathers, Justin Martyr, Irenaeus, Tertullian and others.[228] According to Werner Kümmel, such lan-

---

Philippians (Peabody, MA: Hendrickson, 1995), pp. 140-42. However, the more natural solution seems to be that Polycarp regards all of Paul's letters as intended for every church, even if not directly addressed to them. See Andreas Lindemann, "Paul in the Writings of the Apostolic Fathers," in *Paul and the Legacies of Paul*, ed. William S. Babcock (Dallas: Southern Methodist University Press, 1990), pp. 25-45, esp. pp. 41-42. For an overview of the options, see Michael W. Holmes, "Paul and Polycarp," in *Paul and the Second Century*, ed. Michael Bird and Joseph R. Dodson (London: T & T Clark, 2011), pp. 57-69, at p. 58n10.

[224]*Phil* 3.2.

[225]Paul Hartog, *Polycarp and the New Testament: The Occasion, Rhetoric, Theme, and Unity of the Epistle to the Philippians and Its Allusions to New Testament Literature* (Tübingen: J. C. B. Mohr, 2001), p. 195; Kenneth Berding, *Polycarp and Paul: An Analysis of Their Literary and Theological Relationship in Light of Polycarp's Use of Biblical and Extra-Biblical Literature* (Leiden: E. J. Brill, 2002), p. 187; Michael W. Holmes, "Polycarp's Letter to the Philippians and the Writings That Later Formed the New Testament," in *Reception of the New Testament in the Apostolic Fathers*, p. 226; and Paul V. M. Benecke, "The Epistle of Polycarp," in *New Testament in the Apostolic Fathers*, pp. 84-104.

[226]*Phil.* 3.2.

[227]Helmut Koester, *Introduction to the New Testament*, vol. 2, *History and Literature of Early Christianity* (Philadelphia: Fortress, 1982), p. 307, argues that "for Polycarp there is no apostolic authority other than Paul." But this seems contrary to all the evidence. Not only does Polycarp mention plural "apostles" (*Phil.* 6.3; 9.2), but he knows 1 Peter and 1 John (see below). In addition, Paul himself acknowledges the existence of other apostles (e.g., Gal 2:2).

[228]Denis M. Farkasfalvy, "'Prophets and Apostles': The Conjunction of the Two Terms Before Irenaeus," in *Texts and Testaments*, p. 120.

guage in Polycarp, and other early Christian texts, constitutes the "first steps in the direction of a new Scripture."[229]

But, beyond even this, we have indications that Polycarp regarded Pauline letters as "Scripture." Writing circa A.D. 110, Polycarp appears to cite Paul's letter to the Ephesians, "As it is written in these Scriptures, 'Be angry and do not sin and do not let the sun go down on your anger.'"[230] Although the first part of this quote could come from Psalm 4:4, the two parts together come from Ephesians 4:26. Even though Paul Benecke, in the original Oxford study of the apostolic fathers, affirmed that "the collocation of the two passages in Polycarp is almost certainly due to Ephesians,"[231] other scholars have resisted this conclusion.[232] L. Michael White suggests that Polycarp is only using "Scripture" to refer to the first half of the quote (from Psalms) and not the second half.[233] But there is no indication in the text that Polycarp treats the two halves of the quote any differently— "Scripture" applies to them both equally.[234] Helmut Koester attempts to explain the citation by arguing that Polycarp simply made a mistake and erroneously believed that the entire phrase in Ephesians 4:26 came from Psalm 4:4.[235] However, the argument that Polycarp made a mistake is pure conjecture and ignores the fact that Polycarp has a "very good memory" when it comes to Pauline citations.[236] For this reason, Boudewijn Dehand-

---

[229]Werner G. Kümmel, *Introduction to the New Testament* (London: SCM Press, 1975), p. 485.

[230]Polycarp, *Phil.* 12.1. Latin text: *Modo, ut his scripturis dictum est, irascimini et nolite peccare, et sol non occidat super iracundiam vestram.* Holmes argues that since we cannot be sure of the original Greek terms used by Polycarp then we cannot be sure he intended to cite this passage as Scripture ("Polycarp's Letter to the Philippians," p. 210n99). Holmes's caution is certainly appropriate. However, while there will always be some ambiguity in terms of what Polycarp's original Greek read, the term *scripturis* in Latin is a fairly reliable reference to Scripture. For examples of *scripturis* as the Latin translation of γραφαί ("Scripture"), see Charles M. Nielsen, "Polycarp, Paul, and the Scriptures," *AThR* 47 (1965): 200. It is also interesting to note that James Donaldson, *The Apostolic Fathers: A Critical Acccount of Their Genuine Writings and of Their Doctrines* (London: Macmillan, 1874), p. 243, was so convinced that *scripturis* referred to authoritative Scripture that he argued it must be a later interpolation.

[231]Benecke, "Polycarp," p. 93; cf. Metzger, *Canon of the New Testament*, p. 62.

[232]For a survey of the different options see Berding, *Polycarp and Paul*, pp. 117-19; and Paul Hartog, "Polycarp, Ephesians, and 'Scripture,'" *WTJ* 70 (2008): 255-75.

[233]L. Michael White, *From Jesus to Christianity* (San Francisco: HarperOne, 2004), p. 354 (see also p. 481n72).

[234]Berding, *Polycarp and Paul*, p. 118.

[235]Koester, *Synoptische Überlieferung*, p. 113. Cf. Ernst Käsemann, *Das Neue Testament als Kanon* (Göttingen: Vandenhoeck u. Ruprecht, 1970), p. 67n15.

[236]Berding, *Polycarp and Paul*, p. 118.

schutter considers such a mistake by Polycarp to be "very unlikely" and argues that "The real reason for Köster's reservation seems to be the implications for the history of the Canon."[237] Even Lee McDonald agrees that Polycarp calls Ephesians "Scripture."[238] If so, then we have good reasons to think that Polycarp would have regarded *other* Pauline letters as Scripture. Why would they bear a different level of authority than Ephesians? Indeed, Nielsen argues that Polycarp's letter is a strong indication that by the early second century "a sacred Christian Scripture was emerging with the Pauline corpus as its foundation."[239]

In addition to Paul's epistles, most scholars agree that Polycarp also knew 1 Peter and 1 John, suggesting that he was familiar with a corpus of writings from a number of different apostles.[240] Given the high authority that Polycarp grants to the apostles (as noted above), it is reasonable to think that letters from Peter and John would bear the same authority as letters from Paul. As for whether Polycarp used the canonical Gospels, the evidence is less clear. However, he does appear to quote from some of the Synoptic Gospels on a number of occasions.[241] Benecke even concedes that when it comes to the Lord's prayer (Mt 26:41; Mk 14:38; *Phil. 7.2*), Polycarp's citation "agrees *verbatim* with Matthew and Mark, and appears in a very similar context to that in the Gospels."[242] The fact that Polycarp appears to be aware of the flow and context of the canonical Gospels, instead of just an isolated saying, has led even Koester to admit that Polycarp seems to know these Synoptic passages.[243] Berding also regards it as "almost certain" that Polycarp is citing the Gospel of Matthew here.[244] Although Polycarp does not cite John's Gospel directly, Charles E. Hill has made a compelling case that he knew it—particularly given that fact that he knew 1 John and the

---

[237]Boudewijn Dehandschutter, "Polycarp's Epistle to the Philippians: An Early Example of 'Reception,'" in *New Testament in Early Christianity*, p. 282.

[238]McDonald, *Biblical Canon*, p. 276. See also Nielsen, "Polycarp, Paul, and the Scriptures," pp. 199-216.

[239]Nielsen, "Polycarp, Paul, and the Scriptures," p. 216.

[240]Hartog, "Polycarp," p. 267; Benecke, "Polycarp," pp. 84-104; Holmes, "Polycarp's Letter to the Philippians," p. 226.

[241]E.g., *Phil* 2.3; 7.2.

[242]Benecke, "Polycarp," p. 103 (emphasis original).

[243]Koester, *Synoptische Überlieferung*, pp. 114-15.

[244]Berding, *Polycarp and Paul*, p. 94.

apostle John himself.[245] However, scholars who are committed to the more stringent methodological guidelines mentioned above are reticent to affirm that Polycarp used *any* of these Gospels. After all, it is argued, we cannot be absolutely certain that Polycarp was using the canonical Gospels and not, say, oral tradition.[246] While this is certainly true, it once again raises questions about whether absolute certainty is the most reasonable goal for historical study, particularly given all the contextual factors (Polycarp was an influential bishop who knew Papias and the apostle John himself), which suggest there was a high likelihood that Polycarp would have had access to these Gospels as sources for the teachings of Jesus.[247]

1 Clement. Written at the end of the first century (ca. 96), *1 Clement* is one of the oldest Christian writings apart from the New Testament.[248] And even at this very early stage, the author relies heavily on a number of Paul's letters.[249] At a minimum, scholars are agreed that *1 Clement* certainly uses 1 Corinthians, Romans and Hebrews,[250] and a number of scholars find it probable that he also knew Galatians, Ephesians, Philippians and Titus.[251] Donald Hagner even argues that Clement knew nearly *all* of Paul's letters except 1 and 2 Thessalonians and Philemon.[252] Regardless, Clement possesses some sort of collection of Paul's letters, though the exact number is unclear. Moreover, he uses these letters quite naturally and clearly expects that his audience also has access to the very same ones.[253]

In terms of the authority that Clement attributes to Paul's letters, we must again note the authority he attributes to the apostles. "The Apostles

---

[245]Hill, *Johannine Corpus in the Early Church*, pp. 418-20.

[246]E.g., Benecke, "Polycarp," pp. 101-4; Young, *Jesus Tradition*, pp. 232-37.

[247]This addresses what Bellinzoni describes as the criteria of "accessibility" when assessing whether a writer could have cited a New Testament text; see Bellinzoni, "Gospel of Luke in the Apostolic Fathers," pp. 45-68.

[248]A helpful introduction to this letter can be found in Andrew F. Gregory, "*1 Clement*: An Introduction," in *The Writings of the Apostolic Fathers*, ed. Paul Foster (London: T & T Clark, 2007), pp. 21-31.

[249]The identity of the author of *1 Clement* is unclear; but for our purposes here we shall call the author "Clement." See discussion in Gregory, "*1 Clement*: An Introduction," pp. 23-24.

[250]Andrew F. Gregory, "1 Clement and the Writings That Later Formed the New Testament," in *Reception of the New Testament in the Apostolic Fathers*, pp. 129-57; A. J. Carlyle, "Clement of Rome," in *New Testament in the Apostolic Fathers*, pp. 37-62.

[251]Metzger, *Canon of the New Testament*, p. 42; Carlyle, "Clement of Rome," pp. 37-62. See discussion in Gregory, "1 Clement and the Writings That Later Formed the New Testament," p. 143.

[252]Hagner, *Clement of Rome*, p. 237.

[253]E.g., *1 Clem.* 47:1-3.

received the Gospel for us from the Lord Jesus Christ, Jesus the Christ was
sent from God. The Christ therefore is from God and the Apostles from the
Christ."[254] In addition, he refers to the apostles as "the greatest and most
righteous pillars of the Church."[255] Such statements leave little doubt that he
would have regarded apostolic writings as possessing the very authority of
Christ himself. For this reason he exhorts his audience to read Paul's letters:
"Take up ('Ἀναλάβετε) the epistle of that blessed apostle, Paul. . . . To be sure,
he sent you a letter in the Spirit (πνευματικῶς) concerning himself and
Cephas and Apollos."[256] It is noteworthy that Clement bolsters the authority
of Paul here by not only referring to him as "blessed" but also by expressly
stating that Paul wrote "in the Spirit" (πνευματικῶς). Kirsopp Lake understood this language to mean that Paul wrote "with true inspiration,"[257] and
Alexander Roberts and James Donaldson understood it to mean that Paul
wrote "under the inspiration of the Spirit."[258] While it is possible that such
language in the apostolic fathers can refer simply to ecclesiastical authority,[259]
it is normally used to refer to a level of inspiration that is on par with Scripture.[260] Given that the author of *1 Clement* elsewhere makes a sharp distinction between his own authority and that of the apostles (see above), it
seems reasonable to think that the latter use is in view here.

In addition, Hengel has argued that when Clement exhorts his audience
to "take up" ('Ἀναλάβετε) the letters of Paul, he is most likely referring to
public reading in a worship setting.[261] Such a practice would fit quite well

---

[254]*1 Clem.* 42:1-2.

[255]*1 Clem.* 5:2.

[256]*1 Clem.* 47:1-3. Scholars agree that this passage is a clear reference to 1 Corinthians: Lindemann, *Paulus im ältesten Christentum*, pp. 190-91; Gregory, "1 Clement and the Writings That
Later Formed the New Testament," pp. 129-57; and Hagner, *Use of the Old and New Testaments
in Clement of Rome*, pp. 196-97.

[257]Kirsopp Lake, trans., *The Apostolic Fathers* (2 vols.; London: William Hienemann, 1919), p. 91.

[258]Alexander Roberts and James Donaldson, eds., *The Ante-Nicene Fathers* (Peabody, Mass: Hendrickson, 1885), p. 18.

[259]The main example of this is *1 Clem.* 63:2. However, in this passage it is ambiguous whether the
phrase διὰ τοῦ ἁγίου πνεύματος ("through the Holy Spirit") modifies "the things written," or
whether it describes the means by which the "wanton anger" in a person is rooted out. There
are other examples where the authority of church leaders is emphasized (e.g., Ign. *Trall.* 2:1; *1
Clem.* 59:1), but the term πνευματικῶς is not used. For further discussion, see Craig D. Allert,
High View of Scripture?, pp. 60-65.

[260]E.g., *1 Clem.* 8:1; *Barn.* 14:2; Ign. *Magn.* 9:2; see similar language in Ezekiel 37:1; Matthew
22:43; Revelation 1:10.

[261]Hengel, *Four Gospels*, p. 128 (cf. p. 286n514). Clement's call for the Corinthians to "take up"

with Paul's own commands that his letters be ready publicly to the church (Col 4:16; 1 Thess 5:27; compare 2 Cor 10:9). For a book to be used in such a liturgical fashion was no doubt an indication of its high authority—that was something typically reserved for books that were regarded as Scripture (Lk 4:17-20; Acts 13:15; 15:21).[262] In fact, as we noted above, Justin Martyr informs us that the Gospels were read publicly alongside Old Testament books in worship, a clear indication that they were scriptural documents.[263] If Clement did intend for Paul's letters to be read publicly in worship, then this would be additional evidence that he regarded them as having an authority on par with Scripture.

Hagner also argues that it was very likely that Clement also knew 1 Peter, James and Acts.[264] Inasmuch as Clement regarded any of these writings as apostolic (and we do not know whether he did), then we would expect they would bear the same authority as Paul's letters. This would be particularly likely in the case of 1 Peter because Clement clearly knows Peter is an apostle[265] and places him alongside Paul as "a righteous pillar of the church."[266]

The New Testament. Leaving the world of the apostolic fathers, we consider some critical pieces of evidence from the New Testament itself. One of the earliest examples of New Testament books regarded as Scripture comes from 2 Peter 3:16, in which Paul's letters are regarded as on par with the τὰς λοιπὰς γραφὰς ("the other Scriptures") of the Old Testament. In a fashion quite similar to Ignatius, Polycarp and *1 Clement*, this passage refers not just to a single letter of Paul, but to some sort of collection or corpus of letters (the precise number is unclear) that the author presumes his audience is

---

Paul's letters (ἀναλάβετε) forms a striking parallel to 1 Esdras (I Ezra) 9:45 which asks the recipients to "take up" (ἀναλαβὼν) God's law and read it publicly to God's people.

[262]Gamble, *Books and Readers*, pp. 209-11. Of course, we know there were instances where noncanonical books were read in worship (e.g, Eusebius, *Hist. eccl.* 4.23.11). However, this does not keep us from agreeing with Gamble that "Liturgical reading was the concrete setting from which texts acquired theological authority, and in which that authority took effect" (p. 216).

[263]*1 Apol.* 67.3. Some scholars have argued that the very structure of the Gospels indicates they were intended for liturgical reading: George D. Kilpatrick, *The Origins of the Gospel According to St. Matthew* (Oxford: Clarendon, 1950), pp. 72-100; Michael D. Goulder, *Midrash and Lection in Matthew* (London: SPCK, 1974), pp. 182-83; Phillip Carrington, *The Primitive Christian Calendar: A Study in the Making of the Marcan Gospel* (Cambridge: Cambridge University Press, 1952).

[264]Hagner, *Use of the Old and New Testaments in Clement of Rome*, pp. 238-71. Carlyle, "Clement of Rome," pp. 55-58 is more pessimistic, but I find Hagner's arguments more convincing.

[265]*1 Clem.* 5:4; 47:1-3.

[266]*1 Clem.* 5:4; cf. *1 Clem.* 5:5.

familiar with.[267] On the basis of this passage, David Meade concludes that 2 Peter "clearly articulates a doctrine of 'other,' that is, Christian, scripture, which represents a significant milestone in Christian thought."[268] Meade even argues that the author of 2 Peter includes Petrine texts within this category of Christian Scripture by referring to Paul as "*our* (ἡμῶν) beloved brother" (2 Pet 3:15), a likely reference to the "college" of apostles in which Peter certainly participates (compare 2 Pet 1:16).[269]

Although some critical scholars have argued for a mid-second-century date for 2 Peter, there is little evidence to support such a late date.[270] For scholars who hold to the pseudonymity of 2 Peter, the epistle has generally been dated to the turn of the century (ca. 100–125),[271] and some have suggested an earlier time of A.D. 80–90.[272] Regardless of the position one takes on 2 Peter's authorship, this epistle provides additional evidence that Paul's letters were regarded as Scripture by the turn of the century.

Another passage worthy of consideration is 1 Timothy 5:18: λέγει γὰρ ἡ γραφή, Βοῦν ἀλοῶντα οὐ φιμώσεις, καὶ, Ἄξιος ὁ ἐργάτης τοῦ μισθοῦ αὐτοῦ ("For the Scripture says, 'You shall not muzzle an ox when it treads out the grain,' and 'The laborer deserves his wages.'"). The first citation comes from Deuteronomy 25:4, and the second is identical to a saying of

---

[267]Regarding Pauline letter collections, see David Trobisch, *Die Entstehung der Paulusbriefsammlung: Studien zu den Anfängen christlicher Publizistik (Novum testamentum et orbis antiquus)* (Göttingen: Vandenhoeck & Ruprecht, 1989); Stanley E. Porter, "When and How Was the Pauline Canon Compiled? An Assessment of Theories," in *The Pauline Canon*, ed. Stanley E. Porter (Leiden: E. J. Brill, 2004), pp. 95-127; Harry Y. Gamble, "The Redaction of the Pauline Letters and the Formation of the Pauline Corpus," *JBL* 94 (1975): 403-18; Kenneth L. Carroll, "The Expansion of the Pauline Corpus," *JBL* 72 (1953): 230-37; and Charles H. Buck Jr., "The Early Order of the Pauline Corpus," *JBL* 68 (1949): 351-57.

[268]David Meade, "Ancient Near Eastern Apocalypticism and the Origins of the New Testament Canon of Scripture," in *The Bible as a Human Witness: Hearing the Word of God Through Historically Dissimilar Traditions*, ed. Randall Heskett and Brian Irwin (London: T & T Clark, 2010), p. 318.

[269]Meade, "Ancient Near Eastern Apocalypticism," p. 318.

[270]McDonald, *Biblical Canon*, p. 277, suggests 2 Peter may be as late as ca. 180.

[271]J. N. D. Kelly, *A Commentary on the Epistles of Peter and of Jude* (New York: Harper & Row, 1969), p. 237; C. E. B. Cranfield, *I & II Peter and Jude: Introduction and Commentary* (London: SCM, 1960), p. 149; J. B. Mayor, *The Epistle of St. Jude and the Second Epistle of St. Peter* (London: Macmillan, 1907), cxxvii; Daniel J. Harrington, *Jude and 2 Peter* (Collegeville, MN: Liturgical, 2003), p. 237. Some have tried to push the epistle's date as late as the middle of the second century (e.g., McDonald, *Formation*, p. 277), but this position is decidedly in the minority, and there seems to be little evidence to justify it.

[272]E.g., Richard Bauckham, *Jude, 2 Peter* (Waco, TX: Word, 1983), p. 158; and Bo Reicke, *The Epistles of James, Peter, and Jude* (New York: Doubleday, 1964).

Jesus from Luke 10:7. Of course, there is no way to be sure that 1 Timothy is citing Luke's Gospel in this passage. But the following should be taken into consideration: (1) This citation cannot be explained by appealing to oral tradition because it is clearly referred to as ἡ γραφή.[273] Marshall notes, "A *written* source is surely required, and one that would have been authoritative."[274] (2) While another written source is a possibility (such as Q[275] or an apocryphal gospel[276]) it should be noted that the Greek text in 1 Timothy 5:18 is identical to Luke 10:7 (and *only* to Luke 10:7).[277] Thus, Luke's Gospel fits the evidence in two critical ways: not only does its wording form an exact match with 1 Timothy 5:18, but it is a book that early Christians (at some point) actually regarded as "Scripture." We have no historical evidence that either of these things is true for Q or a hypothetical apocryphal gospel. (3) The known historical connections between Paul and Luke at least provide a plausible scenario for why a Pauline letter would cite Luke's Gospel. In addition to being Paul's traveling companion throughout the book of Acts, Luke is mentioned a number of times in other Pauline letters (Col 4:14; 2 Tim 4:11; Philem 1:24) and clearly has direct connections to the apostolic circle (Lk 1:2). Moreover, there is a regular connection between Paul and Luke's Gospel in the writings of the early church fathers.[278] Some have even suggested that Luke was Paul's amanuensis for 1 Timothy.[279]

All of these considerations, especially taken in tandem, suggest that his-

---

[273]Lorenz Oberlinner, *Kommentar zum ersten Timotheusbrief* (Freiburg im Breisgau: Herder, 1994), p. 254. J. N. D. Kelly, *A Commentary on the Pastoral Epistles*, p. 126; and Martin Dibelius and Hans Conzelmann, *The Pastoral Epistles* (Philadelphia: Fortress, 1972), p. 79, have argued that only the first half of the citation is meant to be "Scripture." But there is nothing in the text that suggests this limitation. In fact, other New Testament examples of double citations—Matthew 15:4; Mark 7:10; Acts 1:20; 1 Peter 2:6; 2 Peter 2:22—have both citations included in the introductory formula (George W. Knight, *The Pastoral Epistles: A Commentary on the Greek Text* [NIGTC; Grand Rapids: Eerdmans, 1992], p. 234). Thus, I. Howard Marshall declares, "Both quotations are envisaged as coming from 'Scripture'" (*A Critical and Exegetical Commentary on the Pastoral Epistles* [ICC; Edinburgh: T & T Clark, 1999], p. 615).

[274]Marshall, *Pastoral Epistles*, p. 616 (emphasis mine).

[275]Anthony T. Hanson, *Pastoral Epistles* (Grand Rapids: Eerdmans, 1982), p. 102.

[276]Kelly, *Pastoral Epistles*, p. 126; Dibelius and Conzelmann, *Pastoral Epistles*, p. 79.

[277]The similar phrase in Matthew 10:10 is still different from Luke 10:7 and 1 Timothy 5:18. Echoes of this phrase also occur in 1 Corinthians 9:14 and *Didache* 13:2. For more, see Anthony E. Harvey, "'The Workman Is Worthy of His Hire': Fortunes of a Proverb in the Early Church," *NovT* 24 (1982): 209-21.

[278]E.g., Irenaeus (*Hist. eccl.* 5.8.3); Origen (*Hist. eccl.* 6.25.6); and the Muratorian Fragment.

[279]C. F. D. Moule, "The Problem of the Pastoral Epistles: A Reappraisal," *BJRL* 47 (1965): 430-52.

torical probabilities ought to weigh in favor of 1 Timothy 5:18 citing Luke's Gospel. John Meier is even more confident: "The only interpretation that avoids contorted intellectual acrobatics or special pleading is the plain, obvious one. [1 Timothy] is citing Luke's Gospel alongside Deuteronomy as normative Scripture for the ordering of the church's ministry."[280] If so, then this suggests that Luke's Gospel was regarded as Scripture (at least by some) by the turn of the century, depending on when one dates 1 Timothy.[281] But even if one wishes to maintain skepticism about the source of the citation in 1 Timothy 5:18, it should still be acknowledged that 1 Timothy at least regards *some* book (and one which contains a known saying of Jesus) to be Scripture alongside the Old Testament. That fact alone should reshape our understanding of when Christians began to consider their own books "Scripture." For this reason, Meade considers 1 Timothy 5:18 to be evidence of an early "canon consciousness."[282]

CONCLUSION

The question we have been asking in this chapter is a simple one. At what point did Christians consider their own books to be "Scripture"? Was this a late-second-century phenomenon largely due to the influence of Irenaeus, as some scholars suggest? The historical evidence surveyed here suggests a very different picture than the one that is typically presented. Not only do others in Irenaeus's own time period already receive many of the New Testament books as Scripture (for example, Muratorian Fragment, Clement of Alexandria, Theophilus of Antioch), but this trend can be traced even further back into the second century. Justin Martyr appears to know the four canonical Gospels and indicates that they were used as Scripture in worship alongside the Old Testament during his day. In addition, Papias, *Barnabas*, Ignatius, Polycarp, *1 Clement*, 2 Peter, and 1 Timothy also seem to

---

[280]John P. Meier, "The Inspiration of Scripture: But What Counts as Scripture?," *Mid-Stream* 38 (1999): 77.

[281]Hanson, *Pastoral Epistles*, p. 13; Kümmel, *Introduction to the New Testament*, p. 387; Marshall, *Pastoral Epistles*, p. 58; Meier, "Inspiration of Scripture," p. 78. Campenhausen's well-known claim that the Pastoral Epistles derive from the time of Polycarp (Campenhausen, *Formation of the Christian Bible*, p. 181) has not been widely accepted and places the letters too late to be so readily received by Irenaeus and the Muratorian Fragment just a short time later; see critique of Campenhausen in Luke Timothy Johnson, *The First and Second Letters to Timothy* (New York: Doubleday, 2001), p. 85; and Kümmel, *Introduction to the New Testament*, pp. 386-87.

[282]Meade, "Ancient Near Eastern Apocalypticism," p. 318.

regard a number of Christian writings as Scripture. They often refer to them expressly as "Scripture" (sometimes introducing them with "it is written") or regard them as possessing apostolic authority—which, functionally, would be on par with the authority of Scripture. While the boundaries of the church's Scriptures during this early time were still fairly fluid (and would not be resolved for centuries), there seems to be little doubt that the church did, in fact, have Scriptures.

It should also be noted that most of the evidence above cannot be explained away simply by appealing to oral tradition. For one, many of the above citations can only be explained on the basis of a written source (for example, *Barnabas* introduced an apparent quote from Mt 22:14 with "it is written"). But, even more than this, much of the evidence we have examined does not consist of citations at all. Rather it consists of an author simply referring to, or mentioning, New Testament books and their role in the life of the church. For instance, Papias defends Mark and Matthew (but does not cite them); Ignatius refers to "every epistle" of the blessed Paul; and 2 Peter 3:16 refers to "all his [Paul's] letters." One should also not forget that the evidence above is not just from a single church father, but from a variety of sources spread over a number of different regions. While any individual piece of evidence might be contested or questioned, it is the extent of the evidence that proves to be the compelling factor.

If we are correct that Christians began to view their books as Scripture much earlier than Irenaeus—perhaps even by the turn of the century—then this provides noteworthy confirmation of the arguments we have been making throughout this volume. We have argued that canon was not a late ecclesiastical development but was something that would have grown naturally and innately out of the earliest Christian movement. Moreover, we argued that even the authors of the New Testament appeared to have some awareness that they were writing Scripture. All of these factors together serve to challenge the "big bang" theory of canon that argues that the canon was forcibly planted within the soil of the church by later ecclesiastical powers (whether Irenaeus or others) who were keen to refute the heresies of their day. Instead, the evidence we have seen here suggests the canon began more like a seed that was present in the soil of the church from the very beginning, growing gradually and consistently over time.

CONCLUSION

Normal science . . . tends to discover
what it expects to discover.

IAN HACKING
preface, *The Structure of Scientific*
Revolutions: 50th Anniversary Edition

⚕

As we draw our study of canon to a close, the distinctive (and perhaps unexpected) focus of this volume has now become apparent. Rather than addressing the traditional question about the boundaries of the canon—Why these twenty-seven books and no others?—this volume has focused on a deeper and more foundational question. Rather than asking which books, we have been asking whether there should even be books. Why is there a New Testament canon at all? While this question might be less interesting to some, the answer has the potential to change the macro paradigm through which we study the origins of the New Testament. Of course, as we have argued throughout the volume, much of modern biblical scholarship has already answered this question. The canon is viewed by many as a later ecclesiastial production, a creation of the second-, third- or even fourth-century church, which is decidely out of sync with the original nature and purpose of Christianity. The early Christian faith, we are told, despised the written word. And even when Christians did write, they had no intention of writing authoritative Scripture-like books. Thus, the idea of a new canon was imposed on the church by some matrix of external forces, whether it be Marcion's heresies, Irenaeus's politics, or Constantine's imperial influence. We have referred to this whole approach as the *extrinsic model* of canon (what Meade calls the "pull") and have argued that it dominates much of modern scholarship.

But dominant positions are not beyond adjustment or correction. It has been the purpose of this volume to offer a well-intended challenge to this extrinsic model. The goal has not been to reject the model in its entirety but to suggest that there were also instrinsic factors at work in the early Christian movement that may have made a new corpus of Scripture a more natural, if not inevitable, development (what Meade calls the "push"). While a volume like this could not address every aspect of the extrinsic model, it has addressed five major tenets that seem to be at its core. These tenets have not been presented as an exhaustive account of the extrinsic model (this model would also hold to many other positions), nor have they been presented as an absolute package (not all adherents to the extrinsic model would hold to each without exception). Nevertheless, these five tenets are commonplace in modern scholarship and often appear together. Let us review these five tenets and our response to each.

The first tenet of the extrinsic model claims that *we must make a sharp distinction between "Scripture" and "canon."* For a variety of reasons, many scholars have coalesced around the idea that the terms "Scripture" and "canon" should be sharply distinguished and that the latter can only be used to describe a final, closed list of books to which nothing can be added and nothing taken away. While this definition of canon is not the exclusive property of the extrinsic model (and is used by some who adhere to other models), it is quite popular among those who view the canon as a later ecclesiastical creation. And the reason for this is not hard to find. This definition insists that this thing we call a "canon" did not, and could not, exist prior to the formal actions of the fourth-century church that restricted and limited which books are acceptable. In other words, this definition not only places the canon at a later date, but also gives the impression that the canon is the result of "a great and meritorious act of the church."[1] In response, we affirmed that this exclusive definition of canon does have some positives. It

---

[1]John Webster, "'A Great and Meritorious Act of the Church'? The Dogmatic Location of the Canon," in *Die Einheit der Schrift und die Vielfalt des Kanons*, ed. John Barton and Michael Wolter (Berlin: Walter de Gruyter, 2003), pp. 96-97.

rightly recognizes that the canon was a long and drawn-out process, and
that a general consesus on the boundaries was not fully realized until the
fourth century. However, it does not give due appreciation to the fact that
even by the second century most of the New Testament books were already seen as fully authoritative. Thus, we argued that the exclusive definition of canon is best rounded out by the functional and ontological
definitions. These three definitions, working in a mutually complementary
fashion, provide the most balanced approach to our understanding of the
term *canon*.

The second tenet of the extrinsic model is that *there was nothing in earliest Christianity that might have led to a canon*. If the canon is a later ecclesiastical idea, then the corollary of this approach is that no one in the earliest stages of the faith would have conceived of it. The idea of a new corpus
of books was the furthest thing from their minds. Thus, we are told, there
was "nothing dictated that there should be a NT."[2] While we would certainly agree that the earliest Christians could not have anticipated the shape
and content of a new corpus of books, that is not the same as suggesting
that there was nothing that might have naturally led to a new corpus of
books. In chapter two we argued that there was a matrix of theological beliefs held by early Christians out of which a canon might have developed
quite naturally. The earliest believers viewed the work of Christ as the great
eschatologial redemption that God promised in the Old Testament by
which Israel would be made new. And, as Meade has argued, "[a] 'New
Israel' . . . will require new Scriptures."[3] In addition, the earliest Christians
conceived of the work of Christ as the inauguration of a new covenant. The
close association between covenants and written texts allowed Delbert
Hillers to argue that when it comes to biblical covenants, "there is a written
document in connection with it, the familiar 'text of the covenant.'"[4] Last,
early Christians had a high view of the apostolic office, viewing the apostles

[2]Harry Y. Gamble, *The New Testament Canon: Its Making and Meaning* (Philadelphia: Fortress, 1985), p. 12.
[3]David Meade, "Ancient Near Eastern Apocalypticism and the Origins of the New Testament Canon of Scripture," in *The Bible as a Human Witness: Hearing the Word of God Through Historically Dissimilar Traditions*, ed. Randall Heskett and Brian Irwin (London: T & T Clark, 2010), p. 315.
[4]Delbert R. Hillers, *Covenant: The History of a Biblical Idea* (Baltimore: Johns Hopkins University Press, 1969), p. 145.

as the very mouthpiece of Christ himself. Thus any document containing apostolic teaching would have been received as an authoritative written text (and the beginning of a canon). Regardless of whether these early Christian beliefs were in fact true (and that is not the issue we are addressing in this volume), they would have, especially taken in tandem, created the ideal environment for a new canon to emerge.

The third tenet of the extrinsic model insists that *early Christians were averse to written documents*. One of the primary reasons that scholars suggest that the canon had to be a later ecclesiastical development is that the earliest Christians were illiterate and uninterested in books. Oral tradition, we are told, was the preferred mode of transmission for the infant church, and written texts were seen with suspicion and skepticism. While we would certainly agree that the earliest Christians were largely illiterate, and that Christian teaching was passed along in oral form, we argued in chapter three that neither of these things necessitates the belief that Christians were averse to written texts. On the contrary, we argued that early Christianity was characterized by a robust *textuality*—the knowledge, use and appreciation of written texts—even though most could not read. Oral and written modes of communications were not mutually exclusive; neither were they hostile to one another. Instead, they often interfaced in a symbiotic and mutually reinforcing manner. Moreover, when we examine the remnants of the earliest Christian literary culture, we see that Christians not only wrote at a very early point but also exhibited a rather developed and sophisticated book technology, as evidenced by scribal handwriting, the use of the *nomina sacra*, and the widespread adoption of the codex. All of these factors suggest that the development of a new corpus of sacred writings would not have been out of sync with the nature of early Christianity.

The fourth tenet of the extrinsic model claims that *the New Testament authors were unaware of their own authority*. Perhaps one of the most common (and unquestioned) assertions made by modern scholars is that the New Testament authors did not conceive of themselves as producing authoritative texts—they were merely producing occasional documents that were only *later* regarded as Scripture. Indeed, such a claim is critical for establishing the canon as an artificial ecclesiastical creation that was at odds with the original purpose of the New Testament authors. However, we argued in chapter four that there are a number of New Testament passages that indicate the authors were quite aware that their books bore apostolic authority, and thereby the very authority of Christ himself. Paul states this apostolic authority quite plainly: "If anyone thinks that he is a prophet, or spiritual, he should acknowledge that the things I am writing to you are a command of the Lord" (1 Cor 14:37-38). Other authors claim this authority more indirectly by purporting to pass down authentic apostolic content (Lk 1:2; Heb 2:3). It does not matter whether these authors referred to their own books with the term "Scripture." That is beside the point. What matters is that these authors viewed their writings as apostolic. And if these writings were apostolic, then they bore the highest authority a book could bear—an authority functionally equivalent to Scripture.

The fifth and final tenet of the extrinsic model that we discussed in this volume is that *the New Testament books were first regarded as Scripture at the end of the second century.* If Christians could never have conceived of a canon, were opposed to the written medium, and did not think of themselves (even when they did write) as penning authoritative books, then we would expect that it would have taken a while for the New Testament writings to attain a scriptural status. It is here that we come to the key issue of the canon's date. Many advocates of the extrinsic model argue that Christian writings were not regarded as Scripture until the end of the second century, most likely due to the influence of Irenaeus, who imposed his innovative ideas upon the church. Although it is certainly true that the end of the second century is the time when the contours of the emerging canon can be seen with more clarity, in chapter five we argued that such a canon could not have popped into existence overnight. It must have roots that extend even further back into the second century—particulary given the fact that Irenaeus was not the only one who had a scriptural collection during this time period. An examination of Justin Martyr, the apostolic fathers and even the New Testament writings themselves indicated that some New Testament writings were viewed as Scripture quite early, even in the first half of the second century. This does not suggest, of course, that there was unity over the boundaries of the New Testament canon by this point. Disagreements over books were not unusual. But, it does suggest that there was a core collection of scriptural books in place from a very early time.

If these five tenets of the extrinsic model really do prove to be problematic, as this volume has argued, then we can begin to consider some implications this might have for modern canonical studies. First, it serves as a simple reminder that historical investigations, like scientific ones, often operate on the basis of models, or what we might call paradigms. Although we like to convince ourselves as historians that we are inherently neutral in our investigations, only collecting the bare facts, the truth of the matter is that we often conduct our investigations on the basis of a predetermined framework. We look at our data through the lens of what we already believe to be true. Ian Hacking has observed this same trend in the scientific community: "Normal science . . . tends to discover what it expects to discover."[5] Now, there is nothing particularly scandalous about this—everyone does (and must) look at the evidence through some lens. The proper response to this reality is not to feign neutrality, but to be willing to acknowledge our model and, more importantly, be willing to question it.

A second implication of this study, and perhaps the most obvious, is that there are enough problems with the extrinsic model to raise serious questions about its viability. This is particularly noteworthy given that a number of the tenets of this model are arguably "consensus" positions within the modern academy. But, as already noted, consensus positions are not necessarily correct simply because they are held by a majority of scholars. Sometimes the dominant model needs to be questioned, or at least tweaked, in order for progress to be made in that field of study. And scholars have to be open to this questioning. Although the extrinsic model is correct about a great many things (as has been acknowledged throughout this volume), its core conviction—that the canon is a later ecclesiastical creation contrary to Christianity's original nature—does not prove to be persuasive in the end.

A third and final implication of this study is that more scholarly consideration should be given to what we have called the intrinsic model. Although our purpose here has not been to prove the intrinsic model (simply critiquing the extrinsic model is not sufficient to do this), this study has at least paved the way for the intrinsic model to be given a fresh look. No doubt some scholars have avoided the intrinsic model due to the mistaken

---

[5]Ian Hacking, in the preface to Thomas S. Kuhn, *The Structure of Scientific Revolutions: 50th Anniversary Edition* (Chicago: University of Chicago Press, 2012), p. xxvi.

belief that it entails some theological commitments to doctrines such as inspiration, or to the special authority of the New Testament books. But, as noted in the introduction, the intrinsic model, at its core, requires no such commitment. The intrinsic model is a historical model, designed to explain how and when the New Testament canon emerged within the early Christian religion. It simply argues that the phenomenon of canon was one that arose early and naturally within the first few stages of Christianity. Indeed, the later church played a key role in shaping and influencing the contours of the canon, and no doubt various "heretical" movements would have also played a part in the canon's development. But the intrinsic model argues that the idea of canon was built into the DNA of the Christian religion and thus emerged quite naturally. In this sense, the canon was like a seedling sprouting from the soil of early Christianity—although it was not fully a tree until the fourth century, it was there, in nuce, from the beginning.

BIBLIOGRAPHY

Achtemeier, Paul J. "Omne Verbum Sonat: The New Testament and the Oral Environment of Late Western Antiquity." *JBL* 109 (1990): 3-27.

———, Joel B. Green and Marianne M. Thompson, eds. *Introducing the New Testament and Its Literature*. Grand Rapids: Eerdmans, 2001.

Ackroyd, P. R., and C. F. Evans, eds. *The Cambridge History of the Bible: From the Beginnings to Jerome*. Cambridge: Cambridge University Press, 1970.

Adamson, James B. *James: The Man and His Message*. Grand Rapids: Eerdmans, 1989.

Adriaanse, H. J. "Canonicity and the Problem of the Golden Mean." In van der Kooij and van der Toorn, *Canonization and Decanonization*, pp. 313-30.

Aichele, George. "Canon, Ideology, and the Emergence of an Imperial Church." In Thomassen, *Canon and Canonicity*, pp. 45-65.

———. *The Control of Biblical Meaning: Canon as Semiotic Mechanism*. Harrisburg, PA: Trinity Press International, 2001.

Aland, Kurt. "The Problem of Anonymity and Pseudonymity in Christian Literature of the First Two Centuries." *JTS* 12 (1961): 39-49.

———. *The Problem of the New Testament Canon*. London: A. R. Mowbury, 1962.

———. *Repertorium der griechischen christlichen Papyri, I, Biblische Papyri*. Berlin: de Gruyter, 1976.

Albl, Martin C. *And Scripture Cannot Be Broken: The Form and Function of the Early Christian Testimonia Collections*. Leiden: Brill, 1999.

Alexander, Loveday. "Ancient Book Production and the Circulation of the Gospels." In Bauckham, *Gospel for All Christians*, pp. 71-111.

———. "Canon and Exegesis in the Medical Schools of Antiquity." In *The Canon of Scripture in Jewish and Christian Tradition*, edited by P. S. Alexander and K. Jean-Daniel, pp. 115-53. Lausanne: Éditions du Zèbre, 2007.

———. "The Living Voice: Skepticism Towards the Written Word in Early Christian and in Greco-Roman Texts." In *The Bible in Three Dimensions*, edited by David J. A. Clines, Stephen E. Fowl and Stanley E. Porter, pp. 221-47. Sheffield: Sheffield Academic Press, 1990.

———. "Memory and Tradition in the Hellenistic Schools." In Kelber and Byrskog, *Jesus in Memory*, pp. 113-53.

———. *The Preface to Luke's Gospel: Literary Convention and Social Context in Luke 1:1-4 and Acts 1:1*. Cambridge: Cambridge University Press, 1993.

Allegro, John M. "Further Messianic References in Qumran Literature." *JBL* 75 (1956): 182-87.

Allen, David L. *Lukan Authorship of Hebrews*. Nashville: B & H Academic, 2010.

Allen, David M. *Deuteronomy & Exhortation in Hebrews: A Study in Re-presentation*. Tübingen: Mohr Siebeck, 2008.

Allert, Craig D. *A High View of Scripture? The Authority of the Bible and the Formation of the New Testament Canon*. Grand Rapids: Baker Academic, 2007.

Allison, Dale C. *The New Moses: A Matthean Typology*. Edinburgh: T & T Clark, 1993.

———. *Constructing Jesus: Memory, Imagination, and History*. Grand Rapids: Baker Academic, 2010.

Alston, William P. *Illocutionary Acts and Sentence Meaning*. Ithaca: Cornell University Press, 2000.

Amphoux, Christian-Bernard. "La finale longue de Marc: un épilogue des quatre évangiles." In *The Synoptic Gospels: Source Criticism and the New Literary Criticism*, edited by Camille Focant, pp. 548-55. Leuven: Leuven University Press, 1993.

Anderson, Øvivind. "Oral Tradition." In Wansbrough, *Jesus and the Oral Gospel Tradition*, pp. 17-58.

Anderson, Paul. *The Christology of the Fourth Gospel*. Tübingen: Mohr Siebeck, 1996.

Annand, Rupert. "Papias and the Four Gospels." *SJT* 9 (1956): 46-62.

Assmann, Aleida, and Jan Assmann, eds. *Kanon und Zensur, Archäologie der literarischen Kommunikation II*. München: Wilhelm Fink Verlag, 1987.

Assmann, Jan. *Das kulturelle Gedächtnis: Schrift, Erinnerung und politische Identität in frühen Hochkulteren*. Munich: C. H. Beck, 1992.

———. "Form as a Mnemonic Device: Cultural Texts and Cultural Memory." In Horsley, Draper and Foley, *Performing the Gospel*, pp. 67-82.

———. *Religion and Cultural Memory*. Translated by Rodney Livingstone. Stanford: Stanford University Press, 2006.

Aune, David E. "Luke 1:1-4: Historical or Scientific *Prooimion?*" In *Paul, Luke and the Graeco-Roman World*, edited by Alf Christopherson, Bruce Longnecker, Jýrg Frey and Carten Claussen, pp. 138-48. Sheffield: Sheffield Academic Press, 2002.

———. "Prolegomena to the Study of Oral Tradition in the Hellenistic World." In Wansbrough, *Jesus and the Oral Gospel Tradition*, pp. 59-196.

———. *Revelation 17-22*. WBC. Nashville: Thomas Nelson, 1998.

Austin, John L. *How to Do Things with Words*. Oxford: Oxford Paperbacks, 1976.

Auwers, J.-M., and H. J. de Jonge, eds. *The Biblical Canons*. Leuven: Leuven University Press, 2003.

Bacon, Benjamin W. "The Five Books of Matthew Against the Jews." *Exp* 15 (1918): 56-66.

———. "The Motivation of John 21:15-25." *JBL* 50 (1931): 71-80.

Bagnall, Roger S. *Early Christian Books in Egypt.* Princeton, NJ: Princeton University Press, 2009.

———. *Everyday Writing in the Graeco-Roman East.* Berkeley: University of California Press, 2011.

Bahn, Eugene. "Interpretive Reading in Ancient Greece." *QJS* 18 (1932): 432-40.

Bailey, Kenneth E. "Informal Controlled Oral Tradition and the Synoptic Gospels." *Them* 20 (1995): 4-11.

Baird, William R. "What Is the Kerygma: A Study of 1 Corinthians 15:3-8 and Galatians 1:11-17." *JBL* 76 (1957): 181-91.

Balás, David L. "Marcion Revisited: A 'Post-Harnack' Perspective." In March, *Texts and Testaments,* pp. 95-107.

Balducelli, Roger. "Professor Riesenfeld on Synoptic Tradition." *CBQ* 22 (1960): 416-21.

Bar-Ilan, Meir. "Illiteracy in the Land of Israel in the First Centuries C.E." In *Essays in the Social Scientific Study of Judaism and Jewish Society,* edited by Simcha Fishbane, Stuart Schoenfeld and Alain Goldschläger, pp. 46-61. Hoboken, NJ: KTAV, 1992.

Barclay, William. *The First Three Gospels.* London: SCM, 1966.

Barnard, Leslie W. *Justin Martyr.* Cambridge: Cambridge University Press, 1967.

———. "Justin Martyr's Eschatology." *VC* 19 (1965): 86-98.

Barnett, P. W. "The Jewish Sign Prophets—A.D. 40–70: Their Intentions and Origin." *NTS* 27 (1980): 679-97.

Barr, James. *Holy Scripture: Canon, Authority and Criticism.* Philadelphia: Westminster, 1983.

———. "Some Semantic Notes on the Covenant." In *Beiträge zur Alttestamentlichen Theologie,* edited by H. Donner, pp. 23-38. Göttingen: Vandenhoeck and Ruprecht, 1977.

———. *The Scope and Authority of the Bible.* Philadelphia: Westminster, 1980.

Barrett, C. K. *A Commentary on the Second Epistle to the Corinthians.* London: A & C Black, 1973.

———. "The First New Testament?" *NovT* 38 (1996): 94-104.

Barth, Karl. *Church Dogmatics.* Edinburgh: T & T Clark, 1975.

Bartholomew, Craig, et al., eds. *Canon and Biblical Interpretation.* Carlisle: Paternoster, 2006.

Bartlet, J. Vernon. "Papias's 'Exposition': Its Date and Contents." In *Amicitiae Corolla,* edited by H. G. Wood, pp. 16-22. London: University of London Press, 1933.

———. "The Epistle of Barnabas." In A Committee of the Oxford Society of Historical Theology, *New Testament in the Apostolic Fathers,* pp. 1-23.

Barton, John. "Canonical Approaches Ancient and Modern." In Auwers and de Jonge, *Biblical Canons,* pp. 199-209.

———. "Marcion Revisited." In McDonald and Sanders, *Canon Debate*, pp. 341-54.

———. *Oracles of God: Perceptions of Ancient Prophecy in Israel After the Exile.* London: Darton, Longman and Todd, 1985.

———. *The Spirit and the Letter: Studies in the Biblical Canon.* London: SPCK, 1997.

Bauckham, Richard. *The Climax of Prophecy: Studies in the Book of Revelation.* Edinburgh: T & T Clark, 1993.

———. "The Delay of the Parousia." *TynBul* 31 (1980): 3-36.

———. *God Crucified: Monotheism and Christology in the New Testament.* Grand Rapids: Eerdmans, 1999.

———, ed. *The Gospel for All Christians: Rethinking the Gospel Audiences.* Grand Rapids: Eerdmans, 1998.

———. *Jesus and the Eyewitnesses: The Gospels as Eyewitness Testimony.* Grand Rapids: Eerdmans, 2006.

———. *Jude, 2 Peter.* Waco, TX: Word, 1983.

———. "Papias and Polycrates on the Origin of the Fourth Gospel." *JTS* 44 (1993): 24-69.

———. "Pseudo-Apostolic Letters." *JBL* 107 (1988): 469-94.

Bauer, Walter. *Orthodoxy and Heresy in Earliest Christianity.* Edited by Robert Kraft and Gerhard Krodel. Translated by Paul J. Achtemeier. Philadelphia: Fortress, 1971.

Baum, Armin D. "The Anonymity of the New Testament History Books: A Stylistic Device in the Context of Greco-Roman and Ancient Near Eastern Literature." *NovT* 50 (2008): 120-42.

Baumgarten, Albert I. *The Flourishing of Jewish Sects in the Maccabean Era: An Interpretation.* Leiden: E. J. Brill, 1997.

Beale, G. K. *The Book of Revelation.* NIGTC. Grand Rapids: Eerdmans, 1999.

———. *1-2 Thessalonians.* IVPNTC. Downers Grove, IL: IVP Academic, 2003.

———. *The Temple and the Church's Mission: A Biblical Theology of the Dwelling Place of God.* Downers Grove, IL: IVP Academic, 2004.

Beard, Mary, ed. *Literacy in the Roman World.* Ann Arbor, MI: Journal of Roman Archaeology, 1991.

———. "Writing and Religion: Ancient Literacy and the Function of the Written Word in Roman Religion." In Beard, *Literacy in the Roman World*, pp. 35-58.

Beatrice, Pier F. "Une citation de l'Évangile de Matthieu dans l'Épître de Barnabé." In Sevrin, *New Testament in Early Christianity*, pp. 231-45.

Beckwith, Roger T. *The Old Testament Canon of the New Testament Church, and Its Background in Early Judaism.* Grand Rapids: Eerdmans, 1986.

Bellinzoni, Arthur J. *The Sayings of Jesus in the Writings of Justin Martyr.* Leiden: E. J. Brill, 1967.

———. "The Gospel of Luke in the Apostolic Fathers: An Overview." In Gregory and Tuckett, *Trajectories Through the New Testament and the Apostolic Fathers*, pp. 45-68.

Benecke, Paul V. M. "The Epistle of Polycarp." In A Committee of the Oxford Society of Historical Theology, *New Testament in the Apostolic Fathers*, pp. 84-104.

Benko, Stephen. "Pagan Criticism of Christianity During the First Two Centuries A.D." In Haase, *ANRW*, vol. 2, pp. 1055-1118.

Berding, Kenneth. *Polycarp and Paul: An Analysis of Their Literary and Theological Relationship in Light of Polycarp's Use of Biblical and Extra-Biblical Literature.* Leiden: E. J. Brill, 2002.

Bernard, John Henry. *A Critical and Exegetical Commentary on the Gospel According to St. John.* Edinburgh: T & T Clark, 1928.

Best, Ernest. *A Commentary on the First and Second Epistles to the Thessalonians.* New York: Harper & Row, 1972.

Bicknell, Edward J. *The First and Second Epistles to the Thessalonians.* London: Methuen and Company, 1932.

Bird, Michael. "Mark: Interpreter of Peter and Disciple of Paul." In *Paul and the Gospels: Christologies, Conflicts, and Convergences*, edited by Michael Bird and Joel Willitts, pp. 30-61. London: T & T Clark, 2011.

———, and Michael Pahl, eds. *The Sacred Text.* Piscataway, NJ: Gorgias, 2010.

Black, Matthew. "The Use of Rhetorical Terminology in Papias on Mark and Matthew." *JSNT* 37 (1989): 31-41.

Blanchard, Alain, ed. *Les débuts du codex.* Turnhout: Brepols, 1989.

Blanck, Horst. *Das Buch in der Antike.* Munich: Beck, 1992.

Blomberg, Craig. *The Historical Reliability of John's Gospel: Issues and Commentary.* Downers Grove, IL: IVP Academic, 2001.

Bock, Darrell L. *Luke: Volume 1: 1:9–9:50.* Grand Rapids: Baker, 1994.

Bockmuehl, Markus, and Donald A. Hagner, eds. *The Written Gospel.* Cambridge: Cambridge University Press, 2005.

Boers, Hendrikus. "The Form-Critical Study of Paul's Letters: I Thessalonians as a Case Study." *NTS* 22 (1976): 140-58.

Bonner, Campbell. *Studies in Magical Amulets.* Ann Arbor, MI: The University of Michigan Press, 1950.

Boring, M. Eugene. "Mark 1:1-15 and the Beginning of the Gospel." *Sem* 52 (1990): 43-81.

Botha, Pieter J. J. "Living Voice and Lifeless Letters: Reserve Towards Writing in the Graeco-Roman World." *HvTSt* 49 (1993): 742-59.

———. "Mark's Story as Oral Traditional Literature: Rethinking the Transmission of Some Traditions About Jesus." *Hervormde Teologiese Studies* 47 (1991): 304-31.

Bousset, Wilhelm. *Die Evangeliencitate Justins Des Märtyrers in Ihrem Wert Für Die Evangelienkritik.* Göttingen: Vandenhoeck & Ruprecht, 1891.

Bovon, François. "The Canonical Structure of Gospel and Apostle." In McDonald and Sanders, *Canon Debate*, pp. 516-27.

———. *L'Evangile et l'Apôtre: Christ inséparable de ses témoins.* Aubonne: Editions du Moulin, 1993.

Bowman, Alan K., and Greg Wolf, eds. *Literacy and Power in the Ancient World.* Cambridge: Cambridge University Press, 1994.

Brakke, David. "Canon Formation and Social Conflict in Fourth Century Egypt: Athanasius of Alexandria's Thirty-Ninth Festal Letter." *HTR* 87 (1994): 395-419.

Brenneman, James E. *Canons in Conflict: Negotiating Texts in True and False Prophecy.* New York: Oxford University Press, 1997.

Brooks, James A. "Clement of Alexandria as a Witness to the Development of the New Testament Canon." *SecCent* 9 (1992): 41-55.

Brown, Raymond E. *An Introduction to the New Testament.* New York: Doubleday, 1997.

Brown, Schuyler. "Concerning the Origin of the *Nomina Sacra.*" *SPap* 9 (1970): 7-19.

———. "The Role of the Prologues in Determining the Purpose of Luke-Acts." In *Perspectives on Luke-Acts*, edited by Charles H. Talbert, pp. 99-111. Edinburgh: T & T Clark, 1978.

Bruce, F. F. *Biblical Exegesis in the Qumran Texts.* London: Tyndale, 1959.

———. *The Book of the Acts.* Grand Rapids: Eerdmans, 1988.

———. *The Epistle to the Galatians: A Commentary on the Greek Text.* Grand Rapids: Eerdmans, 1982.

———. *The Epistle to the Hebrews.* Grand Rapids: Eerdmans, 1990.

———. *The Epistles of John: Introduction, Exposition and Notes.* Grand Rapids: Eerdmans, 1984.

———. *1 & 2 Thessalonians.* Waco, TX: Word, 1982.

———. "Tradition and the Canon of Scripture." In *The Authoritative Word: Essays on the Nature of Scripture*, edited by D. K. McKim, pp. 59-94. Grand Rapids: Eerdmans, 1983.

———. *Tradition: Old and New.* Grand Rapids: Zondervan, 1970.

Bruns, Gerald L. "Canon and Power in the Hebrew Scriptures." *CI* 10 (1984): 462-80.

Buchanan, George W. *To the Hebrews.* Anchor Bible. New York: Doubleday, 1981.

Buck, Charles H., Jr. "The Early Order of the Pauline Corpus." *JBL* 68 (1949): 351-57.

Bultmann, Rudolf. *The Gospel of John.* Philadelphia: Westminster, 1971.

———. *The History of the Synoptic Tradition.* Oxford: Blackwell, 1968.

———. *The Johannine Epistles.* Hermeneia. Philadelphia: Fortress, 1973.

———. "The Significance of the Old Testament for the Christian Faith." In *The Old Testament and the Christian Faith: Essays by Roldolf Bultmann and Others*, edited by Bernhard W. Anderson, pp. 8-35. London: SCM, 1964.

Bumgardner, Charles J. "'As a Brother': 2 Thessalonians 3:6-15 and Ecclesiastical Separation." *DBSJ* 14 (2009): 55-97.

Burge, Gary M. *The Epistles of John.* Grand Rapids: Eerdmans, 1978.

Burridge, Richard A. *What Are the Gospels?* Cambridge: Cambridge University Press, 1992.

Byrskog, Samuel. *Story as History—History as Story: The Gospel Tradition in the Context of Ancient Oral History.* Leiden: E. J. Brill, 2002.

Calvin, John. *Institutes of the Christian Religion.* Edited by John T. McNeill. Translated by Ford Lewis Battles. Philadelphia: Westminster, 1960.

Cameron, Ron. *Sayings Traditions in the Apocryphon of James.* Philadelphia: Fortress, 1984.

Campenhausen, Hans von. *The Formation of the Christian Bible.* Translated by J. A. Baker. London: A&C Black, 1972. Translation of *Die Entstehung der christlichen Bibel.* Tubingen: J. C. B. Mohr, 1968.

Carlyle, A. J. "Clement of Rome." In A Committee of the Oxford Society of Historical Theology, *New Testament in the Apostolic Fathers,* pp. 37-62.

Carmignac, Jean. "II Corinthiens III. 6, 14 et le Début de la Formation du Noveau Testament." *NTS* 24 (1976): 384-86.

Carr, David M. *Writing on the Tablet of the Heart: Origins of Scripture and Literature.* Oxford: Oxford University Press, 2005.

Carrington, Phillip. *The Primitive Christian Calendar: A Study in the Making of the Marcan Gospel.* Cambridge: Cambridge University Press, 1952.

Carroll, Kenneth L. "The Creation of the Fourfold Gospel." *BJRL* 37 (1955–1954): 68-77.

———. "The Earliest New Testament." *BJRL* 38 (1955): 45-57.

———. "The Expansion of the Pauline Corpus." *JBL* 72 (1953): 230-37.

———. "Tatian's Influence on the Developing New Testament." In *Studies in the History and Text of the New Testament in Honor of Kenneth Willis Clark,* edited by Boyd L. Daniels and M. Jack Suggs, pp. 59-70. Salt Lake City: University of Utah Press, 1967.

Carroll, Robert P. "Inscribing the Covenant: Writing and the Written in Jeremiah." In *Understanding Poets and Prophets: Essays in Honour of George Wishart Anderson,* edited by A. Graeme Auld, pp. 61-76. Sheffield: Sheffield Academic Press, 1993.

Carson, D. A. *The Gospel According to John.* Grand Rapids: Eerdmans, 1991.

———, and Douglas J. Moo. *An Introduction to the New Testament.* Grand Rapids: Zondervan, 2005.

Chamblin, Knox. "Revelation and Tradition in the Pauline Euangelion." *WTJ* 48 (1986): 1-16.

Chapa, Juan. "The Early Text of John." In Hill and Kruger, *Early Text of the New Testament,* pp. 140-56.

Chapman, John. *John the Presbyter and the Fourth Gospel.* Oxford: Clarendon Press, 1911.

Chapman, Stephen B. "The Canon Debate: What It Is and Why It Matters." Presented at the Society of Biblical Literature, San Diego, 2007.

———. "How the Biblical Canon Began: Working Models and Open Questions." In Finkelberg and Strousma, *Homer, the Bible, and Beyond,* pp. 29-51.

———. *The Law and the Prophets: A Study in Old Testament Canon Formation.* Tübingen: Mohr Siebeck, 2000.

————. "The Old Testament Canon and Its Authority for the Christian Church." *Ex Auditu* 19 (2003): 125-148.

Charlesworth, James H. *The Beloved Disciple: Whose Witness Validates the Gospel of John?* Valley Forge, PA: Trinity, 1995.

————, Hermann Lichtenberger and Gerbern S. Oegema, eds. *Qumran-Messianism: Studies on the Messianic Expectations in the Dead Sea Scrolls.* Tübingen: Mohr Siebeck, 1998.

Charlesworth, Scott. "Public and Private—Second- and Third-Century Gospel Manuscripts." In Evans and Zacharias, *Jewish and Christian Scripture as Artifact and Canon,* pp. 148-75.

————. "T. C. Skeat, P64+67 and P4, and the Problem of Fibre Orientation in Codicological Reconstruction." *NTS* 53 (2007): 582-604.

Childs, Brevard S. *Biblical Theology of the Old and New Testaments: Theological Reflection on the Christian Bible.* Philadelphia: Augsburg Fortress, 1993.

————. *Introduction to the Old Testament as Scripture.* Philadelphia: Fortress, 1979.

————. *The New Testament as Canon: An Introduction.* London: SCM, 1984.

————. "On Reclaiming the Bible for Christian Theology." In *Reclaiming the Bible for the Church,* edited by Carl E. Braaten and Robert W. Jenson, pp. 1-18. Grand Rapids: Eerdmans, 1995.

Collins, Adela Yarbro. "Numerical Symbolism in Jewish and Early Christian Apocalyptic Literature." In Haase, *ANRW,* vol. 2, pp. 1221-87.

Collins, John J. *Apocalypticism in the Dead Sea Scrolls.* London: Routledge, 1997.

————. "Is a Critical Biblical Theology Possible?" In *The Hebrew Bible and Its Interpreters,* edited by William H. Propp, pp. 1-17. Winona Lake, IN: Eisenbrauns, 1990.

————. "Teacher and Messiah? The One Who Will Teach Righteousness at the End of Days." In Ulrich and VanderKam, *Community of the Renewed Covenant,* pp. 193-210.

Collins, Raymond F. *First Corinthians.* Collegeville, MN: Liturgical, 1999.

Committee of the Oxford Society of Historical Theology, A. *The New Testament in the Apostolic Fathers.* Oxford: Clarendon, 1905.

Conzelmann, Hans. "On the Analysis of the Confessional Formula in 1 Cor 15:3-5." *Int* 20 (1966): 15-25.

————. *Theology of St. Luke.* New York: Harper & Row, 1960.

Coote, Robert P., and Mary P. Coote. *Power, Politics, and the Making of the Bible.* Minneapolis: Fortress, 1990.

Cornell, Tim. "The Tyranny of the Evidence: A Discussion of the Possible Uses of Literacy in Etruria and Latium in the Archaic Age." In Beard, *Literacy in the Roman World,* pp. 7-34.

Cosgrove, Charles H. "Justin Martyr and the Emerging Christian Canon: Observations on the Purpose and Destination of the Dialogue with Trypho." *VC* 36 (1982): 209-32.

Cox, Claude E. "The Reading of the Personal Letter as the Background for the Reading of Scriptures in the Early Church." In Malherbe, Norris and Thompson, *Early Church in Its Context*, pp. 74-91.

Cranfield, C. E. B. *The Gospel According to St. Mark.* Cambridge: Cambridge University Press, 1959.

———. *I & II Peter and Jude: Introduction and Commentary.* London: SCM, 1960.

Croy, N. Clayton. "Where the Gospel Text Begins: A Non-Theological Interpretation of Mark 1:1." *NovT* 43 (2001): 105-27.

Cullmann, Oscar. "The Plurality of the Gospels as a Theological Problem in Antiquity." In *The Early Church*, edited by A. J. B. Higgins, pp. 39-58. London: SCM, 1956.

———. *Salvation in History.* London: SCM, 1967.

———. "The Tradition." In *The Early Church*, edited by A. J. B. Higgins, pp. 59-99. London: SCM, 1956.

Davids, Peter H. *The Letters of 2 Peter and Jude.* Grand Rapids: Eerdmans, 2006.

Davies, Paul. *Whose Bible Is It Anyway?* Sheffield: Sheffield Academic Press, 1995.

Davies, W. D., and Dale C. Allison. *The Gospel According to Saint Matthew.* ICC. Edinburgh: T & T Clark, 1997.

De Boer, Martin C. "The New Preachers in Galatia." In *Jesus, Paul, and Early Christianity*, edited by Margaret M. Mitchell and David P. Moessner, pp. 39-60. Leiden: E. J. Brill, 2008.

DeConick, April. *Recovering the Original Gospel of Thomas: A History of the Gospel and Its Growth.* London: T & T Clark, 2005.

Dehandschutter, Boudewijn. "Polycarp's Epistle to the Philippians: An Early Example of 'Reception.'" In Sevrin, *New Testament in Early Christianity*, pp. 275-91.

Deissmann, Adolf. *Light from the Ancient East.* New York: George H. Doran, 1927.

Dempster, Stephen G. "Canons on the Right and Canons on the Left: Finding a Resolution in the Canon Debate." *JETS* 52 (2009): 47-77.

———. *Dominion and Dynasty: A Biblical Theology of the Hebrew Bible.* Downers Grove, IL: IVP Academic, 2003.

deSilva, David A. *An Introduction to the New Testament: Contexts, Methods, and Ministry Formation.* Downers Grove, IL: IVP Academic, 2004.

Dewey, Joanna. "The Gospel of Mark as Oral Hermeneutic." In Thatcher, *Jesus, the Voice, and the Text*, pp. 71-87.

———. "Oral Methods of Structuring Narrative in Mark." *Int* 43 (1989): 32-44.

———, ed. *Orality and Textuality in Early Christian Literature.* Atlanta: Scholars Press, 1995.

———. "Textuality in an Oral Culture: A Survey of the Pauline Traditions." In Dewey, *Orality and Textuality in Early Christian Literature*, pp. 37-65.

Dibelius, Martin. *From Tradition to Gospel.* Cambridge: J. Clarke, 1971.

———, and Hans Conzelmann. *The Pastoral Epistles.* Philadelphia: Fortress, 1972.

Dillon, Richard J. "Previewing Luke's Project from His Prologue (Luke 1:1-4)." *CBQ* 43 (1981): 205-27.

Dodd, C. H. *The Apostolic Preaching and Its Developments.* New York: Harper, 1949.

———. "The Framework of the Gospel Narrative." *ExpT* 43 (1932–1931): 396-400.

Donaldson, James. *The Apostolic Fathers: A Critical Acccount of Their Genuine Writings and of Their Doctrines.* London: Macmillan, 1874.

Downing, F. Gerald. "Writers' Use or Abuse of Written Sources." In Foster, *New Studies in the Synoptic Problem: Oxford Conference, April 2008,* pp. 523-48.

Drane, John. *Introducing the New Testament.* 3rd ed. Minneapolis: Fortress, 2010.

Dumbrell, William J. *Covenant and Creation.* Grand Rapids: Baker, 1984.

Duncan, J. Ligon. "The Covenant Idea in Melito of Sardis: An Introduction and Survey." *Presb* 28 (2002): 12-33.

Dungan, David L. *Constantine's Bible: Politics and the Making of the New Testament.* 1st ed. Philadelphia: Fortress, 2006.

Dunn, James D. G. "Altering the Default Setting: Re-envisaging the Early Transmission of the Jesus Tradition." *NTS* 49 (2003): 139-75.

———. *Jesus Remembered.* Grand Rapids: Eerdmans, 2003.

———. *Unity and Diversity in the New Testament: An Inquiry into the Character of Early Christianity.* 3rd ed. London: SCM, 2006.

Eddy, Paul R., and Gregory A. Boyd. *The Jesus Legend: A Case for the Historical Reliability of the Synoptic Jesus Tradition.* Grand Rapids: Baker Academic, 2007.

Ehrman, Bart D. *The Apostolic Fathers.* 2 vols. Cambridge, MA: Harvard University Press, 2003.

———. *Forgery and Counterforgery: The Use of Literary Deceit in Early Christian Polemic.* New York: Oxford University Press, 2012.

———. *Jesus: Apocalyptic Prophet of the New Millennium.* New York: Oxford University Press, 1999.

———. *Lost Christianities: The Battles for Scripture and the Faiths We Never Knew.* New York: Oxford University Press, 2002.

———. *The Lost Gospel of Judas Iscariot: A New Look at Betrayer and Betrayed.* New York: Oxford University Press, 2006.

———. *Misquoting Jesus.* San Francisco: HarperCollins, 2005.

———. *The New Testament: A Historical Introduction to the Early Christian Writings.* New York: Oxford University Press, 1997.

———. "The Text as Window: New Testament Manuscripts and the Social History of Early Christianity." In *The Text of the New Testament in Contemporary Research. Essays on the Status Quaestionis,* edited by Bart D. Ehrman and Michael W. Holmes, pp. 361-79. Grand Rapids: Eerdmans, 1995.

———. "The Use and Significance of Patristic Evidence for NT Textual Criticism." In *New Testament Text Criticism, Exegesis, and Early Church History,* edited by Barbara Aland and Joël Delobel, pp. 118-35. Kampen, Netherlands: Kok Pharos, 1994.

Eichrodt, Walther. *Theology of the Old Testament.* Vol. 1. Translated by J. A. Baker. Philadelphia: Westminster, 1961.

Eisenbaum, Pamela M. "Locating Hebrews Within the Literary Landscape of Christian Origins." In Gelardini, *Hebrews*, pp. 213-37.

Ellingworth, Paul. *The Epistle to the Hebrews*. NICNT. Grand Rapids: Eerdmans, 1993.

Ellis, E. Earle. *The Making of the New Testament Documents*. Leiden: E. J. Brill, 2002.

———. "New Directions in the History of Early Christianity." In *Ancient History in a Modern University: Early Christianity, Late Antiquity and Beyond*, vol. 1, edited by T. W. Hillard, R. A. Kearsley, C. E. V. Nixon and A. M. Nobbs, pp. 71-92. Grand Rapids: Eerdmans, 1997.

Enslin, Morton S. "Along Highways and Byways." *HTR* 44 (1951): 67-92.

Epp, Eldon Jay. "The Codex and Literacy in Early Christianity at Oxyrhynchus: Issues Raised by Harry Y. Gamble's *Books and Readers in the Early Church*." In *Critical Review of Books in Religion 1997*, edited by Charles Prebish, pp. 15-37. Atlanta: American Academy of Religion and Society of Biblical Literature, 1997.

———. "Textual Criticism." In Epp, *New Testament and Its Modern Interpreters*, pp. 75-126.

———, and George W. MacRae, eds. *The New Testament and Its Modern Interpreters*. Atlanta: Scholars Press, 1989.

Esler, Philip F. "Collective Memory and Hebrews 11: Outlining a New Investigative Framework." In Kirk and Thatcher, *Memory, Tradition, and Text*, pp. 151-71.

Evans, Craig A. "Aspects of Exile and Restoration in the Proclamation of Jesus and the Gospels." In *Exile: Old Testament, Jewish, and Christian Conceptions*, edited by James M. Scott, pp. 299-328. Leiden: E. J. Brill, 1997.

———. "Covenant in the Qumran Literature." In Porter and de Roo, *Concept of Covenant in the Second Temple Period*, pp. 55-80.

———. "Jesus and the Continuing Exile of Israel." In *Jesus and the Restoration of Israel*, edited by Carey C. Newman, pp. 77-100. Downers Grove, IL: IVP Academic, 1999.

———. "Luke and the Rewritten Bible: Aspects of Lukan Hagiography." In *The Pseudepigrapha and Early Biblical Interpretation*, edited by James H. Charlesworth and Craig A. Evans, pp. 170-201. Sheffield: JSOT Press, 1993.

———. "The Scriptures of Jesus and His Earliest Followers." In McDonald and Sanders, *Canon Debate*, pp. 185-95.

———, and Emanuel Tov, eds. *Exploring the Origins of the Bible: Canon Formation in Historical, Literary, and Theological Perspectives*. Grand Rapids: Baker Academic, 2008.

———, and H. Daniel Zacharias, eds. *Jewish and Christian Scripture as Artifact and Canon*. London: T & T Clark, 2009.

Evans, C. F. "The New Testament in the Making." In Ackroyd and Evans, *Cambridge History of the Bible*, pp. 232-83.

Evans, C. Stephen. "Canonicity, Apostolicity, and Biblical Authority: Some Kierkegaardian Reflections." In Bartholomew et al., *Canon and Biblical Interpretation*, pp. 146-66.

Evans, Christopher. Is 'Holy Scripture' Christian? London: SCM, 1971.

Eve, Eric. The Jewish Context of Jesus' Miracles. London: Sheffield Academic Press, 2002.

Farkasfalvy, Denis. "The Papias Fragments on Mark and Matthew and Their Relationship to Luke's Prologue: An Essay on the Pre-History of the Synoptic Problem." In Malherbe, Norris and Thompson, Early Church in Its Context, pp. 92-106.

———. "'Prophets and Apostles': The Conjunction of the Two Terms Before Irenaeus." In March, Texts and Testaments, pp. 109-34.

Farmer, William R., and Denis M. Farkasfalvy. The Formation of the New Testament Canon. New York: Paulist, 1976.

Fee, Gordon D. The First and Second Letter to the Thessalonians. NICNT. Grand Rapids: Eerdmans, 2009.

———. The First Epistle to the Corinthians. Grand Rapids: Eerdmans, 1987.

———. Papyrus Bodmer II (p66): Its Textual Relationships and Scribal Characteristics. Salt Lake City: University of Utah Press, 1968.

———. "The Text of John in Origen and Cyril of Alexandria: A Contribution to Methodology in the Recovery and Analysis of Patristic Citations." Bib 52 (1971): 357-73.

Fensham, F. C. "Common Trends in Curses of the Near Eastern Treaties and Kudurru-Inscriptions Compared with Maledictions of Amos and Isaiah." ZAW 75 (1963): 155-75.

Ferguson, Everett. "The Covenant Idea in the Second Century." In March, Texts and Testaments, pp. 135-62.

———. "Factors Leading to the Selection and Closure of the New Testament Canon." In McDonald and Sanders, Canon Debate, pp. 295-320.

———. "Review of Geoffrey Mark Hahneman, The Muratorian Fragment and the Development of the Canon." JTS 44 (1993): 691-97.

Filson, Floyd V. "The Significance of the Early House Churches." JBL 58 (1939): 109-12.

———. Which Books Belong in the Bible? A Study of the Canon. Philadelphia: Westminster, 1957.

Finkelberg, Margalit, and Guy G. Strousma, eds. Homer, the Bible and Beyond. Leiden: E. J. Brill, 2003.

Fishbane, Michael A. "Varia Deuteronomica." ZAW 84 (1972): 349-52.

Fisk, Bruce N. "Synagogue Influence and Scriptural Knowledge Among the Christians of Rome." In Porter and Stanley, As It Is Written, pp. 157-85.

Fitzmyer, Joseph A. The Gospel According to Luke. New York: Doubleday, 1985.

———. "'4Q Testimonia' and the New Testament." TS 18 (1957): 513-37.

Fledderman, Harry T. Mark and Q: A Study of the Overlap Texts. Leuven: Peeters, 1995.

Foley, John Miles. Homer's Traditional Art. University Park, PA: Pennsylvania State University Press, 1999.

Folkert, Kendall W. "The 'Canons' of 'Scripture.'" In *Rethinking Scripture: Essays from a Comparative Perspective*, edited by Miriam Levering, pp. 170-79. Albany: State University of New York Press, 1989.

Foster, Paul. "The Epistles of Ignatius of Antioch and the Writings That Later Formed the New Testament." In Gregory and Tuckett, *Reception of the New Testament in the Apostolic Fathers*, pp. 159-86.

———. *The Gospel of Peter: Introduction, Critical Edition and Commentary.* Leiden: Brill, 2010.

———. "The Text of the New Testament in the Apostolic Fathers." In Hill and Kruger, *Early Text of the New Testament*, pp. 282-301.

———. "Who Wrote 2 Thessalonians? A Fresh Look at an Old Problem." *JSNT* 35 (2012): 150-75.

———. *The Writings of the Apostolic Fathers.* London: T & T Clark, 2007.

———, et al., eds. *New Studies in the Synoptic Problem: Oxford Conference, April 2008.* Leuven: Peeters, 2011.

France, R. T. *The Gospel of Mark.* Grand Rapids: Eerdmans, 2002.

———. *The Gospel of Matthew.* NICNT. Grand Rapids: Eerdmans, 2007.

———. *Matthew: Evangelist and Teacher.* Grand Rapids: Zondervan, 1989.

Freedman, David Noel, ed. *The Anchor Bible Dictionary.* 6 vols. New York: Doubleday, 1992.

Fung, Ronald Y. K. *The Epistle to the Galatians.* NICNT. Grand Rapids: Eerdmans, 1988.

———. "Revelation and Tradition: The Origin of Paul's Gospel." *EvQ* 57 (1985): 23-41.

Funk, Robert W. "The Apostolic Parousia: Form and Significance." In *Christian History and Interpretation: Studies Presented to John Knox*, edited by W. R. Farmer, C. F. D. Moule and Reinhold R. Niebuhr, pp. 249-68. Cambridge: Cambridge University Press, 1967.

———. "The Once and Future New Testament." In McDonald and Sanders, *Canon Debate*, pp. 541-57.

Gaffin, Richard B. *Resurrection and Redemption.* Phillipsburg, NJ: P&R, 1978.

Gamble, Harry Y. *Books and Readers in the Early Church.* New Haven, CT: Yale University Press, 1995.

———. "Canon, New Testament." In *ABD*, pp. 205-11.

———. "The Canon of the New Testament." In Epp, *New Testament and Its Modern Interpreters*, pp. 201-43.

———. "Christianity: Scripture and Canon." In *The Holy Book in Comparative Perspective*, edited by Frederick M. Denny and Rodney L. Taylor, pp. 36-62. Columbia: University of South Carolina Press, 1985.

———. "Literacy, Liturgy, and the Shaping of the New Testament Canon." In Horton, *Earliest Gospels*, pp. 27-39.

———. *The New Testament Canon: Its Making and Meaning.* Philadelphia: Fortress, 1985.

————. "The New Testament Canon: Recent Research and the Status Quaestionis." In McDonald and Sanders, *Canon Debate*, pp. 267-94.

————. "The Redaction of the Pauline Letters and the Formation of the Pauline Corpus." *JBL* 94 (1975): 403-18.

Gathercole, Simon. *The Composition of the Gospel of Thomas: Original Language and Influences.* Cambridge: Cambridge University Press, 2012.

Gelardini, Gabriella, ed. *Hebrews: Contemporary Methods, New Insights.* Leiden: E. J. Brill, 2005.

Geldenhuys, J. Norval. *Commentary on the Gospel of Luke.* London: Marshall, Morgan and Scott, 1950.

Georgi, Dieter. "Hebrews and the Heritage of Paul." In Gelardini, *Hebrews*, pp. 241-44.

Gerhardsson, Birger. *Memory and Manuscript with Tradition and Transmission in Early Christianity.* Rev. ed. Grand Rapids: Eerdmans, 1998.

————. *The Reliability of Gospel Tradition.* Peabody, MA: Hendrickson, 2001.

Gevirtz, Stanley. "West-Semitic Curses and the Problem of the Origins of Hebrew Law." *VT* 11 (1961): 137-58.

Given, Mark D. "Paul and Writing." In Porter and Stanley, *As It Is Written*, pp. 237-59.

Gleason, Randall C. "Paul's Covenantal Contrasts in 2 Corinthians 3:1-11." *BSac* 154 (1997): 61-79.

Glover, Richard. "The Didache's Quotations and the Synoptic Gospels." *NTS* 5 (1958): 12-29.

Godley, Alfred D., trans. *Herodotus.* Loeb. Cambridge, MA: Harvard University Press, 1920.

Goldhill, Simon. "The Anecdote: Exploring Boundaries Between Oral and Literate Performances in the Second Sophistic." In Johnson and Parker, *Ancient Literacies*, pp. 96-113.

Goldingay, John. *Models for Scripture.* Grand Rapids: Eerdmans, 1994.

Goodacre, Mark. S. *Thomas and the Gospels: The Case for Thomas's Familiarity with the Synoptics.* Grand Rapids: Eerdmans, 2012.

Goodspeed, Edgar J. *The Formation of the New Testament.* Chicago: University of Chicago Press, 1926.

Goulder, Michael D. *The Evangelist's Calendar: A Lectionary Explanation of the Development of Scripture.* London: SPCK, 1978.

————. "Ingatius' 'Docetists.'" *VC* 53 (1999): 16-30.

————. *Midrash and Lection in Matthew.* London: SPCK, 1974.

Grant, Robert M. "The Bible of Theophilus of Antioch." *JBL* 66 (1947): 173-96.

————. *Early Christianity and Society: Seven Studies.* New York: Harper & Row, 1977.

————. *The Formation of the New Testament.* New York: Harper & Row, 1965.

————. *Irenaeus of Lyons.* London: Routledge, 1997.

————. "Scripture and Tradition in St. Ignatius of Antioch." *CBQ* 25 (1963): 322-35.

———. *Theophilus of Antioch: Ad Autolycum*. Oxford: Oxford University Press, 1970.

Grayston, K. "'Logos' in 1 John 1:1." *ExpT* 86 (1974/1975): 279.

Green, E. M. B. *2 Peter Reconsidered*. London: Tyndale, 1960.

Green, Gene L. *Jude and 2 Peter*. BECNT. Grand Rapids: Baker Academic, 2008.

Green, Joel B. *The Gospel of Luke*. Grand Rapids: Eerdmans, 1997.

———, and Michael C. McKeever. *Luke-Acts and New Testament Historiography*. Grand Rapids: Baker Academic, 1994.

Gregory, Andrew F. "*1 Clement*: An Introduction." In Foster, *Writings of the Apostolic Fathers*, pp. 21-31.

———. "1 Clement and the Writings That Later Formed the New Testament." In Gregory and Tuckett, *Reception of the New Testament in the Apostolic Fathers*, pp. 129-57.

———. *The Reception of Luke and Acts in the Period Before Irenaeus*. Tübingen: Mohr Siebeck, 2003.

———. "What Is Literary Dependence?" In Foster, *New Studies in the Synoptic Problem: Oxford Conference, April 2008*, pp. 87-114.

———, and Christopher Tuckett, eds. *The Reception of the New Testament in the Apostolic Fathers*. Oxford: Oxford University Press, 2005.

———, and Christopher Tuckett. "Reflections on Method: What Constitutes the Use of the Writings That Later Formed the New Testament in the Apostolic Fathers?" In Gregory and Tuckett, *Reception of the New Testament in the Apostolic Fathers*, pp. 61-82.

———, and Christopher Tuckett, eds. *Trajectories Through the New Testament and the Apostolic Fathers*. Oxford: Oxford University Press, 2005.

Grindheim, Sigurd. "The Law Kills But the Gospel Gives Life: The Letter-Spirit Dualism in 2 Cor 3:5-18." *JSNT* 84 (2001): 97-115.

Grudem, Wayne. "Scripture's Self-Attestation and the Problem of Formulating a Doctrine of Scripture." In *Scripture and Truth*, edited by D. A. Carson and John D. Woodbridge, pp. 19-59. Grand Rapids: Baker, 1992.

Guelich, Robert A. "'The Beginning of the Gospel': Mark 1:1-15." *BR* 27 (1982): 5-15.

———. "The Gospel Genre." In *Das Evangelium und die Evangelien*, edited by Peter Stuhlmacher, pp. 183-219. Tübingen: Mohr Siebeck, 1983.

———. *Mark 1–8:26*. Dallas: Word Books, 1989.

Gundry, Robert H. "ΕΥΑΓΓΕΛΙΟΝ: How Soon a Book?" *JBL* 115 (1996): 321-25.

———. *Mark: A Commentary on His Apology for the Cross*. Grand Rapids: Eerdmans, 1993.

———. *Matthew: A Commentary on His Handbook for a Mixed Church Under Persecution*. 2nd ed. Grand Rapids: Eerdmans, 1994.

Güterbock, Hans Gustav. "Mursili's Accounts of Suppiluliuma's Dealings with Egypt." *RHA* 18 (1960): 59-60.

Guthrie, Donald. *New Testament Introduction*. Downers Grove, IL: IVP Academic, 1990.

Hacking, Ian. "Preface." In Thomas S. Kuhn, *The Structure of Scientific Revolutions: 50th Anniversary Edition*. Chicago: University of Chicago Press, 2012.

Haelst, Joseph van. *Catalogue des Papyrus Littéraires Juifs et Chrétiens*. Paris: Publications de la Sorbonne, 1976.

Hafemann, Scott J. "The Covenant Relationship." In *Central Themes in Biblical Theology: Mapping Unity in Diversity*, edited by Scott Hafemann and Paul House, pp. 20-65. Grand Rapids: Baker Academic, 2007.

———. *Paul, Moses, and the History of Israel: The Letter/Spirit Contrast and the Argument from Scripture in 2 Corinthians 3*. Tübingen: J. C. B. Mohr, 1995.

———. *2 Corinthians*. NIVAC. Grand Rapids: Zondervan, 2000.

Hägg, Tomas. "Canon Formation in Greek Literary Culture." In Thomassen, *Canon and Canonicity*, pp. 109-28.

Hagner, Donald A. *Hebrews*. NIBC. Peabody, MA: Hendrickson, 1993.

———. "The Sayings of Jesus in the Apostolic Fathers and Justin Martyr." In *Gospel Perspectives: The Jesus Tradition Outside the Gospels*, edited by David Wenham, pp. 233-68. Sheffield: JSOT Press, 1985.

———. *The Use of the Old and New Testaments in Clement of Rome*. Leiden: E. J. Brill, 1973.

Hahneman, Geoffrey M. *The Muratorian Fragment and the Development of the Canon*. Oxford: Clarendon, 1992.

———. "The Muratorian Fragment and the Origins of the New Testament Canon." In McDonald and Sanders, *Canon Debate*, pp. 405-15.

Haines-Eitzen, Kim. *Guardians of Letters: Literacy, Power, and the Transmitters of Early Christian Literature*. Oxford: Oxford University Press, 2000.

Halverson, John. "Oral and Written Gospel: A Critique of Werner Kelber." *NTS* 40 (1994): 180-95.

Handley, Eric W., and Ute Wartenburg, eds. *The Oxyrhynchus Papyri*. Vol. 64. London: Egypt Exploration Society, 1997.

Hanson, Anthony Tyrrell. *The Pastoral Epistles*. Grand Rapids: Eerdmans, 1982.

Harnack, Adolf von. *History of Dogma*. Vol. 2. New York: Dover, 1961.

———. *Marcion: Das Evangelium von fremden Gott*. Leipzig: J. C. Hinrichs, 1924.

———. *Origin of the New Testament and the Most Important Consequences of a New Creation*. London: Williams & Northgate, 1925.

———. "Probabilia über die Addresse und den Verfasser des Hebräerbriefs." *ZNW* 1 (1900): 16-41.

———. "Theophilus von Antiochia und das Neue Testament." *ZKG* 11 (1889–1890): 1-21.

Harrington, Daniel J. *Jude and 2 Peter*. Collegeville, MN: Liturgical Press, 2003.

———. "The Reception of Walter Bauer's Orthodoxy and Heresy in Earliest Christianity During the Last Decade." *HTR* 77 (1980): 289-98.

———. "Theophilus von Antiochia und das Neue Testament." *ZKG* 11 (1889–1890): 1-21.

Harris, James Rendel. *Testimonies.* Cambridge: Cambridge University Press, 1916.

Harris, William V. *Ancient Literacy.* Cambridge, MA: Harvard University Press, 1989.

Hartog, Paul. *Polycarp and the New Testament: The Occasion, Rhetoric, Theme, and Unity of the Epistle to the Philippians and Its Allusions to New Testament Literature.* Tübingen: Mohr Siebeck, 2001.

———. "Polycarp, Ephesians, and 'Scripture.'" *WTJ* 70 (2008): 255-75.

Harvey, Anthony E. "Review of *Midrash and Lection in Matthew* by M. G. Goulder." *JTS* 27 (1976): 188-95.

———. "'The Workman is Worthy of His Hire': Fortunes of a Proverb in the Early Church." *NovT* 24 (1982): 209-21.

Hatch, William H. P. "The Position of Hebrews in the Canon of the New Testament." *HTR* 29 (1936): 133-51.

Havelock, Eric. *Preface to Plato.* Cambridge, MA: Harvard University Press, 1963.

Hays, Richard B. *Echoes of Scripture in the Letters of Paul.* New Haven: Yale, 1989.

Head, Peter M. "Is P4, P64, and P67 the Oldest Manuscript of the Four Gospels? A Response to T. C. Skeat." *NTS* 51 (2005): 450-57.

———. "Some Recently Published NT Papyri from Oxyrhynchus: An Overview and Preliminary Assessment." *TynBul* 51 (2000): 1-16.

Heard, Richard. "The ΑΠΟΜΝΗΜΟΝΕΥΜΑΤΑ in Papias, Justin, and Irenaeus." *NTS* 1 (1954): 122-33.

———. "Papias' Quotations from the New Testament." *NTS* 1 (1954): 130-34.

Hearon, Holly. "Implications of Orality for the Study of the Biblical Text." In Horsley, Draper and Foley, *Performing the Gospel*, pp. 3-20.

Heckel, Theo K. *Vom Evangelium des Markus zum viergestaltigen Evangelium.* Tübingen: J. C. B. Mohr, 1999.

Hengel, Martin M. *Die Johanneische Frage: Ein Lösungsversuch mit einem Beitrag zur Apolalyse von Jörg Frey.* Tübingen: Mohr Siebeck, 1993.

———. *The Four Gospels and the One Gospel of Jesus Christ.* Harrisburg, PA: Trinity Press International, 2000.

———. *Studies in the Gospel of Mark.* London: SCM, 1985.

———. "The Titles of the Gospels and the Gospel of Mark." In Hengel, *Studies in the Gospel of Mark*, pp. 64-84.

Henne, Philippe. "La Datation du canon de Muratori." *RB* 100 (1993): 54-75.

Hezser, Catherine. *Jewish Literacy in Roman Palestine.* Tübingen: Mohr Siebeck, 2001.

Hilgenfeld, Adolf. *Kritische Untersuchungen Über Die Evangelien Justin's, Der Clementinischen Homilien Und Marcion's.* Halle: C. A. Schwetschke, 1850.

Hill, Charles E. "The Debate over the Muratorian Fragment and the Development of the Canon." *WTJ* 57 (1995): 351-59.

———. "Did the Scribe of P52 Use the *Nomina Sacra*? Another Look." *NTS* 48 (2002): 587-92.

———. "God's Speech in These Last Days: The New Testament Canon as an Eschatological Phenomenon." In *Resurrection and Eschatology: Theology in Service of the Church*, edited by Lane G. Tipton and Jeffrey C. Waddington, pp. 203-54. Phillipsburg, NJ: P&R, 2008.

———. "Ignatius and the Apostolate." In *Studia Patristica*, edited by M. F. Wiles and E. J. Yarnold, vol. 36, pp. 246-48. Leuven: Peeters, 2001.

———. "Ignatius, 'The Gospel,' and the Gospels." In Gregory and Tuckett, *Trajectories Through the New Testament and the Apostolic Fathers*, pp. 267-85.

———. "'In These Very Words': Methods and Standards of Literary Borrowing in the Second Century." In Hill and Kruger, *Early Text of the New Testament*, pp. 261-81.

———. "Intersection of Jewish and Christian Scribal Culture: The Original Codex Containing P4, P64, and P67, and Its Implications." In *Among Jews, Gentiles, and Christians in Antiquity and the Middle Ages*, edited by Reidar Hvalvik and John Kaufman, pp. 75-91. Trondheim: Tapir Academic Press, 2011.

———. "Justin and the New Testament Writings." In *Studia Patristica*, edited by Elizabeth Livingstone, vol. 30, pp. 42-48. Leuven: Peeters, 1997.

———. *The Johannine Corpus in the Early Church*. Oxford: Oxford University Press, 2004.

———. "Was John's Gospel Among Justin's Apostolic Memoirs?" In Parvis and Foster, *Justin Martyr and His Worlds*, pp. 88-94.

———. "What Papias Said About John (and Luke): A New Papias Fragment." *JTS* 49 (1998): 582-629.

———. *Who Chose the Gospels? Probing the Great Gospel Conspiracy*. Oxford: Oxford University Press, 2010.

———, and Michael J. Kruger, eds. *The Early Text of the New Testament*. Oxford: Oxford University Press, 2012.

Hillers, Delbert R. *Covenant: The History of a Biblical Idea*. Baltimore: Johns Hopkins University Press, 1969.

Hoffman, Daniel. "The Authority of Scripture and Apostolic Doctrine in Ignatius of Antioch." *JETS* 28 (1985): 71-79.

Hoffmann, R. Joseph. *Marcion: On the Restitution of Christianity: An Essay on the Development of Radical Paulinist Theology in the Second Century*. Chico, CA: Scholars Press, 1984.

Holmes, Michael William. *1 & 2 Thessalonians*. Grand Rapids: Zondervan, 1998.

———. "Paul and Polycarp." In *Paul and the Second Century*, edited by Michael Bird and Joseph R. Dodson, pp. 57-69. London: T & T Clark, 2011.

———. "Polycarp's *Letter to the Philippians* and the Writings That Later Formed the New Testament." In Gregory and Tuckett, *Reception of the New Testament in the Apostolic Fathers*, pp. 187-228.

———. "Polycarp of Smyrna, Epistle to the Philippians." In Foster, *Writings of the Apostolic Fathers*, pp. 108-25.

Hölscher, Gustav. *Kanonisch und Apocryph. Ein Kapitel aus der Geschichte des altestamentlichen Kanons.* Naumburg: Lippert, 1905.

Holtz, T. "Paul and Oral Gospel Tradition." In Wansbrough, *Jesus and the Oral Gospel Tradition*, pp. 380-93.

Hooker, Morna D. *The Gospel According to St. Mark.* London: A & C Black, 1991.

Horbury, William. "'Gospel' in Herodian Judea." In Bockmuehl and Hagner, *Written Gospel*, pp. 7-30.

————. "The Wisdom of Solomon in the Muratorian Fragment." *JTS* 45 (1994): 149-59.

Horsfall, Nicholas. "Statistics or States of Mind?" In Beard, *Literacy in the Roman World*, pp. 59-78.

Horsley, Richard A. "'Like One of the Prophets of Old': Two Types of Popular Prophets at the Time of Jesus." *CBQ* 47 (1985): 435-63.

————, Jonathan A. Draper and John Miles Foley, eds. *Performing the Gospel: Orality, Memory, and Mark.* Minneapolis: Fortress, 2006.

Horton, Charles, ed. *The Earliest Gospels.* London: T & T Clark, 2004.

Horton, Michael S. *Covenant and Eschatology: The Divine Drama.* Louisville: Westminster John Knox, 2002.

————. *God of Promise: Introducing Covenant Theology.* Grand Rapids: Baker, 2006.

Howard, George. "The Tetragram and the New Testament." *JBL* 96 (1977): 63-83.

Hübner, Hans. *Biblische Theologie des Neuen Testaments.* Vol. 1: Prolegomena. Göttingen: Vandenhoeck & Ruprecht, 1990.

Hughes, Philip E. *A Commentary on the Epistle to the Hebrews.* Grand Rapids: Eerdmans, 1990.

————. *Paul's Second Epistle to the Corinthians.* Grand Rapids: Eerdmans, 1962.

Hurd, John C. "Reflections Concerning Paul's 'Opponents' in Galatia." In *Paul and His Opponents*, edited by Stanley E. Porter, pp. 129-48. Leiden: E. J. Brill, 2005.

Hurtado, Larry W. *The Earliest Christian Artifacts: Manuscripts and Christian Origins.* Grand Rapids: Eerdmans, 2006.

————. "The Earliest Evidence of an Emerging Christian Material and Visual Culture: The Codex, the Nomina Sacra, and the Staurogram." In *Text and Artifact in the Religions of Mediterranean Antiquity: Essays in Honour of Peter Richardson*, edited by Stephen G. Wilson and Michael Desjardins, pp. 271-88. Waterloo: Wilfrid Laurier University Press, 2000.

————. "Greco-Roman Textuality and the Gospel of Mark: A Critical Assessment of Werner Kelber's *The Oral and Written Gospel.*" *BBR* 7 (1997): 91-106.

————. "Manuscripts and the Sociology of Early Christian Reading." In Hill and Kruger, *Early Text of the New Testament*, pp. 49-62.

————. "The New Testament in the Second Century: Texts, Collections, and Canon." In *Transmission and Reception: New Testament Text-Critical and Exegetical Studies*, ed. Jeff Childers and D. C. Parker, pp. 3-17. Piscataway, NJ: Gorgias Press, 2006.

———. "The Origin of the *Nomina Sacra*: A Proposal." *JBL* 117 (1998): 655-73.

———. "P52 (P.Rylands Gk. 457) and the *Nomina Sacra*: Method and Probability." *TynBul* 54 (2003): 1-14.

Inge, William Ralph. "Ignatius." In A Committee of the Oxford Society of Historical Theology, *New Testament and the Apostolic Fathers*, pp. 61-83.

Iverson, K. R. "Orality and the Gospels: A Survey of Recent Research." *CBR* 8 (2009): 71-206.

Jacobson, Anders-Christian, ed. *Religion and Normativity*. Vol. 1 of The Discursive Fight Over Religious Texts in Antiquity. Aarhus: Aarhus University Press, 2009.

Jensen, Peter. *The Revelation of God*. Downers Grove, IL: IVP Academic, 2002.

Jeremias, Joachim. *The Parables of Jesus*. New York: Scribner, 1955.

Jewett, Robert. *The Thessalonian Correspondence: Pauline Rhetoric and Millenarian Piety*. Philadelphia: Fortress, 1986.

Johns, Loren L. "Was 'Canon' Ever God's Will?" In *Jewish and Christian Scriptures: The Function of "Canonical" and "Non-Canonical" Religious Texts*, edited by James H. Charlesworth and Lee McDonald, pp. 41-45. London: T & T Clark, 2010.

Johnson, Luke Timothy. *The First and Second Letters to Timothy*. New York: Doubleday, 2001.

———. *The Letter of James*. Anchor Bible. New York: Doubleday, 1995.

———. *The Writings of the New Testament*. 3rd ed. Minneapolis: Fortress, 2010.

Johnson, Marshall D. *The Purpose of Biblical Genealogies, with Special Reference to the Setting of the Genealogies of Jesus*. Cambridge: Cambridge University Press, 1969.

Johnson, William A. *Bookrolls and Scribes in Oxyrhynchus*. Toronto: University of Toronto Press, 2004.

———. "Towards a Sociology of Reading in Classical Antiquity." *American Journal of Philology* 121 (2000): 593-627.

Johnson, William H., and Holt N. Parker, eds. *Ancient Literacies: The Culture of Reading in Greece and Rome*. Oxford: Oxford University Press, 2009.

Jones, Peter R. "The Apostle Paul: Second Moses to the New Covenant Community. A Study in Pauline Apostolic Authority." In *God's Inerrant Word*, edited by John Warwick Montgomery, pp. 219-41. Minneapolis: Bethany Fellowship, 1974.

Jonge, H. Jan de. "The New Testament Canon." In Auwers and de Jonge, *Biblical Canons*, pp. 309-19.

Judge, Edwin A. *The Social Pattern of Christian Groups in the First Century*. London: Tyndale, 1960.

Kalin, Everett R. "Early Traditions About Mark's Gospel: Canonical Status Emerges as the Story Grows." *CurTM* 2 (1975): 332-41.

———. "The Inspired Community: A Glance at Canon History." *CTM* 42 (1971): 205-8.

Kannaday, Wayne C. *Apologetic Discourse and the Scribal Tradition: Evidence of the*

Influence of Apologetic Interests on the Text of the Canonical Gospels. Atlanta: Society of Biblical Literature, 2004.

Käsemann, Ernst. *Das Neue Testament als Kanon.* Göttingen: Vandenhoeck u. Ruprecht, 1970.

Katz, Peter. "The Johannine Epistles in the Muratorian Canon." *JTS* 8 (1957): 273-74.

Keener, Craig S. *The Gospel of John.* Peabody, MA: Hendrickson, 2003.

———. *The Historical Jesus of the Gospels.* Grand Rapids: Eerdmans, 2009.

Keith, Chris. *Jesus' Literacy: Scribal Culture and the Teacher from Galilee.* London: T & T Clark, 2011.

———. "A Performance of the Text: The Adulteress's Entrance into John's Gospel." In *The Fourth Gospel and Ancient Media Culture,* edited by Anthony LeDonne and Tom Thatcher, pp. 49-69. London: T & T Clark, 2011.

———. "Prolegomena on the Textualization of Mark's Gospel: Manuscript Culture, the Extended Situation, and the Emergence of Written Gospels." In *Keys and Frames: Memory and Identity in Ancient Judaism and Early Christianity,* edited by Tom Thatcher. Atlanta: Society of Biblical Literature, forthcoming.

Kelber, Werner H. *The Oral and the Written Gospel: The Hermeneutics of Speaking and Writing in the Synoptic Tradition, Mark, Paul, and Q.* Philadelphia: Fortress, 1983.

———, and Samuel Byrskog, eds. *Jesus in Memory: Traditions in Oral and Scribal Perspectives.* Waco, TX: Baylor University Press, 2009.

Kelhoffer, James A. "'How Soon a Book' Revisited: ΕΥΑΓΓΕΛΙΟΝ as a Reference to 'Gospel' Materials in the First Half of the Second Century." *ZNW* 95 (2004): 1-34.

———. *Miracle and Mission: The Authentication of Missionaries and Their Message in the Longer Ending of Mark.* Tübingen: Mohr Siebeck, 2000.

Kelly, J. N. D. *A Commentary on the Epistles of Peter and of Jude.* New York: Harper & Row, 1969.

———. *A Commentary on the Pastoral Epistles.* Peabody, MA: Hendrickson, 1960.

———. *Early Christian Doctrines.* San Francisco: HarperCollins, 1978.

Kelsey, David H. *The Uses of Scripture in Recent Theology.* Philadelphia: Fortress, 1975.

Kennedy, George A. "An Introduction to the Rhetoric of the Gospels." *Rhetoric* 1 (1983): 17-31.

———. *A New Testament Interpretation Through Rhetorical Criticism.* Chapel Hill, NC: University of North Carolina, 1984.

Kenyon, Frederic G. *Books and Readers in Ancient Greece and Rome.* 2nd ed. Oxford: Clarendon, 1932.

———. *The Chester Beatty Biblical Papyri: Descriptions and Texts of Twelve Manuscripts on Papyrus of the Greek Bible.* Vol. 1. London: Emery Walker, 1933–1937.

Kilpatrick, George D. *The Origins of the Gospel According to St. Matthew.* Oxford: Clarendon, 1950.

Kinzig, Wolfram. "καινὴ διαθήκη: The Title of the New Testament in the Second and Third Centuries." *JTS* 45 (1994): 519-44.

Kirk, Alan. "Manuscript Tradition as a Tertium Quid: Orality and Memory in Scribal Practices." In Thatcher, *Jesus, the Voice, and the Text*, pp. 215-34.

———. "Memory, Scribal Media, and the Synoptic Problem." In Foster, *New Studies in the Synoptic Problem: Oxford Conference, April 2008*, pp. 459-82.

———. "Social and Cultural Memory." In Kirk and Thatcher, *Memory, Tradition, and Text*, pp. 1-24.

———, and Tom Thatcher, eds. *Memory, Tradition, and Text: Uses of the Past in Early Christianity*. Atlanta: Society of Biblical Literature, 2005.

Kitchen, Kenneth A. *On the Reliability of the Old Testament*. Grand Rapids: Eerdmans, 2003.

Klauck, Hans-Josef. *Ancient Letters and the New Testament: A Guide to Context and Exegesis*. Waco, TX: Baylor University Press, 2006.

Klijn, Albertus F. J. *Jewish-Christian Gospel Tradition*. Leiden: E. J. Brill, 1992.

Kline, Leslie L. "Harmonized Sayings of Jesus in the Pseudo-Clementine Homilies and Justin Martyr." *ZNW* 66 (1975): 223-41.

Kline, Meredith G. *Kingdom Prologue: Genesis Foundations for a Covenantal Worldview*. Overland Park, KS: Two Age Press, 2000.

———. "The Old Testament Origins of the Gospel Genre." *WTJ* 38 (1975): 1-27.

———. *The Structure of Biblical Authority*. 2nd ed. Eugene, OR: Wipf & Stock, 1997.

———. *Treaty of the Great King*. Grand Rapids: Eerdmans, 1963.

Kloppenborg, John S. "An Analysis of the Pre-Pauline Formula in 1 Cor 15:3b-5." *CBQ* 40 (1978): 351-67.

———. *The Formation of Q*. Philadelphia: Fortress, 1987.

Knight, George William. *The Pastoral Epistles: A Commentary on the Greek Text*. Grand Rapids: Eerdmans, 1992.

Knoch, Otto. *Die "Testamente" des Petrus und Paulus*. Stuttgart: KBW, 1973.

Knohl, Israel. *The Messiah Before Jesus: The Suffering Servant of the Dead Sea Scrolls*. Berkeley: University of California Press, 2000.

Knox, John. *Marcion and the New Testament: An Essay in the Early History of the Canon*. Chicago: University of Chicago Press, 1942.

Koester, Craig R. *Hebrews*. Anchor Bible. New York: Doubleday, 2001.

Koester, Helmut. *Ancient Christian Gospels: Their History and Development*. London: SCM, 1990.

———. "Apocryphal and Canonical Gospels." *HTR* 73 (1980): 105-30.

———. "The Extracanonical Sayings of the Lord as Products of the Christian Community." *Semeia* 44 (1988): 57-78.

———. *From Jesus to the Gospels: Interpreting the New Testament in Its Context*. Minneapolis: Fortress, 2007.

———. "From the Kerygma Gospel to the Written Gospels." *NTS* 35 (1989): 361-81.

————. *History and Literature of Early Christianity.* Vol. 2 of Introduction to the New Testament. Philadelphia: Fortress, 1982.

————. *Synoptische Überlieferung bei den apostlischen Vätern.* Berlin: Akademie-Verlag, 1957.

————. "The Text of the Synoptic Gospels in the Second Century." In *Gospel Traditions in the Second Century. Origins, Recensions, Text, and Transmission,* edited by William L. Petersen, pp. 19-37. Notre Dame: University of Notre Dame Press, 1989.

————. "Written Gospels or Oral Tradition?" *JBL* 113 (1994): 293-97.

Köhler, Wolf-Dietrich. *Die Rezeption des Matthäusevangeliums in der Zeit vor Irenäus.* Tübingen: J. C. B. Mohr, 1987.

Kolenkow, Anitra B. "The Genre Testament and Forecasts of the Future in the Hellenistic Jewish Milieu," *JSJ* 6 (1975): 57-71.

Kooij, Arie van der, and Karel van der Toorn, eds. *Canonization and Decanonization.* Leiden: E. J. Brill, 1998.

Körtner, Ulrich H. J. "Markus der Mitarbeiter des Petrus." *ZNW* 71 (1980): 160-73.

Köstenberger, Andreas J. *John.* BECNT. Grand Rapids: Baker, 2004.

Kraft, Robert A. "The 'Textual Mechanics' of Early Jewish LXX/OG Papyri and Fragments." In *The Bible as Book: The Transmission of the Greek Text,* edited by Scot McKendrick and Orlaith O'Sullivan, pp. 51-72. London: British Library, 2003.

Kraus, Thomas J., and Tobias Nicklas, eds. *New Testament Manuscripts: Their Texts and Their World.* Leiden: E. J. Brill, 2006.

Krosney, Herbert. *The Lost Gospel: The Quest for the Gospel of Judas Iscariot.* Hanover, PA: National Geographic Society, 2006.

Kruger, Michael J. "The Authenticity of 2 Peter." *JETS* 42 (1999): 645-71.

————. *Canon Revisited: Establishing the Origins and Authority of the New Testament Books.* Wheaton, IL: Crossway, 2012.

————. "Early Christian Attitudes Toward the Reproduction of Texts." In Hill and Kruger, *Early Text of the New Testament,* pp. 63-80.

————. "Manuscripts, Scribes, and Book Production Within Early Christianity." In *Christian Origins and Classical Culture: Social and Literary Contexts for the New Testament,* edited by Stanley E. Porter and A. W. Pitts, pp. 15-40. Leiden: E. J. Brill, 2012.

Kümmel, Werner G. *Introduction to the New Testament.* Nashville: Abingdon, 1973.

Kürzinger, Josef. *Papias Von Hierapolis Und Die Evangelien Des Neuen Testaments.* Regensburg: F. Pustet, 1983.

Kyrtatus, Dimitris. "Historical Aspects of the Formation of the New Testament Canon." In Thomassen, *Canon and Canonicity,* pp. 29-44.

Ladd, George Eldon. *Jesus and the Kingdom: The Eschatology of Biblical Realism.* New York: Harper & Row, 1964.

Lake, Kirsopp, trans. *The Apostolic Fathers.* 2 vols. London: William Hienemann, 1919.

Lampe, G. W. H. "Scripture and Tradition in the Early Church." In *Scripture and Tradition*, edited by Frederick William Dillistone, pp. 21-52. London: Lutterworth, 1955.

Lane, William L. "Covenant: The Key to Paul's Conflict with Corinth." *TynBul* 33 (1982): 3-29.

————. *The Gospel According to St. Mark*. Grand Rapids: Eerdmans, 1974.

————. *Hebrews 1–8*. WBC. Waco, TX: Word, 1991.

Lange, Armin. "Oracle Collection and Canon: A Comparison Between Judah and Greece in Persian Times." In Evans and Zacharias, *Jewish and Christian Scripture as Artifact and Canon*, pp. 9-47.

Lemcio, Eugene E. "Ephesus and the New Testament Canon." *BJRL* 69 (1986): 210-34.

Levine, Lee I. "The Second Temple Synagogue: The Formative Years." In *The Synagogue in Late Antiquity*, edited by Lee I. Levine, pp. 7-31. Philadelphia: ASOR, 1987.

Lieberman, Saul. *Hellenism in Jewish Palestine*. 2nd ed. New York: Jewish Theological Seminary, 1962.

Lierman, John. *The New Testament Moses*. Tübingen: Mohr Siebeck, 2004.

Lieu, Judith. *Christian Identity in the Jewish and Graeco-Roman World*. Oxford: Oxford University Press, 2004.

————. "How John Writes." In Bockmuehl and Hagner, *Written Gospel*, pp. 171-83.

Lightfoot, J. B. *The Apostolic Fathers*. 2 vols. London: MacMillan, 1889.

————. *Essays on the Work Entitled Supernatural Religion*. London: MacMillan, 1889.

————. *St. Paul's Epistle to the Philippians*. Peabody, MA: Hendrickson, 1995.

Lim, Timothy H. *Holy Scripture in the Qumran Commentaries and Pauline Letters*. Clarendon: Oxford University Press, 1997.

Lincoln, Andrew T. "The Beloved Disciple as Eyewitness and the Fourth Gospel as Witness." *JSNT* 85 (2002): 3-26.

Lindemann, Andreas. "Paul in the Writings of the Apostolic Fathers." In *Paul and the Legacies of Paul*, edited by W. S. Babcock, pp. 25-45. Dallas: Southern Methodist University Press, 1990.

————. *Paulus im ältesten Christentum: Das Bild des Apostels und die Rezeption der paulinischen Theologie in der frühchristlichen*. Tübingen: Mohr Siebeck, 1979.

Linnemann, Eta. *Parables of Jesus: Introduction and Exposition*. London: SPCK, 1975.

Lints, Richard. *The Fabric of Theology*. Grand Rapids: Eerdmans, 1993.

Llewelyn, Stephen R. "The Development of the Codex." In *A Review of the Greek Inscriptions and Papyri Published in 1982–83*, edited by Stephen R. Llewelyn and R. A. Kearsley, pp. 249-56. Vol. 7 of New Documents Illustrating Early Christianity. North Ryde, Canada: Macquarie University Ancient History Documentary Research Center, 1994.

Longman, Tremper, III, and Daniel G. Reid. "Jesus: New Exodus, New Conquest." In *God Is a Warrior*, pp. 91-118. Grand Rapids: Zondervan, 1995.

Longenecker, Richard. *Galatians*. Dallas: Word, 1990.

Lord, Albert. "The Gospels as Oral Traditional Literature." In *The Relationships Among the Gospels: An Interdisciplinary Dialogue*, edited by William O. Walker Jr., pp. 33-91. San Antonio: Trinity University Press, 1978.

———. *The Singer of Tales*. Cambridge, MA: Harvard University Press, 1960.

Lowe, Malcolm, and David Flusser. "Evidence Corroborating a Modified Proto-Matthean Synoptic Theory." *NTS* 29 (1983): 25-47.

Lührmann, Dieter. "Q: Sayings of Jesus or Logia?" In *The Gospels Behind the Gospels: Current Studies on Q*, edited by Ronald A. Piper, pp. 97-116. Leiden: E. J. Brill, 1995.

Luijendijk, A. *Greetings in the Lord: Early Christians in the Oxyrhynchus Papyri*. Cambridge, MA: Harvard University Press, 2008.

Lundhaug, Hugo. "Canon and Interpretation: A Cognitive Perspective." In Thomassen, *Canon and Canonicity*, pp. 67-90.

Macdonald, Michael C. A. "Literacy in an Oral Environment." In *Writing and Ancient Near Eastern Society: Papers in Honour of Alan R. Millard*, edited by P. Bienkowski, C. B. Mee and A. E. Slater, pp. 49-118. London: T & T Clark, 2005.

Mack, Burton L. *What Is Rhetorical Criticism?* Minneapolis: Augsburg Fortress, 1990.

Malherbe, Abraham J. *The Letters to the Thessalonians*. New York: Doubleday, 2000.

———. *Social Aspects of Early Christianity*. Philadelphia: Fortress, 1983.

———, Frederick W. Norris and James W. Thompson, eds. *The Early Church in Its Context: Essays in Honor of Everett Ferguson*. Leiden: E. J. Brill, 1998.

Mann, Christopher S. *Mark*. Anchor Bible. New York: Doubleday, 1986.

Manson, Thomas W. "The Gospel of St. Matthew." In *Studies in the Gospels and Epistles*, edited by Matthew Black, pp. 68-104. Edinburgh: T & T Clark, 1962.

March, W. E., ed. *Texts and Testaments: Critical Essays on the Bible and the Early Church Fathers*. San Antonio: Trinity University Press, 1980.

Marcus, Joel. *Mark 1-8: A New Translation with Introduction and Commentary*. Anchor Bible. New York: Doubleday, 2000.

Marshall, I. Howard. *A Critical and Exegetical Commentary on the Pastoral Epistles*. ICC. Edinburgh: T & T Clark, 1999.

———. *The Epistles of John*. Grand Rapids: Eerdmans, 1978.

———. *The Gospel of Luke*. NIGTC. Grand Rapids: Eerdmans, 1978.

———. "The Last Supper." In *Key Events in the Life of The Historical Jesus*, edited by Darrell L. Bock and Robert L. Webb, pp. 481-588. Tübingen: Mohr Siebeck, 2009.

———. *Luke: Historian and Theologian*. Grand Rapids: Zondervan, 1970.

———. *1&2 Thessalonians*. NCBC. Grand Rapids: Eerdmans, 1983.

Martin, Ralph P. "Authority in the Light of the Apostolate, Tradition and the Canon." *EvQ* 40 (1968): 66-82.

———. *2 Corinthians*. WBC. Waco, TX: Word, 1986.

Martin, Victor, and Rudolf Kasser. *Papyrus Bodmer XIV-XV*. 2 vols. Geneva: Bibliotheca Bodmeriana, 1961.

Marxsen, Willi. *Introduction to the New Testament: An Approach to Its Problems*.
Philadelphia: Westminster, 1968.

Massaux, Édouard. *The Influence of the Gospel of Saint Matthew on Christian Literature Before Saint Irenaeus*. 2 vols. Translated by Norman J. Belval and Suzanne
Hecht. Macon, GA: Mercer University Press, 1994. [Original French title: *Influence de L'Évangile de Saint Matthieu sur la littérature chrétienne avant Saint
Irénée*. Lueven: Lueven University Press, 1986.]

———. "Le texte du Sermon sur la Montagne de Matthieu utilisé par Saint Justin."
ETL 28 (1952): 411-48.

Mattila, Sharon L. "A Question Too Often Neglected." *NTS* 41 (1995): 199-217.

Mayor, Joseph B. *The Epistle of St. James*. London: Macmillan, 1892.

———. *The Epistle of St. Jude and the Second Epistle of St. Peter*. London: Macmillan,
1907.

McCarthy, Dennis J. *Treaty and Covenant*. Rome: Biblical Institute Press, 1981.

McComiskey, Thomas E. *The Covenants of Promise: A Theology of the Old Testament
Covenants*. Grand Rapids: Baker, 1985.

McCown, C. C. "Codex and Roll in the New Testament." *HTR* 34 (1941): 219-50.

McDonald, Lee M. *The Biblical Canon: Its Origin, Transmission, and Authority*.
Peabody, MA: Hendrickson, 2007.

———. *Forgotten Scriptures: The Selection and Rejection of Early Religious Writings*.
Louisville: Westminster John Knox, 2009.

———. *The Formation of the Christian Biblical Canon*. Peabody, MA: Hendrickson,
1995.

———. "Identifying Scripture and Canon in the Early Church: The Criteria
Question." In McDonald and Sanders, *Canon Debate*, pp. 416-39.

———. "The Integrity of the Biblical Canon in Light of Its Historical Development."
BBR 6 (1996): 95-132.

———, and James A. Sanders, eds. *The Canon Debate*. Peabody, MA: Hendrickson,
2002.

McGrath, James F. "Written Islands in an Oral Stream: Gospel and Oral Traditions."
In *Jesus and Paul: Global Perspectives in Honor of James D. G. Dunn*, ed. B. J.
Oropeza, pp. 3-12. London: T & T Clark, 2009.

McKenzie, Steven L. *Covenant*. St. Louis: Chalice, 2000.

Meade, David. "Ancient Near Eastern Apocalypticism and the Origins of the New
Testament Canon of Scripture." In *The Bible as a Human Witness: Hearing the
Word of God Through Historically Dissimilar Traditions*, edited by Randall
Heskett and Brian Irwin, pp. 302-21. London: T & T Clark, 2010.

———. *Pseudepigrapha and Canon*. Tübingen: J. C. B. Mohr, 1986.

Meeks, Wayne A. *The First Urban Christians: The Social World of the Apostle Paul*.
New Haven, CT: Yale University Press, 1983.

————. *The Prophet-King: Moses Traditions and the Johannine Christology*. Leiden: E. J. Brill, 1967.

Meier, John P. "The Inspiration of Scripture: But What Counts as Scripture?" *Mid-Stream* 38 (1999): 71-78.

Mendenhall, George E. "Covenant." In *ABD*, pp. 1179-1202.

————. "Covenant Forms in Israelite Tradition." *BA* 17 (1954): 50-76.

————. *Law and Covenant in Israel and the Ancient Near East*. Pittsburgh: The Biblical Colloquium, 1955.

Menoud, Philippe H. "Revelation and Tradition: The Influence of Paul's Conversion on His Theology." *Int* 7 (1953): 131-41.

Metzger, Bruce M. *The Canon of the New Testament: Its Origin, Development and Significance*. Oxford: Clarendon, 1987.

————. *Early Versions of the New Testament: Their Origin, Transmission and Limitations*. Oxford: Clarendon, 1977.

————. *An Introduction to the Apocrypha*. New York: Oxford University Press, 1977.

————. "Literary Forgeries and Canonical Pseudepigrapha." *JBL* 91 (1972): 3-24.

————. *Manuscripts of the Bible: An Introduction to Greek Palaeography*. New York: Oxford University Press, 1981.

————. "Patristic Evidence and the Textual Criticism of the New Testament." In *New Testament Studies: Philological, Versional, and Patristic*, pp. 167-88. Leiden: E. J. Brill, 1980.

————. *A Textual Commentary on the Greek New Testament*. Stuttgart: German Bible Society, 1994.

Meyer, Ben F. "Many (=All) Are Called, But Few (=Not All) Are Chosen." *NTS* 36 (1990): 89-97.

Millard, Alan. *Reading and Writing in the Time of Jesus*. New York: New York University Press, 2000.

Moessner, David P. "'Eyewitnesses,' 'Informed Contemporaries,' and 'Unknowing Inquirers': Josephus' Criteria for Authentic Historiography and the Meaning of ΠΑΡΑΚΟΛΟΥΘΕΩ." *NT* 38 (1996): 105-22.

————. "How Luke Writes." In Bockmuehl and Hagner, *Written Gospel*, pp. 149-70.

Morris, Leon. *The Epistles of Paul to the Thessalonians*. TNTC. Grand Rapids: Eerdmans, 1974.

————. *The First Epistle of Paul to the Corinthians*. TNTC. Grand Rapids: Eerdmans, 1975.

————. *The Gospel According to John*. NICNT. Grand Rapids: Eerdmans, 1995.

————. *The Gospel According to Matthew*. Grand Rapids: Eerdmans, 1992.

Moule, C. F. D. *The Birth of the New Testament*. London: Adam & Charles Black, 1981.

————. "The Problem of the Pastoral Epistles: A Reappraisal." *BJRL* 47 (1965): 430-52.

Mournet, Terence C. *Oral Tradition and Literary Dependency*. Tübingen: Mohr Siebeck, 2005.

————. "The Jesus Tradition as Oral Tradition." In Kelber and Byrskog, *Jesus in Memory*, pp. 39-52.

Murray, John. "The Attestation of Scripture." In *The Infallible Word*, edited by Ned B. Stonehouse and Paul Wooley, pp. 1-54. Philadelphia: P&R, 1946.

Murray, Oswyn. *Early Greece*. London: Fontana, 1993.

Mussies, Gerard. "Parallels to Matthew's Version of the Pedigree of Jesus." *NovT* 28 (1986): 32-47.

Mutschler, Bernard. *Irenäus als johanneischer Theologe*. Tübingen: Mohr Siebeck, 2004.

Neusner, Jacob. "History and Purity in First-Century Judaism." *HR* 18 (1978): 1-17.

Newton, Michael. *The Concept of Purity at Qumran and in the Letters of Paul*. Cambridge: Cambridge University Press, 1985.

Nicholson, Ernest W. *God and His People: Covenant Theology in the Old Testament*. Oxford: Oxford University Press, 1986.

Niederwimmer, Kurt. "Johannes Markus un die Frage nach dem Verfasser des zweiten Evangeliums." *ZNW* 58 (1967): 172-88.

Nielsen, Charles M. "Polycarp, Paul, and the Scriptures." *AThR* 47 (1965): 199-216.

Nienhuis, David R. *Not by Paul Alone: The Formation of the Catholic Epistle Collection and the Christian Canon*. Waco, TX: Baylor University Press, 2007.

Nolland, John. *The Gospel of Matthew: A Commentary on the Greek Text*. NIGTC. Grand Rapids: Eerdmans, 2005.

————. *Luke 1:1–9:20*. WBC. Dallas, TX: Word Publishing, 1989.

Nongbri, Brent. "The Use and Abuse of P52: Papyrological Pitfalls in the Dating of the Fourth Gospel." *HTR* 98 (2005): 23-48.

Nordheim, Eckhard von. *Das Testamente als Literaturgattung im Judentum der hellenistische-romischen Zeit*. Vol 1 of Die Lehre Der Alten. Leiden: E. J. Brill, 1980.

Oberlinner, Lorenz. *Kommentar zum ersten Timotheusbrief*. Freiburg im Breisgau: Herder, 1994.

O'Callaghan, Jose. *Nomina Sacra in Papyrus Graecis Saeculi III Neotestamentariis*. Rome: Biblical Institute Press, 1970.

O'Connell, Jake H. "A Note on Papias's Knowledge of the Fourth Gospel." *JBL* 129 (2010): 793-94.

Olson, Daniel C. "Matthew 22:1-14 as Midrash." *CBQ* 67 (2005): 435-53.

Ong, Walter J. *The Presence of the Word: Some Prolegomena for Cultural and Religious History*. New Haven, CT: Yale University Press, 1967.

Osborn, Eric F. *Irenaeus of Lyons*. Cambridge: Cambridge University Press, 2001.

————. *Justin Martyr*. Tübingen: Mohr Siebeck, 1973.

————. "Teaching and Writing in the First Chapter of the *Stromateis* of Clement of Alexandria." *JTS* 10 (1959): 335-43.

Overbeck, Franz. "Über die Anfänge der partristischen Literatur." *Historische Zeitschrift* 48 (1882): 417-72.

Paap, A. H. R. E. *Nomina Sacra in the Greek Papyri of the First Five Centuries*. Leiden: E. J. Brill, 1959.

Pagels, Elaine. *Beyond Belief: The Secret Gospel of Thomas.* New York: Random House, 2003.

Paget, James Carleton. "The *Epistle of Barnabas* and the Writings That Later Formed the New Testament." In Gregory and Tuckett, *Reception of the New Testament in the Apostolic Fathers*, pp. 229-49.

————. *The Epistle of Barnabas: Outlook and Background.* Tübingen: Mohr Siebeck, 1994.

Pahl, Michael. "The 'Gospel' and the 'Word': Exploring Some Early Christian Patterns." *JSNT* 29 (2006): 211-27.

Pao, David. *Acts and the Isaianic New Exodus.* Tübingen: Mohr Siebeck, 2000.

Parker, David. *The Living Text of the Gospels.* Cambridge: Cambridge University Press, 1997.

Parker, Holt N. "Books and Reading Latin Poetry." In Johnson and Parker, *Ancient Literacies*, pp. 186-229.

Parry, Adam M., ed. *The Making of Homeric Verse: The Collected Papers of Milman Parry.* Oxford: Clarendon, 1971.

Parvis, Sara, and Paul Foster, eds. *Justin Martyr and His Worlds.* Minneapolis: Fortress, 2007.

Pearson, Birger A. "1 Thessalonians 2:13-16: A Deutero-Pauline Interpolation." *HTR* 64 (1971): 79-94.

Peckham, John C. "The Canon and Biblical Authority: A Critical Comparison of Two Models of Canonicity." *TrinJ* 28 (2007): 229-49.

Peer, Willie van. "Canon Formation: Ideology or Aesthetic Quality?" *British Journal of Aesthetics* 36 (1996): 97-108.

Perlitt, Lothar. *Bundestheologie im Alten Testament.* Neukirchen Vluyn: Neukirchener Verlag, 1969.

Petersen, William L. "The Diatesseron and the Fourfold Gospel." In Horton, *Earliest Gospels*, pp. 50-68.

————. *Tatian's Diatessaron: Its Creation, Dissemination, Significance, and History in Scholarship.* Leiden: E. J. Brill, 1994.

————. "Textual Evidence of Tatian's Dependence upon Justin's ΑΠΟΜΝΗΜΟΝΕΨΜΑΤΑ." *NTS* 36 (1990): 512-34.

————. "Textual Traditions Examined: What the Text of the Apostolic Fathers Tells Us About the Text of the New Testament in the Second Century." In Gregory and Tuckett, *Reception of the New Testament in the Apostolic Fathers*, pp. 29-46.

————. "What Text Can New Testament Textual Criticism Ultimately Reach?" In *New Testament Textual Criticism, Exegesis, and Early Church History: A Discussion of Methods*, edited by Barbara Aland and Joël Delobel, pp. 136-52. Kampen, Netherlands: Kok Pharos, 1994.

Poirier, John C. "Scripture and Canon." In Bird and Pahl, *Sacred Text*, pp. 83-98.

Porter, Stanley E. *Handbook of Classical Rhetoric in the Hellenistic Period.* Leiden: E. J. Brill, 1997.

————. "When and How Was the Pauline Canon Compiled? An Assessment of Theories." In *The Pauline Canon*, edited by Stanley E. Porter, pp. 95-127. Leiden: E. J. Brill, 2004.

————, and Jacqueline C. R. de Roo, eds. *The Concept of Covenant in the Second Temple Period*. Leiden: E. J. Brill, 2003.

————, and Christopher D. Stanley, eds. *As It Is Written: Studying Paul's Use of Scripture*. Atlanta: Society of Biblical Literature, 2008.

Powell, Mark Allan. *Introducing the New Testament: A Historical, Literary, and Theological Survey*. Grand Rapids: Baker Academic, 2009.

Poythress, Vern S. *The Shadow of Christ in the Law of Moses*. Phillipsburg, NJ: P&R, 1991.

Pritchard, James B., ed. *The Ancient Near East: An Anthology of Texts and Pictures*. Princeton, NJ: Princeton University Press, 2010.

Provan, Iain. "Canons to the Left of Him: Brevard Childs, His Critics, and the Future of Old Testament Theology." *SJT* 50 (1997): 1-38.

————. "Ideologies, Literary and Critical: Reflections on Recent Writings on the History of Israel." *JBL* 114 (1995): 585-606.

Pryor, John W. "Justin Martyr and the Fourth Gospel." *SecCent* 9 (1992): 153-67.

Puech, Émile. "Messianism, Resurrection, and Eschatology at Qumran and in the New Testament." In Ulrich and VanderKam, *Community of the Renewed Covenant*, pp. 235-56.

Räisänen, Heikki. *Beyond New Testament Theology: A Story and a Program*. London: SCM, 1990.

Rathke, Heinrich. *Ignatius von Antiochen und die Paulusbriefe*. Berlin: Akademie-Verlag, 1967.

Reicke, Bo. *The Epistles of James, Peter, and Jude*. Anchor Bible. New York: Doubleday, 1964.

————. *The Roots of the Synoptic Gospels*. Philadelphia: Fortress, 1986.

Rendtorff, Rolf. *Theologie des Altens Testaments: Ein kanonischer Entwurf*. Neukirchen-Vluyn: Neukirchener Verlag, 1999.

Richards, E. Randolph. "The Codex and the Early Collection of Paul's Letters." *BBR* 8 (1998): 151-66.

Ricoeur, Paul. "The 'Sacred' Text and the Community." In *The Critical Study of Sacred Texts*, edited by Wendy D. O'Flaherty, pp. 271-76. Berkeley: Graduate Theological Union, 1979.

Ridderbos, Herman N. *Bultmann*. Philadelphia: P&R, 1960.

————. *The Coming of the Kingdom*. Phillipsburg, NJ: P&R, 1962.

————. *The Gospel of John*. Grand Rapids: Eerdmans, 1997.

————. *Paul: An Outline of His Theology*. Grand Rapids: Eerdmans, 1975.

————. *Redemptive History and the New Testament Scripture*. Phillipsburg, NJ: P&R, 1988.

Riddle, Donald W. "Textual Criticism as a Historical Discipline." *ATR* 18 (1936): 220-33.

Riekert, Stephanus J. P. K. "Critical Research and the One Christian Canon Comprising Two Testaments." *Neot* 14 (1981): 21-41.

Robbins, Vernon K. "The Claims of the Prologues and Greco-Roman Rhetoric: The Prefaces to Luke and Acts in Light of Greco-Roman Rhetorical Strategies." In *Jesus and the Heritage of Israel*, edited by David P. Moessner, pp. 63-83. Harrisburg, PA: Trinity Press International, 1999.

———. "Interfaces of Orality and Literature in the Gospel of Mark." In Horsley, Draper and Foley, *Performing the Gospel*, pp. 125-46.

Roberts, Alexander, and James Donaldson, eds. *The Ante-Nicene Fathers*. Peabody, MA: Hendrickson, 1885.

Roberts, Colin H. "Books in the Greco-Roman World and in the New Testament." In Ackroyd and Evans, *Cambridge History of the Bible*, pp. 48-66.

———. "An Early Papyrus of the First Gospel." *HTR* 46 (1953): 233-37.

———. *Manuscript, Society and Belief in Early Christian Egypt*. London: Oxford University Press, 1979.

———. "An Unpublished Fragment of the Fourth Gospel in the John Rylands Library." *BJRL* 20 (1936): 45-55.

———. "Two Biblical Papyri in the John Rylands Library, Manchester." *BJRL* 20 (1936): 219-44.

———, and T. C. Skeat. *The Birth of the Codex*. London: Oxford University Press, 1987.

Roberts, John H., and Andreas B. Du Toit. *Preamble to New Testament Study*. Vol. 1 of Guide to the New Testament. Pretoria: N. G. Kerkboekhandel Transvaal, 1979.

Robertson, Archibald, and Alfred Plummer. *The First Epistle of St. Paul to the Corinthians*. ICC. Edinburgh: T & T Clark, 1961.

Robertson, O. Palmer. *The Christ of the Covenants*. Phillipsburg, NJ: P&R, 1980.

———. *Covenants: God's Way with His People*. Philadelphia: Great Commission, 1978.

Robinson, James M. *The Secrets of Judas: The Story of the Misunderstood Disciple and His Lost Gospel*. San Francisco: HarperSanFrancisco, 2006.

———, Paul Hoffmann and John S. Kloppenborg, eds. *The Critical Edition of Q*. Minneapolis: Fortress, 2000.

Robinson, Thomas A. *Ignatius of Antioch and the Parting of the Ways: Early Jewish-Christian Relations*. Grand Rapids: Baker Academic, 2009.

Rodgers, Peter. "The Text of the New Testament and Its Witnesses Before 200 A.D.: Observations on P90 (P.Oxy. 3523)." In *The New Testament Text in Early Christianity: Proceedings of the Lille Colloquium, July 2000*, edited by C. B. Amphoux and J. K. Elliott, pp. 83-91. Lausanne: Éditions Du Zèbre, 2003.

Roetzel, Calvin. "The Judgment Form in Paul's Letters." *JBL* 88 (1969): 305-12.

Russell, Ronald. "The Idle in 2 Thess 3:6-12: An Eschatological or a Social Problem?" *NTS* 34 (1988): 105-19.

Sanday, William. "A Commentary on the Gospels Attributed to Theophilus of Antioch." In *Studia Biblica et Ecclesiastica*, ed. S. R. Driver, T. K Cheyne and W. Sanday, pp. 89-101. Oxford: Clarendon, 1885.

Sanders, E. P. *Judaism: Practice and Belief 63BCE-66CE*. London: SCM, 1992.

———. *Paul and Palestinian Judaism*. Minneapolis: Fortress, 1977.

———. *The Tendencies of the Synoptic Tradition*. Cambridge: Cambridge University Press, 1969.

———, and Margaret Davies. *Studying the Synoptic Gospels*. London: SCM, 1989.

Sanders, Henry A. "The Beginnings of the Modern Book." *University of Michigan Quarterly Review* 44 (1938): 95-111.

Sanders, James A. *Torah and Canon*. Philadelphia: Fortress, 1972.

Sanders, Jack T. "Paul's 'Autobiographical' Statements in Galatians 1–2." *JBL* 85 (1966): 335-43.

Sandnes, Karl Olav. *Paul—One of the Prophets? A Contribution to the Apostle's Self-Understanding*. Tübingen: Mohr Siebeck, 1997.

Sarna, Nahum. "Bible." In *Encyclopedia Judaica*, vol. 3, ed. Fred Skolnik, p. 832. Macmillan Reference, 2006.

Schiffman, Lawrence H. "Communal Meals at Qumran." *RQ* 10 (1979): 45-56.

Schmidt, Daryl. "1 Thess. 2.13-16: Linguistic Evidence for Interpolation." *JBL* 102 (1983): 269-79.

Schmidt, Karl Ludwig. *Der Rahmen Der Geschichte Jesu: Literarkritische Untersuchungen Zur Ältesten Jesusüberlieferung*. Berlin: Trowitzsch, 1919.

Schnackenburg, Rudolf. *The Gospel According to St. John*. London: Burns and Oates, 1982.

Schneemelcher, Wilhelm, ed. *New Testament Apocrypha*. 2 vols. Translated by Robert McLachlan Wilson. Louisville: Westminster John Knox, 1991.

Schneider, Bernardin. "The Meaning of St. Paul's Antithesis 'The Letter and the Spirit.'" *CBQ* 15 (1953): 163-207.

Schoedel, William R. *Ignatius of Antioch*. Philadelphia: Fortress, 1985.

———, and R. L. Wilken, eds. *Early Christian Literature and the Classical Intellectual Tradition: In Honorem Robert M. Grant*. Paris: Beauchesne, 1979.

Schreiner, Thomas. *New Testament Theology: Magnifying God in Christ*. Grand Rapids: Baker Academic, 2008.

———. *Paul: Apostle of God's Glory in Christ*. Downers Grove, IL: IVP Academic, 2001.

Schrenk, Gottlob. "βίβλος, βιβλίον." *TDNT* 1:615-20.

———. "γράφω." *TDNT* 1:768.

Schubart, Wilhelm. *Das Buch bei den Griechen und Römern*. Edited by E. Paul. 2nd ed. Heidelberg: Schneider, 1962.

Schweitzer, Albert. *The Quest of the Historical Jesus*. New York: MacMillan, 1968.

Scott, Bernard B. *Hear Then the Parable: A Commentary on the Parables of Jesus*. Minneapolis: Fortress, 1989.

Searle, John R. *Speech Acts: An Essay in the Philosophy of Language*. Cambridge: Cambridge University Press, 1970.

Segovia, Fernando F. "The Final Farewell of Jesus: A Reading of John 20:30–21:25." *Sem* 53 (1991): 167-90.

Seitz, Christopher. *The Goodly Fellowship of the Prophets: The Achievement of Association in Canon Formation*. Grand Rapids: Baker Academic, 2009.

Semler, Johann Salomo. *Abhandlung von freier Untersuchung des Canon*. 4 vols. Halle: 1771–1775. Repr., Gütersloh: Mohn, 1967.

Sevrin, J. M., ed. *The New Testament in Early Christianity*. Leuven: Leuven University Press, 1989.

Sheppard, Gerald T. "Canon." In *Encyclopedia of Religion*, vol. 3, edited by Lindsay Jones, pp. 62-69. Detroit: Thomson Gale, 1987.

———. "Canonization: Hearing the Voice of the Same God Through Historically Dissimilar Traditions." *Ex auditu* 1 (1985): 106-14.

Shiner, Whitney. "Memory Technology and the Composition of Mark." In Horsley, Draper and Foley, *Performing the Gospel*, pp. 147-65.

———. *Proclaiming the Gospel: First Century Performance of Mark*. Harrisburg, PA: Trinity Press International, 2003.

Sibinga, J. Smit. "Ignatius and Matthew." *NovT* 8 (1966): 263-83.

Skarsaune, Oskar. "Justin and His Bible." In Parvis and Foster, *Justin Martyr and His Worlds*, pp. 53-76.

Skeat, T. C. "'Especially the Parchments': A Note on 2 Timothy iv.13." *JTS* 30 (1979): 173-77.

———. "Irenaeus and the Four-Gospel Canon." *NovT* 34 (1992): 194-99.

———. "The Oldest Manuscripts of the Four Gospels?" *NTS* 43 (1997): 1-34.

———. "The Origin of the Christian Codex." *ZPE* 102 (1994): 263-68.

Skeen, Judy. "Not as Enemies, but Kin: Discipline in the Family of God—2 Thessalonians 3:6-10." *RevExp* 96 (1999): 287-94.

Smith, Charles Foster, trans. *Thucydides*. Loeb. Cambridge, MA: Harvard University Press, 1980.

Smith, D. Moody. "When Did the Gospels Become Scripture?" *JBL* 119 (2000): 3-20.

Smith, Jonathan Z. "Canons, Catalogues, and Classics." In van der Kooij and van der Toorn, *Canonization and Decanonization*, pp. 295-311.

Smith, Wilfred C. *What Is Scripture? A Comparative Approach*. London: SPCK, 1993.

Snyder, H. Gregory. "Review of *Jewish Literacy in Roman Palestine*, by C. Hezser." *RBL* 8 (2002): 4.

Souter, Alexander. *The Text and Canon of the New Testament*. London: Duckworth, 1954.

Spivey Robert A., and D. Moody Smith. *Anatomy of the New Testament*. New York: McMillan, 1989.

Staerk, Willy. "Der Schrift- und Kanonbegriff der jüdischen Bibel." *ZST* 6 (1929): 101-19.

Stählin, Otto. *Clemens Alexandrinus*. 4 vols. Leipzig: J. C. Hinrichs, 1905.

Stanley, Christopher D. "The Importance of 4QTanhumim (4Q176)." *RevQ* 60 (1992): 569-82.

———. *Paul and the Language of Scripture: Citation Technique in the Pauline Epistles and Contemporary Literature.* Cambridge: Cambridge University Press, 1992.

Stanton, Graham N. "Form Criticism Revisited." In *What About the New Testament?*, edited by Morna D. Hooker and Colin J. A. Hickling, pp. 13-27. London: SCM, 1975.

———. "The Fourfold Gospel." *NTS* 43 (1997): 317-46.

———. *Jesus and Gospel.* Cambridge: Cambridge University Press, 2004.

———. *Jesus of Nazareth in New Testament Preaching.* SNTSMS 27. Cambridge: Cambridge University Press, 1974.

———. "Jesus Traditions and Gospels in Justin Martryr and Irenaeus." In Auwers and de Jonge, *Biblical Canons*, pp. 353-70.

———. "What Are the Gospels? New Evidence from Papyri." In Stanton, *Jesus and Gospel*, pp. 192-206.

———. "Why Were Early Christians Addicted to the Codex?" In Stanton, *Jesus and Gospel*, pp. 165-91.

Stein, Robert H. *Mark.* BECNT. Grand Rapids: Baker Academic, 2008.

Stettler, Christian. "The 'Command of the Lord' in 1 Cor 14:37—A Saying of Jesus?" *Bib* 87 (2006): 42-51.

Steudel, Annette. "אחרית הימים in the Texts from Qumran." *RevQ* 16 (1993): 225-46.

Stonehouse, Ned B. *The Origins of the Synoptic Gospels.* Grand Rapids: Baker, 1963.

Stott, John R. W. *The Letters of John.* Grand Rapids: Eerdmans, 1996.

Stuhlhofer, Franz. *Der Gebrauch Der Bibel Von Jesus Bis Euseb: Eine Statistische Untersuchung Zur Kanonsgeschichte.* Wuppertal: R. Brockhaus, 1988.

Stuhlmacher, Peter. *Das Paulinische Evangelium.* Göttingen: Vandenhoeck & Ruprecht, 1968.

Suggs, M. Jack. "The Use of Patristic Evidence in the Search for a Primitive New Testament Text." *NTS* 4 (1957–1958): 139-47.

Sundberg, Albert C. "The Biblical Canon and the Christian Doctrine of Inspiration." *Int* 29 (1975): 352-71.

———. "Canon Muratori: A Fourth-Century List." *HTR* 66 (1973): 1-41.

———. "The Making of the New Testament Canon." In *The Interpreter's One-Volume Commentary on the Bible*, ed. George A. Buttrick and Charles M. Laymon, pp. 1216-24. Nashville: Abingdon, 1971.

———. "Towards a Revised History of the New Testament Canon." *Studia Evangelica* 4 (1968): 452-61.

Talmon, Shemaryahu. "The Community of the Renewed Covenant: Between Judaism and Christianity." In Ulrich and VanderKam, *Community of the Renewed Covenant*, pp. 3-24.

———. "Oral Tradition and Written Transmission, or the Heard and the Seen Word in Judaism of the Second Temple Period." In Wansbrough, *Jesus and the Oral Gospel Tradition*, pp. 121-58.

Taylor, Vincent. *The Gospel According to St. Mark.* Grand Rapids: Baker, 1981.

Thatcher, Tom. "Beyond Texts and Traditions: Werner Kelber's Media History of Christian Origins." In Thatcher, *Jesus, the Voice, and the Text*, pp. 2-26.

———, ed. *Jesus, the Voice, and the Text: Beyond the Oral and Written Gospel*. Waco, TX: Baylor University Press, 2008.

Theissen, Gerd. *The New Testament: A Literary History*. Minneapolis: Fortress, 2012.

Thiede, Carston Peter. "Papyrus Magdalen Greek 17 (Gregory-Aland P64): A Reappraisal." *ZPE* 105 (1995): 13-20.

Thielman, Frank. "The New Testament Canon: Its Basis for Authority." *WTJ* 45 (1983): 400-410.

Thomassen, Einar, ed. *Canon and Canonicity: The Formation and Use of Scripture*. Copenhagen: Museum Tusculanum Press, 2010.

Thompson, John A. *The Ancient Near Eastern Treaties and the Old Testament*. Grand Rapids: Tyndale Press, 1964.

Tov, Emanuel. "Scribal Features of Early Witnesses in Greek Scripture." In *The Old Greek Psalter: Studies in Honour of Albert Pietersma*, edited by Robert J. V. Hiebert, Claude E. Cox and Peter J. Gentry, pp. 125-48. Sheffield: Sheffield Academic Press, 2001.

———. *Scribal Practices and Approaches Reflected in the Texts Found in the Judean Desert*. Leiden: E. J. Brill, 2004.

Traube, Ludwig. *Nomina Sacra: Versuch einer Geschichte der christlichen Kürzung*. Munich: Beck, 1907.

Trebilco, Paul R. *The Early Christians in Ephesus from Paul to Ignatius*. Tübingen: Mohr Siebeck, 2004.

Trebolle-Barrera, Julio C. "Origins of a Tripartite Old Testament Canon." In McDonald and Sanders, *Canon Debate*, pp. 128-45.

Treu, Kurt. "Die Bedeutung des Griechischen für die Juden im römischen Reich." *Kairos* 15 (1973): 123-44.

Trevett, Christine. "Approaching Matthew from the Second Century: The Under-Used Ignatian Correspondence." *JSNT* 20 (1984): 59-67.

Trites, Allison. *The New Testament Concept of Witness*. Cambridge: Cambridge University Press, 1977.

Trobisch, David. *Die Entstehung der Paulusbriefsammlung: Studien zu den Anfängen christlicher Publizistik (Novum testamentum et orbis antiquus)*. Göttingen: Vandenhoeck & Ruprecht, 1989.

———. *The First Edition of the New Testament*. Oxford: Oxford University Press, 2000.

———. *Paul's Letter Collection: Tracing the Origins*. Minneapolis: Fortress, 1994.

Tuckett, Christopher M. "Form Criticism." In Kelber and Byrskog, *Jesus in Memory*, pp. 21-38.

———. *Nag Hammadi and the Gospel Tradition*. Edinburgh: T & T Clark, 1986.

———. "'Nomina Sacra': Yes and No?" In Auwers and de Jonge, *Biblical Canons*, pp. 431-58.

———. "P52 and the *Nomina Sacra.*" *NTS* 47 (2001): 544-48.

———. "The Synoptic Tradition in the Didache." In Sevrin, *New Testament in Early Christianity*, pp. 197-230.

Turner, Cuthbert H. "Marcan Usage: Notes Critical and Exegetical on the Second Gospel V. The Movements of Jesus and His Disciples and the Crowd." *JTS* 26 (1925): 225-40.

Turner, Eric G. *Greek Manuscripts of the Ancient World*. London: Institute of Classical Studies, 1987.

———. *Greek Papyri: An Introduction*. Oxford: Clarendon Press, 1968.

———. "Scribes and Scholars." In *Oxyrhynchus: A City and Its Texts*, ed. Patricia J. Parsons, Alan K. Bowman, R. A. Coles and Nikolaos Gonis, pp. 256-61. London: Egypt Exploration Society, 2007.

———. *The Typology of the Early Codex*. Philadelphia: University of Pennsylvania Press, 1977.

Turner, Nigel. "The Literary Charcter of New Testament Greek." *NTS* 20 (1974): 107-14.

Ulrich, Eugene. "The Notion and Definition of Canon." In McDonald and Sanders, *Canon Debate*, pp. 21-35.

———. "Qumran and the Canon of the Old Testament." In Auwers and de Jonge, *Biblical Canons*, pp. 57-80.

———, and James C. VanderKam, eds. *The Community of the Renewed Covenant: The Notre Dame Symposium on the Dead Sea Scrolls*. Notre Dame: University of Notre Dame Press, 1994.

Unnik, Willem C. van. "De la régle μήτε προσθεῖναι μήτε ἀφελεῖν dans l'histoire du canon." *VC* 3 (1949): 1-36.

———. "ἡ καινὴ διαθήκη—A Problem in the Early History of the Canon." *Studia Patristica* 4 (1961): 212-27.

VanderKam, James C. "Apocalyptic Tradition in the Dead Sea Scrolls and the Religion of Qumran." In *Religion in the Dead Sea Scrolls*, edited by John J. Collins and Robert A. Kulger, pp. 113-34. Grand Rapids: Eerdmans, 2000.

Vanhoozer, Kevin J. *The Drama of Doctrine: A Canonical-Linguistic Approach to Christian Theology*. Louisville: Westminster John Knox, 2005.

———. *First Theology: God, Scripture & Hermeneutics*. Downers Grove, IL: IVP Academic, 2002.

Vansina, Jan M. *Oral Tradition as History*. Madison, WI: University of Wisconsin Press, 1985.

Verheyden, Jozef. "Assessing Gospel Quotations in Justin Martyr." In *New Testament Textual Criticism and Exegesis, Festschrift J. Delobel*, edited by Adelbert Denaux, pp. 361-78. Leuven: Peeters, 2002.

———. "The Canon Muratori: A Matter of Dispute." In Auwers and de Jonge, *Biblical Canons*, pp. 487-556.

Vermes, Geza. *The Dead Sea Scrolls: Qumran in Perspective*. Philadelphia: Fortress, 1977.

Vielhauer, Philipp, and Georg Strecker. "Jewish-Christian Gospels." In Schneemelcher, *New Testament Apocrypha*, 1:134-78.

Vogels, Walter. "La structure symétrique de la Bible chrétienne." In Auwers and de Jonge, *Biblical Canons*, pp. 295-304.

Vos, Geerhardus. *Biblical Theology*. Edinburgh: Banner of Truth, 1975.

———. "Hebrews, the Epistle of the Diatheke." In *Redemptive History and Biblical Interpretation: The Shorter Writings of Geerhardus Vos*. Phillipsburg, NJ: P&R, 1980.

Wachtel, Klaus. "P64/67: Fragmente des Matthäusevangeliums aus dem 1. Jahrhundert?" *ZPE* 107 (1995): 73-80.

Walls, Andrew F. "Papias and Oral Tradition." *VC* 21 (1967): 137-40.

Walton, John H. *Ancient Israelite Literature in Its Cultural Context*. Grand Rapids: Zondervan, 1989.

———. *Covenant: God's Purpose, God's Plan*. Grand Rapids: Zondervan, 1994.

Wanamaker, Charles A. *The Epistles to the Thessalonians*. NIGTC. Grand Rapids: Eerdmans, 1990.

Wansbrough, Henry, ed. *Jesus and The Oral Gospel Tradition*. Edinburgh: T & T Clark, 2004.

Ward, Richard F. "Pauline Voice and Presence as Strategic Communication." In Dewey, *Orality and Textuality in Early Christian Literature*, pp. 95-107.

Warfield, B. B. "The Formation of the Canon of the New Testament." In *The Inspiration and Authority of the Bible*, pp. 411-16. Phillipsburg, NJ: P&R, 1948.

Wasserman, Tommy. "The Early Text of Matthew." In Hill and Kruger, *Early Text of the New Testament*, pp. 83-107.

Waszink, J. Hendrik. *Tertullian: The Treatise Against Hermogenes*. New York: Newman Press, 1956.

Watson, Francis. "Bible, Theology and the University: A Response to Philip Davies." *JSOT* 71 (1996): 3-16.

———. *Paul and the Hermeneutics of Faith*. London: T & T Clark, 2004.

———. *Text and Truth: Redefining Biblical Theology*. Grand Rapids: Eerdmans, 1997.

Weatherly, Jon A. "The Authenticity of 1 Thessalonians 2:13-16: Additional Evidence." *JSNT* 42 (1991): 79-98.

Weber, Max. *The Sociology of Religion*. Boston: Beacon Press, 1993.

Webster, John B. "'A Great and Meritorious Act of the Church'? The Dogmatic Location of the Canon." In *Die Einheit der Schrift und die Vielfalt des Kanons*, edited by John Barton and Michael Wolter, pp. 95-126. Berlin: Walter de Gruyter, 2003.

Weir, J. Emmette. "The Identity of the Logos in the First Epistle of John." *ExpT* 86 (1974–1975): 118-20.

Westcott, Brooke F. *A General Survey of the History of the Canon of the New Testament*. London: MacMillan, 1870.

White, John L. "Introductory Formulae in the Body of the Pauline Letter." *JBL* 90 (1971): 91-97.

White, L. Michael. *From Jesus to Christianity.* San Francisco: Harper, 2004.

Whittaker, John. "The Value of Indirect Tradition in the Establishment of Greek Philosophical Texts or the Art of Misquotation." In *Editing Greek and Latin Texts. Papers Given at the Twenty-Third Annual Conference on Editorial Problems, University of Toronto 6-7 November 1987,* edited by John Grant, pp. 63-95. New York: AMS, 1989.

Wikgren, Allen Paul. "ΑΡΧΗ ΤΟΥ ΕΥΑΓΓΕΛΙΟΥ." *JBL* 61 (1942): 11-20.

Wilckens, Ulrich. *Die Missionsreden der Apostelgeschichte.* 3rd ed. Neukirchen-Vluyn: Neukirchener Verlag, 1974.

Wilken, Robert L. "Pagan Criticism of Christianity: Greek Religions and Christian Faith." In Schoedel and Wilken, *Early Christian Literature,* pp. 117-34.

Willis, John T. "Isaiah 2:2-5 and the Psalms of Zion." In *Writing and Reading the Scroll of Isaiah: Studies of an Interpretive Tradition,* edited by Craig C. Broyles and Craig A. Evans, pp. 295-316. Leiden: E. J. Brill, 1997.

Winter, Bruce W. "'If a Man Does Not Wish to Work . . .' A Cultural and Historical Setting for 2 Thessalonians 3:6-16." *TynBul* 40 (1989): 303-15.

Witherington, Ben, III. *Jesus, Paul and the End of the World.* Downers Grove, IL: IVP Academic, 1992.

Wolterstorff, Nicholas. *Divine Discourse: Philosophical Reflections on the Claim That God Speaks.* Cambridge: Cambridge University Press, 1995.

Wrede, William. *The Origin of the New Testament.* Translated by James S. Hill. London and New York: Harper & Bros., 1909.

Wright, N. T. *Jesus and the Victory of God.* Minneapolis: Fortress, 1996.

———. *The Last Word: Beyond the Bible Wars to a New Understanding of the Authority of Scripture.* San Francisco: HarperSanFrancisco, 2005.

———. *The New Testament and the People of God.* Minneapolis: Fortress, 1992.

Wuellner, Wilhelm. "Greek Rhetoric and Pauline Argumentation." In Schoedel and Wilken, *Early Christian Literature,* pp. 177-88.

Yarbrough, Robert W. "The Date of Papias: A Reassessment." *JETS* 26 (1983): 181-91.

———. *1-3 John.* BECNT. Grand Rapids: Baker Academic, 2008.

Young, Frances M. *Biblical Exegesis and the Formation of Christian Culture.* Cambridge: Cambridge University Press, 1997.

Young, Stephen E. *Jesus Tradition in the Apostolic Fathers.* Tübingen: Mohr Siebeck, 2011.

Zahn, Theodor. *Geschichte des neutestamentlichen Kanons.* Erlangen: A. Deichert, 1888-1892.

Zumstein, Jean. "La naissance de la notion d'Écriture dans la littérature johannique." In Auwers and de Jonge, *Biblical Canons,* pp. 371-94.

Author Index

Achtemeier, Paul, 78

Aland, Kurt, 16

Albl, Martin, 95

Alexander, Loveday, 88, 90, 92, 96, 107-8

Allen, David, 149

Allert, Craig, 30, 33

Allison, Dale, 144, 146

Allison, David, 52

Assmann, Jan, 72-73, 75, 90

Barr, James, 30, 47-48, 80

Barrett, C. K., 54

Barton, John, 30, 35, 43, 101-2, 121-22, 153-54

Bauckham, Richard, 105-6, 114, 136, 183, 186

Baum, Armin, 130-31

Baur, F. C., 104

Beale, Greg, 145, 160

Beard, Mary, 87

Beatrice, Pier, 188

Bellinzoni, Arthur, 155, 157

Benecke, Paul, 195-96

Berding, Kenneth, 196

Best, Ernest, 125

Bock, Darrell, 142

Bovon, François, 53-54

Bruce, F. F., 123, 152

Buchanan, George, 148

Bultmann, Rudolf, 82, 152

Byrskog, Samuel, 72, 105, 107

Cameron, Ron, 105, 184

Campenhausen, Hans von, 67, 156

Carmignac, Jean, 65

Carroll, Kenneth, 156

Chapman, Stephen, 32

Charlesworth, Scott, 173

Childs, Brevard, 18, 27, 34-36, 45

Collins, Raymond, 128

Cornell, Tim, 84

Davies, W. D., 52, 144, 146

Dehandschutter, Boudewijn, 195-96

Deissmann, Adolf, 91-92

Dempster, Stephen, 33, 36

Dewey, Joanna, 88-89

Dibelius, Martin, 82, 112

Donaldson, James, 198

du Toit, Andreas, 132

Dungan, David, 19, 32

Eichrodt, Walter, 58

Enslin, Morton, 48

Evans, C. F., 48, 79, 105, 112

Evans, Christopher, 18

Evans, Craig A., 104, 143

Farkasfalvy, Denis, 194

Fee, Gordon, 125

Ferguson, Everett, 21, 66-67

Filson, Floyd, 42

Fitzmyer, Joseph, 141, 143

Foster, Paul, 175, 189

Fung, Ronald, 124

Funk, Robert, 80

Gaffin, Richard, 53

Gamble, Harry, 30, 47-48, 95

Goulder, Michael, 193

Grant, Robert, 166, 191

Green, Gene, 75

Green, Joel, 139

Guelich, Robert, 131, 133

Hacking, Ian, 204, 209

Hafemann, Scott, 111

Hagner, Donald, 148, 197, 199

Hahneman, Geoffrey, 30, 104, 159, 163

Harnack, Adolf von, 15, 18-20, 35-36, 38, 54, 62

Harris, William, 83, 85

Havelock, Eric, 84

Hengel, Martin, 132, 134, 167, 172, 198

Hill, Charles, 75, 159, 161, 191, 193, 196

Hillers, Delbert, 61, 77, 206

Hurtado, Larry, 158, 180

Jensen, Peter, 64-65

Johns, Loren, 18

Keener, Craig, 138

Keith, Chris, 86

Kelber, Werner, 84-85, 103, 109-10, 112

Kelhoffer, James, 178

Kelsey, David, 30, 38-39

Kline, Meredith, 60-63

Koester, Helmut, 19, 156, 174, 177-78, 195-96

Köhler, Wolf-Dietrich, 187

Kümmel, Werner, 194-95

Kyrtatus, Dimitris, 156

Lake, Kirsopp, 198

Lim, Timothy, 95

Lints, Richard, 52

Lord, Albert, 84, 103

Marshall, I. Howard, 140, 142, 151, 201

Marxsen, Willi, 144

McDonald, Lee, 18, 30, 37, 104-5, 119, 130, 153, 156, 196

Meade, David, 22, 36, 116, 200, 205-6

Meier, John, 202

Mendenhall, George, 62

Moessner, David, 141-42

Morris, Leon, 129

Moule, C. F. D., 69

Mournet, Terence, 89

Mutschler, Bernard, 168

Nienhuis, David, 31

Ong, Walter, 84, 103

Overbeck, Franz, 81-82

Pagels, Elaine, 20, 157

Paget, Carleton, 187-89

Pahl, Michael, 56

Pao, David, 56

Parker, Holt, 90

Parry, Milman, 84, 103

Peterson, William, 174, 176-77

Plummer, Alfred, 128

Powell, Mark, 120

Provan, Iain, 31, 36, 42

Ridderbos, Herman, 137

Riekert, Stephanus, 36
Roberts, Alexander, 198
Roberts, Colin, 98, 173
Roberts, John, 132
Robertson, Archibald, 128
Schleiermacher, Friedrich, 82
Schneemelcher, Wilhelm, 120
Schreiner, Thomas, 114-15
Seitz, Christopher, 64
Sheppard, Gerald, 36
Shiner, Whitney, 105
Skarsaune, Oskar, 174-75

Skeat, T. C., 101, 161
Smith, D. Moody, 52, 119, 121
Spivey, Robert, 121
Stanton, Graham, 99-100, 162, 174
Stein, Robert, 131
Stott, John, 152
Sundberg, Albert, 29, 33-34, 163-64
Talmon, Shemaryahu, 88
Theissen, Gerd, 116-17, 132
Turner, Eric, 181
Ulrich, Eugene, 30

Vanhoozer, Kevin, 42
Verheyden, Joseph, 164
Vermes, Geza, 58
Vogels, Walter, 63-64
Walton, John, 58
Wanamaker, Charles, 129
Warfield, Benjamin, 41
Watson, Francis, 42, 82, 96
White, L. Michael, 195
Wright, N. T., 50, 57, 113, 121, 135
Zahn, Theodor, 35-36
Zumstein, Jean, 137

Subject Index

Acts, book of, 56, 63-64
Against Heresies, 99, 159
anonymity of authorship,
  130-31
Apocalypse of Peter, 37, 162
apocalyptic imagery, 113, 115
apocrypha, New Testament,
  17, 37, 98, 162-63, 167, 201
apostles, 67-69
  and revelation, 122
  authority of, 126, 129,
    206-7
  credentials of, 140-41, 151
  deaths of, 75
  preaching of, 131
  teaching of, 69-71, 73, 76,
    121, 128, 133, 150, 152,
    190-92
apostolic fathers, 68, 176-181,
  208
apostolic tradition, 121,
  124-25, 132-33, 138-39, 147
authority of NT authors,
  119-21, 153-54, 207-8
book production, Christian,
  100-101, 118
canon
  books excluded from
    the, 37
  criticism (canonical), 36
  church and the, 17, 21-22,
    24, 31, 33-34, 38, 44-45
  divine authority of,
    40-41
  exclusive definition of,
    29-34, 42-45
  functional definition of,
    34-40, 42-45
  Old Testament, 50
  ontological definition of,
    40-45
  order of, 145-46
canonization process, 21-22,
  34-35, 38-39, 43
Catholic Epistles, 147-53
Celsus, 84-85

Cicero, 90
1 Clement, 68, 197-99, 202
Clement of Alexandria, 66,
  167-68
Clement of Rome, 148
commands/commandments
  of God, 126-27
Constantine, 19, 204
Council of Trent, 32
covenant theology, 57-59
covenants, 59, 61-62, 65-67,
  110, 206-7
David, 50, 52-53
Decalogue, 60
Diatesseron, 165
divino instrumento versus
  instrumentum, 66
Epistle of Barnabas, 187-89,
  202-3
eschatology, 51, 77, 112-16,
  206
Eusebius, 166
*Exposition of the Lord's
  Oracles,* 106
extended situation
  (zehrdente Situation),
  75-76
extrinsic model, 18-23, 28, 33,
  47, 80, 117, 156, 205
eyewitness testimony, 107,
  151
form criticism, 81-82, 112,
  178
formula citandi, 172
Galen, 107
genealogy, 144-45
Gospel of Thomas, 98
Gospels, 30-46, 32, 63, 85-86,
  114, 157, 159, 161-62, 171,
  173-75, 179, 186
Greek language, NT style of,
  91-92
Griesbach hypothesis, 179
handwritten scripts, 98-99
Hermogenes, 166
Herodotus, 105-6

historical criticism, 41-42
historiography, 105-6
Ignatius of Antioch, 68, 148,
  189-93, 202-3
inscriptional curse, 60-61,
  63, 153
intrinsic model, 21-23, 57, 79,
  154, 205, 209-10
Irenaeus, 20, 24, 69, 99,
  156-61, 163, 165, 168-69,
  181-82, 193, 202-4, 208
Jesus' relation to canon, 48,
  51-52
John (Evangelist), 135-36, 138,
  151-52, 182, 193
Justin Martyr, 68, 88, 169-76,
  199, 202, 208
kingdom of God, 49, 51, 59,
  113-14
letter/Spirit distinction,
  109-11
literacy, 24, 82-84, 87-88, 103,
  117, 207
literary dependence, 179
living voice, 107-9
Lucian, 84, 106
Luke (Evangelist), 138-43,
  148
Marcion(ism), 18-19, 38, 82,
  94, 154, 157-58, 204
Mark (Evangelist), 148
Martial, 93
Matthew (Evangelist),
  143-46
Melito of Sardis, 65-66
membrana, 93-95
Messiah/Messianic
  expectations, 49-51, 55-56,
  77
Minucius Felix, 84
Montanists/anti-Montanists,
  66
Muratorian fragment,
  162-64
nomina sacra, 101-2, 207
oral history, 106

oral religion, 79-80
oral tradition, 72, 86, 101,
    109, 178, 192
orality, 70, 81, 84, 87, 89,
    103-4
Origen, 67, 148
OT citations in the NT,
    54-57, 94-95, 134-35, 137-38,
    149
Papias, 104-9, 171, 182-87, 193,
    202-3
Paul (apostle), 64, 109-12, 193
    credentials of, 123
Pauline corpus, 32, 86,
    123-29, 157, 175, 189-90,
    198-99
Peter (apostle), 68, 73, 75,
    133-34, 149-51, 183
Philip the Evangelist, 182

Pliny, 90
Polybius, 105
Polycarp, 160, 182, 193-97,
    199, 202
prophetic judgment, 128-29
public reading, 172-73
Q (document), 93, 179, 185, 201
Quintilian, 93
Qumran community, 57-58,
    95, 115-16
rhetoric, 92, 107
Second Temple Judaism,
    49-50, 58, 74
Seneca, 108
Shepherd of Hermas, 37, 98
Sibylline Oracles, 161
sociohistorical theory, 83, 117
speech-act philosophy,
    44-45

Tatian, 165-66, 169
Tertullian, 66
testamentary genre, 73-74
Tetragrammaton, 102
textuality, 24, 87, 89, 91,
    94-95, 101, 103, 117, 178, 181,
    207
Theophilus (biblical figure),
    142
Theophilus of Antioch,
    164-66
Thucydides, 105-6
Timothy, 148
two-source hypothesis, 179
written documents, 62, 65,
    75, 81, 107-8
    mode of transmission,
        90

Scripture Index

OLD TESTAMENT

Genesis
2:4, *144*
5:1, *144*
12:1-3, *57*
15:18, *57*
17:2, *57*

Exodus
2:1-10, *146*
3:1, *146*
4:10, *110*
14, *146*
16, *146*
17:14, *70*
19:3, *146*
19:12-13, *146*
20:2, *53*
23:20, *135*
24:7, *61*
24:12, *146*
24:13, *146*
24:18, *146*
25:16, *60, 62*
31:18, *110*
34:2, *146*
34:28, *57, 61*

Leviticus
4:13, *127*
5:17, *127*
27:34, *127*

Numbers
11, *146*
15:39, *127*
27:12, *146*

Deuteronomy
1:24, *146*
1:41, *146*
1:43, *146*
4:2, *61, 62, 64, 66, 127,*
  184
4:13, *61*
5:5, *146*
6:17, *127*
8:6, *127*
9:9, *146*
10:2, *60*
11:28, *127*
12:32, *61*
18, *55*
18:18, *54, 55*
25:4, *200*
27-30, *57*
28:58, *137*
29:21, *61*
30:16, *127*
31:9, *60*
31:10-13, *61*

Joshua
1:2, *64*
3:14-17, *49*
22:3, *127*
24:26, *60*

Judges
3:4, *127*

1 Samuel
8:8, *53*
12:6, *53*

2 Samuel
7:23, *53*

2 Kings
23:2, *61*

1 Chronicles
1-2, *52*
3:1-24, *50*

2 Chronicles
34:21, *137*
34:30, *61*
36:23, *145*

Ezra
7:11, *127*

Nehemiah
9:9-10, *53*
10:29, *127*

Psalms
19:8, *127*
78:12-14, *53*
135:9, *53*

Proverbs
30:5-6, *61*

Isaiah
2, *56*
2:2-3, *56*
2:2-5, *56*
11:1, *55*
11:4, *55*
11:16, *53*
30:8, *70*
40:1-11, *49*
40:3, *51, 133, 135*
40:9, *56, 124*
42:1, *135*
44:3, *51*
49:6, *49, 57*
52:7, *56, 124, 133,*
  135
52:8, *49*
52:13–53:12, *49*
55:3, *57*
58:6, *56*
59:21, *59*
61:1, *124, 133, 135*
61:1-2, *51, 55, 56, 57*
61:2, *56*

Jeremiah
25:13, *138*
30:2, *70*
31:27-28, *59*
31:31, *59, 62, 77*
31:31-40, *49*
31:33, *110, 111*

Ezekiel
1:6, *161*
1:22, *161*
10:1, *161*
10:20, *161*
11:19, *110*
36:24-28, *49*
36:26, *111*
36:36, *59*
37:1, *198*

Daniel
1, *161*
2, *161*

Hosea
1:2, *132*
11:1, *51, 53, 146*

Amos
9:11-15, *49*

Habakkuk
2:2, *70*

Zephaniah
3:14-20, *49*

Zechariah
14:9, *49*

Malachi
3:1, *135*

APOCRYPHA

Tobit
14:5-7, *49*

Wisdom of Solomon
1, *49*

3:7, *49*
11–19, *50*

Sirach
4, *50, 145*
39:1, *50, 145*
50:1-21, *50*

Baruch
2:7-10, *49*
3:6-8, *49*
4:36-37, *49*

1 Maccabees
1:15, *58*
1:57, *61*
2:20, *58*
4:8-11, *58*
8:30, *61, 184*

2 Maccabees
1:27-29, *49*
2:5-18, *49*
2:18, *49*
4, *49*
8:14-18, *58*

New Testament

Matthew
1, *143*
1:1, *52, 144*
1:2-17, *144*
2:1-18, *146*
2:14-15, *51*
2:15, *146*
2:23, *146*
3:1-7, *51*
3:13, *146*
3:13-17, *146*
3:15, *192*
5:1, *51, 146*
5:28, *165*
5:32, *165*
5:44, *165*
6:3, *165*
7:21, *114*
8:11, *114*
9:9, *143*
9:13, *189*
10:2, *113*

10:3, *143*
10:10, *201*
10:14, *67*
10:20, *67*
11:5, *55*
12:6, *53*
12:28, *114*
14:13-20, *146*
15:4, *201*
15:6, *125*
16:28, *113*
19:12, *192*
20:16, *187*
22:1-14, *188*
22:14, *187, 188, 203*
22:43, *198*
24:34, *113*
26:28, *59*
26:41, *196*
28:18-20, *76, 145*

Mark
1–8, *131*
1–14, *133*
1:1, *56, 131, 132, 133*
1:1-15, *131, 135*
1:2, *135*
1:3, *133, 135*
1:4-8, *133*
1:10-11, *135*
1:14, *132*
1:15, *51, 132*
1:16, *134*
3:14-15, *67*
7:10, *201*
7:13, *125*
7:19, *130*
8:35, *132*
9:1, *113*
9:7, *55*
10:7, *165*
10:29, *132*
13:10, *76, 132*
13:14, *130*
13:30, *113*
14:9, *132*
14:24, *59*
14:25, *114*
14:29, *132*
14:38, *196*
15–16, *133*
15:34, *113*

15:43, *114*
16:7, *134*

Luke
1:1, *92*
1:1-2, *139, 140*
1:1-4, *72, 130, 138, 139*
1:1–9:20, *139, 141*
1:2, *139, 140, 141, 142, 147, 148, 151, 152, 201, 208*
1:3, *71*
1:72, *59*
2:25, *49*
2:38, *49*
3:2, *125*
3:3, *56*
4:16-30, *51*
4:17-19, *124*
4:17-20, *126, 199*
4:18-19, *55, 56, 57*
4:20, *93*
4:21, *114*
4:44, *56*
5:1, *125*
7:22-23, *55*
8:1, *56*
8:12-15, *141*
8:39, *56*
9:2, *56*
9:27, *113*
9:31, *51*
10:7, *143, 201*
10:18, *186*
12:3, *56*
12:39-40, *114*
14:16-24, *188*
17:20-21, *114*
18:27, *165*
20:44, *53*
21:32, *113*
22:20, *59*
22:44, *166*
24:19, *51*
24:39, *192*
24:44, *50, 140, 145*
24:46-47, *56*
24:47, *56, 57, 76*
24:48, *139, 140, 151*

John
1:1, *53, 151, 152*

1:14, *192*
1:17, *111*
1:18, *170*
1:35-40, *136*
1:41, *49*
2:17, *138*
2:17-22, *137*
2:22, *130*
3:3, *170*
3:8, *192*
3:16, *170*
4:25, *49*
5:4, *166*
6:14, *55*
6:31, *138*
6:32, *51*
6:45, *138*
7:40, *55*
7:52, *53*
7:53–8:11, *166*
8:17, *138*
10:34, *138*
12:14, *138*
12:14-16, *137*
12:16, *138*
13:23, *136*
14:26, *67*
15:25, *138*
15:26, *137*
15:26-27, *137*
15:27, *136, 137, 140, 151*
17:8, *67*
17:16, *192*
19:26, *136*
19:35, *136*
20:25, *170*
20:27, *170*
20:30, *138*
20:30-31, *137, 138*
20:30–21:25, *137*
20:31, *71, 138, 152*
21, *136*
21:15-25, *136*
21:20, *136*
21:24, *130, 135, 136, 137, 138, 151, 152*
21:24-25, *137*

Acts
1:1, *72, 141*
1:6, *49*
1:7-8, *76*

1:8, *56, 64, 139, 151*
1:20, *201*
1:21-22, *151*
1:22, *140, 151*
2:43, *147*
3:15, *139, 151*
3:22-23, *51*
3:23-24, *55*
4:20, *151*
4:30, *147*
4:31, *125*
5:12, *147*
5:32, *139, 151*
5:37, *49*
6:2, *125*
6:4, *140, 152*
6:8, *147*
7:37, *55*
7:38, *185*
8:5, *56*
8:14, *125*
9:1-9, *123*
9:20, *56*
10:34-43, *133*
10:36, *133*
10:36-37, *55*
10:37, *56, 133, 140*
10:38, *133*
10:39, *133*
10:39-41, *139, 151*
10:41-42, *68*
10:42, *56*
11:1, *125*
12:12-17, *134*
13:15, *126, 199*
14:3, *147*
15:12, *147*
15:21, *56, 126, 199*
16:3, *148*
16:4, *141*
17:14, *148*
19:13, *56*
20:17-35, *74*
20:25, *56*
21:8-9, *182*
26:16, *139, 140, 142, 151*
28:31, *56*

Romans
1:5, *76*
2:7-9, *166*
2:29, *111*

3:2, *185*
3:7, *166*
4, *192*
6:17, *86*
7:6, *111*
7:8-13, *127*
8:2, *111*
9:6, *125*
10:15, *56*
11:27, *59*
13:9, *127*
15:19, *147*
16:5, *190*
16:21, *148*

1 Corinthians
4:17, *148*
5:9, *92*
5:9-11, *129*
7:12, *127*
7:19, *127*
9:14, *201*
10:2, *146*
10:11, *51*
11:2, *86, 126, 141*
11:23, *86, 123, 125, 141*
11:23-25, *127*
11:25, *59*
14:36, *56, 125*
14:37, *127, 150, 153*
14:37-38, *126, 127, 128, 208*
15:1-3, *125*
15:3, *86, 123, 141*
15:3-4, *95*
15:3-5, *86*
15:3-8, *123*
15:32, *190*
15:33, *129*
16:5-6, *76*
16:8, *190*

2 Corinthians
1:19, *148*
2:16, *110*
2:17, *56*
3, *110*
3:1-11, *110*
3:3, *110*
3:5-18, *110*
3:6, *59, 65, 109, 110, 128*

3:8, *110*
3:9, *110*
3:14, *59, 64, 65*
4:2, *56*
5:20, *65*
10:9, *63, 87, 126, 199*
10:10, *126*
12:12, *147*

Galatians
1–2, *123*
1:1, *123, 127*
1:6, *123*
1:9, *86, 125*
1:11, *124*
1:11-12, *124*
1:11-17, *123*
1:17-20, *123*
2:2, *194*
3:7-9, *76*
3:10, *93*
3:14, *51*
3:15, *64*
3:17-18, *111*
4:24-26, *111*

Ephesians
1:1, *190*
2:11-22, *76*
2:15, *127*
2:20, *71*
4:26, *195*
6:2, *127*

Philippians
2, *196*
3, *194*
3:1, *92*
4:9, *86*

Colossians
1:7, *76*
1:25, *125*
2:6-8, *86, 125*
4:14, *201*
4:16, *63, 87, 92, 120, 126, 199*

1 Thessalonians
1:8, *56*
2:13, *56, 86, 115, 124, 125, 127, 141, 152*

2:13-16, *124*
4:2, *125*
4:2-8, *125*
4:3, *125*
4:8, *125*
4:15-17, *113, 114, 115*
5:2, *114*
5:27, *63, 87, 115, 126, 199*

2 Thessalonians
2:8, *55*
2:15, *69, 77, 86, 126*
3:6, *86, 125, 126, 128, 129*
3:6-10, *129*
3:6-12, *128*
3:6-15, *129*
3:6-16, *128*
3:14, *69, 77, 128, 129*

1 Timothy
1:3, *190*
2:1-2, *166*
2:1-7, *76*
3:16, *76*
5:18, *122, 143, 200, 201, 202*
6:20, *86*

2 Timothy
1:14, *86*
1:18, *190*
2:9, *125*
4:11, *201*
4:12, *190*
4:13, *93*
4:17, *76*

Titus
1:14, *127*
3:1, *166*

Philemon
1:24, *201*

Hebrews
1–8, *148*
1:2, *51, 53*
2:1-4, *147*
2:3, *208*
2:3-4, *147*

4:12, *125*
5:12, *166*
7:22, *59*
8:8, *59*
9:19, *93*
10:29, *59*
11, *104*
12:9, *166*
12:29, *166*
13:7, *125*
13:23, *148*

1 Peter
1:1, *150*
2:6, *201*
4:3, *166*
5:13, *134*

2 Peter
1:1, *150*
1:13-15, *74*
1:16, *200*
1:16-18, *150*

1:19, *166*
1:21, *166*
2:21, *86, 141*
2:22, *201*
3:1, *150*
3:2, *68, 149, 150*
3:4-10, *114*
3:15, *200*
3:16, *122, 150, 199, 203*

1 John
1:1, *151, 152*
1:1-2, *151*
1:1-4, *151*
1:2, *148*
1:4, *152*
1:5, *152*

Jude
3, *71, 86, 141*

Revelation
1:1, *153*

1:1-3, *153*
1:3, *87, 126, 153*
1:10, *198*
1:11, *71*
1:16, *55*
4:5, *160*
4:6-8, *160, 161*
7:1, *160, 161*
7:9, *76*
8:5, *160*
9:14-15, *160*
11:5, *55*
11:19, *160*
14:6, *76*
15:4, *76*
16:18, *160*
17–22, *61, 63, 184*
19:15, *55*
20:8, *160*
22:18, *138*
22:18-19, *63, 66, 153*